The Snake at the Mouth of the Cave

EXPLORING TALMUDIC NARRATIVES

TOURO COLLEGE & UNIVERSITY SYSTEM
Where Knowledge and Values Meet

מגיד
MAGGID

Moshe Sokol

The Snake at the Mouth of the Cave

Exploring Talmudic Narratives

Touro College and University System
Maggid Books

The Snake at the Mouth of the Cave
Exploring Talmudic Narratives

First Edition, 2021

Maggid Books
An imprint of Koren Publishers Jerusalem Ltd.

POB 8531, New Milford, CT 06776-8531, USA
& POB 4044, Jerusalem 9104001, Israel

www.maggidbooks.com

Cover photo: Hallucinating with the beauty of the unknown lower antelope, Arizona, United States; designed by Unaihuiziphotography – Freepik.com

The publication of this book was made possible through the generous support of *The Jewish Book Trust.*

ISBN 978-1-59264-547-3, *hardcover*

A CIP catalogue record for this title is available from the British Library

Printed and bound in the United States

בס"ד

Touro College and University System
pays tribute to

RABBI DR. MOSHE SOKOL

DEAN, LANDER COLLEGE FOR MEN

Dean Sokol is an outstanding Rav, scholar and academician who is respected by his peers and beloved by his students.

This volume is yet another of his contributions to the corpus of Rabbinic scholarship. His insights will undoubtedly enhance understanding of the Talmud and advance Torah knowledge.

Contents

Acknowledgments

This volume originated in a series of lectures delivered to students at the Lander College for Men, and to members of the Yavneh Minyan of Flatbush. I am grateful to them not only for the opportunity to develop these ideas, but for their unflagging interest, and for their wonderful contributions to the discussion of these rich texts. This book would not have been possible without them.

The Touro College and University System has been my academic home for almost all of my professional life, and I am grateful to its leadership for nurturing my career, and for nurturing the Lander College for Men, where it has been my good fortune to serve as dean and professor for two decades. I owe a special debt of gratitude to Dr. Alan Kadish, president and CEO, and Rabbi Moshe Krupka, executive vice president, not only for their magnificent leadership of the Touro system, but also for their role in making the publication of this book possible. I likewise owe a debt of gratitude to the Yavneh Minyan of Flatbush, where I have served as rabbi for some thirty years, and to its president, Amichai Ziegler and members of the board, not only for their leadership of a shul with such exemplary qualities, but also for their role in making the publication of this book possible as well.

I have shared chapters of this book, or discussed its content, with many people, and I am grateful to each of them for their comments, insights, and suggestions. These include Dr. Stanley Boylan, Dr. Michael

Shmidman, Dr. Steven Huberman, Rabbi Moshe Bamberger, Dr. David Shatz, Dr. David Arnow, Dr. Kenneth Danishefsky, Prof. Raizy Shmulewitz, Mr. Michael Schussheim, and Dr. Zev Eleff.

Members of the Lander College for Men staff have also been extremely helpful, and I wish to thank Mr. Yeshaya Metal, the librarian, who invested much time in helping me track down sources, Mrs. Rachel Horowitz, Mrs. Susan Moskowitz, Mrs. Annette Schwartz, and especially Mrs. Elana Raskas Deutsch, for her extensive assistance with the text.

The Koren/Maggid Books team has been a pleasure to work with. Rabbi Aryeh Sklar, my talented and erudite editor, devoted countless hours to the manuscript, and he did a superb job in every possible respect. I am likewise grateful to Mrs. Debbie Ismailoff, Mrs. Ita Olesker, and especially to Rabbi Reuven Ziegler, who oversees the press, and whose sage counsel and good cheer have been helpful from the very beginning of the project.

Some of my most avid and helpful readers have been members of my family: my wife Chaya Sarah Sokol; and my children Rabbi Zvi Sokol and his wife Dr. Dina Sokol; Estee Schwab and her husband Rabbi Daniel Schwab; Dr. Aliza Rosenwasser and her husband Rabbi Uri Rosenwasser; Yona Sokol and his wife Zehava Sokol; and Dr. Yosef Sokol and his wife Devorah Sokol. They and their wonderful children have been the light of my life. No words can express my gratitude, love, and respect for them.

I am likewise grateful to my beloved brother Steven Sokol and sister Raisy Barnett, with her husband David Barnett, who provided love and encouragement to me throughout our lives together, and especially during the long process of bringing this book to life

One of my earliest childhood memories is that of my Zaydie Rabbi Dov Zvi Slomowitz as an elderly man sitting long hours before a Gemara while we children played around the house. His love of Gemara, and the life he led, remain an inspiration to me so many decades later. I hope he would find joy in this volume about passages from the Gemara he held so dear. My parents Albert and Shirley Sokol raised me in his footsteps to love God, Torah, wisdom, and truth, and whatever I have achieved in life is due in no small measure to them. May they live many more years in good health, with *naḥat* from their children, grandchildren, and great-grandchildren.

My gratitude to my wife Chaya Sarah Sokol knows no bounds. She possesses a remarkable soul and an impeccable moral compass, and not a day goes by that I do not learn from her. Her parents, of blessed memory, Isaac and Helen Wagh, were God-fearing people of great faith and integrity who courageously built a family together during challenging times. Their character shines forth in Chaya Sarah, and may the two of us continue to share our lives together in love, good health, and *naḥat* for many decades to come.

Finally, I wish to thank God for the many gifts He has given me and my family. He is the source of all good, and of all the wisdom whose depths this volume seeks to plumb. I know that I am, in the words of the Talmud, like a dog that licks at the sea of His Torah. I hope that in this book I have drawn up and savored at least a few precious drops from that infinite sea.

Introduction

When reading the Talmud, one is often struck by the great amount of aggada, the non-halakhic teachings about theology, ethics, spirituality, psychology, health, and many other topics, interspersed throughout the text. Countless works have been written about the Talmud over the ages, but the majority of these works are about the halakhic portions of the Talmud; this is to be expected, given the overwhelming importance of halakha and halakhic discourse to traditional Judaism. Classic yeshiva curricula likewise, and perhaps for good reason, focus almost exclusively on the halakhic portion of the Talmud. Yet if the talmudic rabbis devoted so much attention to aggada, it was clearly important to them as well. In fact, if one includes all the non-halakhic midrashim, which extensively cite the rabbis of the Talmud, it becomes apparent that these rabbis treasured aggada a great deal indeed. Despite this, there remains a relative paucity of commentary and scholarship on aggada, especially in the English language, and especially about that portion of aggada in which the rabbis tell stories. While in Israel there has been a recent spurt of interest in, and publications about, aggadic narrative, this has not been matched in the United States or England. This volume seeks to contribute to that literature.

Why write about aggadic narratives? The talmudic rabbis often told stories because stories are a compelling form of human communication, dating back almost to the origins of humankind. Let us remember that the Torah itself contains more narrative than law. Well-told stories grab our interest, for we identify with the characters whose stories are told, and grow by entering their world. The stories I have elected to analyze in this volume are gripping. They include tales of sin, redemption, success and failure, interpersonal conflict, alienation, human pain and triumph, love, fear, anger, and spiritual yearning. I hope the narrative energy of these stories captures the readers of this volume as it has captured me, and that I can successfully convey through my interpretations the wisdom the talmudic rabbis themselves sought to convey.

The first set of three chapters constitutes a trilogy, all devoted to R. Eliezer b. Hyrcanus, perhaps the greatest student of the leader who re-established Jewish religious life after the destruction of the Temple in 70 CE, R. Yoḥanan b. Zakkai. The first chapter tells of R. Eliezer's youth, longing for Torah study and growth as a scholar. The second tells of his excommunication at the hands of his friends and colleagues, all over a debate about the halakhic status of a particular oven. The last chapter tells of the pathos-filled attempt on the part of R. Eliezer's students and colleagues to reconcile with him on his deathbed. During this encounter, R. Eliezer compares his own unquenchable yearning for Torah knowledge to that of a thirsty dog lapping at the sea, driven to acquire ever more knowledge, but who only barely touches the infinite surface of the Talmud's sea. I have been tempted to name this book *Lapping at the Sea: Studies in Talmudic Stories* for as much as we readers yearn to uncover the true depths of talmudic stories, we sometimes feel as if we are merely lapping at the surface of the sea.

The fourth chapter continues with the theme of excommunicated scholars, and analyzes the story of Akavya b. Mahalalel, who refused to retract four of his halakhic positions despite pressure from the majority of the Sages, and examines in some depth his personality, his approach to halakha, and his fate.

The second set of three stories are another trilogy, about the great master R. Yoḥanan bar Nappaḥa, who lived in *Eretz Yisrael* and is traditionally thought to be the main compiler of the Talmud Yerushalmi. The fifth chapter depicts a crucial decision point in R. Yoḥanan's early life, when he, unlike his closest friend and colleague, chose to remain in the study hall and not enter the world of business despite his grinding poverty. The sixth chapter, which catches him mid-career, revolves around his complex and evolving relationship with his close student-turned-colleague and brother-in-law, Reish Lakish, and ends with the death of both. The seventh and last chapter in this trilogy focuses on R. Yoḥanan in his old age, and in a disastrous encounter with another great Sage, R. Kahana.

The eighth chapter picks up on the theme of loss in the sixth chapter, which described the intense pain R. Yoḥanan felt with the death of Reish Lakish. This chapter provides a fresh analysis of the famous and strange tale of Ḥoni, the magic worker, who slept for seventy years, only to awaken to a world that would not accept him. Both R. Yoḥanan and Ḥoni die bereft of the relationships that made life worth living for them.

Some of these texts are well-known, and others less so, but all provide remarkably rich and dramatic stories which revolve around a common theme: The costs of living a deeply principled life, and the complex ways in which human nature, past experiences, and future hopes and anxieties shape difficult, principled choices. All the protagonists in these stories were men with profound commitments to the Jewish people, as well as to Torah and halakhic truth as they saw it, and were willing to make the greatest personal sacrifices to realize or preserve their vision. Yet these choices were not made in a vacuum. The authors of these aggadot portray these great men as human beings with pasts and with concerns and needs all their own, as all human beings possess. These aggadot explore this nexus in various ways, between principle and past, between human nature and elevated aspiration.

I have been blessed over the years with many wonderful Talmud teachers, and they taught me to interrogate every word, phrase, line, and textual unit (*sugya*) of the Talmud. Why does the text use this word rather than that word? Why do the rabbis ask this question when they could have asked another, or why are they silent when they should have asked a question but did not? Why do they give one answer when they could have given another? Does the author of this teaching contradict himself with another teaching? The list of questions to be asked of the text could be very long indeed. My teachers taught me that each word, phrase, and line of the Talmud was crafted with the utmost care, bespeaks the religious heights of its authors, and is precious beyond words. My aim in this volume is to apply exactly this same approach to the study of talmudic narratives. I might add that my years in graduate school studying classical philosophical texts reinforced a similarly rigorous interrogation of text, although of course without the reverence with which I was taught to hold the Talmud.

What methods do I use in analyzing these narratives? Essentially, I ask of the texts many questions, and propose answers based upon my understanding of the narrative itself, the intellectual history of the period in which the protagonists of the narrative lived, various Jewish sources, and insights from such diverse fields as psychology, literature, cultural studies, philosophy, and more. Of course, I draw regularly on the classical rabbinic commentaries to the Talmud, as well as upon contemporary scholarship. However, the overall readings of the texts offered in this volume are very much my own. I wish to stress that I offer no more than theories about what these narratives might mean, theories which are designed to be faithful to the language of the texts and to answer the questions I raise. I can never be confident that these readings are true – whatever that might even mean – nor do I wish to claim that they are. Rather, my aim is to explain these often-puzzling texts in ways that make sense to me. If other readers of these narratives find these explanations helpful to them too, I will be more than gratified. Of course, readers who seek alternative accounts of the text must themselves take up the challenge of answering the very questions which led me to the interpretations I offer.

Each chapter in this volume begins with a brief introduction, followed by the texts in the original language, along with their English translations in boldface type and brief commentary in lightface, based on the *Koren Talmud Bavli* (Jerusalem: Steinsaltz Center and Koren Publishers Jerusalem, 2012–2019), also available at www.sefaria.org. The overall exposition here is that of a retelling of the story with a running commentary full of observations, questions, and potential answers, and includes a very extended analysis and discussion. My goal is to provide an overarching account of the narrative and its aims through this method of exposition. Since the chapters tend to be long, they are divided into parts to make it easier for the reader.

In attempting to interpret these challenging narratives, I will offer many suggestions about the inner lives, thoughts, feelings, and attitudes of their protagonists. These men are the heroes of the Talmud, whose views on the Torah have shaped Judaism for millennia, and whose biographies are compelling. I cannot stress enough that the inner lives of such extraordinary men are outside the reach of a limited reader living in the twenty-first century, so far removed from talmudic culture, times, Torah knowledge, and religious heights. Some would argue that no contemporary reader can truly hope to understand what these exceptional persons were really like. I take this claim very seriously. What I seek to achieve in this volume is an understanding not of these men themselves, *but an understanding of what the texts might teach the reader about these men.* My working assumption is that the author of the story formed it the way he did because he believed that it had much to teach the reader about the protagonists in question, and thereby about human nature, Torah study, the service of God, ethical values, human relationships, the purposes of life, and so on. The redactors of the Talmud likewise chose to include these stories in the Talmud itself because they too believed that these stories had much to teach future generations. While there may be elements of humor or playfulness in these stories, I begin with the premise that they seek to convey messages of import, and my goal is to unpack what these lessons might have been. Of course, this too is a daunting task, but nevertheless a more modest one than entering into the hearts and minds of the talmudic greats.

It is worth noting here that sometimes the texts themselves cast negative light on their protagonists, either directly or by implication. Let us first remember that these negative aspersions are cast by authors who themselves often lived long after the protagonists themselves, and so we, the readers of these texts, are not encountering the protagonist himself, but a later author's version of the protagonist. Moreover, the author often tells the story for his own purposes and with his own agenda, often to teach his readers an ethical or religious lesson important to him, and that may color his presentation. Thus, the true character of the talmudic heroes who are the subjects of these stories remains hidden from us even if the story appears in the Talmud itself. We must remember that our task is to analyze the protagonist's motives and behavior *as they appear in the text,* not as he truly is. This entails confronting that text honestly, without flinching from its sometimes-negative implications, all the while recognizing that we are interpreting not the protagonist himself, but the Talmud's version of him.

That said, my tendency in this book is to offer a generous reading of the protagonists, even as presented in the text, when that is possible. This is not to say that I fail to confront these sometimes-negative implications, but only that I wish to give the men who are subjects of this volume the benefit of the doubt. While I recognize that not all scholars adopt this posture, I choose to do so for multiple reasons. First, these were men who devoted their lives to Torah study and service of God, as is evidenced throughout the Talmud. They were clearly God- and Torah-infatuated, for which reason their behavior and choices were likely less negative than might first appear. Second, the moral and religious lessons they taught, recorded in the Talmud, frequently reflect exemplary moral and spiritual aspirations and sensitivities. Moreover, the authors of the talmudic texts we examine in this volume were themselves Torah scholars who would likely appreciate the great religious achievements of their heroes, as can be seen in the talmudic tradition, "R. Zeira taught in the name of Rava bar Zimuna: If the earlier scholars were sons of angels, we are the sons of men, and if the earlier scholars were sons of men, we are like donkeys."[1] Therefore, where the stories these authors tell appear to cast aspersions on their protagonists, it seems fair to assume that they would do so in moderation, even if the authors wish to make (or score) an ethical or religious point. Some might suggest that the criticisms they make or imply are relative to the stature in which the author of the text held the subject of the criticism. The greater the stature, the more intense the criticism, even if the misbehavior alleged is, in reality, only slight. That may or may not be, but in any case, for all these reasons, where a reading of the text allows for a generous but plausible interpretation, I favor it. Of course, plausibility is, in some respects, in the eye of the beholder, and the reader will have to judge if my readings meet that bar. Note, however, that even a more generous interpretation must not be a whitewash, and that too I assiduously seek to avoid. The authors of

1. Shabbat 112b. See also Eiruvin 53a.

these texts time and again force us to confront the shortcomings of all human beings, even what they perceive to be the shortcomings of truly great men as well. This is a crucial element in the texts' legacy.

While the majority of classic rabbinic literature on the Talmud focuses on its halakhic content, there is also a very long and distinguished history of rabbinic commentary to the aggada going back to the *Geonim*. Some of these are included in the compendium *Ein Yaakov*, by Rabbi Jacob ibn Ḥabib, the fifteenth-to-sixteenth-century Spanish scholar. A recent Hebrew edition of this work includes citations to additional, and also more recent, rabbinic commentary to aggadic passages.[2] There is, as well, a substantial and ever-growing body of academic literature of considerable merit which analyzes rabbinic narratives. Some rabbis in the classical tradition incline toward a plain reading of the text; others to rationalist readings of the narratives, interpreting them as naturalistically as possible, including those with apparently supernatural elements; others to a more mystical approach; and others to allegorical readings, Rabbi Judah Loew, the Maharal of Prague, being a distinguished example of the latter.[3] In this volume, I attempt to make sense of the narratives with categories of thought that are meaningful to me, a person living and educated in the twenty-first century, drawing upon both classical and academic sources. The interpretations I suggest do not assume a body of esoteric knowledge like the mystical, nor the allegorical approach of the Maharal, as valuable and illuminating as some might find them to be. I prefer the rationalist approach, but will use metaphor if the text itself seems to call for such a reading.

One example of my use of metaphor is when an aggadic narrative includes within it a halakhic dialogue or exposition. I have found upon reflection that such technical halakhic discourse often serves the deeper narrative purposes of the aggada itself, and will make this suggestion repeatedly throughout the book. This is not to say that the halakhic discourse was really not halakhic but aggadic, for that is not the case. The rabbis really were debating points of law. However, my contention is that

2. *Ein Yaakov HaMefo'ar* (Jerusalem: Mekhon HaMefo'ar, 2008).

3. For a survey of medieval approaches to aggada, see Marc Saperstein, *Decoding the Rabbis* (Cambridge, 1980), ch. 1.

the author of the aggada appropriated this pre-existing discourse for his own narrative purposes. The reader will be the ultimate judge of its value.

Another point to make is that the method I use is not comparative or source-critical. By that I mean that I do not compare the sometimes-varying versions of the same narrative that appear in different rabbinic texts, nor do I examine how the narrative might have developed over time or changed across geography, as expressed in the different texts and their provenances. While this can be revealing, it is not my purpose. As do other scholars in the field, I take the text which appears in a classical source as a self-sufficient literary unit, and seek to understand what its particular author (or editor) might have meant to convey.[4] While I draw on sources external to the narrative being analyzed, the focus is always on the text itself in its traditional form.

The Talmud has endured for millennia, and is studied with unflagging commitment and energy across the world today by more people than ever in Jewish history, in widely varying contexts – primarily in yeshivas, but also in synagogues, study halls, and university classrooms. Despite many predictions to the contrary, the study of Talmud flourishes, a testament to the stature of its authors and editors, to its transcendent value, and to the enduring commitment of the Jewish people to its wisdom. The talmudic conversation will continue long into the future, and I pray that this volume will contribute its own small voice to that conversation.

4. For an overview of contemporary methods used in the analysis of aggadic narratives, see Moshe Lavee, "Welfare and Education vs. Leadership and Redemption: The Stories about Rabbi and Rabbi Hiyya as an Example of the Image of the Tannaitic Past in the Babylonian Talmud," *JSIJ* 8 (2009): 52–55 (Heb.).

Chapter 1

The Making of R. Eliezer

Pirkei DeRabbi Eliezer, Chapters 1–2

INTRODUCTION

R. Eliezer b. Hyrcanus, who lived at the end of the first and beginning of the second centuries, was among the greatest of the *Tanna'im,* the rabbinic Sages who lived from 10 CE until approximately 220 CE, and one of the outstanding students of R. Yoḥanan b. Zakkai, the man most responsible for the survival of Judaism after the destruction of the Second Temple. R. Yoḥanan b. Zakkai described his star student as a "sealed well which does not lose a drop placed in it"; such were the powers of R. Eliezer's recall.[1] Indeed, R. Yoḥanan b. Zakkai is reported to have said: "If all the Sages of Israel were in one scale of a balance, and Eliezer ben Hyrcanus in the other, he would outweigh them all."[2] R. Eliezer's

1. *Pirkei Avot* 2:11, translation from *The Koren Sacks Siddur* (Jerusalem: Koren Publishers, 2010), 648. All translations of *Pirkei Avot* in this volume are from the *Koren Sacks Siddur.*
2. Ibid., 2:12.

teachings are cited with great frequency in the Mishna and Talmud, and he played a pivotal role in carrying forward Torah teachings into the generation following the destruction of the Temple. One of his many students was the illustrious R. Akiva, himself among the most remarkable figures of the rabbinic era.

Yet, despite these towering achievements, R. Eliezer was excommunicated by his colleagues for insisting on the truth of one of his teachings regardless of being overruled by all of his colleagues, and he went to his death a solitary, tragic figure, alienated from his students and friends. This chapter is the first of three depicting the most important events in R. Eliezer's life, his early beginnings, the great conflict with his colleagues, and their final attempt at reconciliation on R. Eliezer's deathbed.

The lengthy selection we will focus on in this chapter is one of the most extensive and sustained ancient biographical accounts we possess of any of the great rabbinic Sages of the Mishna and Talmud. Several very similar versions of the story appear elsewhere in rabbinic literature, but this analysis will focus on the richest and most detailed, that which appears in *Pirkei DeRabbi Eliezer*. This late midrash collects many teachings attributed to R. Eliezer (hence the title of the collection), and begins with two biographical chapters about R. Eliezer himself.[3] Our discussion here will likewise be divided into two parts, corresponding to these two chapters. The story it tells is fascinating not only because of its inherent drama and the importance of its subject, but because it adumbrates the character traits of the man who would become one of the greatest and most controversial Sages of the rabbinic period. In other words, it permits us to begin to answer the question of how R. Eliezer became the man he did. The story also subtly but beautifully delineates the complex and evolving human relationship between R. Eliezer and R. Yoḥanan b. Zakkai, his great master. Finally, the story brings to brilliant light the intense spiritual yearning that can make a person great.

3. A summary of other versions of the story appears in J. Eisenstein, *Otzar Midrashim* (New York, 1915), 27.

PART ONE
R. ELIEZER LEAVES HOME TO STUDY WITH R. YOḤANAN B. ZAKKAI

Pirkei DeRabbi Eliezer, chapter 1

א) מעשה ברבי אליעזר בן הורקנוס, שהיו לאביו חורשים והיו חורשים על גבי המענה, והוא היה חורש בטרשין. ישב לו והיה בוכה. אמר לו אביו, מפני מה אתה בוכה? שמא מצטער אתה שאתה חורש בטרשין? עכשיו אתה חורש על גבי המענה. ישב לו על גבי המענה והיה בוכה. אמר לו מפני מה אתה בוכה? שמא מצטער אתה שאתה חורש על גבי המענה? אמר לו, לאו. ולמה את בוכה? אמר לו, שאני מבקש ללמד תורה. אמר לו והלא בן עשרים ושמונה שנים אתה, ואתה מבקש ללמד תורה. אלא קח לך אשה ותוליד לך בנים ואתה מוליכן לבית הספר. עשה שתי שבתות ולא טעם כלום עד שנגלה לו אליהו זכור לטוב, ואמר לו, בן הורקנוס, למה אתה בוכה? אמר לו מפני שאני מבקש ללמד תורה. אמר לו, אם אתה מבקש ללמד תורה, עלה לירושלים אצל רבן יוחנן בן זכאי. עמד והלך אצל רבן יוחנן בן זכאי. ישב לו והיה בוכה. אמר לו, מפני מה אתה בוכה? אמר לו, מפני שאני מבקש ללמד תורה. אמר לו, בן מי אתה? ולא הגיד לו.

(1) The following befell R. Eliezer, son of Hyrcanus.

His father had plowmen who were plowing arable ground, while he was plowing a stony plot; he sat down and wept.

His father said to him: Why do you weep? Perhaps you are distressed because you plow a stony plot? Now behold you shall plow arable soil!

He sat down on the arable ground and wept. His father said to him: Why do you weep? Perhaps you are distressed because you plow arable land?

He replied to him: No. [His father] said to him: [Then] why do you weep? He answered him: Because I desire to learn Torah.

[His father] said to him: Are you not twenty-eight years old – yet you desire to learn Torah? No; take for yourself a wife and have sons and you will take them to school.

He fasted two weeks, not tasting anything, until Elijah – may he be remembered for good – appeared to him and said to him: Son of Hyrcanus! Why do you weep?

He replied: Because I desire to learn Torah. [Elijah] said to him: If you desire to learn Torah, go to Jerusalem to R. Yoḥanan b. Zakkai.

He got up and went up to Jerusalem to R. Yoḥanan b. Zakkai and sat down and wept. [R. Yoḥanan] said to him: Why do you weep? He answered him: Because I wish to learn Torah. [R. Yoḥanan] said to him: Whose son are you? But he did not tell him.

ב) אמר לו, מימיך לא למדת קריאת שמע ולא תפלה ולא ברכת המזון? אמר לו לאו. אמר לו עמד ואלמדך שלשתן. ישב והיה בוכה. אמר לו, בני, מפני מה אתה בוכה? אמר לו, שאני מבקש ללמד תורה. והיה אומר לו שתי הלכות כל ימי השבוע, והיה חוזר לו עליהן ומדבקן. עשה שמונה ימים ולא טעם כלום עד שעלה ריח פיו לפני רבן יוחנן בן זכאי, והעמידו מלפניו. ישב והיה בוכה. אמר לו מפני מה אתה בוכה? אמר לו, מפני שהעמדתני מלפניך כאדם שמעמיד מלפניו מכה שחין. אמר לו, בני, כשם שעלה ריח פיך מלפני, כך יעלה ריח חקי תורה מפיך לשמים. אמר לו, בני, בן מי אתה? אמר לו בן הורקנוס אני. אמר לו, והלא בן גדולי עולם אתה, ולא היית מגיד לי! אמר לו, חייך, היום אתה סועד אצלי. אמר לו, כבר סעדתי אצל אכסניא שלי. אמר לו, ומי הוא אכסניא שלך? אמר לו, רבי יהושע בן חנניה, ורבי יוסי הכהן.

(2) [R. Yoḥanan] asked him: Did you ever learn to read the *Shema*, or the [main] Prayer, or the Grace after Meals?

He replied: No. He arose and [R. Yoḥanan] taught him those three [prayers].

[Eliezer] sat down and wept. [R. Yoḥanan] said to him: My son, why do you weep? He replied: Because I desire to learn Torah. [R. Yoḥanan] taught him two rules of halakha every day of the week, and on Shabbat [Eliezer] reviewed them and assimilated them.

He fasted for eight days, not tasting anything, until the odor of his mouth was noticed by R. Yoḥanan b. Zakkai, who had him removed from his presence. He sat down and wept.

[R. Yoḥanan] said to him: My son, why do you weep? He answered: Because you removed me from your presence like one who removes a person with a skin affliction from his presence.

[R. Yoḥanan] said to him: My son, just as the odor of your mouth has ascended before me, so may the odor of the [savory smell of the] laws of the Torah ascend from your mouth to heaven. He said to him: My son, whose son are you? He replied: I am the son of Hyrcanus.

[R. Yoḥanan] said: Are you not the son of one of the great men of the world, and you did not tell me? He [continued and] said: By your life! You are eating with me today. [Eliezer] answered: I have eaten already with my host. [R. Yoḥanan] asked: Who is your host? He replied: R. Yehoshua b. Ḥananya and R. Yosei the Priest.

(ג) שלח ושאל לאכסניא שלו, אמר להם, אצלכם סעד אליעזר היום? אמרו לו, לאו. והלא יש לו שמונה ימים שלא טעם כלום. אחרי כן הלכו רבי יהושע בן חנניה ורבי יוסי הכהן ואמרו לו לרבן יוחנן בן זכאי, והלא יש לו שמונה ימים שלא טעם כלום.

(3) [R. Yoḥanan] sent a message to his hosts, and said to them: Did Eliezer eat with you today? They answered: No. It has surely been eight days for him without tasting anything! Afterward, R. Yehoshua b. Ḥananya and R. Yosei the Priest went and said to R. Yoḥanan b. Zakkai: It has surely been eight days for him without tasting anything![4]

The midrash opens with what appears to be a lovely scene, of farmers working the fields. However, that halcyon image is quickly undermined with the appearance of Eliezer the son of Hyrcanus. He is the son of the owner of the fields, and is assigned to plow a stony, difficult plot, unlike the rest of the workers, who are assigned better land. Even more

4. Gerald Friedlander, trans., *Pirkei DeRabbi Eliezer* (London, 1916), with modifications.

strikingly, we first encounter him sitting and crying. Eliezer was not a child then; as the midrash tells the reader later, he was all of twenty-eight years old, not the age where crying is typical. Hyrcanus, Eliezer's father, asks Eliezer why he is crying, and proposes an answer of his own, which is that Eliezer was assigned a stony plot rather than an arable plot to plow. This is a reason for crying that Hyrcanus can understand, and so to remedy the problem he tells Eliezer that he can move on to a better plot of land. Much to Hyrcanus's surprise, Eliezer continues to cry. Hyrcanus presses Eliezer on this, perhaps thinking that his son prefers not to plow at all. Eliezer finally blurts out the truth to his father Hyrcanus: He is crying because he seeks to study Torah.

Hyrcanus cannot even begin to understand this as a reason for tears. He utterly dismisses his son's desire, and tells him that as a twenty-eight-year-old man, he should first marry and have children. When the children grow up, then he can take them to school to study Torah. Hyrcanus shows no sympathy whatsoever for his son's yearning for Torah; from his perspective, it is time for Eliezer to get on with his life. As a farmer, Hyrcanus understands the importance of tilling the fields, earning a living, marrying, and procreating, all very "grounded" activities. However, he cannot even begin to fathom the value of abstract Torah study. As will become even clearer as the story unfolds, father and son live in radically different worlds, one pragmatic and material, the other spiritual and ideal. There can be no real communication between them, so different, even incommensurate, are their values. Father ridicules son, and son continues to cry. Father makes no attempt to sympathize with or understand son, and son makes no attempt to explain himself to father.

This perspective may help answer a puzzling question about the story. Why did Hyrcanus assign his son a stony plot of land to plow in the first place? After all, the other workers – and they were not even family! – were assigned far better soil. Why discriminate against his very own son? Is it not likely that Hyrcanus sensed all along that his son yearned for more than the life of a farmer, even if he had never acted upon or articulated that desire? If so, it is quite plausible that Hyrcanus would want to "cure" his "effete" son, by forcing him to "toughen up" with hard manual labor on the farm.

Eliezer responds to his father's harsh words by fasting for two weeks, a very long fast indeed. Why does he fast? Is it an expression of pure spiritual yearning, for an otherworldly life of Torah, far away from the physical entanglements of a farmer? Is it a symptom of the depression and frustration he may feel, because he is unable to realize his spiritual yearning, and because he is persistently misunderstood and even ridiculed by his intransigent father? It seems likely that his fasting is of a piece with his crying, both an expression of frustration, sadness, and unrequited yearning. As we shall see, both Eliezer's crying and his fasting persist.

The result of this two-week-long fast is the appearance to Eliezer of no less a figure than Elijah the Prophet. Elijah asks him the very same question, using the very same words, as did his father: "Why are you crying?" The answer is exactly the same: "Because I seek to learn Torah." It is as if Elijah, in using the same words as Hyrcanus, stands in place of the father who does not understand his son, while Elijah of course does. For Elijah tells him that if he wishes to study Torah, he must take action, and that action is to leave his family and farm and to go up to Jerusalem[5] to study Torah with the great master R. Yoḥanan b. Zakkai. If Elijah is a new father figure for Eliezer, he immediately transfers that role to R. Yoḥanan b. Zakkai, who will eventually, as we shall see, take on the more enduring role of father in earnest. Elijah the Prophet comes and goes; Eliezer needed far more than that. Interestingly, Elijah addresses Eliezer not by his name, but by his patronymic, and calls him "son of Hyrcanus." Why does he not use the name Eliezer, or Eliezer the son of Hyrcanus, a more formal means of address? At one level, this is acutely ironic, for Eliezer has rejected his father and his father's values. Why then use the patronymic? Perhaps Elijah means to stress exactly this point, and in effect say: "You are the son of Hyrcanus, yet you still cry! Why and how could that be? You are the son of a wealthy, successful farmer. What are you missing? What could lead you to tears? Of course, I, the prophet, know the answer to these questions. You are the son of Hyrcanus, yet you are not really his son, and you must seek another father, and I will help you do so."

5. This story is set before the destruction of the Temple and the sacking of Jerusalem.

It is worth observing that in rabbinic literature, Elijah the Prophet typically appears to distinguished scholars or other great people. Eliezer is a twenty-eight-year-old farmer who, as we shall see, is an utter Jewish ignoramus at this stage in his life, yet Elijah appears to him nevertheless. The author of the midrash clearly means to teach his reader about the power of sheer yearning for Torah. Great Torah knowledge alone does not necessarily bring Elijah, for many extraordinary scholars never had such a vision. Yet intense yearning for Torah, even by the ignorant, is powerful and meaningful enough to bring Elijah himself. Would that all the midrash's readers could yearn for Torah like Eliezer! Or, so the author of the midrash implies.

On the face of it the choice of R. Yoḥanan b. Zakkai as a teacher for Eliezer seems odd. R. Yoḥanan b. Zakkai was the leading Torah scholar of his generation, and, as we shall see, Eliezer was ignorant of even the most basic of Jewish fundamentals. It would be as if someone without even an elementary-school education had been sent to study with a Nobel laureate in biology at Rockefeller University, which lacks even an undergraduate college. Of course, it turns out that it was a perfect choice, and Elijah, being a prophet, could understand just how apt a choice it was. But only Elijah could divine that. The reader must remain puzzled and in suspense, until the story as it unfolds illuminates the mystery.

The midrash now writes that Eliezer got up and went to R. Yoḥanan b. Zakkai. This spatial change is significant. So far, the only position in which we have seen Eliezer is a sitting one. Now, thanks to the encouragement and advice of Elijah the Prophet, Eliezer can finally stand, take action, move, and travel. He is no longer paralyzed, locked in tearful place. Yet the first thing Eliezer does upon arriving at the yeshiva of R. Yoḥanan b. Zakkai is sit – and cry. This is the second time we find in the midrash Eliezer crying. An exact recapitulation of the question of both Hyrcanus, as father one, and Elijah, as father two, ensues, when R. Yoḥanan, father three, asks Eliezer: "Why are you crying?" Eliezer now provides exactly the same answer he gave to fathers one and two: "Because I seek to learn Torah."

The reader no doubt wonders just why Eliezer sits and cries. He has left the farms and the narrow material world of his family and sits at the feet of the greatest Torah master of all. It would seem as if his deepest yearning is about to be realized. Should this not be a time for rejoicing rather than crying? Part of the answer may be that he has not yet been accepted into R. Yoḥanan b. Zakkai's yeshiva, just as the student lacking an elementary-school education might well not be accepted to Rockefeller University. His yearning for Torah has not yet been requited, and he fears that it never will be, for he clearly lacks the qualifications of all R. Yoḥanan b. Zakkai's other students. His cry may express that fear. Moreover, sometimes tears come with any powerful emotional experience, and what could be more powerful an experience for Eliezer than meeting the great R. Yoḥanan b. Zakkai at his yeshiva, his yearning for Torah now closer than ever to realization? Finally, there may be another factor at play as well. For what, after all, is Eliezer's primary qualification for admission? Surely it was not his Torah knowledge, which was sorely lacking. Rather, it was the sheer intensity of his yearning, its depth and authenticity. On the basis of an entrance exam alone, Eliezer would certainly fail. But when it comes to the quest for Torah, there are other criteria for admission that may matter more than knowledge amassed, and that is the desire to amass knowledge. This was Eliezer's greatest strength, and this he allowed himself to express.

R. Yoḥanan b. Zakkai next asks this crying young man who his father is, and Eliezer refuses to answer. This raises two questions: Why does R. Yoḥanan b. Zakkai ask who Eliezer's father is, and why does Eliezer refuse to answer? It is possible that such a question was common at that time and place. How better to gain insight into a person than by understanding who is father is, how he was raised, and with what values?[6] Even today, a person's identity is profoundly shaped by the family in which he or she was raised. Of course, in modern times in the West, people have been far freer to create their own new identities, and are less shaped by the family traditions of the past, even if they can

6. To this very day, Jews are called up to read the Torah by their name and their father's name, a practice common from time immemorial. For one example of this in Western literature, recall how Odysseus identifies himself throughout his long journey in *The Odyssey*, as "Odysseus the son of Laertes" (adding, interestingly, his geographic origin as well, Ithaca).

never fully leave those identities behind. In this respect, Eliezer, who rejects his family and past, is a harbinger of the modern world.

Even more striking is R. Eliezer's refusal to answer. First, on the face of it, refusing to answer the master's question seems like an imprudent strategy for gaining admission to the yeshiva. Moreover, how could this young, ignorant man deign to disregard the request of the greatest scholar and leader of the generation? In part, this speaks to the toughness of mind so characteristic of R. Eliezer throughout his life, beginning with his rejection of his father's life, a characteristic that will become even more apparent with the unfolding of the story in this chapter and the next two. But why be tough of mind about this particular request?

Three answers suggest themselves. Perhaps most importantly, he wanted to demonstrate to R. Yoḥanan b. Zakkai the sincerity of his quest, that he was alone in the world, with no father whose name he could mention, since all he wanted was to study Torah. Put differently, his only defining hallmark was his overwhelming yearning to study Torah. While fathers generally help define a person's identity, that was not true of Eliezer, who wanted to communicate to R. Yoḥanan b. Zakkai that his identity was no more nor less than the sum total of his desire for Torah. His father, whose life he had rejected, was totally irrelevant to who Eliezer was. Secondly, he may have wanted to study Torah anonymously, undistracted by family ties and entanglements once publicized. Finally, it is possible that Eliezer wanted to be accepted to the yeshiva on his own merit, not because of the wealth and social status of his father. If R. Yoḥanan b. Zakkai were to learn the identity of his father early on, and if Eliezer thought that R. Yoḥanan b. Zakkai might accept and encourage him because of that, then Eliezer would forever doubt his own value, and R. Yoḥanan b. Zakkai himself might never fully appreciate the value of his student. Like many young men and women throughout history, Eliezer was determined to make it on his own.[7] It is remarkable that R. Yoḥanan b. Zakkai does not press Eliezer on this, despite Eliezer's apparent insolence, which reflects the sensitivity R. Yoḥanan b. Zakkai consistently displays, especially as the story

7. Contemporary debates about the value of affirmative action in university admissions policies reflect the same tension.

unfolds. Instead, R. Yoḥanan b. Zakkai comments that Eliezer is ignorant, that he has never learned about the obligation to recite *Shema,* or about prayer, or about the blessings to be made after eating a meal, an observation Eliezer himself confirms.

It seems fair to ask how R. Yoḥanan b. Zakkai would have made this inference, as Eliezer had not uttered a single word since his arrival, except to say that he wants to study Torah. What could have betrayed his ignorance? Apparently, it was his dress and demeanor. Eliezer had come straight from the farm, and was no doubt dressed the part of a farmer far from the urban center of Jerusalem. It seems that men of that occupation, class, time, and place were typically ignorant.[8] It is surely striking that this ignorance extended even to the rudiments of Jewish life, including the recital of *Shema* and prayer. Now the midrash does not make clear in what exactly his ignorance consisted. It seems unlikely that he could not even recite *Shema,* and more likely that he had not learned many of the laws governing its recital. In any case, R. Yoḥanan b. Zakkai tells Eliezer to stand, no doubt out of respect for the Torah and to "uplift" his despairing student, and that he would teach him these three subjects, which he does. After the lesson, we find Eliezer sitting yet again, and crying yet again. This is the fourth time the midrash records that Eliezer cried. Not surprisingly, R. Yoḥanan b. Zakkai wonders why, and asks him "My son, why are you crying?"

Note that for the very first time in the story, R. Yoḥanan b. Zakkai addresses Eliezer as "my son." This reflects a crucial new stage in the ever-evolving relationship between R. Yoḥanan b. Zakkai and Eliezer. Eliezer has already rejected father one, Hyrcanus. Father two, Elijah, had

8. Note that the Mishna in Yoma 1:6 describes the ignorance of even some of the high priests, those who needed others to read to them, since they themselves were illiterate. In the previous mishna, the high priest and the people of the court would weep on Yom Kippur, since there was necessity to perform certain actions to prove the high priest was not a Sadducee. The ignorance of the high priest is often attributed to the sale of the position. For a discussion and relevant sources see B. Alon, *Sages* (Jerusalem, 2007), vol. 1, 232–37 (Heb.). The Talmud in Sota 22a defines an *am haaretz* as someone who fails to educate his children to study Torah, a definition which surely characterizes Hyrcanus. Note too that R. Akiva, R. Eliezer's most extraordinary student, was himself raised ignorant, hardly an uninteresting parallel.

transferred paternity to R. Yoḥanan b. Zakkai, who now, for the first time, feels and expresses this new role. R. Yoḥanan b. Zakkai saw in Eliezer the intense yearning for Torah, his solitary and painful quest, and he has by now actually taught him Torah and made him into his student. Thus, R. Yoḥanan b. Zakkai takes Eliezer under his fatherly wing.

But why the seemingly excessive crying? Eliezer's answer is in some ways a non sequitur. "I am crying because I want to learn Torah." How does that answer the question? And has he not already begun the process of studying Torah? Apparently, Eliezer was not yet satisfied with the lesson received, perhaps because he felt it was too rudimentary for him, despite his relative ignorance. Perhaps he thought that R. Yoḥanan b. Zakkai only meant to teach him the basics of Jewish practice so that he could function better as a farmer, but what he really wanted was to learn all the Torah, in its infinite breadth and depth. We cannot know for sure, but his frustration endured.

In response, R. Yoḥanan b. Zakkai teaches Eliezer two laws a week, *prima facie* a modest amount of material indeed, yet over the course of the week, Eliezer reviewed and assimilated these two laws. But how much would there have been to review if only two laws were taught? What the text probably means is that he taught Eliezer two areas of law, two broad subjects. In any case, the Hebrew verb used in the text to describe Eliezer's response to his lessons, here translated as "assimilated," is *medabekan,* which literally means "he attached them." This is an interesting and unusual term in context, which can be interpreted in two ways, horizontally and vertically. Interpreted horizontally, it might mean that Eliezer drew connections between two laws he had just learned, or more broadly across the body of his knowledge, integrating his new knowledge with what he already knew. This is key to all learning and retention. Isolated facts are rarely well understood or retained for long. Interpreted vertically, however, this might mean that Eliezer "attached them" to himself. That is, Eliezer internalized them, reflected about their meaningfulness to him. Both meanings, of course, could co-exist.

In any case, we next learn that Eliezer fasts, yet again, for a total of eight days. Unfortunately, this bears repercussions for the smell of his breath, which, in the event, became malodorous in the extreme.

R. Yoḥanan b. Zakkai, unable to tolerate the stench, kept Eliezer at a distance, which in turn so upset Eliezer that, yet again, he sits and cries, the fifth instance of a crying Eliezer in the midrash. R. Yoḥanan b. Zakkai, apparently oblivious to Eliezer's distress at being kept at a distance, asks him the same question he asked before, "Why are you crying?" Note that this time he does not employ the endearment "my son," perhaps because he is baffled and exasperated by Eliezer's persistent tears, which might border on the histrionic. After all, R. Yoḥanan has accepted him warmly to the yeshiva, or at least so it would seem to him.

But that is not how Eliezer saw it, and he answers R. Yoḥanan b. Zakkai's question accusatorily: "Because you had me removed from your presence as if I were afflicted with a skin condition." That appears to be a harsh comment, from a young neophyte outsider to the great master of the generation, and is of a piece with the tough-mindedness which emerges again and again as one of Eliezer's most distinctive traits. It also seems to emerge from Eliezer's drive not only to study Torah, so paramount in his life, but also be fully accepted by R. Yoḥanan b. Zakkai as the true father he sought, unlike the father who could not understand him, and whom he abandoned in the fields. For R. Yoḥanan b. Zakkai to distance himself from Eliezer because of something so inconsequential to Eliezer as bad breath, is tantamount to a rejection of Eliezer as a son. Would a loving father reject a son with bad breath? More importantly, wouldn't a loving father attempt to discover just what caused this affliction? Is he not eating, or not eating well? Is he suffering for some reason? What Eliezer was really accusing R. Yoḥanan b. Zakkai of was a failure to look after his well-being, to care about him not only as his student, but as a son. It is also possible that Eliezer was looking not only for a new father, but a new family, and he wistfully hoped that the yeshiva would play that role. Perhaps R. Yoḥanan b. Zakkai's distancing meant not only that Eliezer had not found his new father, but that he would also never be fully integrated and accepted into the elite new family of the yeshiva.

This accusation appears to have struck home, for R. Yoḥanan b. Zakkai responds: "My son, just as the odor of your mouth has ascended before me, so may the smell of the statutes of the Torah ascend [as a savory odor] from your mouth to heaven." First, R. Yoḥanan b. Zakkai uses the endearment "my son" once again. Moreover, for the first time, he gives Eliezer a blessing, just as a caring father would. He accepts lowly Eliezer's critique lovingly, further demonstration of the exceptional humanity and sensitivity of R. Yoḥanan b. Zakkai, who takes the lemon of Eliezer's bad breath and transforms it into the lemonade of a beautiful blessing. The content of the blessing is itself meaningful in its own right. For R. Yoḥanan may well surmise that Eliezer's malodorous breath is linked in some way to his yearning for Torah knowledge, and a correct surmise that would be, as we shall see. Of course, that very yearning is the source of all the vast Torah knowledge Eliezer will acquire, whose savor will ascend to the heavens. The bad odor that derives from his quest for Torah is thus a marker for exactly the force that elevates the sweet smell of Torah knowledge to God.

There is yet another dimension to his blessing as well. The term for "odor" or "smell" here is a translation of the Hebrew word *re'aḥ*. In the context of smells "rising to heaven," the imagery of the Torah's description of the Tabernacle sacrifices is invoked, that of the *re'aḥ niḥo'aḥ,* the savory smells of the offerings being "experienced" by God. No doubt R. Yoḥanan b. Zakkai is alluding to the great sacrifices Eliezer must have made to abandon completely his former life in order to study Torah under his wings. R. Yoḥanan b. Zakkai may likewise be alluding to the very real physical sacrifice of fasting, which he might have suspected as the cause of Eliezer's bad breath.

Their relationship thus achieved a certain intimacy it lacked before, and R. Yoḥanan b. Zakkai has learned more about his mysterious new student. This may have led R. Yoḥanan b. Zakkai to ask Eliezer the very same question that was rebuffed before: "Whose son are you?" Eliezer is now able to answer this question, given what has now transpired between them. R. Yoḥanan b. Zakkai responds to his answer with some surprise: "Are you not the son of one of the great men of the world, and you did not tell me? By your life, today you will eat with me!" How are we to interpret R. Yoḥanan b. Zakkai's invitation to dinner? Why did R. Yoḥanan b. Zakkai wait until now to invite him? Do only students from wealthy families merit invitations? While that is indeed possible, it is also possible that R. Yoḥanan b. Zakkai could invite Eliezer only if and when Eliezer was willing to share his past with him. An invitation reflects intimacy, and intimacy must be reciprocal. Eliezer must first open himself to his master before his master would open himself and his home to him.

Eliezer's response to the invitation is, on its face, nothing less than astonishing: He lies. He tells R. Yoḥanan b. Zakkai that he has already eaten with his host. R. Yoḥanan b. Zakkai inquires about this claim, and discovers it to be false, which, of course, we, the readers, already know. Eliezer has not eaten for eight days, for which reason his breath is malodorous.

The question begs itself: Why does Eliezer lie? We cannot know the answer to this question with any certainty, because the text does not explain itself, but we can conjecture. In part this is no doubt an expression of Eliezer's independent streak, his autonomy and individualism.[9] As we saw before, he insists on making it on his own, succeeding on his own terms. He does not want to be the favored house guest of R. Yoḥanan b. Zakkai merely because he stems from a wealthy family, whose identity he has now divulged, and whose wealth and values he has radically rejected. This is ironic, because, as we have seen, he seeks a new father, while at the same time rejecting his new father's overtures. Yet the rejection still makes deep psychological sense, because he wants his new father to value him for exactly what he is – a seeker of Torah – and not because of what he has rejected, the wealth and standing of his past.

Worthy of note is the change in R. Yoḥanan b. Zakkai. For the first time he inquires after the physical well-being of his new student/son, proactively sending messengers to ascertain whether or not he has eaten. This marks a new stage in R. Yoḥanan b. Zakkai's evolution as teacher/father. Teachers might think their primary responsibility is to teach, and that may be so. But a true teacher, a true master, will also take responsibility for the overall well-being of the student who has come to study under his wings, exactly like a father who takes responsibility for the overall well-being of his son. This is a crucial role, which R. Yoḥanan b. Zakkai finally undertakes. R. Yoḥanan b. Zakkai continues to evolve, from a teacher only, to a teacher who calls Eliezer "my son," to a teacher who not only calls Eliezer "my son," but finally acts that way too.

9. These same characteristics emerge with great force and clarity in the texts we will analyze in the next two chapters of this volume.

This concludes the beginning of Eliezer's development into the great scholar he became. Part 2 of this chapter (which is an analysis of chapter 2 of *Pirkei DeRabbi Eliezer*) picks up many years later, with Eliezer now a more mature, developed scholar, and transports us momentarily back to the farm from which he came.

PART TWO

R. ELIEZER EMERGES AS A GREAT SCHOLAR AND RECONCILES WITH HIS FATHER

Pirkei DeRabbi Eliezer, chapter 2

א) אמרו בניו של הורקנוס לאביהם, עלה לירושלים ונדה את בנך אליעזר מנכסיך. ועלה לירושלים לנדותו, ומצא שם יום טוב לרבן יוחנן בן זכאי. והיו כל גדולי המדינה סועדין אצלו, בן ציצית הכסת, ונקדימון בן גוריון, ובן כלבא שבוע.

(1) The sons of Hyrcanus said to their father: Go up to Jerusalem and exclude your son Eliezer from your possessions.

He went up to Jerusalem to exclude [i.e., to disinherit] him, and he found a festival being celebrated there by R. Yoḥanan b. Zakkai. All the magnates of the district were dining with him – ben Tzitzit HaKesat, Nakdimon ben Guryon, and ben Kalba Savua.

ב) ולמה נקרא שמו בן ציצית הכסת, שהיה מסב למעלה מגדולי ירושלים. אמרו על נקדימון בן גוריון, שהיה לו מזון שלשה סאים קמח לכל אחד ואחד שהיו בירושלים. אמרו עליו על בן כלבא שבוע, שהיה לו בית ארבע כורין של גנות טוחנין בזהב. אמרו לו, הרי אביו של רבי אליעזר בא. אמר להם, עשו לו מקום, ועשו לו מקום והושיבו אותו אצלו. ונתן עיניו ברבי אליעזר, אמר לו, אמור לנו דבר אחד מהתורה. אמר לו, רבי, אמשול לך משל, למה הדבר דומה? לבור הזה שאינו יכול להוציא מים יותר ממה שהיה מוציא. כך אני איני יכול לומר דברי תורה יותר ממה שקיבלתי ממך.

(2) Why was his name called ben Tzitzit HaKesat? Because he reclined [in a chair (kiseh)] higher than the [other] magnates

of Jerusalem. They said regarding Nakdimon ben Guryon that he had [stored] provisions containing three *se'a* of fine flour for every inhabitant of Jerusalem. They said regarding ben Kalba Savua that he had [a space the size of] gardens measuring four *kor* in which he would grind gold.

They said [to R. Yoḥanan]: Behold, the father of R. Eliezer has arrived. He said to them: Prepare a place for him. They prepared a place for him, and they sat him next to [R. Yoḥanan].

[R. Yoḥanan] fixed his gaze on R. Eliezer, [and] said to him: Tell us some words of the Torah. [R. Eliezer] answered him saying: Rabbi, I will tell you a parable. To what can the matter be compared? To this sealed well, which cannot yield more water than what it has received; likewise am I unable to speak words of the Torah more than what I have received from you.

(ג) אמר לו, אמשול לך משל למה הדבר דומה, למעין זה שהוא נובע ומוציא מים, ויש בכוחו להוציא מים יותר ממה שהוא מכניס. כך אתה יכל לומר דברי תורה יותר ממה שקבלו מסיני. אמר לו, שמא ממני אתה מתבייש, הריני עומד מאצלך. עמד רבן יוחנן והלך לו לחוץ, והיה רבי אליעזר יושב ודורש ופניו מאירות כאור החמה, וקרנותיו יוצאות כקרנותיו של משה, ואין אדם יודע אם יום ואם לילה. בא רבן יוחנן מאחוריו ונשקו על ראשו. אמר לו, אשריכם אברהם .יצחק ויעקב שיצא זה מחלציכם.

(3) [R. Yoḥanan] said to him: I will [also] tell you a parable. To what can the matter be compared? To this spring which flows and sends forth water, and it is able to produce more water than it receives [from the rain]; so too you can speak words of the Torah more than what they received at Sinai. [R. Yoḥanan continued and] he said to him: Lest you should feel embarrassed on my account, behold, I will stand away from you. R. Yoḥanan stood up and went outside. R. Eliezer sat down and expounded. His face shone like the light of the sun and his rays beamed like the rays of Moses, such that no one knew whether it was day or night. They went and said to R. Yoḥanan b. Zakkai: Come and see R. Eliezer sitting and expounding, his face shining like the light of the sun and his rays beaming like the rays of Moses, such

that no one knows whether it is day or night. He came from [his place] behind him and kissed him on his head, and said to him: Happy are you, Abraham, Isaac, and Jacob, because this one has come forth from your loins.

ד) אמר הורקנוס, למי אמר כך. אמרו לו, לאליעזר בנך. אמר להם, לא כך היה לו לומר, אלא אשרי אני שיצא זה מחלצי. היה רבי אליעזר יושב ודורש, ואביו עומד על רגליו. כיון שראה אביו עומד על רגליו, נבהל. אמר לו, אבא, שב, שאיני יכול לומר דברי תורה ואתה עומד על רגליך. אמר לו, בני, לא על כך באתי, אלא לנדותך מנכסי. ועתה שבאתי לראותך וראיתי כל השבח הזה, הרי אחיך מנודים מהם, והם נתונים לך במתנה.

(4) Hyrcanus his father said: To whom does [R. Yoḥanan] speak such a thing? They said to him: To Eliezer your son. He said to them: [R. Yoḥanan] should not have said it like that, but rather, "Happy am I because he has come forth from my loins."

R. Eliezer would sit and expound, and his father would stand upon his feet. When [Eliezer] saw his father standing upon his feet, he became agitated and said to him: My father! Be seated, for I cannot utter the words of the Torah when you are standing upon your feet. [Hyrcanus] replied to him: My son, it was not for this reason that I came, but my intention was to exclude you from my possessions. Now that I have come and I have witnessed all this praise, behold, your brothers are excluded and their portion is given to you as a gift.

(ה) אמר לו, והרי אני איני שוה כאחד מהם. אילו קרקעות בקשתי מלפני הקדוש ברוך הוא, היה לפניו לתן לי, שנאמר, (תהלים כד, א): "לה' הָאָרֶץ וּמְלוֹאָהּ תֵּבֵל וְיֹשְׁבֵי בָהּ". ואילו כסף וזהב בקשתי, היה נותן לי, שנאמר, (חגי ב, ח): "לִי הַכֶּסֶף, וְלִי הַזָּהָב נְאֻם ה' צְבָאוֹת". אלא לא בקשתי מלפני הקדוש ברוך הוא אלא תורה בלבד, שנאמר, (תהלים קיט, קכח): "עַל־כֵּן, כָּל־פִּקּוּדֵי כֹל יִשָּׁרְתִּי כָּל־אֹרַח שֶׁקֶר שָׂנֵאתִי".

(5) [Eliezer] replied: Behold, I am not equal to one of them. If I had asked the Holy One, blessed be He, for land, it would be possible for Him to give this to me, as it is said, "The earth is the

> Lord's, and the fullness thereof" (Ps. 24:1). Had I asked the Holy One, blessed be He, for silver and gold, He could have given them to me, as it is said, "The silver is Mine, and the gold is Mine" (Hag. 2:8). But I asked the Holy One, blessed be He, that I might be worthy [to learn the] Torah only, as it is said, "Therefore I esteem all precepts concerning all things to be right; and I hate every false way" (Ps. 119:128).

Hyrcanus's children remained at home over these many years working the fields like dutiful sons, while Eliezer has long since absconded to Jerusalem, away from the hard work of the farmer. No doubt Hyrcanus's sons suspect that Eliezer has amounted to very little, for he was like them once, completely unlearned. Moreover, they must have resented his abandonment of the farms to live what they took to be a life of leisure. For both these reasons, they ask Hyrcanus to travel to Jerusalem and prohibit Eliezer from deriving any benefit from their father's vast holdings. If to be a son means to carry on his father's traditions, his fealty to land and soil, to carry on his labors, then Eliezer has proven himself to be no son. Eliezer and his father and brothers live in entirely different worlds, with different values, between which there can be no communication, no discussion, and Hyrcanus agrees to their request.

He arrives in Jerusalem to discover a celebratory feast in progress, at which some of the wealthiest and most distinguished citizens of Jerusalem are assembled together with R. Yoḥanan b. Zakkai. No reason is given for the celebration, and it might have marked a family *simḥa*, or even a fundraising dinner for R. Yoḥanan's yeshiva. Whatever its purpose, when Hyrcanus walks into the room, R. Yoḥanan b. Zakkai is immediately informed that "the father of Rabbi Eliezer has arrived." Note that for the first time in this story Eliezer is called "Rabbi," marking his development as a scholar, a significant milestone in R. Eliezer's life, and in the story we are told. R. Yoḥanan b. Zakkai now tells those around him to make room for Hyrcanus at the head of the table, at a place of honor right next to R. Yoḥanan himself. Why did R. Yoḥanan b. Zakkai do this? Part of the reason may simply be that R. Yohanan accorded him honor because of his wealth. But why then sit him at the very head of the table, next to R. Yohanan himself? Other guests were wealthier and more prominent than he was. In all likelihood, R. Yohanan knew that Eliezer and his father were estranged. He also probably suspected that *kavod,* honor, is a currency that a wealthy farmer from the hinterlands would appreciate. By according Hyrcanus *kavod,* R. Yoḥanan b. Zakkai was probably seeking to bridge the gap between father and son. Hyrcanus will feel more part of Eliezer's new world if that world brings him honor too. Moreover, what father would not take legitimate pride in the accomplishments of a successful son?

Probably with the same goal in mind, R. Yoḥanan b. Zakkai asks Eliezer to share words of Torah with the assembled guests. By demonstrating to Hyrcanus just how much honor his son had achieved, that would bring honor to the father of such a scholar too. Parental pride in a son's achievements might overcome parental resentment of a son who abandons his parent's ways. Yet, while the plan was beautifully conceived, R. Eliezer, perhaps characteristically, abruptly and surprisingly blocks its implementation: He refuses to speak. Now this is a very public, even brazen, refusal to obey the great R. Yoḥanan b. Zakkai on the part of a junior scholar and in front of all the distinguished guests. How could R. Eliezer have done so?

At one level, of course, this is not the only time R. Eliezer disdains conventional behavior in a Torah context, and it foreshadows his great confrontation with the Rabbis over the status of the purity of an oven, called the *tanur shel akhnai,* the subject of the second chapter in this series on R. Eliezer. Moreover, it echoes the the young Eliezer's rejection of his biological father Hyrcanus. Yet even still, why confront R. Yoḥanan b. Zakkai in so public a fashion? R. Eliezer justifies his behavior through classically rabbinic discourse. He offers a *mashal,* a parable: Just as a sealed well can yield no more water than was initially placed into it, so too I, said R. Eliezer, cannot teach any Torah I possess which has not been placed into me by you, my great teacher. Why then do you ask me to teach words of Torah? I can do no more than repeat the words of Torah you have taught me.

The use of the metaphor of a sealed well is revealing, for recall the mishna in *Pirkei Avot* cited earlier, in which R. Yoḥanan b. Zakkai himself praises R. Eliezer for being like a sealed well that loses not a drop of water placed into it, so remarkable was R. Eliezer's recall. R. Eliezer's great strength, his approach to Torah study, is here already apparent even at this stage of his development. While this will become even more manifest over the following two chapters of this volume, it is worth stressing even now that R. Eliezer's predilection for recall of Torah taught was not merely the product of his no doubt prodigious memory. Rather, it was also the product of a deep ideological commitment to the purity of the transmission of Oral Law from one generation to the next. Remember that R. Yoḥanan b. Zakkai is described as a student of Hillel[10] and that it was Hillel who brought from Babylonia to *Eretz Yisrael* methods for creativity in halakhic interpretation of the Torah, the "Seven Hermeneutical Principles."[11] Shammai disagreed and favored the ancient traditions of halakha, without unnecessary recourse to such creative methods of interpretation. R. Yoḥanan b. Zakkai in Yavne, follower of the school of Hillel, stressed the creative power of great Torah scholars to confront new realities, especially in response to the disastrous destruction of the Holy Temple and the loss of Jewish sovereignty. R. Eliezer dissented from such creativity. Torah was revealed by God to Moses at Sinai, then transcribed by Moses, and the Oral Law which explained and accompanied the Written Law was transmitted from one generation of Torah scholars to the next. Preserving that tradition in its entirety was the most certain method of preserving Torah truth, for any investment of human creativity into the process of halakhic decision making brings with it the risk of error, and therefore of misinterpreting God's will. After all, what could matter more than getting God's will right?

In this respect, R. Eliezer, although educated by R. Yoḥanan b. Zakkai, identified more with elements of the approach of Shammai to the *mesora*, the faithful rendering of tradition, than with the approach of Hillel, and focused with his prodigious memory on preserving the great traditions of the Oral Law transmitted from generation

10. Sukka 28a; Bava Batra 134a.

11. For more on Hillel's bringing of these rules, called the *middot shehaTorah nidreshet bahen*, to *Eretz Yisrael*, and how he applied it to a specific halakhic doubt, see Tosefta Pesaḥim 4:13–14.

to generation with as little human intervention as possible.[12] This is not to say that Shammai, Shammai's school, and R. Eliezer himself never invested independent human reason to resolve halakhic challenges. That would be impossible, and all parties to the talmudic tradition did. The question was to what extent, and how much that creative effort was valorized, or avoided when possible.[13] With this background we can better understand R. Eliezer's refusal to share Torah teachings with the assembled. If his Torah is no more than the Torah of his master R. Yoḥanan, then why should he repeat his master's Torah in the presence of the master himself?

One answer might be that R. Yoḥanan wished him to demonstrate just how well he had absorbed his master's teachings, how broad and clear his knowledge was. Yet that does not satisfy R. Eliezer, perhaps because he wanted to make a public point about his deeply held ideology of Torah study. As we shall soon see, another reason emerges as well. In any case, R. Yoḥanan b. Zakkai refuses to accept his student's demur-

---

12. For a discussion of Hillel and Shammai, their schools and approaches to Torah see Binyamin Lau, *The Sages* (Tel Aviv, 2007), vol. 1, 151–200 (Heb.). For an extensive discussion of R. Eliezer, his approach to Torah study and his relationship to the school of Shammai, see Y. D. Gilat, *R. Eliezer ben Hyrcanus: A Scholar Outcast* (Ramat Gan, 1984), especially chs. 1 and 15. Medieval commentators puzzled over the question of why R. Eliezer identified with Shammai if he had been a student of R. Yoḥanan b. Zakkai, who was himself a student of Hillel. Some suggest that R. Yoḥanan b. Zakkai transferred his allegiance to Shammai later in life, but Nahmanides in his commentary to Shabbat 12a suggests an alternative answer, which seems to me most likely. R. Yoḥanan b. Zakkai, true follower of Hillel, taught all competing traditions, for which Hillel was much praised (see Eiruvin 13b). While he himself probably favored his own master, Hillel, R. Eliezer, who heard both positions fairly presented, favored Shammai. This interpretation best accounts for the text which is the subject of this chapter. This also explains why R. Eliezer sometimes cites Hillel despite following Shammai (see Yevamot 26a and Eduyot 2:4). While both R. Yoḥanan b. Zakkai and R. Eliezer placed great emphasis on prodigious recall, R. Yoḥanan b. Zakkai, student of Hillel, remained open to the creativity that Shammai and R. Eliezer did not.
13. Students of Talmud know the story told about how even Moses could not understand the creative teachings of R. Akiva. This brilliantly exemplifies the Yavne school's emphasis on creativity, fully realized by R. Akiva, who, ironically, was one of the great students of R. Eliezer (see Menaḥot 29b for more on this story). Of course, R. Akiva was also the student of R. Yehoshua, R. Eliezer's main antagonist in the oven of *akhnai* confrontation.

ral, and he refuses to do so on ideological grounds as well. In short, he denies R Eliezer's theory of Torah study and articulates his own position, by denying the aptness of R. Eliezer's parable, and offering his own. He insists that Torah study may be more aptly compared not to a sealed well preserving the water placed into it, but rather to a spring, which yields more water than placed into it by any outsider, from its own flowing resources. R. Yoḥanan draws a direct lesson: You, R. Eliezer, can and must teach more Torah than was ever received at Sinai.

Note first that R. Yoḥanan expresses no anger at his young student for refusing publicly to obey his request. This is a continuing manifestation of the sensitivity and humanity of R. Yoḥanan b. Zakkai. He respects and cares for his student, like a father for his son. Second, R. Yoḥanan b. Zakkai, true to Hillel and his school, valorizes human creativity over mere preservation of tradition, as important as that is. He puts this in very sharp terms, encouraging him to go beyond the pure revelation at Sinai, to add his own insights to the great flow of tradition. Surely the waters of a gushing spring are fresher than old, even well-preserved, waters from a sealed well. He, in effect, argues for the vitality of human creativity in the process of Torah study, despite the risk of error. *Pirkei DeRabbi Eliezer*, the late midrash we are analyzing, vividly depicts this early clash about the ideals of Torah study.

R. Yoḥanan b. Zakkai next makes a fascinating point. He suggests that R. Eliezer might be embarrassed at teaching Torah in his master's presence, and offers to leave the room. There is deep wisdom in this insight, and in his offer. In order for a student to flourish, the master must give him or her room to do so. A teacher who constantly hovers over the student, who thereby implies that the student can succeed only if he becomes a replica of the master, will in the end suffocate that student. Every human being has unique gifts. The great teacher must help a student cultivate and realize those gifts, even if they are different from those of the master, and must liberate the student to flourish in his or her own ways. This may mean that the student will come to see things differently from the master, even disagree with him or her. Yet that is as it should be. Students require great teachers to teach them knowledge they did not know, and to teach them methodologies for acquiring new knowledge and insight, and then those teachers must leave their students to their own talents and devices. A great teacher must know when to abscond. And this is especially true of a teacher who is also a father to the student brought under his or her wing.

This is exactly what R. Yoḥanan b. Zakkai does, and its impact on R. Eliezer is nothing short of remarkable. Once R. Yoḥanan leaves the room, R. Eliezer begins to teach, and "his face shone like the light of the sun, and his rays beamed like the rays of Moses, so that no one knew whether it was day or night." The reference to Moses, and the brilliance of the glow, calls to mind the revelation at Sinai, and what the assembled guests witnessed was nothing short of a new quasi-Sinaitic revelation. In effect, R. Eliezer is portrayed here as his generation's Moses, and R. Eliezer has taken his mentor's words – that he teach more than was revealed at Sinai – seriously indeed. Everyone in the room was dazzled. However, upon reflection, his performance raises a very troubling question. Was R. Eliezer not ideologically opposed to such novel insights? Did he not valorize the retentive over the creative? Is he then not guilty of rank inconsistency?

In some ways, this may be a key to understanding R. Eliezer's confounding personality. One might have thought that R. Eliezer favored the retentive over the creative because the retentive capitalized exactly on his distinctive intellectual gifts. However, such a claim would be reductionist and simplistic, for two reasons. No doubt, of course, R. Eliezer had a wonderful memory, but what he remembered did not come without effort. In fact, R. Eliezer says of himself, recalling his student days, "No one ever arrived before me in the study hall, and I never slept in the study hall, neither a full sleep nor a nap. I never left behind anyone in the study hall when I left, I never spoke words of a secular nature, and I never said anything I had never heard from my teachers."[14] R. Eliezer's memory was at least in part due to prodigious effort. Whatever gifts he had were pushed to their very limits. Those individuals blessed with a photographic memory see something once, then recall it with ease. Such was apparently not the case with R. Eliezer.

Second, and more importantly, according to our midrash, R. Eliezer had extraordinary creative gifts as well, for he became, for that moment,

14. Sukka 28a.

like the spring in R. Yoḥanan's parable, pouring forth new insight after new insight, brilliant enough to illuminate the room. Why then did R. Eliezer never exploit this talent during his long life? Because he believed that it was the wrong way to study Torah, that it risked contaminating the purity of Torah's inter-generational transmission, teacher to teacher, all the way back to Sinai: "I never said anything I had never heard from my teachers." On this telling, R. Eliezer was a heroic figure, and a tragic one. No doubt exercising the greatest of self-control, he suppressed the creative talents and insights bubbling up within him, insisting on the discipline of teaching only what he had been taught. Imagine the psychic cost of such suppression! R. Eliezer's tragedy was not only that he suffered the excommunication of his peers. No less a tragedy for him personally was that he possessed extraordinary creative gifts, and no doubt continued to conceive brilliant new insights into Torah, yet in disciplined service to his vision of Torah, he suppressed his creativity and new insights for the whole of his mature life in Torah. Here ideology is not a product of personality or talent, but its enemy.

R. Yoḥanan's departure from the celebration liberated for R. Eliezer, if only momentarily, those inner gifts he had long suppressed. The genie had left the bottle, but R. Eliezer, with his unimaginable inner discipline and drive, subsequently managed to put it back in the bottle forever. One wonders if the toughness, the contrarian side of R. Eliezer, the anger which the Talmud describes as the product of his excommunication,[15] were all exacerbated by the inner tension which must have pursued R. Eliezer throughout his life, as he struggled to suppress the creativity with which he was gifted.

How does R. Yoḥanan b. Zakkai respond to his student's brilliant demonstration? Does he feel threatened? Decidedly not. In an act of the greatest love and self-restraint, R. Yoḥanan b. Zakkai approaches Eliezer from behind, remaining invisible to him, and he kisses him on the head. R. Yoḥanan says to R. Eliezer, "Fortunate are you, Abraham, Isaac, and Jacob, that such a person has come from your loins." R. Yoḥanan

15. See chapters 2 and 3 of this volume for more evidence and discussion of this claim. The analysis in this chapter suggests that these characteristics go back to his youth, and that they became more prominent as a result of this tension.

remains hidden from view, leaving space for his blossoming student, while acknowledging to him, and to all the assembled guests, including Hyrcanus his father, just how precious his student is. For the first time, R. Yoḥanan kisses R. Eliezer, completing the evolution of their father-teacher/son relationship. Moreover, and continuing to deepen the theme of paternity, R. Yoḥanan asserts that Eliezer's ultimate parents are surely not Hyrcanus, nor even himself, but Abraham, Isaac, and Jacob, his ultimate spiritual fathers. Hyrcanus and R. Yoḥanan both are but links in a chain whose origins go back to the fathers of all Jews, the Patriarchs themselves.

The reader reflects about the long journey R. Eliezer has taken, and his evolving relationship with R. Yoḥanan, and with this kiss from behind is left with an enduring and powerful image of both love and restraint.

Following the exchange between R. Eliezer and his father/master R. Yoḥanan, the author of the text turns the reader's attention to the relationship between R. Eliezer and his biological father, Hyrcanus, from father three to father one. What impact will all these developments have on Hyrcanus, and on how Hyrcanus feels about his son? Has R. Eliezer's attitude toward his father evolved? Is reconciliation possible? Will they finally succeed in communicating?

Hyrcanus hears R. Yoḥanan say about the speaker that Abraham, Isaac, and Jacob are fortunate to have such a man come from their loins, and asks just who that man is. When he is told by the assembled that the man was none other than his son R. Eliezer (which, of course, Hyrcanus knew all along), Hyrcanus responds that R. Yoḥanan should better have said, referring to Hyrcanus himself (instead of, or in addition to, the Patriarchs), "Fortunate am I that such a person descends from my loins." In other words, Hyrcanus wishes a share in the credit for the achievements of his now distinguished son. Has Hyrcanus undergone a dramatic conversion, and suddenly become a lover and supporter of Torah study? This is hardly likely. Rather, one currency Hyrcanus understands is honor, and the impressive honor now shown for R. Eliezer, should, he maintains, belong also to him. While his comment may also reflect the legitimate joy that a father experiences with the success of a child, the very self-referential expression of that joy – "Fortunate am I" – suggests that there is more to it than that.

R. Eliezer continues to sit and teach Torah, while Hyrcanus stands. This, of course, is a reversal of the natural order, where the son would stand out of respect for the father. Here the father stands out of respect for the son. Note that we once again find R. Eliezer sitting, but consider the transformation in the significance of that posture. Eliezer as a young man sat in despair, crying and fasting. R. Eliezer now sits regally, in full command of the Torah, brilliantly revealing new insights like Moses at Sinai, before an assembled congregation of admirers, including his own father, who now stands in respect. He has found a new and loving father and has been fully accepted into the elite family of the yeshiva. Sitting can connote two very different conditions indeed.

When R. Eliezer notices that his father stands while he sits, he becomes agitated, and asks his father to sit, protesting that he cannot teach Torah while his father stands, which would be a sign of disrespect for his father. What are we to make of this? Why was R. Eliezer so agitated about implying disrespect for his father? After all, his father had been an obstacle to his dreams of Torah study from the very beginning. Indeed, while R. Eliezer may not have known this, the very purpose of Hyrcanus's visit to Jerusalem was to disown him!

Part of the answer may be halakhic. R. Eliezer knew the stringencies of the biblical obligation to honor a father, and would have been dismayed if his behavior even bordered on their violation. However, as the ensuing dialogue implies, there is more to it than that. R. Eliezer is now an older and wiser man, and his dream of Torah scholarship has finally been realized. I would suggest that R. Eliezer has come to accept his father for who he is. With all Hyrcanus's limitations, he is still R. Eliezer's father. At this new stage in his life, R. Eliezer is finally able to respect Hyrcanus as a father, has put the anguish of the past behind him, understands his father for who he is, strengths and weaknesses alike, and affirms Hyrcanus's place in his life. Just as R. Eliezer's relationship with his dominant spiritual father, R. Yoḥanan b. Zakkai, evolved over time, so too, and perhaps commensurately, did his relationship with his biological father, Hyrcanus, evolve, and also heal. In the end, R. Eliezer's relationships with both his fathers are complex, for R. Eliezer not only affirms but also rejects each, of course in different ways and degrees. As always, sons must find their own way in the world.

Hyrcanus responds to R. Eliezer's request that he sit by blurting out the truth, that he had come to Jerusalem to disown him financially, but now that he sees "all the praise" R. Eliezer has garnered, he's changed his mind. In a complete turnaround, Hyrcanus states that he will disown not R. Eliezer, but his sons back on the farm, and that he, R. Eliezer, will inherit his wealth. By attributing his abrupt *volte-face* to "praise" for R. Eliezer, rather than the value of the Torah R. Eliezer has acquired, Hyrcanus reveals his hand. The motivator is pride in his son's accomplishments, once again. Hyrcanus's change of heart is not a change of ideals, but a change in calculus. He determines that he will derive greater praise by supporting R. Eliezer than by disowning him, in the coin of praise, which is obviously the currency most meaningful to him. As much as his son R. Eliezer has changed, as a Torah scholar and a son, Hyrcanus remains much the same, with the same values he started with, even if he is now willing to support R. Eliezer in his studies. Some people, it seems, can never really change.

Strikingly, R. Eliezer rejects Hyrcanus's offer, saying that he doesn't require, or even want, Hyrcanus's wealth. If he had wanted material goods, he would have asked for them from God, whose capacity to bestow them is unlimited. All he ever sought from God was Torah. This sentence is the perfect *summa* of R. Eliezer's life, up until this moment, and to its tragic end, which we shall see.

Thus, the story, and this chapter in R. Eliezer's life, ends. Is this a happy or tragic ending? Surely it is happy, in that R. Eliezer has come to realize his deepest ambition, to devote his life to Torah, and to achieve the knowledge for which he yearned. Consider, then, the sheer power of his inspiring drive for Torah knowledge, and how it formed his life. Moreover, he makes peace with his father, and accepts his father for who he is, just as Hyrcanus makes peace with the alternative life his son has chosen. While all this is true, the picture it draws is not complete. Although R. Eliezer and Hyrcanus have reconciled, their reconciliation is no more than superficial. While he takes pride in R. Eliezer's achievements, Hyrcanus still fails to truly understand his son or to appreciate the values to which he has devoted his life. Father and son speak different languages, live in incommensurate worlds, with no possibility of deep communication between them. It is tragic, too, in that, as we saw, R. Eliezer's tough-mindedness and stubbornness made his extraordinary accomplishments possible, as did his extreme commitment to the importance of purity in the intergenerational Torah transmission. Yet it was precisely those qualities, and precisely that ideology, both apparent even in his youth, which ultimately led to his eventual excommunication and tragic end. R. Eliezer's greatest strengths ultimately unraveled his great life.

Chapter 2

The Day R. Eliezer Was Excommunicated: A Debate over the Oven of *Akhnai*

Bava Metzia 59b

INTRODUCTION

The previous chapter explored the early years of R. Eliezer, as depicted in *Pirkei DeRabbi Eliezer*. This chapter examines the culmination of R. Eliezer's many years of study and teaching in the tragic conflict over the halakhic status of a particular kind of oven. All of R. Eliezer's colleagues took one position, he another, and although he adduces divine miracles to prove his position, and a voice from heaven even ratifies it, his colleagues nevertheless refuse to concede. R. Eliezer in turn refuses to concede to his colleagues, and as a result they excommunicate him, with disastrous consequences for all involved. This aggada is among the most famous in all the Talmud, and scores of studies have been written about it over the years. While my approach in this chapter builds upon the work of others, it nevertheless is distinctive in that it seeks to place this aggada into the context of R. Eliezer's early life, and his deathbed encounter with his colleagues and students. This strategy provides a more unified and integrated portrait of R. Eliezer's life, at least based upon these texts, which in turn provides a fresh perspective on the events told in this chapter, and in the other two chapters of the trilogy as well. Each illuminates the others.[1]

Much of the discussion about this aggada focuses on the theory of halakha which is debated between R. Eliezer and the Sages. While I shall address this to some extent as well, my focus will be on the aggada's context, a talmudic discussion of the terrible wrong of *onaat devarim*, of offending and hurting another person's feelings. The oven of *akhnai* story is included in this larger discussion as an example of the importance of the law prohibiting hurting another person's feelings, and the human costs that flow from violating this prohibition. This focus leads naturally to an examination of the interpersonal tensions and conflicts depicted in the aggada. As we shall see, these in part grow out of R. Eliezer's past, and foreshadow the dramatic deathbed scene depicted in Sanhedrin 68a, the subject of the next chapter in this volume, the final one in the trilogy on R. Eliezer. This chapter is divided into two parts, the first dealing with the controversy over the oven, the second dealing with its aftermath.

1. Jeffrey Rubenstein, in his *Talmudic Stories: Narrative Art, Composition and Culture* (Baltimore, 1999), 34–63, provides an excellent analysis, although my emphasis on R. Eliezer's responsibility for his fate is different from his, as is my situating this aggada in the context of R. Eliezer's early life and his deathbed encounter. In his first endnote on this story (pp. 314–15) he provides a comprehensive listing of sources on this aggada, to which I would add the valuable discussion in Y. Brandes, *Aggada LeMaase* (Jerusalem, 2011), vol. 2, 72–82 (Heb.). In addition, for a useful discussion of traditional sources on this aggada, see Yitzchak Englard, "The Oven of *Akhnai*: Various Interpretations of an Aggadah," *Annual of Research in Jewish Law* I (1974), 45–56 (Heb.), and in English, "Majority Tradition and Individual Truth," *Tradition* 15:1–2 (1975), 137–52.

Bava Metzia 59b

וזה הוא תנור של עכנאי מאי עכנאי אמר רב יהודה אמר שמואל שהקיפו דברים כעכנא זו וטמאוהו תנא באותו היום השיב רבי אליעזר כל תשובות שבעולם ולא קיבלו הימנו. אמר להם אם הלכה כמותי חרוב זה יוכיח נעקר חרוב ממקומו מאה אמה ואמרי לה ארבע מאות אמה אמרו לו אין מביאין ראיה מן החרוב חזר ואמר להם אם הלכה כמותי אמת המים יוכיחו חזרו אמת המים לאחוריהם אמרו לו אין מביאין ראיה מאמת המים. חזר ואמר להם אם הלכה כמותי כותלי בית המדרש יוכיחו הטו כותלי בית המדרש ליפול גער בהם רבי יהושע אמר להם אם תלמידי חכמים מנצחים זה את זה בהלכה אתם מה טיבכם לא נפלו מפני כבודו של רבי יהושע ולא זקפו מפני כבודו של ר"א ועדיין מטין ועומדין.

And this is known as **the oven of *akhnai*.** The Gemara asks: **What** is the relevance of ***akhnai,*** a snake, in this context? **Rav Yehuda said** that **Shmuel said:** It is characterized in that manner due to the fact **that** the Rabbis **surrounded** it **with** their **statements like this snake,** which often forms a coil when at rest, **and deemed it impure.** The Sages **taught: On that day,** when they discussed this matter, **Rabbi Eliezer answered all** possible **answers in the world** to support his opinion, **but** the Rabbis **did not accept** his explanations **from him.** After failing to convince the Rabbis logically, Rabbi Eliezer **said to them: If** the ***halakha*** is **in accordance with my** opinion, **this carob** tree **will prove** it. The **carob** tree **was uprooted from its place one hundred cubits, and some say four hundred cubits.** The Rabbis **said to him: One does not cite** halakhic **proof from the carob** tree. Rabbi Eliezer **then said to them: If** the ***halakha*** is **in accordance with my** opinion, **the stream will prove** it. The water in **the stream turned backward** and began flowing in the opposite direction. **They said to him: One does not cite** halakhic **proof from a stream.** Rabbi Eliezer **then said to them: If** the ***halakha*** is **in accordance with my** opinion, **the walls of the study hall will prove** it. **The walls of the study hall leaned** inward and began **to fall. Rabbi Yehoshua scolded** the walls and **said to them: If Torah scholars are contending** with

each other in matters of ***halakha,*** **what** is the **nature** of **your** involvement in this dispute? The Gemara relates: The walls **did not fall because of** the **deference** due **Rabbi Yehoshua, but they did not straighten because of** the **deference** due **Rabbi Eliezer, and they still remain leaning.**

חזר ואמר להם אם הלכה כמותי מן השמים יוכיחו יצאתה בת קול ואמרה מה לכם אצל ר"א שהלכה כמותו בכ"מ. עמד רבי יהושע על רגליו ואמר (דברים ל, יב) לא בשמים היא מאי לא בשמים היא אמר רבי ירמיה שכבר נתנה תורה מהר סיני אין אנו משגיחין בבת קול שכבר כתבת בהר סיני בתורה (שמות כג, ב) אחרי רבים להטות אשכחיה רבי נתן לאליהו א"ל מאי עביד קוב"ה בההיא שעתא א"ל קא חייך ואמר נצחוני בני נצחוני בני.

Rabbi Eliezer **then said to them: If** the *halakha* is **in accordance with my** opinion, **Heaven will prove** it. **A Divine Voice emerged** from Heaven **and said: Why are you** differing **with Rabbi Eliezer, as** the *halakha* is **in accordance with** his opinion **in every place** that he expresses an opinion? **Rabbi Yehoshua stood on his feet and said:** It is written: **"It is not in heaven"** (Deuteronomy 30:12). The Gemara asks: **What** is the relevance of the phrase **"It is not in heaven"** in this context? **Rabbi Yirmeya says:** Since **the Torah was already given at Mount Sinai, we do not regard a Divine Voice, as You already wrote at Mount Sinai, in the Torah: "After a majority to incline"** (Exodus 23:2). Since the majority of Rabbis disagreed with Rabbi Eliezer's opinion, the *halakha* is not ruled in accordance with his opinion. The Gemara relates: Years after, **Rabbi Natan encountered Elijah** the Prophet and **said to him: What did the Holy One, Blessed be He, do at that time,** when Rabbi Yehoshua issued his declaration? Elijah **said to him:** The Holy One, Blessed be He, **smiled and said: My children have triumphed over Me; My children have triumphed over Me.**

אמרו אותו היום הביאו כל טהרות שטיהר ר"א ושרפום באש ונמנו עליו וברכוהו ואמרו מי ילך ויודיעו אמר להם ר"ע אני אלך שמא ילך אדם

שאינו הגון ויודיעו ונמצא מחריב את כל העולם כולו. מה עשה ר״ע לבש שחורים ונתעטף שחורים וישב לפניו ברחוק ארבע אמות אמר לו ר״א עקיבא מה יום מיומים אמר לו רבי כמדומה לי שחבירים בדילים ממך.

The Sages **said:** On **that day,** the Sages **brought all the ritually pure** items **deemed pure by** the ruling of **Rabbi Eliezer** with regard to the oven **and burned them in fire, and** the Sages **reached a consensus in his regard and ostracized him. And** the Sages **said: Who will go and inform him** of his ostracism? **Rabbi Akiva,** his beloved disciple, **said to them: I will go, lest an unseemly person go** and inform him in a callous and offensive manner, **and he would thereby destroy the entire world. What did Rabbi Akiva do? He wore black and wrapped himself in black,** as an expression of mourning and pain, **and sat before** Rabbi Eliezer **at a distance of four cubits,** which is the distance that one must maintain from an ostracized individual. **Rabbi Eliezer said to him: Akiva, what** is different about **today from other days,** that you comport yourself in this manner? Rabbi Akiva **said to him: My teacher, it appears to me that** your **colleagues are distancing** themselves **from you.** He employed euphemism, as actually they distanced Rabbi Eliezer from them.

אף הוא קרע בגדיו וחלץ מנעליו ונשמט וישב על גבי קרקע. זלגו עיניו דמעות לקה העולם שליש בזיתים ושליש בחטים ושליש בשעורים ויש אומרים אף בצק שבידי אשה טפח תנא אך גדול היה באותו היום שבכל מקום שנתן בו עיניו ר״א נשרף. ואף ר״ג היה בא בספינה עמד עליו נחשול לטבעו אמר כמדומה לי שאין זה אלא בשביל ר״א בן הורקנוס עמד על רגליו ואמר רבונו של עולם גלוי וידוע לפניך שלא לכבודי עשיתי ולא לכבוד בית אבא עשיתי אלא לכבודך שלא ירבו מחלוקות בישראל נח הים מזעפו.

Rabbi Eliezer, **too, rent his garments and removed his shoes,** as is the custom of an ostracized person, **and he dropped** from his seat **and sat upon the ground.** The Gemara relates: **His eyes shed tears,** and as a result **the** entire **world was afflicted: One-third of** its **olives** were afflicted, **and one-third of** its **wheat, and**

one-third of its **barley. And some say** that **even dough** kneaded **in a woman's hands spoiled.** The Sages **taught: There was great anger on that day, as any place that Rabbi Eliezer fixed his gaze was burned. And even Rabban Gamliel,** the *Nasi* of the Sanhedrin at Yavne, the head of the Sages who were responsible for the decision to ostracize Rabbi Eliezer, **was coming on a boat** at the time, and **a large wave swelled over him** and threatened **to drown him.** Rabban Gamliel **said: It seems to me that this is only for the sake of Rabbi Eliezer ben Hyrcanus,** as God punishes those who mistreat others. Rabban Gamliel **stood on his feet and said: Master of the Universe, it is revealed and known before You that neither was it for my honor** that **I acted** when ostracizing him, **nor was it for the honor of the house of my father** that **I acted; rather,** it was **for Your honor, so that disputes will not proliferate in Israel.** In response, **the sea calmed from its raging.**

אימא שלום דביתהו דר״א אחתיה דר״ג הואי מההוא מעשה ואילך לא הוה שבקה ליה לר״א למיפל על אפיה ההוא יומא ריש ירחא הוה ואיחלף לה בין מלא לחסר איכא דאמרי אתא עניא וקאי אבבא אפיקא ליה ריפתא. אשכחתיה דנפל על אנפיה אמרה ליה קום קטלית לאחי אדהכי נפק שיפורא מבית רבן גמליאל דשכיב אמר לה מנא ידעת אמרה ליה כך מקובלני מבית אבי אבא כל השערים ננעלים חוץ משערי אונאה.

The Gemara further relates: **Imma Shalom, the wife of Rabbi Eliezer, was the sister of Rabban Gamliel. From that incident forward, she would not allow Rabbi Eliezer to lower his head** and recite the *taḥanun* prayer, which includes supplication and entreaties. She feared that were her husband to bemoan his fate and pray at that moment, her brother would be punished. **A certain day was** around the day of **the New Moon, and she** inadvertently **substituted a full** thirty-day month **for a deficient** twenty-nine-day month, i.e., she thought that it was the New Moon, when one does not lower his head in supplication, but it was not. **Some say** that **a pauper came and stood at the door,** and **she took bread out to him.** The result was that she left her husband momentarily unsupervised. When she returned, **she found him** and saw **that he had lowered his head** in prayer. **She said to him: Arise; you** already **killed my brother. Meanwhile,** the sound of **a** *shofar* **emerged from the house of Rabban Gamliel** to announce **that** the *Nasi* **had died.** Rabbi Eliezer **said to her: From where did you know** that your brother would die? **She said to him: This is** the tradition that **I received from the house of the father of** my **father: All the gates** of Heaven are apt to be **locked, except for the gates** of prayer for victims **of** verbal **mistreatment.**

PART ONE

A SEARING DEBATE OVER THE OVEN OF *AKHNAI*

The mishna in Kelim 5:10 records a dispute between R. Eliezer and the Sages about the halakhic status of a particular oven, called according to some texts *akhnai*, and according to others *ḥakhinai*.[2] Whatever its true name, there is little question about what it was. This oven was formed out of sections of hardened clay a few inches in diameter, with sand placed between each section. Once assembled, the surface was plastered to keep everything in place, a design which made the oven portable, since it could easily be assembled and disassembled for traveling. R. Eliezer maintained that because the oven was constructed in sections divided by sand it had the halakhic status of a broken vessel, which can never become impure, as only whole vessels can. The Sages maintained that since the surface was plastered and the oven could be used for baking, it had the status of a whole vessel and could become impure.[3]

The Talmud begins its discussion by asking about the meaning of the term *akhnai*. Now, if the name derives from the name of its

2. See *Tosafot*, Bava Metzia 59b, s.v. *zeh tanur*. The Talmud Yerushalmi used the latter, and it may have been the name of the person who produced them. The Talmud Bavli, whose text we are studying in this chapter, used the former. While *akhnai* may also have been the name of the person who produced these ovens, the Bavli interprets the name figuratively as well, as we shall see.

3. When the laws of purity were carefuly observed, an impure vessel could not be used, and in the case of an impure oven, food prepared therein could not be eaten either.

producer, why ask about the meaning of the term? It is possible, of course, that the Bavli had no tradition that it was named after its producer, and so asked the question it did. More likely, however, the Bavli sought some deeper, figurative meaning to this oven whose significance cast shock waves throughout the rabbinic world of the time. This seems evident from the answer cited by R. Yehuda in the name of Shmuel, that the Sages "surrounded R. Eliezer with words like a snake," and deemed the oven impure. This interpretation is made possible by the meaning of the Aramaic word "*akhnai,* a snake which coils to attack its prey.[4] Thus the very name of the oven not only foreshadowed the clash between R. Eliezer and the Sages, but foreshadowed the aggressive and destructive treatment meted out to R. Eliezer by the Sages: his excommunication. Thus, the name itself integrates the unfolding story into the larger talmudic discussion of *onaat devarim,* paining someone with words.

Following this amoraic prologue, the Talmud cites an earlier *baraita* which tells the basic story. R. Eliezer had marshaled all the arguments he could in support of his lone position against all the scholars who opposed him, to no avail, so he adverts to supernatural means to prove his point. He proclaims that the carob tree standing outside the study hall will prove him correct, at which point the carob tree promptly moved one hundred *amot*[5] from its place.[6] The Sages respond that mobile carob trees do not constitute acceptable evidence in a halakhic debate. R. Eliezer next attempts another supernatural proof, and proclaims that the stream of water flowing outside the study hall will prove him right, at which point the stream reverses course and flows backward. The Sages

4. This interpretation assumes either that the name given to the oven antedated the actual debate, and the mishna uses terms that R. Eliezer and the Sages did not themselves use, or that the name always was *akhnai,* but it took on another meaning in the course of history.

5. About 150 feet.

6. The *baraita* itself records another tradition, that it moved not one hundred but four hundred *amot.* This no doubt reflects not only the classic rabbinic focus on exact measurements, but also the desire of the author of the *baraita* to reinforce the veracity of the tale itself, by recording two exacting traditions regarding the distance the tree moved. Moreover, such focus on detail lends an aura of authenticity to a story that might appear fantastical to some.

respond, again, that streams of water likewise do not constitute acceptable evidence in a halakhic debate.

R. Eliezer then tries one final supernatural gambit, and proclaims that the walls of the study hall will prove him right, at which point they start to fall. This stirs the ire of R. Yehoshua, R. Eliezer's closest companion and halakhic sparring partner, who responds in anger to the tottering walls, "If Torah scholars are contending with each other in matters of halakha, what is the nature of your involvement in this dispute?" Interestingly, R. Yehoshua intervenes only here. The walls are personified and addressed, but not the carob tree or the stream of water. Why the difference? Before answering this question, let us examine the next few lines of the story. The author of the *baraita* reports that out of respect for R. Yehoshua the walls did not fall, while out of respect for R. Eliezer, they did not aright themselves either, but rather remained tilted. This commentary on the events described adds a crucial new perspective. The walls, "inanimate" objects, are concerned with the dignity of the contending scholars, and seek compromise. This contrasts with the human beings in the story, who do not show similar concern for the dignity of the other, notably the Sages toward R. Eliezer, and who refuse any compromise to preserve the feelings of their adversaries. The author seems to imply that human beings have much to learn from mere walls. That said, the tension these walls symbolize is never fully resolved, and they remain tilted as a graphic and physical reminder of the irreconcilable contest between R. Eliezer and the Sages, whose repercussions have endured throughout the ages, much as the tilted walls endured too.

This perspective in turn sheds light on the question raised above, for it leads us to inquire about the symbolic significance of all three supernatural signs. When R. Eliezer called upon the walls of the study hall to prove his position, and they begin to fall, it is likely that R. Eliezer was implying that the very survival of the Torah, whose study is housed within, was at stake. If the Sages cannot agree with his position, then Torah will collapse, crushed under the collapse of the study hall itself. And the scholars studying within? They too would be killed by the falling walls. So convinced was R. Eliezer of his rectitude, that he was asserting in effect that there could be no future to Torah, and to Torah scholars, if his adversaries failed to agree with him. R. Eliezer had called upon the walls of the study hall to prove this dire prediction correct, as if they were part of the halakhic process which takes place within their very confines.

Yet R. Yehoshua, great follower of Hillel and advocate of halakhic creativity, could not agree, for argument and debate would always be of the essence of Torah learning. He addresses the walls directly, telling them that they are not protagonists in the search for halakhic truth, even if they house it. The symbolism of the falling walls, which alludes to the death of Torah and its scholars, is quite different from the symbolism of the moving tree and the reversal of the flowing waters. In the latter two miracles, no mortal threats are implied. As is well known, both trees and water are symbols of Torah, and the life it provides.[7] If so, with the marching of the tree, R. Eliezer meant to signal that Torah cannot remain where it belongs if his colleagues fail to agree with him. Likewise, with the reversal of the stream's flow, R. Eliezer meant to suggest that the natural life-flow of the Torah will be disturbingly altered. Yet despite these setbacks, no mortal threats are made, and Torah study could still take place in the study hall, even if impeded, and scholars would still remain alive within. R. Yehoshua therefore saw no need yet to interject. R. Eliezer was scoring points, but had not yet threatened the woof and warp of Torah study. Everything changed with the collapse of the walls. For R. Yehoshua, R. Eliezer had now gone too far. While R. Yehoshua knows R. Eliezer will not listen to him, he believes the walls will, and indeed they do. That is why he addresses them directly.

It seems fair to ask at this point whether or not the events described so far in the *baraita* actually took place. Did the tree move, the water reverse course, and the walls fall? One answer, of course, is that they did. We know from other sources that R. Eliezer was gifted in the art of sorcery, and he may have applied his skill here as well.[8] Another

---

7. For the symbolism of the tree, see, e.g., Proverbs 3:18, "It [the Torah] is the tree of life for those who grasp it"; for the symbolism of water, see, e.g., Bava Kamma 17a, "There is no water except Torah."
8. See Sanhedrin 68a, which describes how R. Eliezer magically moved thousands of

very interesting possibility is proposed by Rabbenu Ḥananel, the eleventh-century commentator cited in the sixteenth-century anthology of medieval commentaries to the Talmud, the *Shita Mekubetzet*, on our passage. He comments that all the events described in the *baraita* took place in a dream. A scholar in the study hall, while observing the sharp debates between R. Eliezer and the Sages, dozed off and dreamt all the events described. The author of the *baraita* recorded the dream because he believed, like many of his compatriots of that era, that dreams contain an element of prophecy, and are worthy of preserving.[9] As we shall see, this approach is significant for understanding the jurisprudential implications of the debate.

In any case, R. Eliezer possesses one final recourse to vindicate his position, following the failure of his previous attempts: He appeals to God Himself. "If I am right," he proclaims, "may the heavens prove it!" A *bat kol*, a voice from the heavens, asserts, "Why are you differing with R. Eliezer? The law is always in accordance with his opinion." This heavenly endorsement goes well beyond the case at hand, and affirms R. Eliezer's supremacy and authority in all areas of halakha. What could be more potent than that? We have here no mere symbolic affirmation of R. Eliezer's, but an explicit heavenly endorsement of every one of R. Eliezer's countless disputed halakhic teachings. Surely there could be no better evidence for R. Eliezer's halakhic standing than God Himself. The case should be closed, but it isn't.

In one of the most famous passages in all the Talmud, the *baraita* recounts that R. Yehoshua stood on his feet, affirmed the autonomy of human reasoning, and declared, quoting Deuteronomy, "The Torah is not in the heavens!"[10] Thus ends the *baraita*. The Talmud now asks what the

---

planted cucumbers from one place to another. While use of such magic is generally forbidden, the Talmud there explains that it is permitted for purposes of instruction. R. Eliezer may have believed that the stakes were so high in his dispute here with the Sages that he could suspend that prohibition temporarily, as Elijah the Prophet did at Mt. Carmel.

9. This interpretation is one in a long line of authorities who interpret certain fantastical aggadot as dreams. See chapter 7 of this volume for a list and discussion, and Z. H. Chajes, *Mevo HaTalmud*, ch. 28.

10. Deuteronomy 30:12.

meaning of R. Yehoshua's teaching is, and cites the later Sage R. Yirmeya as teaching that once the Torah was revealed at Sinai, scholars pay no attention to heavenly voices, because the Torah, itself revealed at Sinai, teaches that one must always follow the majority.[11] The Talmud next recounts that R. Natan happened upon Elijah the Prophet and asked him what God was up to during the dramatic confrontation between R. Eliezer and R. Yehoshua, to which Elijah responds, "The Holy One, Blessed Be He, smiled and said, 'My children have triumphed over Me; My children have triumphed over Me.'" With this divine comment the first portion of the aggada is brought to a close. What follows next, the subject of part 2 of this chapter, is a description of the catastrophic impact of these events on all the parties involved.

What are we to make of all this? These passages have been the subject of a vast literature, mostly focusing on the theory of Jewish law. For our purposes, let us first recall that R. Eliezer asserted of himself on several occasions in the Talmud that he never taught a halakha that he did not first hear from his teachers.[12] According to this self-testimony, why does our *baraita*, alongside many other sources,[13] depict R. Eliezer as engaged in classic halakhic argumentation?[14] It is of course possible that he was recapitulating the arguments he heard from his teachers,[15] or that he adduced his own arguments to support the position he received. Nevertheless, his reliance on halakhic arguments is of limited import, for they would not have been decisive if they contradicted the teachings of his predecessors, to which he retained absolute fidelity.

As we saw in chapter 1 of this volume, R. Eliezer maintained that the most reliable method for assuring the divine truth of a halakhic teaching is the authority of its sources, whose oral traditions go back to Sinai itself. Unnecessary halakhic novelty is dangerous, because it risks missing God's intent. Rather, prophecy should serve as a model

11. Exodus 23:2.
12. See, for example, Sukka 28a.
13. See, for example, Mishna Pesaḥim 6:2.
14. Our *baraita* states explicitly that R. Eliezer offered every possible answer in the world to support his position.
15. See Mishna Nega'im 9:3.

for halakhic reasoning. Just as a prophet derives his teachings from God Himself, the Sages, their successors in Jewish history, must aspire to that very certainty and authenticity. R. Eliezer maintained that this can be best achieved by adhering to the purity of the intergenerational transmission of the law. Truth can be best preserved through fealty to ancient halakhic traditions, following his great mentor, Shammai.[16] Reasoning may be best used to explain or justify an already received teaching, or perhaps to adjudicate a case for which there is no clear precedent. However, it should be avoided to the extent possible in generating halakhic novellae, for human reasoning is often flawed, and relying on often flawed reasoning risks getting God's will wrong. For this reason, as we saw in the previous chapter, R. Eliezer valorizes prodigious memory, and compares the ideal Torah teacher to a sealed reservoir which never loses a drop stored within it, rather than to a flowing spring. Of course, preservation of the past became all the more compelling after the destruction of the Holy Temple and the exile of those surviving Torah scholars to Yavne and elsewhere.

Both R. Yehoshua and R. Eliezer were students of the great R. Yoḥanan b. Zakkai, and they were key figures in his escape from besieged Jerusalem to establish a Torah center in Yavne, out of which all post-Temple Judaism would regenerate.[17] As we saw, R. Yoḥanan b. Zakkai advocated a model of Torah study which stressed the importance of human creativity in responding to new challenges, and whose metaphor for a Torah scholar was not the sealed reservoir but the flowing spring. R. Yehoshua followed in this tradition, as did the Sages. Ironically, R. Eliezer, student of R. Yoḥanan b. Zakkai, who would never teach what he hadn't been taught by his master, nevertheless rejected the very model of Torah study advocated by the master himself.[18]

In any case, this background sheds much light on the rationale behind the controversy between R. Eliezer and the Sages. Nevertheless, it does not go far enough, as two questions must be still answered. First,

16. See Gilat, *R. Eliezer ben Hyrcanus,* ch. 1, for an extensive summary of some of these ancient traditions.
17. See Gittin 56a.
18. See chapter 1 for a fuller discussion of these issues and the relevant sources.

why do the Sages not follow the divine voice? Even if halakhic creativity is a virtue, surely they also wish to get God's will right. Secondly, why does R. Eliezer resist the majority point of view? Was it not widely accepted that the majority opinion must be followed?

One answer to the first question is that the Sages were convinced about two points. First, they were convinced that there was no possibility of error on their part. There was a large body of scholars who took the position they did only after the most careful consideration and analysis of all the competing arguments. Let us remember that R. Eliezer challenged them again and again with his arguments, in the hope he could persuade them he was correct, all to no avail. They had taken human reasoning as far as it possibly could go, and they knew that according to the canons of human reasoning they were right. Second, they were also convinced that it was God's will that human beings exercise fully their capacity to reason, and that they must follow the manifest conclusions of their arguments and analysis, irrespective of God's own view of the matter. They maintained that God has a vision for human perfection, and that perfection, at least in part, consists in human beings actualizing the fullness of their intellectual capacities in sorting out God's Torah. That precisely is God's will, for which reason God is depicted as smiling even while "vanquished," for His "children" have fulfilled His "meta-will," His will that they figure out for themselves what God wants. Of course, if they hadn't done an adequate job of analysis, and nevertheless chose to subvert God's will, He would have been very unhappy indeed. But that was not the case in this dispute.[19] This distinction, between adequate and inadequate analysis, is of course a crucial one. While some readers of this famous aggada see in it an unqualified endorsement of human autonomy in halakhic decision making, I do not believe there is evidence to support this more radical conclusion. In practice this distinction severely limits the real-life exercise of full autonomy in halakhic decision making, because how often can one be absolutely certain one is right? Moreover,

19. This account essentially follows that of Rabbi Nissim of Gerona, in his *Derashot HaRan,* ed. Aryeh Feldman (Jerusalem: 1987), 44. However, the formulation of this position here is mine. For different explanations of the position of R. Yehoshua and the Sages in traditional sources, see Y. Englard, "The Oven of *Akhnai.*"

in the case at hand, a large body of scholars, indeed all of them except one, were convinced of their rectitude. How often does this occur today? While we do have an endorsement of human autonomy here, and that is a crucial theological point, it is not an unqualified endorsement, which is a crucial practical point.[20]

Moreover, according to the proposal of Rabbenu Ḥananel discussed above, there is no evidence for even this qualified endorsement of autonomy, since the entire episode took place in a dream. Indeed, one reason Rabbenu Ḥananel may have offered his interpretation is precisely because he was troubled by how the Sages could have violated God's will as revealed by the divine voice. According to his proposal, they did not.

Let us now turn to the second question I posed above: Why did R. Eliezer not regard himself as bound by majority rule? The answer is an obvious one: Majority rule is binding only in a court of law, but this debate took place in the study hall (or just outside it). The extensive laws governing the rebellious elder based on Deuteronomy 17:8–13 obtain only in a judicial context,[21] which was not the case here. R. Eliezer should have been free to dissent. But this, in turn, raises another question: Why the tremendous tumult about this debate, if R. Eliezer is free to dissent? Why does R. Eliezer insist on supernatural proofs, even a divine voice, to prove his point, and, especially puzzling, why do the Sages excommunicate him for his failure to concede?

We cannot answer these questions with any certainty, for the text itself is opaque. Nahmanides, in his commentary to this passage, suggests that R. Eliezer was excommunicated because of the lack of respect he showed the majority in adducing supernatural support for his dissent, and the general breakdown in rabbinic authority likely to result.[22] However, there may be more to it than that, and I would suggest that the debate here was a culmination – indeed, an explosive one – of a longstanding

20. For a much fuller discussion of these issues, see Moshe Sokol, *Judaism Examined* (Touro College Press, 2013), 263–304.

21. This is evident from the verses themselves, and is so codified by Maimonides in *Mishneh Torah, Hilkhot Mamrim* 1:1–2.

22. He also considers a second explanation, that the Sages relied on an oral tradition, which R. Eliezer, on the basis of his autonomous reason, sought to subvert. The explanation I suggest below runs in a different direction.

tension between R. Eliezer and the Sages. The great debates between Hillel and Shammai, and their respective schools, were resolved in Yavne, especially under the leadership of R. Yoḥanan b. Zakkai's successor, Rabban Gamliel, to favor Hillel. R. Eliezer, who was more closely aligned with the approach of Shammai, resisted the stress on halakhic creativity first developed by Hillel, who pioneered the use of methods whereby to derive new halakhot from the Torah, then developed more fully by Hillel's successors, until it reached its peak in the creativity of R. Akiva.[23] These longstanding, deeply held and deeply felt differences boiled over in the debate over this oven. R. Eliezer chose in this debate to stake his claim without compromise and to prove the validity of his approach to Torah study unequivocally, through supernatural means. Note that the heavenly voice sides with R. Eliezer not only about this case, but universally. It asserted that his approach to Torah study, going back to Shammai, and not that of the Sages, is correct. The Sages, on the other hand, were deeply committed to consolidating halakha around the approach of Hillel, and thereby consolidating halakhic authority and methodology, especially in the tenuous and fragile years after the destruction of the Temple and the demise of the Sanhedrin that sat in Jerusalem. They could brook no dissent, for, to them, the very future of Jewish life was at stake.

R. Eliezer was thus a lonely dissident against not only the Sages themselves, but also the creative halakhic methods they carried forward from Hillel, codified at Yavne. He remained loyal to Shammai's conservative respect for ancient tradition despite the overwhelming turn toward Hillel.[24] We see once again the tough-mindedness and individualism of R. Eliezer, manifest in his earliest youth, discussed in the chapter

23. For a fuller discussion, see Lau, *The Sages* (Tel Aviv, 2008), vol. 2, 83–106.

24. See Mishna Yadayim 4:3 for a moving expression of this. When R. Yosei b. Durmaskit visited R. Eliezer, he was asked what new laws were discussed in the study hall in Yavne. When R. Eliezer heard that the Sages there by majority rule had come to a certain decision, he cried and said, "Go and tell them that they should not follow their majority, because I have a tradition from R. Yoḥanan b. Zakkai, who heard it from his master, who heard it from his master back to the halakha revealed by God to Moses at Sinai" that the majority position in this matter is incorrect. Note R. Eliezer's crying (reminding us of the passage in *Pirkei DeRabbi Eliezer*), and his rejection of majority rule based upon ancient tradition.

preceding this one. The very R. Eliezer who rebelled against his father and left home to study Torah, the very R. Eliezer who refused to reveal his identity to his new teacher, the very R. Eliezer who refused R. Yoḥanan b. Zakkai's public request to teach new Torah, here refuses to accept the prevailing wisdom of the day, brought to a head in the dispute over the oven. The child is the parent of the adult.

This leads us back to a consideration of the name of the oven and its symbolic significance. I suggest elsewhere in this volume that halakhic debates embedded in talmudic narratives are often symbolic and serve the narrative itself.[25] Halakha thus functions as a kind of code to convey the aggada's deeper themes. Interestingly, the Talmud itself adopts such a posture here, interpreting the name of the oven in question as a symbol of *onaat devarim*. I'd like to take this further, and suggest that the content of the debate, and not just the name of the oven whose status is debated, is being alluded to as well. Our oven is made up of sections separated by mere sand, and superficially plastered over. Can a broken oven be united by superficial plaster? Can a broken halakhic process of unresolved debate and argument in the post-destruction world be united by the superficial patch of human reason enforced by majority rule? Who is to say the creative reasoning of the majority is correct, especially if there are good reasons to think the majority is dead wrong, reasons including no less than the voice of God Himself? R. Eliezer maintained that following the divine will about His own law must be the only criterion for adjudicating the truth, and that the majority's use of human reason contrary to divine truth cannot patch up unresolved, fractured debate. The broken oven symbolizes a broken system for adjudicating halakhic debate. Only a whole vessel, a whole oven, can become impure, but a broken oven remains pure, and that is exactly R. Eliezer's position. However, the Sages maintain that majority rule following perfect use of human reason is efficacious. The oven is whole, it functions as an oven, and therefore can become impure.

25. See chapters 5 and 6 particularly, and elsewhere in this volume.

PART TWO

THE AFTERMATH: R. ELIEZER'S EXCOMMUNICATION

Let us recall that God is quite satisfied with the position of the Sages. He smiles, despite their contravention of His will, and no divine-human tension exists. However, the same cannot be said for human-human tension, for while God is satisfied with the Sages, the Sages most definitely are not satisfied with R. Eliezer. Without waiting for even a day to pass, they take aggressive action. First, they confiscate all vessels deemed pure by R. Eliezer and they proceed to burn them, following which they vote to excommunicate him.[26] The question then arises as to who would inform R. Eliezer of his sorry new status, and R. Akiva volunteers for the unenviable task. The reason he gives is interesting: He feared that if the wrong person notified R. Eliezer, he would destroy the entire world.[27] As we shall see, R. Akiva's fears were not wholly unfounded.

R. Akiva role's in R. Eliezer's life will be a focus of our attention in the next chapter, which discusses R. Eliezer's deathbed encounter with R. Akiva and his colleagues. Suffice it to note for now that aside from being one of R. Eliezer's closest and greatest students, R. Akiva was a man of great personal compassion and love. One of his most famous teachings is that the great principle of the whole of the Torah is love of one's fellow,[28] and he and no one else of his thousands of students took the trouble to visit and care for a sick student.[29] R. Akiva probably felt that for both these reasons he was best equipped to break the terrible news

26. The exact form the excommunication took is much discussed by the commentators. Some suggested that it was the more extreme form, called *ḥerem,* which entailed no communication with R. Eliezer at all, including Torah study, with others suggesting a somewhat milder form, called *niddui,* which might technically permit such communication. This plays out in the deathbed scene we shall take up in the next chapter of this volume, when R. Eliezer asks his students why they did not come to study Torah with him. See *Tosafot,* s.v. *vekara,* and Nahmanides, ad loc.

27. The antecedent to the pronoun "he," in "he would destroy the entire world" is not altogether clear. It might refer to R. Eliezer, or to the person who notifies him. The ensuing story suggests that it might well have referred to R. Eliezer himself.

28. Genesis Rabba 24:7, *Sifra Kedoshim* 4:12, Y. Nedarim 9:4 (30b), Rashi on Leviticus 19:18.

29. Nedarim 50a.

to R. Eliezer. How does he do so? He dresses in black, shrouds his head in black, and sits before his master at a distance of four *amot,* some six feet. Nonverbal communication preceded verbal communication, and even before R. Akiva says a word to R. Eliezer, he has signaled to him that something is amiss, since these are signs both of mourning, and of the social distance consequent upon excommunication.

Remarkably, R. Akiva's behavior conveys two conflicting messages. By sitting at a distance, he demonstrates that he has accepted the decree of the Sages. Yet mourners traditionally wear black, and by wearing black himself, R. Akiva mourns, expressing his deep empathy for the suffering of the great master. R. Akiva embodies graphically the ambivalence he felt about the tragedy in which he himself was a willing if emotionally conflicted participant. While R. Akiva no doubt believed that he and his colleagues had done the right thing, he still felt deeply the pain that action had caused his beloved master, and he wanted his master to know that. Note that R. Akiva remains silent, and does not talk until addressed by R. Eliezer, much as those visiting a mourner remain silent until spoken to by the mourner himself. This is not only an expression of empathy and tact, but in this case is likely also an atonement for what the Sages did to R. Eliezer. They choked R. Eliezer with their words. R. Akiva is at first silent.

R. Eliezer immediately suspects something, and asks R. Akiva why today is different from other days, a question which suggests that R. Eliezer never anticipated so harsh a reaction from his colleagues. R. Akiva, responding with great sensitivity and tact, says, "It appears to me that your colleagues are distancing themselves from you." R. Eliezer then rents his clothes, removes his shoes, and sits on the ground, all markers of his excommunication and of mourning. Remarkably, and uncharacteristically, he does not argue with R. Akiva, does not attempt to fight the excommunication, nor does he even complain, at least explicitly. He silently accepts the decision, admits defeat, and acts accordingly, for what practical alternative did he have?

While R. Eliezer may have had no practical alternative, that did not mitigate the pain his excommunication brought him. The Talmud relates that tears poured from his eyes, and as a result the whole world was afflicted, losing one-third its olive, wheat, and barley crops. Some say that even the dough kneaded in the hands of women was spoiled. R. Eliezer's bitter tears here recall the tears he shed so frequently, at home with a father who failed to understand his aspirations for Torah, and in the yeshiva of R. Yoḥanan b. Zakkai, until he was fully accepted into its midst.[30] Thus, the inner core of steel we have seen in R. Eliezer joins paradoxically to a life of the most intense emotions. Those everflowing early tears subside, but return yet again in this moment of crisis.

Note that it was not the excommunication itself which wrought this havoc, but only R. Eliezer's pain. The crops were doing just fine until R. Eliezer broke down in tears. This reinforces the overarching theme of the aggada, that of *onaat devarim,* of causing pain to another human being. Destruction follows immediately. Interestingly, the destruction limned here is to the natural order. Let us remember that R. Eliezer subverted the natural order to bring proofs to his position, causing carob trees to move and water to flow backward. However, the Sages refused to accept proofs from this subversion. A consequence of both R. Eliezer's subversion, and the Sages refusal to acknowledge its significance, leads to a further and very dangerous subversion, destruction of crops, and even bread. Does the Talmud mean to suggest that both R. Eliezer and the Sages, in their own different ways, failed to respect nature and its subversions? It is apparent that the "natural" consequence of those failures was the destruction of the natural order.

The intense pain R. Eliezer felt sheds further light on the symbolism of the name of the oven, the debate over whose halakhic status felled R. Eliezer and led him to bitter tears. The sectional, "broken" oven may symbolize not only the fractured nature of halakhic disagreement, as I suggested above, but it may also symbolize R. Eliezer himself, broken by the crushing snake of majority rule. When R. Eliezer says that the broken oven is pure, he is asserting that he, the man broken by excommunication, is nevertheless pure, his Torah vouched for by God Himself. However, the Sages maintain that the oven is not really broken at all, because its surface is plastered, and it functions like an oven. They mean to say, "You, R. Eliezer, are like the oven in question. You continue to function as the scholar you are, yet you refuse to concede to the majority.

30. See the previous chapter regarding this.

Like the oven, you function as a scholar, and are therefore, like a functioning oven, impure. You can achieve purity only if you allow youself to be broken, by submitting to the will of the majority."

The harm caused by R. Eliezer's banning did not end with crops and dough, as bad as that was. The Talmud adds that "there was great anger on that day, as any place R. Eliezer fixed his gaze upon was burned." This is quite different from the destruction of the crops described above, as that occurred as a consequence of R. Eliezer's tears, without any direct intervention by R. Eliezer himself. Here R. Eliezer gazes, apparently in anger, and that angry gaze destroys.[31] It is hard not to recall a previous burning, by the Sages, of the vessels that R. Eliezer had decided were pure. Now, that burning is turned against the world of the Sages themselves. The consequence of paining R. Eliezer fits the crime.

What is the origin of R. Eliezer's anger? Of course, and most immediately, the ban under which he was placed. However, as we shall see in the next chapter, R. Eliezer evinces anger toward his son, and toward his students, when they visit him on his deathbed. Likewise, R. Eliezer shows anger toward R. Akiva even before the ban. A mishna records an extensive debate between R. Yehoshua and R. Eliezer about which elements of the Pesach sacrificial order may be performed on Shabbat, and R. Akiva interjects in support of R. Yehoshua.[32] According to the Talmud, R. Eliezer takes offense at R. Akiva remarks, perhaps because of the tone, as Rashi there suggests, and responds, in a play on words based upon the content of the debate, that R. Akiva's own fate is to be slaughtered like a sacrifice.[33] This too implies, at the very least, extreme irritation.[34] Readers of the chapter on R. Eliezer's origins may not be surprised by this. The flintiness, tough-mindedness, and willingness to defy his great master suggests a man who does not suffer fools

31. An alternative explanation is that the anger is not R. Eliezer's but God's. However, God is not mentioned here, and the most natural reading of the text is that R. Eliezer is angry. Moreover, God is depicted as smiling. Why then would He be angry?
32. Mishna Pesaḥim 6:1.
33. Pesaḥim 69a. Tragically, his prediction proved true. See the next chapter for further discussion of this passage.
34. R. Eliezer taking offense here is reminiscent of R. Yoḥanan taking offense in his relationship with both Reish Lakish and R. Kahana, discussed in chapters 6 and 7.

gladly. In this regard he may have been similar to his great mentor Shammai, who would hold no truck with bothersome people.[35]

Perhaps more importantly, however, R. Eliezer knew that the ban placed upon him would make it nigh impossible for him to teach the vast knowledge of Torah that he possessed to his student, acquired through unimaginable diligence. As we shall see vividly in the next chapter, for a man with R. Eliezer's passionate love of Torah, that was the unkindest cut of all.

R. Eliezer's suffering and anger destroy not only crops and dough and ignite fires but, the Talmud goes on to report, they also endanger the life of Rabban Gamliel, his brother-in-law. As it happened, Rabban Gamliel was traveling in a ship, and a great wave threatened to drown those within. Now, why is Rabban Gamliel singled out? His name does not even appear in the context of the debate, unlike that of his colleague, R. Yehoshua. The answer of course is that Rabban Gamliel was the *nasi*, the head of the preeminent post-destruction Torah center in Yavne and the leader of the Jewish community. As such, no doubt he bore some responsibility for the decision to ban R. Eliezer. Moreover, as brother-in-law to R. Eliezer, who would know more than anyone else the pain this ban would cause, should he not have intervened on behalf of a family member?

Rabban Gamliel's response to the threat is telling indeed. With the great wave looming, he says, "It seems to me that this is only for the sake of Eliezer, the son of Hyrcanus."[36] It is as if he sensed that R. Eliezer's flowing tears poured into the sea and became the ferocious wave that threatened his very life. He stood on his feet and declared, "Master

35. Shabbat 31a.

36. Note that R. Eliezer loses his title "Rabbi," and in some editions of the Talmud, R. Eliezer's name itself is elided, where Rabban Gamliel calls him "the son of Hyrcanus." This would reflect R. Eliezer's loss of status; not only is he banned, but he loses his very name. This is ironic, because R. Eliezer abandoned his father in search of Torah, yet it is the Torah he found which returns to him the name of his father. One wonders if Rabban Gamliel means to subtly criticize R. Eliezer by calling him "son of Hyrcanus." As we saw in the previous chapter, Hyrcanus was motivated by the need for honor. Does Rabban Gamliel mean to suggest that R. Eliezer's refusal to accept the Sages' decision was motivated by the same need?

of the Universe, it is revealed and known before You that it was neither for my honor, nor for the honor of the house of my father that I acted, but only for Your honor, so that disputes will not proliferate in Israel." The historical context for understanding this *apologia* is crucial. Rabban Gamliel lived after the destruction of the Temple, and he succeeded R. Yoḥanan b. Zakkai as head of the yeshiva in Yavne, and as leader of the Jewish people. Unlike R. Yoḥanan b. Zakkai, he was descended from the great line of Jewish leadership going back to Hillel, and his succession marked a restoration of that illustrious past.

One of the central goals of Rabban Gamliel's leadership was the unification of Jewish practice following the trauma of the destruction of the Temple and Jerusalem. Differences of opinion abounded, many related to the ongoing disputes between the schools of Hillel and Shammai, and Jewish life risked permanent schism. Despair over the loss of the Temple, perennial debate, and the geographic scattering of scholars because of persecution threatened the very survival of the Jewish people. Rabban Gamliel asserted his authority to prevent that catastrophic result, and under his leadership at Yavne, halakha was consolidated according to Hillel rather than Shammai. His style of leadership was thought by some to be overbearing, and based upon his harsh treatment of R. Yehoshua,[37] he was even temporarily deposed.[38]

Of course, this consolidation would not have been met without resistance, and R. Eliezer, who, as we have seen, remained more closely affiliated with the school of Shammai, opposed Rabban Gamliel on certain key fronts. For example, the loss of the Temple threatened the very possibility of Jewish worship, which had revolved around the sacrificial order. Rabban Gamliel understood that a new mode of formal worship must replace the sacrifices, and according to one key source, under his leadership the *Amida*, the central pillar of Jewish liturgy, was standardized.[39] Further, Rabban Gamliel taught that it must be recited daily. However, in a disagreement of paramount importance to daily

37. Berakhot 27b.
38. For a discussion of Rabban Gamliel's tenure, accomplishments, and conflicts, see Lau, *The Sages*, vol. 2, 87–136.
39. Megilla 17b.

Jewish life, R. Eliezer dissented, and opposed making the recitation of the *Amida* routine.[40] While Rabban Gamliel and R. Eliezer were brothers-in-law, deep differences divided them.

The motives of authoritarian leaders are sometimes, and for good reason, suspect. How much is altruistic, and how much is about personal power and ego? Rabban Gamliel's poignant declaration on the ship was meant to affirm the integrity and good intentions of his strong leadership style, and of his support of the ban against R. Eliezer. For Rabban Gamliel, the very survival of post-Temple Judaism was at stake, and harsh measures were required to consolidate halakha and Jewish ritual practice. Note that the Talmud reports that Rabban Gamliel "stood on his feet" when he made this declaration. This echoes R. Yehoshua, who likewise stood on his feet to declare that Torah is not in heaven, while it sharply contrasts with R. Eliezer, who sinks to the ground upon learning of his excommunication. Posture physically marks both victory and defeat.

What happens to Rabban Gamliel? God responds; he is saved from the terrifying wave and survives to live another day. This seems like a divine endorsement not only of the ban, but of Rabban Gamliel's motives as well.

The Talmud next relates that following his excommunication, Imma Shalom, R. Eliezer's wife and the sister of Rabban Gamliel, never permitted her husband to fall on his face in painful personal prayer.[41] She was afraid that the intensity of his prayer would result in the death of her brother, a fear that ultimately proved justified. By way of background to the events that follow, recall that on Rosh Ḥodesh, the first day of the new lunar month, this special prayer is not said. It turns out that Imma Shalom erred in calculating the correct date of Rosh Ḥodesh, and thinking that it was Rosh Ḥodesh when it wasn't, she let her husband out of her sight. When she returned, she discovered him fallen on his face, reciting the prayer. His posture is now even lower. After the ban he sat on the floor; now he falls on his face, a symbol of his further degradation. Posture marks not only victory and defeat, but degradation

40. Mishna Berakhot 4:3.

41. This is a reference to *Taḥanun,* recited in the daily liturgy after the prayer leader repeats the *Amida.*

too. She immediately tells R. Eliezer to get up, and charges him with killing her brother. With the death of one of his tormenters, R. Eliezer can now, finally, get up. The first day of the month symbolically marks a new first day in R. Eliezer's life, for his suffering has now been vindicated. Just as the new moon has arisen from the darkness of night, from the defeat of its absence in the skies, so too has R. Eliezer risen from his own personal defeat.

The Talmud also records another version of this story. According to this version, a poor person comes to the door begging for food, and while she is away tending to the poor person's needs, R. Eliezer falls on his face and recites the prayer. The end result is the same. Following the charge she levels against her husband, they hear the sound of a shofar, blown to inform the community of the terrible news that Rabban Gamliel has died. Imma Shalom was right. R. Eliezer in turn asks her how she knew, and she responds by citing a moving tradition going back to her distinguished grandfather, himself a leader of the Jewish community. While all the gates of heaven may be locked, he taught, the gate for those who have been hurt by others remains forever open to their prayers, and to their pain. Imma Shalom opens the gate for a suffering person at her door, and the prayers of R. Eliezer, yet another suffering person, travel through the open gates of the house, and through the gates of heaven itself.

On one level, this is a grave human and family tragedy. Rabban Gamliel's intentions in supporting the ban must have been good, for God accepted his declaration and stopped the wave that threatened to drown him. Likewise, it is highly unlikely that R. Eliezer prayed to harm his brother-in-law, as he seems surprised to learn of his death. Yet Rabban Gamliel inflicted enormous pain upon R. Eliezer in supporting the ban, and R. Eliezer's expression of that pain in prayer resulted in Rabban Gamliel's death. In an ironic, even bitter twist, the name of the woman who tried but failed to make peace and prevent R. Eliezer from praying is none other than Imma Shalom, which means "mother of peace." Good mother that she was, she attempted to bring peace between two warring factions of her family, yet her husband remained excommunicated and her brother died.

At another level, this is a grave national tragedy. R. Eliezer, whom R. Yoḥanan b. Zakkai favored above all his students as the greatest master of his generation,[42] was banned from the community of scholars, his vast and as yet unshared knowledge of Torah lost forever to Judaism.[43] Rabban Gamliel, one of the preeminent leaders who made the survival of Judaism and the Torah possible after the destruction of the Temple and of Jerusalem, dies before his time.

Finally, it is also a tragedy of ideas. Hegel, in his *Lectures on Aesthetics*, writes, "The original essence of tragedy consists then in the fact that within such a conflict each of the opposed sides, if taken by itself, has justification, while on the other hand each can establish the true and positive content of its own aim and character only by negating and damaging the equally justified power of the other. Consequently, in its moral life, and because of it, each is just as much involved in guilt."[44] Tragedy occurs when right opposes right, when each party to a conflict takes his position without acknowledging the power of the position of his or her opponent.

R. Eliezer believed that the unimpeachable authority of intergenerational transmission of Torah, in contrast with the fallibility of human reasoning, was the best way to live according to God's will. Following the destruction of the Temple and demise of Jerusalem's Sanhedrin, such tradition was the only hope of keeping to God's word and will. However, Rabban Gamliel and all the Sages maintained that God wants human beings to exercise their creativity in interpreting His word, and to follow the majority in ascertaining which creative interpretations become law. How better to ensure the flourishing of Torah in a new world? This was a momentous clash of ideas. For Rabban Gamliel and the Sages, there could be no compromise, nor could there be compromise for R. Eliezer, lone dissident in a sea of rabbinic opposition. There was just too much at stake for all of them.

What makes this conflict different from classic Hegelian tragic conflict is that it is likely that each side recognized the force behind the position of his opponent. No doubt R. Eliezer acknowledged the value of human reasoning in halakha, for he himself engaged in it, and there are

42. *Pirkei Avot* 2:12.

43. For more on this, see the discussion in the next chapter.

44. T. M. Knox, trans., *Hegel's Aesthetics: Lectures on Fine Art* (Oxford: Clarendon, 1975), 1196.

times when no clear traditional precedent exists. Yet he could not abide by the unlicensed valorization of such intellectual autonomy. Likewise, no doubt Rabban Gamliel and the Sages recognized the importance of intergeneration transmission of Torah, for they themselves spent so much of their lives studying the traditions of the past and transmitting them to their students. Thus, each recognized the force of their opponents' views. Yet, despite this, they could not compromise one iota in their absolute commitment to their own view of Torah. This uncompromising absoluteness with which they held their positions led to the unraveling of their lives.

That said, this analysis may lead to a possible answer to the question raised earlier. If God Himself endorsed Rabban Gamliel's insistence that his motives were pure, and did not object to the ban itself, why then does Rabban Gamliel die when God hears R. Eliezer's prayers? Surely this is one of the most puzzling features of the story.[45]

Implicit in the Hegelian analysis of tragedy is the claim that each party to the conflict is doing something wrong. According to this view, even if Rabban Gamliel were justified in promulgating the ban, and even if it were good public policy to do so, he is still wronging R. Eliezer. The good of the ban overrides the harm it causes, but to override the harm is not to eliminate it. Even morally good actions may still possess an element of moral wrong. Now most of us would not be culpable for that wrong, since on balance we did the right thing. Nevertheless, great people like Rabban Gamliel may be called to task even for behavior which was justified, because of the wrong still inherent in it. An analogy to this principle might found in the comments of *Tosafot*,[46] who seek to reconcile two conflicting teachings about whether or not voluntary fasting is a discouraged practice in Judaism. He suggests that the good of fasting (which brings repentance and increases religious fervor) overrides the

45. One possible answer to this question is that while God may have supported the ban initially, He might have wanted Rabban Gamliel to lift it after the passage of time. Rabban Gamliel dies because he kept the ban in place for too long. However, we have no evidence anywhere in the Talmud that R. Eliezer ever recanted, except, perhaps, at his death. Nor does it seem likely, knowing what we know about him, that he ever would. Why then blame Rabban Gamliel for not lifting the ban?

46. *Tosafot,* Taanit 11a, s.v. *amar Shmuel.*

wrong in fasting (the denial of the pleasures of God's world), and fasting is virtuous, but the person who fasts is still regarded as a sinner.[47]

A second answer to this question turns on a deeper understanding of the behavior of Rabban Gamliel himself.[48] Even if Rabban Gamliel had been right to support the ban against his brother-in-law, and even if his motives were pure, we might fairly ask *how he felt* about causing such intense pain to R. Eliezer. Surely he should have felt awful about what he did, acutely unhappy that his principles were such as to bring grief to a family member and to such a great Torah scholar. Surely he should have cried the same bitter tears that R. Eliezer himself cried over the ban, tears in empathy and distress. Let us remember that R. Akiva dresses as a mourner when approaching R. Eliezer with the terrible news of his ban, vividly expressing his feelings of loss. What of Rabban Gamliel? Surely Rabban Gamliel acted on his principles, and for the best of intentions, but true principles and good intentions must never eliminate a moral agent's sheer humanity. A parent may rightly decide, with the best of motives, that his or her child must undergo serious and painful surgery. But how would a parent *feel* about that decision? What parent wouldn't feel terrible about the necessity for causing a beloved child to suffer, even if it was for his or her greater good?

Of course, we do not know with any certainty how Rabban Gamliel felt. Yet we do know that he was punished with his death, though again, keep in mind that God seems to have supported both his decision and his motives. We also know that there is no evidence that Rabban Gamliel ever expressed pain over his tragic dilemma, over the suffering he caused his brother-in-law. Finally, the Talmud reports of an accusation that his great colleague R. Yehoshua made against him. After Rabban Gamliel had been deposed from his position as *nasi*, he sought out R. Yehoshua to make amends for the harshness with which he had treated him. When Rabban Gamliel arrived at R. Yehoshua's home and saw the blackened walls, he commented that he hadn't been aware that

47. For further discussion and analysis of this idea, see Sokol, *Judaism Examined,* chs. 2 and 12, especially pp. 54–55.

48. See also Martha Nussbaum, *The Fragility of Goodness* (Cambridge, 1986), chs. 2 and 3, commenting on several Greek tragedies.

R. Yehoshua's trade was that of a blacksmith. R. Yehoshua responds, "Woe unto the generation that you are its leader, and you do not even know the suffering of its scholars, how they make a living and how they feed themselves."[49]

Rabban Gamliel was among the very greatest Jews of his era, an outstanding scholar and leader, yet, at least according to R. Yehoshua, he did not empathize with the suffering of his colleagues. Here too, it seems more than likely that Rabban Gamliel was so convinced of his rectitude that he may have allowed his noble convictions to override his empathy for R. Eliezer.

Sometimes there is a cost to living a principled life, for living a principled life may come at the expense of living an emotionally sensitive one. This may be the deeper meaning behind the consequences of the tragic debate over the oven of *akhnai*. Rabban Gamliel had been right. Nevertheless, the gates of heaven are never closed to the prayers of those hurt, and they were not closed to R. Eliezer. If Rabban Gamliel did not sufficiently feel the torment he caused R. Eliezer, then he would be relentlessly pursued by that torment, until it brought his death. For those who suffer like R. Eliezer, the gates of heaven are never closed.

---

49. Berakhot 28a.

Chapter 3

R. Eliezer on His Deathbed: Is Reconciliation Possible?

Sanhedrin 68a

INTRODUCTION

R. Eliezer was one of the towering Sages of the tannaitic period, yet, as we saw in the previous chapter, he was excommunicated by his colleagues for refusing to submit to majority rule. The consequences of his dissent sent shock waves throughout the rabbinic world, and R. Eliezer's own brother-in-law, Rabban Gamliel, the head of the Jewish community, died as a result. R. Eliezer himself remained ostracized from his colleagues and students, unable to share the vast repository of Torah knowledge he had acquired. This rupture was not only human and personal, but also ideological, as R. Eliezer on the one hand, and his colleagues and students on the other, advocated opposing visions of the ideal nature of Torah study and halakhic decision making. R. Eliezer's closest colleague, R. Yehoshua, would have nothing to do with him, and perhaps even more painfully, neither would his prized student, R. Akiva.

Years pass, and his colleagues and students learn that R. Eliezer is very ill, indeed on his deathbed. They visit him in an apparent last-ditch effort to reconcile and to heal the wounds of that devastating excommunication. Has R. Eliezer changed over the years and might he retract his position? Have his students and colleagues changed? Is reconciliation possible given the bitterness of the split, and the deep convictions and temperaments of the parties to the conflict? The powerful and deeply moving aggada that we will analyze in this chapter, from a tannaitic source, seeks to answer these questions. The chapter unfolds in three parts. The first examines the initial encounter and dialogue between R. Eliezer and his interlocutors. The second part analyzes a very puzzling halakhic exchange which leads up to R. Eliezer's death, and the striking reaction of his visitors to the very last word he utters before dying. The third and final part examines the complex relationship between R. Eliezer and his great student R. Akiva, as it emerges from this aggada, especially its conclusion, and from other correlated rabbinic sources.

Sanhedrin 68a

כשחלה ר׳ אליעזר נכנסו ר׳ עקיבא וחביריו לבקרו הוא יושב בקינוף שלו והן יושבין בטרקלין שלו ואותו היום ע״ש היה ונכנס הורקנוס בנו לחלוץ תפליו גער בו ויצא בנזיפה אמר להן לחביריו כמדומה אני שדעתו של אבא נטרפה אמר להן דעתו ודעת אמו נטרפה היאך מניחין איסור סקילה ועוסקין באיסור שבות כיון שראו חכמים שדעתו מיושבת עליו נכנסו וישבו לפניו מרחוק ד׳ אמות.

When Rabbi Eliezer took ill, Rabbi Akiva and his colleagues came to visit him. He was sitting on his canopied bed [*bekinof*], **and they were sitting in his parlor** [*biteraklin*]; they did not know if he would be able to receive them, due to his illness. **And that day was Shabbat eve, and** Rabbi Eliezer's **son Hyrcanus entered to remove his phylacteries,** as phylacteries are not worn on Shabbat. His father **berated him, and he left reprimanded.** Hyrcanus **said to his** father's **colleagues: It appears to me that father went insane,** since he berated me for no reason. Rabbi Eliezer heard this and **said to them: He,** Hyrcanus, **and his mother went insane. How can they neglect** Shabbat preparations with regard to **prohibitions** punishable by **stoning,** such as lighting the candles and preparing hot food, **and engage in** preparations concerning **prohibitions by rabbinic decree,** such as wearing phylacteries on Shabbat? **Since the Sages perceived** from this retort **that his mind was stable, they entered and sat before him at a distance of four cubits,** as he was ostracized (see *Bava Metzia* 59b). It is forbidden to sit within four cubits of an ostracized person.

א״ל למה באתם א״ל ללמוד תורה באנו א״ל ועד עכשיו למה לא באתם א״ל לא היה לנו פנאי אמר להן תמיה אני אם ימותו מיתת עצמן אמר לו ר׳ עקיבא שלי מהו אמר לו שלך קשה משלהן נטל שתי זרועותיו והניחן על לבו אמר אוי לכם שתי זרועותיי שהן כשתי ספרי תורה שנגללין.

Rabbi Eliezer **said to them: Why have you come? They said to him: We have come to study Torah,** as they did not want to say that they came to visit him due to his illness. Rabbi Eliezer **said to them: And why have you not come until now? They said to him: We did not have spare time.** Rabbi Eliezer **said to them: I would be surprised if these** Sages **die their own death,** i.e., a natural death. Rather, they will be tortured to death by the Romans. **Rabbi Akiva said to him: How will my** death come about? Rabbi Eliezer **said to him: Your** death will be **worse than theirs,** as you were my primary student and you did not come to study. Rabbi Eliezer **raised his two arms and placed them on his heart,** and he **said: Woe to you, my two arms, as they are like two Torah scrolls that are** now **being rolled up,** and will never be opened again.

הרבה תורה למדתי והרבה תורה לימדתי הרבה תורה למדתי ולא חסרתי מרבותי אפילו ככלב המלקק מן הים הרבה תורה לימדתי ולא חסרוני תלמידי אלא כמכחול בשפופרת ולא עוד אלא שאני שונה שלש מאות הלכות בבהרת עזה ולא היה אדם ששואלני בהן דבר מעולם ולא עוד אלא שאני שונה שלש מאות הלכות ואמרי לה שלשת אלפים הלכות בנטיעת קשואין ולא היה אדם שואלני בהן דבר מעולם חוץ מעקיבא בן יוסף פעם אחת אני והוא מהלכין היינו בדרך אמר לי רבי למדני בנטיעת קשואין

אמרתי דבר אחד נתמלאה כל השדה קשואין אמר לי רבי למדתני נטיעתן למדני עקירתן אמרתי דבר אחד נתקבצו כולן למקום אחד.

I have learned much Torah, and I have taught much Torah. I have learned much Torah, and I have not taken away from my teachers, i.e., I have not received from their wisdom, **even like a dog lapping from the sea. I have taught much Torah, and my students have taken away from me,** i.e., they have received from my wisdom, **only like** the tiny amount that **a paintbrush** removes **from a tube** of paint. **Moreover, I can teach three hundred** *halakhot* **with regard to a snow-white leprous mark** [*baheret*], **but no person has ever asked me anything about them.** He could not find a student who could fully understand him in those matters. **Moreover, I can teach three hundred** *halakhot*, **and some say** that Rabbi Eliezer said **three thousand** *halakhot*, **with regard to the planting of cucumbers** by sorcery, **but no person has ever asked me anything about them, besides Akiva ben Yosef.** Rabbi Eliezer described the incident: **Once he and I were walking along the way,** and **he said to me: My teacher, teach me about the planting of cucumbers. I said one statement** of sorcery, and **the entire field became filled with cucumbers. He said to me: My teacher, you have taught me** about **planting them; teach me** about **uprooting them. I said one statement and they all were gathered to one place.**

אמרו לו הכדור והאמוס והקמיע וצרור המרגליות ומשקולת קטנה מהו אמר להן הן טמאין וטהרתן במה שהן מנעל שעל גבי האמוס מהו אמר להן הוא טהור ויצאה נשמתו בטהרה עמד רבי יהושע על רגליו ואמר הותר הנדר הותר הנדר.

After these comments, the Sages **asked him** questions of *halakha*: **What is** the *halakha*, with regard to ritual impurity, of **a ball** made of leather and stuffed with rags, **and** likewise **a last,** the frame on which a shoe is fashioned, which is made of leather and stuffed with rags, **and** likewise **an amulet** wrapped in leather, **and a pouch for pearls,** wrapped in leather, **and a small weight,** which is wrapped in leather? Rabbi Eliezer **said to them: They are susceptible to impurity, and their purification is** effected by immersing them in a ritual bath **as they are,** as there is no need to open them up. They asked him further: **What is** the *halakha* with regard to **a shoe that is on a last?** Is it considered a complete vessel, which needs no further preparation, and is therefore susceptible to impurity? Rabbi Eliezer **said to them: It is pure, and** with this word, **his soul left** him **in purity. Rabbi Yehoshua stood on his feet and said: The vow is permitted; the vow is permitted;** i.e., the ostracism that was placed on Rabbi Eliezer is removed. Rabbi Akiva was not present at the time of his death.

למוצאי שבת פגע בו רבי עקיבא מן קיסרי ללוד היה מכה בבשרו עד שדמו שותת לארץ פתח עליו בשורה ואמר (מלכים ב ב, יב) אבי אבי רכב ישראל ופרשיו הרבה מעות יש לי ואין לי שולחני להרצותן אלמא מרבי אליעזר גמרה גמרה מרבי אליעזר ולא סברה הדר גמרה מרבי יהושע ואסברה ניהליה היכי עביד הכי והאנן תנן העושה מעשה חייב להתלמד שאני דאמר מר (דברים יח, ט) לא תלמד לעשות לעשות אי אתה למד אבל אתה למד להבין ולהורות.

At the conclusion of Shabbat, Rabbi Akiva encountered the funeral procession on his way **from Caesarea to Lod.** Rabbi Akiva **was striking his flesh** in terrible anguish and regret **until his blood flowed to the earth. He began to** eulogize Rabbi Eliezer **in the row** of those comforting the mourners, **and said: "My father, my father, the chariot of Israel and its horsemen"** (II Kings 2:12)**. I have many coins, but I do not have a money changer** to whom **to give them,** i.e., I have many questions, but after your death I have no one who can answer them. The Gemara returns to the matter at hand: **Apparently,** Rabbi Akiva **learned** the *halakhot* of gathering cucumbers through sorcery **from Rabbi Eliezer,** not from Rabbi Yehoshua. The Gemara answers: **He learned it from Rabbi Eliezer but he did not understand it. Later he learned it from Rabbi Yehoshua, and** Rabbi Yehoshua **explained it to him.** The Gemara asks: **How could** Rabbi Eliezer **have performed that** act of sorcery? **But didn't we learn** in the mishna that **one who**

performs an act of sorcery **is liable?** The Gemara answers: Performing sorcery not in order to use it, but in order **to teach oneself** the *halakhot* **is different,** and it is permitted; **as the Master says** that it is derived from the verse: **"You shall not learn to do** like the abominations of those nations. There shall not be found among you ... one who uses divination, a soothsayer, an enchanter, or a sorcerer" (Deuteronomy 18:9–10), so that **you shall not learn,** i.e., it is prohibited for you to learn, in order **to do, but you may learn,** i.e., it is permitted for you to learn, in order **to understand** the matter yourself **and teach** it to others.

PART ONE

R. ELIEZER'S STUDENTS COME FOR A VISIT

The Talmud begins by reporting that when R. Eliezer became ill, R. Akiva and his friends came to visit him, just before Shabbat begins. While this is hardly an optimal time for visiting, they may have feared that the end was so close they could not delay for a moment. From the text it is apparent that many friends came to visit, among them R. Yehoshua, who was R. Eliezer's close colleague and another seminal teacher for R. Akiva. Yet the Talmud centers the visit on R. Akiva. This suggests that the crucial encounter here is between R. Eliezer and his remarkable student, R. Akiva, and that all other figures, as distinguished as they might be, remain hidden in R. Akiva's shadow. In part 3 of this chapter, we will examine why that might be.

R. Eliezer is resting under his canopied bed, and the visitors at first remain at a distance, in the parlor, perhaps because they were unsure if he was well enough to greet them. In any case, they observe Hyrcanus,[1] R. Eliezer's son, enter the room to help his father remove his tefillin from his head and arm, which in that era were worn throughout the day, except on Shabbat. The visitors observe that R. Eliezer expresses great anger at his son for so doing, who as a result leaves the room sharply rebuked. Hyrcanus, in turn, comments to the visitors outside that it seems to him

1. This is the same name as R. Eliezer's father, an interesting choice on R. Eliezer's part, since R. Eliezer had abandoned his father's home and values to study Torah, and was even threatened by him with disinheritance. See chapter 1 of this volume.

that his father has lost his mind, leaving to them to conjecture that this might be due to his extreme illness and advanced age. R. Eliezer's hearing had apparently remained sharp, however, as he overhears his son's comment, and he responds tartly, "He and his mother have lost their minds." I'm not the one suffering from dementia, he meant to say – they are! Shabbat has almost begun, and the candles are yet to be lit. If they delay just a bit, they will light the Shabbat candles too late, violating biblical prohibitions, while the prohibition against wearing tefillin on Shabbat is only rabbinic in origin.[2] Foolishly, they have focused on the wrong issue, worrying about the removal of tefillin rather than making sure the candles are lit on time.[3]

R. Eliezer's rejoinder makes it amply clear that he has lost none of his mental acuity despite his illness and age. The same toughness of mind and inability to suffer fools gladly, the same fierce intellectualism and commitment to truth that characterized his life until this point, all remain alive and well despite his physical deterioration. R. Eliezer the man is unchanged, from his earliest youth, to his confrontation with the Sages in the fiery debate over the oven of *akhnai*, to this interaction with his son, and, as we shall soon see, to his final encounter with his colleagues and students.

While the events described so far may well have taken place exactly at the time described, the eve of Shabbat, it is difficult to avoid reflecting about the symbolic significance of the Sabbath eve, and the way in which this symbolic reading reinforces the narrative theme. Sabbath eve is transitional, moments in time when secular time slides into sacred time. The weekday ends, and the holy Sabbath begins. R. Eliezer too now lives in transitional time. The week of his life is ending, and he is about to enter the sacred space of the World to Come. The time is liminal, because it is neither altogether sacred nor altogether profane. The shadows are lengthening, tefillin must be removed to mark the end of

2. *Tosafot*, s.v. *he'akh*, discuss some of the halakhic aspects of this claim.
3. *Tosafot* and the Maharsha assume that the issue here is candle lighting, and Rashi mentions this as one of two possibilities. Since candle lighting is typically the last thing done before Shabbat, and therefore the most likely to be late, I follow this interpretation throughout the chapter.

the week, and candles are not yet lit to mark the arrival of Shabbat. He is between one time and another, this world and the next. His visitors enter this liminal space, and in the mistiness of that time seek to leverage change in R. Eliezer.

If the time of the visit carries symbolic weight, so too might the lighting of the candles. To light the candles is to assert that a future of light and sacredness is around the bend of time. Yet R. Eliezer's own son did not light that candle, but rather sought to remove the past marker of weekday time, R. Eliezer's tefillin. This is not what R. Eliezer wanted. R. Eliezer sought a new illuminated future as he was phasing into the World to Come, symbolized by the lighting of his candle, not a mere elimination of the sacred weekday past.

Perhaps, too, the light is a metaphor for R. Eliezer's own life. R. Eliezer was angry that the candles were not yet lit. Is this at a deeper level anger at himself? If the candle is a metaphor for R. Eliezer's life, then his anger is that the candle of his life has not yet been lit; his life has not yet been fully realized. The darkness of Torah ignorance surrounds him, which he could have dispelled by his vast knowledge. The darkness of his death, and his unlit, not fully realized life await him, thwarted by an undeserved ban. R. Eliezer may be angry at himself, and that anger may have been vented at his son, who insists on removing his tefillin, rather than lighting his candle.

And from R. Eliezer's perspective, would he not have had good reason to be angry at his son? Could Hyrcanus not have studied more Torah from his father, stood in for the lost brilliance of R. Akiva and R. Eliezer's other students? So much of R. Eliezer's knowledge will die with him, for lack of a good student. And his son couldn't even get straight the distinction between laws of biblical and rabbinic origin! R. Eliezer's anger at his inability to teach what he knew may have been projected onto his son, triggered by the unexpected appearance of his erstwhile colleagues and students.

The story now continues, and the visitors, having observed that R. Eliezer's wits are about him, enter his room, careful to sit the requisite six feet away required by the ban. In so doing they graphically convey to R. Eliezer that the ban still stands, and that they have not changed their position despite the passage of time. R. Eliezer asks them why they have come, and they answer that they wish to study Torah. R. Eliezer then asks the obvious question: What took you so long? Why did you not visit all these long years of the ban to study? Their answer is surprising: We did not have time.

On the face of it, this entire dialogue is puzzling. Surely R. Eliezer knew that they came to visit because he was so ill. Surely they knew that the explanation they gave for the visit, to study Torah, would subject them to exactly the critical question R. Eliezer asked, "Where were you all this time?" Surely they would know that their answer to this question was hardly adequate. They did not have time? What kind of excuse is that? These extraordinary men spent all their days studying Torah. Could they not have found the time to study with R. Eliezer, the greatest master of all? And what did they mean when they said they came to study Torah? Did they really intend to engage in halakhic discourse by R. Eliezer's deathbed?

Perhaps the best way to read this is as a dialogue by indirection, in which each party spoke in veiled language. R. Eliezer knew full well why they came, and in effect was asking them all along, with more than a tinge of sarcasm, why they came just now and never before. His question was, in reality, an implied critique, made explicit only after he had set them up, trapping them with the answer he expected. If you really do want to study Torah, where have you been? In short, R. Eliezer meant to attack them from the beginning. The visitors allowed themselves to fall for this trap, however, because they meant in earnest what they said, that they came to study Torah. But what Torah did they mean to study by R. Eliezer's very deathbed? I would suggest that the Torah they came to study was the Torah of life. That is, they wanted to learn how a master like R. Eliezer would die, how he coped with his tragic ban, and whether or not he regretted his actions. They wanted to learn whether reconciliation between them was possible, whether peace could be found, whether R. Eliezer had tempered his views. As we shall see, the technical halakhic questions they will ask him would all be aimed at answering these deep questions of life.

What did the visitors mean by their answer that they did not have time? Some commentators suggest that they wished to respond with tact, providing an excuse for not visiting without mentioning the real but painful reason for their long absence, that R. Eliezer remained under the ban.[4] On this reading, they did their best to avoid hurting R. Eliezer's feelings, the very cause for all the terrible consequences of the ban. However, is that explanation fully satisfying? Given R. Eliezer's temperament and sharp mind, surely they would not expect him to be mollified by so flimsy an excuse. If they had decided to lie for the sake of truth, why use such a shaky one? Perhaps what they really meant was to provide an excuse so absolutely lame that R. Eliezer would take it to be tantamount to an admission of at least partial guilt. If they had nothing better to say than the obviously silly explanation that they had no time, then they were in effect conceding at least the partial error of their ways. R. Eliezer was not fooling them, and they were not fooling him. Each party to the dialogue in their own way alluded indirectly to their inner feelings and beliefs.

Whatever the meaning of their response, R. Eliezer's immediate retort was not only angry, but frightening, even shocking. He says that he would be surprised if any of his visitors died a natural death.[5] R. Akiva, his erstwhile star student, next asks what his death will be like, and R. Eliezer answers that his will be even worse than theirs.[6] The same R. Eliezer whose prayers brought the death of his brother-in-law Rabban Gamliel, and whose gaze destroyed one-third of the produce of the land, predicted the unnatural death of his visitors. While we shall have more to say about R. Akiva and his death toward the end of this chapter, even now it seems fair to say that R. Eliezer's anger has never really subsided. His anger at his son is likely also in part an expression of the general anger he continued to feel over his unjust treatment at the hands of the Sages. While R. Eliezer may not directly have borne a grudge, that old anger may have remained long present in his life.

R. Eliezer next lifts his arms, holds them upright against his heart, and in a bitter cry says, "Woe unto you my two arms, as they are like

4. See *Yad Rama*, ad loc.

5. Interestingly enough, R. Akiva himself makes a similar claim, regarding a student who took pleasure in besting a colleague. See Menaḥot 98b.

6. As we shall see, R. Eliezer had already foretold a terrible death for R. Akiva. Why, then, did R. Akiva ask yet again? Did he hope that R. Eliezer had softened his prediction over time? If so, that hope was rapidly dashed.

two Torah scrolls that are now being rolled up." R. Eliezer knows that he is about to die, and with his death will be lost forever that vast store of Torah knowledge he had through almost superhuman effort acquired, but could not teach due to the ban. He vividly demonstrates with his very body the tragedy of his soon-to-be-lost knowledge. His arms are like Torah scrolls placed next to his heart. It is difficult to avoid remembering that this is the same heart which so passionately beat for knowledge of Torah, the heart whose yearning for Torah drove him to abandon his home, drove him to be the first student in the study hall and the last one out, and drove him to become perhaps the leading master of his generation. The teaching of a *baraita* resonates deeply: "When R. Eliezer died, the Torah scroll was buried."[7] R. Eliezer's arms, the two Torah scrolls in his metaphor, were with his death closed forever, and those Torah scrolls, like his arms, would be buried with him.

Following this dramatic enactment of his inner feelings of despair, R. Eliezer compares himself to his students: "I have learned much Torah and I have taught much Torah. I have learned much Torah, but I have not received from their wisdom even like a dog lapping from the sea. I have taught much Torah, and my students have received from me no more than the tiny amount that a paintbrush removes from a tube of paint." Both he and his students have learned little from their respective masters, yet they are nevertheless different. He, in relation to his masters, is like a dog lapping at the sea, while his students, in relation to him, are like a paintbrush in a tube of paint. What is the meaning of this switch in metaphors? Moreover, why does he compare himself to a dog, while comparing his students to a paintbrush? If he wishes to criticize his students, shouldn't the metaphors be reversed? Shouldn't he compare his students to dogs, rather less flattering, and compare himself to a vehicle for beauty, a paintbrush?

At one level, of course, he means modestly to convey the difference in knowledge between his masters and himself. Their knowledge is as vast as the sea, and his as limited as a tube of paint. Nevertheless, could he not have used a more pleasing metaphor for himself than a slurping dog? Several answers to these questions suggest themselves. First, a very

7. Sota 49b.

thirsty dog has an insatiable desire for drink. He is unstoppable, driven with an animal's need and lust, slurping madly, with little regard for conventions of civility. He simply must have water. R. Eliezer means to convey that his desire for Torah is no less driven, by an almost animal-like need and lust for knowledge of God's wisdom. He is unstoppable, will arise early in the morning to study, and leave the study hall later than anyone else. He abandons his family, farm, and wealth, will fast for days on end, and will cry in despair again and again, only to "doggedly" seek more Torah. He may sacrifice civility and conventional behavior, good manners and conformity, all in his driven lust for the truth of God's word. Upon reflection, R. Eliezer has employed a brilliantly apt metaphor for his own life and aspirations.

Contrast this image with a paintbrush in a tube. The paintbrush is inanimate and immobile. It does nothing at all of its own accord, unless it is moved by an external force. It desires nothing, yearns for nothing, and makes no sacrifices to acquire paint. Someone must move it around within the tube, and then extract it, to use the paint which adheres to its surface. A dog consumes the water it drinks, unlike the paintbrush, on whose surface the paint remains, only to be removed when used. R. Eliezer thus means to say that the Torah he learns penetrates deep within him. However, the Torah his students learn remains only a superficial possession, like paint atop the paintbrush, and does not enter into the depths of their hearts, minds, and souls. Moreover, like the paintbrush acquiring paint because it is moved by an outside source, their motivation to study is not intrinsic, does not derive from an internal understanding of its true value. Rather, it is extrinsic, derived from how they think it will benefit them, either in honors accrued, social status, or wealth. Something outside itself must move it to collect the paint, that hand of another, unlike the dog, who races of its own need to the sea.

What is water used for? It is the sustenance of life, and Torah is compared to it. Paint is used for superficial, aesthetic purposes, especially since the paint and tube mentioned here are often used for makeup. R. Eliezer slurped up Torah in his driven need for the life-sustaining purposes of acquiring God's wisdom. His students studied because they wanted to look pretty, because of the aesthetic intellectual pleasure it gave them, the beauty of a neat argument or deft reply, or because of the honor they received. R. Eliezer's need for Torah was existential. His students' need for Torah was aesthetic and self-serving. Moreover, a paintbrush, even if used for makeup, implies creativity, and that is exactly what R. Eliezer rejected in Torah study. The goal of Torah study is preservation of the past, not creation of the new.

On this analysis, R. Eliezer's switch of metaphors implies a devastating critique of his students. At one level, what he may have meant to say was this: If you loved Torah like I do, if your need for the truth of God's Torah was as driven and as mindless of conventions as mine, you would never have placed me under a ban. You did so only because you are like effete paintbrushes in a tube, and that is your failure, not mine.

PART TWO
HALAKHIC DISCOURSE AND THE MEANING OF LIFE

The second part of this chapter enters the world of halakhic discourse, first in the words of R. Eliezer himself, and then in a dialogue between R. Eliezer and his visitors. Throughout this book I have suggested that in talmudic narratives, the Sages often used halakhic language as a kind of code to communicate symbolically deeper themes which they preferred to communicate only indirectly. They lived in the world of halakhic discourse, and would have chosen that discourse to express their otherwise veiled inner thoughts, feelings, and aspirations. I would suggest that the aggada analyzed in this chapter provides an excellent example of this hypothesis.

The narrative continues with R. Eliezer providing two examples of the extensive halakhic knowledge he possesses, bemoaning the sad reality that these are laws about which no one has asked him, thus leaving that knowledge to be buried with him in his grave. The first example is the set of laws governing white leprous marks, certainly arcane, about which he knows three hundred halakhot. Why this example? Surely there are many other areas of halakha in which R. Eliezer possesses vast knowledge not yet taught. Does he mean to allude to himself as the person smitten with such leprosy, banned by his colleagues like a leper who halakhically must leave town? Does he mean to recollect how his own master, R. Yoḥanan b. Zakkai, treated him like a leper shortly after he arrived at the yeshiva? As we saw in chapter 1, Eliezer had fasted, R. Yoḥanan b. Zakkai was repelled by his halitosis, and Eliezer reproaches his master for treating him like someone who has a leprous skin disease. He, alas, knows the fullness of the pain of the exiled leper, in all its excruciating three hundred details.[8]

The second example he provides is from the laws governing the practice of planting cucumbers using sorcery, forbidden under Torah law, about which he can teach three hundred laws – and some report that he actually said three thousand laws! He laments that no one has ever even bothered to ask him about them, with one exception, and that was R. Akiva, his erstwhile prize student. R. Eliezer then recounts an incident which took place when he and R. Akiva were walking along the road, a memory of the good times, when master and student still spent productive and pleasant time together. R. Akiva asked his master to teach him about the laws of planting cucumbers, perhaps because they passed a field of cucumbers. R. Eliezer, master of the laws governing sorcery, deployed his knowledge to magically fill the entire field with cucumbers. R. Akiva then asks him to teach the laws regarding the use of sorcery for uprooting cucumbers, with which R. Eliezer complies, and after uttering a few words the cucumbers all magically gathered to one place in the field.

Before analyzing this, we might first inquire as to how R. Eliezer could have used sorcery to plant and uproot cucumbers, when such activities are biblically forbidden. The Talmud itself later raises this question, and answers that the practice of sorcery is permitted for pedagogical purposes. If a teacher wishes to explain exactly what the Torah forbids, he may demonstrate it to a willing pupil. While this explanation is a compelling one, it leads to the following observation. R. Eliezer is willing to skirt the law, and use altogether legitimate loopholes, to teach the truth of the Torah *as he saw it*. This bespeaks his entire career.

8. Note, too, that the laws of *nega'im* were becoming increasingly less relevant (see Ketubot 77b), and so with R. Eliezer's death the laws might become extinct with the disease. Also, these laws may have been regarded as among the most difficult in the Oral Law (see, e.g., Sanhedrin 38b and Ḥagiga 11a). With R. Eliezer's death, who then could master them?

R. Eliezer did not regard himself as bound by majority rule in the seminal debate over the oven of *akhnai*, and from a technical perspective, his dissent was permissible, since the Sanhedrin had not formally ruled. Nevertheless, common practice, and for very good reason, was to submit to the majority. Yet R. Eliezer broke with that practice, and again skirted the law, out of his uncompromising commitment to the purity of Torah knowledge. This same tendency is likewise reflected in his frequent alignment with the House of Shammai over the House of Hillel, which by then had already become dominant.[9] It seems fair to say that R. Eliezer lived at the margins. The Talmud's justification of R. Eliezer's behavior thus speaks brilliantly to his very character and *modus vivendi*.

But what are we to make of flying cucumbers? Why does R. Eliezer choose this as an example of the extraordinary knowledge he possesses? In part, this is probably meant to serve as an indictment of R. Akiva. R. Akiva knew better than anyone else just how much Torah R. Eliezer had amassed, for he had been R. Eliezer's star student, and was the only person to have been interested enough to inquire about, and learn, the laws governing sorcery and cucumbers. Nevertheless, R. Akiva supported the ban, and even elected to inform him of its provenance. In effect, this provides an explanation for why R. Eliezer had predicted a more terrible death for R. Akiva than anyone else. R. Eliezer may well have believed that in some measure R. Akiva deserved that death.

It is also likely that on R. Eliezer's deathbed, ill and very aged as he was, his last encounter with students and colleagues triggered bittersweet memories. He remembered a halcyon time in his life, when he and R. Akiva his beloved student strolled together on the road, when R. Akiva would ask him the most esoteric questions, and when he in turn would draw upon his vast storehouse of knowledge to offer answers. Those were the days when he and R. Akiva chatted together about what they both loved most, God's Torah. Alas, those days are long gone.

Yet there may be another dimension to this as well. R. Eliezer here is a kind of wizard, making cucumbers fly at his command. R. Eliezer's own powers over halakha and over his students is in a way wizard-like, almost magical. In the good days, his students would ask him about

9. For discussion and sources, see previous chapter.

any matter of law, and he would answer them with total clarity, drawing upon his extraordinary knowledge. He could plant his students with that unending knowledge, and uproot them at will. If R. Eliezer is a kind of Torah wizard, then his students were like cucumbers, over whom he had complete control – complete control, that is, until the ban. In recalling the episode with the cucumbers, he is reminding his student R. Akiva and the others of his magical mastery of Torah, and his magical mastery over them, as if they were no more than mere cucumbers in his magisterial hands.

At this point R. Eliezer's visitors ask him a series of questions about an equally arcane area of halakha. These laws are quite technical and involved, and I beg the reader's indulgence as I attempt to explain them. The effort required to understand them will, I hope, be amply rewarded by the conclusion of this part of the chapter.[10] The first question involves the halakhic status of leather objects designed from the start to be filled, such as a leather ball designed to be stuffed with wool for use as a toy, or a leather shoe last, designed to be stuffed, and around which a new shoe is shaped. As Rashi understands it, this case was the subject of a debate between R. Eliezer and the Sages.[11] The general rule is that a vessel is considered a halakhic vessel, a *keli,* and may become impure (if an impurity is transferred to it), only if it can contain something within it. However, here we have a vessel (the leather pouch, for example) designed from its very outset to be filled. Therefore, the pouch never contains anything besides the stuffing. The question is whether the stuffing is considered to be a part of the pouch itself, as if the pouch were one solid unit including the stuffing, like a sponge ball, or whether the pouch and stuffing are two separate entities. If the answer is that the filling is considered to be part of the pouch, then this vessel has no room to contain anything else. Therefore, it does not have the status of a *keli,* and could not become impure. If, on the other hand, the filling is not considered to be part of the pouch itself, then the pouch is a *keli,* for it does contain something, namely, the stuffing. Therefore, it could

10. My discussion here throughout follows Rashi's understanding of this difficult text.

11. Mishna Kelim 23:1. *Tosafot* here, s.v. *vetoharasan,* point out that this debate is not explicit in the mishna, but may be inferred from the Tosefta.

become impure. The Sages maintain that it does not have the status of a *keli,* because the stuffing is considered part of the pouch, and therefore could never become impure. R. Eliezer maintains that the stuffing is not considered part of the pouch, for which reason it does have the status of a *keli,* and can become impure.

The next issue revolves around the status of objects whose leather pouch was torn, rendering the interior visible. In this case, even the Sages would agree that the object can become impure. Now, in order for an impure object to become pure, it must be immersed in the purifying waters of a *mikve.* However, no object (or person) may become pure by immersion in a *mikve* unless the entire surface of the object immersed comes into contact with the water, without any impediment. The question at hand is whether or not the stuffing is considered an impediment which must be removed from the leather pouch in order for the pouch to become pure by immersion in the *mikve.* R. Eliezer maintained that the stuffing does not count as an impediment, since it enables the pouch to perform its function, and that it need not be removed before the immersion. The Sages disagree. They maintain the stuffing in a now dysfunctional object counts as an impediment, and must be removed prior to immersion.

The visitors next ask a third and final question. What is the halakha regarding a fully finished shoe not yet removed from the last on which it was made? Now in order for an object to achieve the status of a *keli,* it must be fully finished. Here we have a finished shoe, but one not yet functional, since the shoemaker has not yet removed it from the last. Does such a shoe have the status of a *keli*? The Sages maintained that since the shoe is complete, requiring no further professional adjustments, it does have that status, and therefore can become impure. However, R. Eliezer maintains that since the shoe is not yet functional, as it remains on the last, it does not have the status of a *keli,* and is therefore pure.[12]

After R. Eliezer asserts that the shoe on the last is pure, he dies abruptly. The very last word he utters in this world is "pure," and

12. Note the interesting parallel between this debate, and the debate between R. Yoḥanan and Reish Lakish about what makes a vessel finished, analyzed in chapter 6 of this volume.

the Talmud asserts that R. Eliezer thus left the world in purity. Next, R. Yehoshua immediately stands and publicly proclaims, twice for emphasis, that the ban is now lifted. R. Eliezer has indeed left the world in purity. Of course, it is no accident that R. Yehoshua is the Sage who lifts the ban, and that he stands while doing so. First, he was R. Eliezer's closest colleague before the ban, and the two of them together secreted R. Yoḥanan b. Zakkai out of a besieged Jerusalem to establish the Torah center in Yavne that made post-destruction Jewish life possible.[13]

Perhaps even more importantly, let us recall that during the bitter oven of *akhnai* controversy, after the heavenly voice endorsed R. Eliezer, it was R. Yehoshua who got up and pronounced, "The Torah is not in heaven." This scene at R. Eliezer's death is thus a perfect recapitulation of the events at the initial ban. The ban is, as it were, relived and reversed. With great pathos and power, R. Yehoshua himself stands and proclaims, "The vow is lifted, the vow is lifted."

But why should the mere happenstance utterance of the word "pure" by R. Eliezer achieve the lifting of the vow? How can the Talmud assert that he left the world in purity for that reason alone? Is there some magical power to his utterance of the word "pure" over his halakhic status? Moreover, why did his visitors persist in asking such involved technical questions just as R. Eliezer was about to die? Rashi here suggests that these questions were probative, as they wanted to ascertain whether or not R. Eliezer had finally recanted the position he took about the oven of *akhnai*. But then why not ask him about that law directly, as the debate here is so different?

For all these reasons I would like to suggest that this halakhic dialogue is a code for a series of existential questions that the visitors intended to probe. Sometimes it is easier to communicate by indirection, and R. Eliezer's visitors chose not to confront him directly. They preferred to use the language and halakhic categories they knew and loved, in order to speak about difficult and painful matters so close to their hearts.[14]

---

13. See Gittin 56a.
14. Some years after I developed this analysis I came across a recent volume by A. Beitner, *The Tales of Yavne* (Ramat Gan: 2011), 81–83 (Heb.), who also interprets these halakhic dialogues metaphorically, but differently from how I present it here.

Let us first observe that the crucial halakhic category here is a *keli,* a vessel. An object has this status only if it is capable of containing something within it. But is not a *keli* a metaphor for the human condition? For to be a person is to possess, to hold something within, and for the Sages and R. Eliezer there can be no more important entity to be held within a human being than God's Torah. To be a person is to possess Torah. And why is a human being created? For no reason other than to possess Torah. This, after all, was what these great men devoted their lives to, the intense study of Torah. And, this is exactly analogous to the ball in the debate between R. Eliezer and the Sages. The ball was made to be filled with wool, and a person is created to be filled with Torah.

The Sages maintained that the stuffing of the ball is part of its very essence, and therefore the ball does not have the status of a *keli.* A person and the Torah he possesses are one. And if the Torah that person possesses is flawed, then the person is flawed too. They meant to say: "R. Eliezer, your Torah is flawed; you refuse to follow the majority. Since you and the Torah are one, if your Torah is flawed, so too are you, and your excommunication was and remains justified." R. Eliezer disagreed. Although a human being is created to possess Torah, the Torah he possesses is not identical with the person who possesses it. Even if the Torah is flawed, the person may be pure. He meant to say, "You disagree with my halakhic position, but you cannot draw the conclusion that I am fundamentally flawed. A person and his Torah are not one entity but two, and you excommunicated me unjustly."

The second debate revolved around a ball or shoe last whose leather pouch was torn. Such an object requires immersion in a *mikve,* and the question was whether or not the stuffing must be removed. Does it count as an impediment or not? R. Eliezer maintained that the stuffing does not count as an impediment, while the Sages maintained that it does. Now if a *keli,* here the leather pouch, is a metaphor for a person, then a torn leather pouch is a metaphor for a torn person. This torn person is none other than R. Eliezer himself, and that tear can mean one of two things. It might mean that R. Eliezer is flawed, like the torn pouch, flawed by virtue of his character, his temperament, or his ideological convictions regarding Torah study. Not only is he flawed, but, like the leather pouch, he is impure. How can R. Eliezer then purify himself?

The Sages maintain that the only way he can purify himself is by removing the impediment, and in his case the impediment is his position on the oven of *akhnai*. In short, he must recant.

However, R. Eliezer maintains that his position on the oven of *akhnai* is Torah, even if it was rejected by the Sages. His position represents an ancient tradition endorsed by God Himself. Even if the Sages have the right to reject it, that position does not lose the status of Torah. And in principle, Torah can never serve as an impediment to purity. Torah is the quintessence of purity itself, and can never impede the purity of the human being who possesses it.

A second reading of the torn leather pouch is that it is a metaphor not for R. Eliezer's flaws, but for his mental state. R. Eliezer is a broken man, torn asunder by the trauma of excommunication. The Sages maintain that the only path to the purity of healing is by recanting his position on the oven to remove the impediment preventing his healing, and R. Eliezer maintains that Torah can never prevent healing. On either reading, however, the basic debate is the same. R. Eliezer maintains that his position on the oven is Torah, and Torah can never impede purity.

This brings us to the third enigmatic question they pose: What is the status of a shoe not yet removed from its last? According to the Sages, it is a finished object, with the status of a *keli*, and can therefore become impure. R. Eliezer insists that since it is not yet removed from the last it is not yet finished, does not have the status of a *keli*, and remains pure. I have suggested that all the objects in question throughout these halakhic debates are metaphors for the human condition in general, and for R. Eliezer himself in particular, and the shoe in question here is no different. R. Eliezer is on the very cusp of death. He is, as it were, the shoe about to be removed from its last, ready to enter the World to Come. Is he, at this moment, a finished object? The Sages maintain that at this final moment in R. Eliezer's life no change is possible, for he is about to die. His life is, de facto, over, he has lived as he chose, and he will die with the bitter consequences of those choices.

R. Eliezer insists, however, that the shoe has not yet left its last, and that his life is not yet over. He is still a work in progress, as is all life, until death irrevocably strikes. But death has not yet struck, and perhaps, just perhaps, he might change his mind. He insists that he is pure, just as the shoe is, for neither is finished. Both remain on the last, where a slight adjustment can still be made. R. Eliezer meant to say, "Never condemn a man before his time," for life, as the ancient Greek philosopher Heraclitus taught, is forever in flux. Human beings change, and change and change again, and so might he. R. Eliezer thus taught, in the coded language of halakha, "I am pure, because I am a work in progress, and it is therefore always possible that I will change my views."

The assertion of purity triggered R. Yehoshua's dramatic lifting of the ban. The word "pure" has no magical power. Rather, R. Yehoshua and the other visitors heard in R. Eliezer's last word an admission that perhaps, in the end, he might have been wrong, that he is a fallible human being, whose views are not final until he can no longer express any views at all. This marks a deep change in R. Eliezer. While he never admits that he was wrong, he finally admits the *possibility* that he was wrong, and that difference made all the difference in the world. The ban was finally lifted. Of course, it was lifted too late to change his life, but it was not lifted too late to change his legacy. For the author of this aggada, R. Eliezer is readmitted to the circle of scholars whose teachings shaped Judaism for millennia to come.

PART THREE

R. ELIEZER, R. AKIVA, AND THE FINAL END TO THE OVEN OF *AKHNAI* TRAGEDY

I noted at the outset of this chapter that R. Akiva is the central figure in this deathbed encounter with R. Eliezer, for the Talmud introduces the story by stating that "R. Akiva and his friends" visited, eliding the names of all the other visitors, including R. Akiva's second great teacher, R. Yehoshua, a close colleague of R. Eliezer himself. R. Eliezer later informs R. Akiva that his death will be worst of all, and finally we now encounter R. Akiva, in the aftermath of R. Eliezer's death.

After Shabbat ends, the mourners carry R. Eliezer's coffin from Caesarea to Lod, and R. Akiva meets up with the funeral procession. He strikes his flesh with such anguish that his blood flowed to the earth, and then proceeds to eulogize him, first citing the verse from II Kings 2:12, "My father, my father, the chariot of Israel and its horsemen." "I have many coins to exchange," he cries out, many questions of Torah to ask, "but no money changer to whom to give them," no one to answer my many questions. With these profoundly pained comments, the story ends. We must ask ourselves why the story both begins and ends with R. Akiva.

By way of answering this crucial question, let us begin by asking several others. First, why was R. Akiva not traveling together with the funeral procession, in mourning for his great master? Why did he just meet up with it on the way? Did he leave R. Eliezer's house early? Second, what is the meaning of the money changer metaphor? In ancient times, a money changer typically took foreign coins, and changed them into local currency. How exactly is that relevant to the role R. Eliezer played in R. Akiva's life of Torah study? Rashi explains that R. Akiva was saying he had many questions to ask, but no one to answer them. However, how does that speak to the actual ancient practice of a money changer?

Third, how is it halakhically permissible for R. Akiva to mourn as he does? The Torah seems to forbid exactly this behavior, as in, "You shall not make gashes in your flesh for the dead" (Lev. 19:28). Some suggest that the verse refers only to gashes, not other forms of self-mortification, while others suggest that R. Akiva did so not in mourning over personal loss, which would be forbidden, but out of the permissible anguish he felt at the loss of so extraordinary a source of Torah knowledge.[15] Whatever interpretation one follows, however, the analogy to R. Eliezer himself, the sorcerer who moves the cucumbers, seems clear. Both use legitimate loopholes to skirt the law for higher purposes. R. Akiva steps into the footsteps of his master immediately following the master's death, as if to say, "Even now, you remain my teacher."

This similarity between R. Akiva and R. Eliezer turns our attention to the crucial question of their relationship, and the similarities and differences between them. At one level, the similarities are profound. First, they both began their lives in radical Jewish ignorance. As we saw in chapter 1, it was not until the age of twenty-eight, and moti-

15. See *Tosafot* here, and *Tosafot*, Yevamot 13b, s.v. *de'amar.*

vated by a burning desire for Torah, that R. Eliezer left home to study in the yeshiva of R. Yoḥanan b. Zakkai. At that stage in his life, he was ignorant of even the rudiments of halakha. Likewise, according to many sources, R. Akiva did not begin to study Torah until he was forty years old, and retrospectively characterized himself in those early years as an *am haaretz*, a person ignorant of Jewish law.[16] Both were driven by an insatiable thirst for Torah, which led them to make many personal, if different, sacrifices, and both eventually achieved greatness.

Despite these similarities, the trajectories of their lives clearly diverged. As we have seen, R. Eliezer's greatest strength in Torah study was his memory, and his commitment to preserving all the ancient halakhic traditions he received from his masters going back to Sinai. R. Akiva's greatest strength in Torah study was his halakhic creativity, his ability to derive or link new laws to every letter of the Torah. So extraordinary was this creativity that, according to a well-known aggada, even Moses himself, who received the Torah at Sinai, failed to understand it.[17] This clash came to the fore in the debate over the oven of *akhnai*, as we saw in the previous chapter. However, the differences do not end here.

R. Eliezer demanded absolute respect for a master, and would teach nothing he had not heard from him, while the very first time R. Akiva speaks openly to R. Eliezer, his own great teacher, was to disagree with him. This so upset R. Eliezer that he predicted R. Akiva's death, a point I shall return to shortly.[18] While R. Eliezer had a very negative attitude toward gentiles,[19] R. Akiva, in a passage I shall cite just below, stressed that all human beings should be beloved because

16. *Avot DeRabbi Natan*, version A, 6, and Pesaḥim 49b. For a recent review of the sources regarding R. Akiva's origins and turn toward Torah see R. Hammer, *Akiva: The Man, Legend, and Legacy* (Rishon LeTzion: 2015), 21–53 (Heb.).
17. Menaḥot 29b.
18. Pesaḥim 69a. For sources on R. Eliezer's attitude toward respect of a master, see Gilat, *R. Eliezer ben Hyrcanus*, 163–65.
19. For sources, see Gilat, ibid., 450–55. Thus, R. Eliezer maintains that a Torah scroll written by a gentile must be burned (Gittin 45b), and that a red heifer may not be purchased from gentile idol worshippers, which the Talmud explains as grounded in the view that such persons are suspected of bestiality (Mishna Para 2:1 and Avoda Zara 23a).

they were created in the image of God.[20] R. Akiva possessed a boundless optimism in the face of adversity,[21] while R. Eliezer responded to adversity, as we have seen, first by crying, in his earliest years, and later in anger. In general, R. Eliezer appears to have modeled a life of *yira*, of the greatest fear of God, an austere posture which led him to advocate asceticism in various aspects of life, especially with respect to marital intimacy.[22] R. Akiva, on the other hand, seemed to model a life of love for human beings, of all Jews, and of God, best exemplified in his famous teaching recorded in the mishna in *Pirkei Avot*:

> He used to say: Beloved is man, for he was created in the image of God. As a gesture of special love, it was made known to him that he was created in the image of God.... Beloved are Israel for they are called God's children.... Beloved are Israel, for they were given a precious vessel [the Torah].[23]

R. Akiva thus advocates love to all human beings and especially to Jews. This loving posture seems to have characterized his relationship with his wife as well, described powerfully in various sources.[24] Finally, of course, it extended to God, and, as we shall see, R. Akiva died a martyr's death while teaching his students the meaning of true love of God "with all your soul."[25]

While these contrasts are generalizations, requiring more analysis for accurate nuance, it is fair to say that the overall portrait is of two great figures who started their lives in similar circumstances, but diverged dramatically as they each matured. We must now ask how R. Eliezer

20. See below. For additional sources, see Hammer, *Akiva*, 135–39.

21. See, for example, Makkot 24a–24b. For a collection of sources on this theme, see Meir Soloveichik, "Rabbi Akiva's Optimism," *Azure* 30 (2007): 91–109.

22. See Gilat, *R. Eliezer ben Hyrcanus*, 417–21, for sources. Especially noteworthy are the severely restricted practices during sexual intercourse ascribed to R. Eliezer by his wife in Nedarim 20a–b.

23. *Pirkei Avot* 3:18.

24. Ketubot 62b–63a.

25. Berakhot 61b.

took to his student R. Akiva's independent ways. As we saw, R. Eliezer, more than most, prized a student's loyalty to his master.

The first clue emerges from a passage alluded to earlier. R. Eliezer and R. Yehoshua were once vigorously debating which elements of the sacrifice of the Paschal lamb must be completed before Shabbat begins, when the eve of Passover is Friday.[26] The arguments proved inconclusive, until R. Akiva interjected with his own powerful argument. R. Eliezer responds, with a play on words, that R. Akiva's fate will be the same as the sacrificial lamb of the Passover offering: both will be slaughtered.[27] This disturbing response precisely foreshadows the equally disturbing comment R. Eliezer makes to R. Akiva, discussed above, that his death will be worse than the premature deaths of all his colleagues. Why did R. Eliezer attack R. Akiva so harshly?

The Talmud Yerushalmi makes a very interesting and important observation about R. Akiva's intervention in the argument of his two teachers.[28] According to the Yerushalmi, for the first thirteen years that R. Akiva studied in the yeshiva of R. Eliezer in Lod, R. Eliezer paid him no attention, and said not a word to him. The argument R. Akiva unleashed here contained the very first words R. Akiva ever uttered to R. Eliezer. Now, assuming the sources describing the early origins of R. Eliezer are consistent with this source, we will recall that R. Eliezer himself fiercely sought full acceptance into the yeshiva of R. Yoḥanan b. Zakkai, and was deeply offended when his master kept him at a distance due to the halitosis which resulted from his prolonged fasting. Yet here, R. Eliezer, now a great master himself, pays no attention to a student who, just like his own youthful self, arrives at the yeshiva with limited background, but an insatiable desire to learn. What R. Eliezer sought in his master, R. Eliezer himself did not provide to his student. Is this a reflection of R. Eliezer's tough-minded personality, and of his unyielding quest for Torah study at the very highest, rather than elementary, levels? Is he more the elite scholar than the pedagogue?

26. Mishna Pesaḥim 6:1.

27. Pesaḥim 69a.

28. Y. Pesaḥim 6:3, 42a.

As plausible as these explanations may be, it is impossible to say for certain.

In any case, the Yerushalmi's comment may shed light on why R. Eliezer responded so harshly to R. Akiva's role in the discussion. Who is this young student to interject himself in an argument between his two great masters, R. Eliezer and R. Yehoshua? How could he side with R. Yehoshua over him, when he, R. Eliezer, is the bearer of the great ancient traditions of the Oral Law? Surely human reason cannot adjudicate this dispute. R. Eliezer is certain he is correct, because he knows exactly what his masters taught him, and what their masters in turn were taught, going all the way back to Sinai. Yes, he too deploys arguments in the debate, but that is only to reinforce a position that he knows to be correct for traditional, not logical, reasons, and even if his arguments fail him, he is certain of the rectitude of his position. And here this junior student, convinced of the power and autonomy of human reason, throws himself into the debate with yet another argument, when he should know that arguments count for little against an oral tradition which goes back to Sinai. And how can he show disrespect for his great masters by even interjecting himself into the debate? Torah scholars must show the utmost respect for their masters, and never even teach a halakha not heard from them. Yet R. Akiva has the gall to side with R. Yehoshua, not only on this matter, but on R. Yehoshua's whole theory of halakha, of affirmation of the value of creativity and independence. From this perspective, it is hardly surprising that R. Eliezer was so upset with his student. The debate here foreshadowed the great debate over the oven of *akhnai*, the die has been cast, and for R. Eliezer, R. Akiva is on the wrong side.

What may have exacerbated these feelings was a recognition by R. Eliezer that R. Akiva was so much like him, that they shared a common history, and a common passionate yearning for Torah. Both in their own ways were capable of skirting conventional practice, R. Eliezer in rejecting the majority, and R. Akiva with his breathtakingly novel readings of the Torah. R. Eliezer may have initially seen in R. Akiva a younger version of himself, profoundly identified with him, and took R. Akiva to be a kind of spiritual child, even if they did not converse with one another. He might have meant to insist that R. Akiva make it in the yeshiva on his own, just as he, R. Eliezer, chose to conceal his wealthy father's identity when he first arrived at R. Yoḥanan b. Zakkai's yeshiva, so that he too would make it on his own.

Are R. Akiva and R. Eliezer mirror images of one another, born alike, yet eventually separated by profound differences in *weltanschauung*, personality, and approach to the service of God and to the study of His Torah? If so, the disloyalty in R Akiva's support of the opposition may have hurt even more. For this reason, R. Eliezer predicts so terrible a death for R. Akiva, after he hears the very first words R. Akiva utters in the study hall.

Here we must recall the depiction of R. Eliezer's early years in *Pirkei DeRabbi Eliezer*, discussed in the first of this trilogy of chapters on R. Eliezer. In front of a number of distinguished guests assembled at a party, R. Yoḥanan b. Zakkai had asked his student to deliver words of Torah. R. Eliezer refuses, on the grounds that no scholar should ever teach but what he heard from his own masters. However, once R. Yoḥanan b. Zakkai leaves the room, R. Eliezer's begins to teach brilliant new insights into Torah, and his face "shone like the light of the sun, his rays beamed like the rays of Moses, so that no one knew whether it was day or night." R. Eliezer possessed all the creative talents anyone could wish for, exactly the creative talents that he would see in his student R. Akiva. Yet over the course of his life in Torah, R. Eliezer would suppress this creativity bubbling up within, the fresh new insights emerging like water from an ever-flowing fountain (to use the metaphor of R. Yoḥanan b. Zakkai himself), in self-sacrificial service to the ideal of pure tradition. Imagine the difficulty of that suppression, and the psychological costs R. Eliezer might have paid!

Yet R. Akiva, his great student, chose to nurture that very creativity rather than suppress it. In a sense, R. Akiva is the man R. Eliezer himself would have been, had R. Eliezer not adhered to a different and far more restrictive vision of Torah study. In observing R. Akiva, he was observing not only his mirror image, but also his own alter ego, the man he could have become, but with unimaginable self-sacrifice chose not to. Might this not have shaped his attitude toward R. Akiva from the moment R. Akiva opened his mouth, to the time he publicly sided with R. Eliezer's opponents?

Despite these differences, their relationship endured for years until the oven of *akhnai* tragedy, witnessed by the conversation R. Eliezer reports that he held with R. Akiva about the cucumbers. This must have taken place before the oven of *akhnai* debate, yet after R. Akiva first spoke up in the study hall. R. Akiva continues to study under his great master, who chooses, despite R. Akiva's interjection in the study hall, to continue to teach him. R. Eliezer no doubt recognized the prodigious talents of his star student. Perhaps he hoped that R. Akiva would eventually come to see the error of his ways. Yet R. Akiva did not. He sides with the Sages in the oven of *akhnai* debate, and volunteers to inform R. Eliezer of the ban. Their paths have now parted forever, until the pathos-filled encounter at R. Eliezer's deathbed. It is likely that R. Eliezer's feelings toward his student remained ambivalent. Surely R. Eliezer would never forget his dire prediction about R. Akiva's end.

If R. Eliezer's feelings toward his student were ambivalent, one must now ask how R. Akiva felt about R. Eliezer. How did he react to the ominous warnings about his terrible death? How did he react to a master whom he no doubt respected to the heavens, but with whom he deeply disagreed? The unusual metaphor of the money changer is revealing. Money changers were typically used by foreign travelers, who needed to exchange their coins for the currency of the realm. If the coins remained unchanged, they could not be used. This metaphor makes it apparent that R. Akiva regards himself as a foreign traveler. The Torah he brings to the table is a foreign coin too, for it is the product of his human reasoning, of his capacity to derive laws from the letters of the Torah that even Moses himself did not see or understand. R. Eliezer, on the other hand, is the money changer. He possesses the coins of the realm, the authentic traditions by which he measures the true value of R. Akiva's alien currency, his strange new ideas.

This metaphor thus brilliantly reflects R. Akiva's own ambivalence. First, he concedes that his ideas are alien to the ancient traditions of halakha mastered by his teacher R. Eliezer; he recognizes that their utility in that traditional Torah world is suspect, and requires validation by R. Eliezer. Yet, at the same time, he asserts that the Torah he brings does have value, are coins of worth in the currency of scholars who share his approach to Torah study, even if not validated by R. Eliezer himself.

He affirms the importance of R. Eliezer's Torah, and R. Eliezer's validation of his Torah, but only on R. Eliezer's home turf, not on his own. This metaphor aligns perfectly with the image of R. Akiva when he informs R. Eliezer that his colleagues banned him. On the one hand, R. Akiva dressed in black, vividly expressing the empathy and pain he felt for his great master. On the other hand, he approaches no closer than four cubits, reflecting the ban. R. Akiva feels deeply his teacher's tragedy, but nevertheless at the same holds him at a distance.

How does a student revere a master while at the same time fundamentally part ways with him? Is reverence still possible in the face of rejection? R. Akiva learned so much from his master, but his master in turn both held R. Akiva close to him with his teachings, yet rejected him at the same time. Surely it is likely that R. Akiva himself would both hold onto and reject his master at the same time as well. Is this why R. Akiva did not accompany the funeral procession from the start? Might he have left his master's presence immediately after R. Eliezer foretells his awful death? The complexity of R. Eliezer's feelings about R. Akiva were likely matched by the complexity of R. Akiva's feelings toward R. Eliezer. Surely such is often the way of human relationships.

We are finally ready to examine what I would argue is the last chapter in the saga of R. Eliezer and R. Akiva, and that is the story of R. Akiva's martyrdom. R. Akiva was captured by the Romans for teaching Torah publicly, and the Talmud reports:

> **When they took Rabbi Akiva out to be executed, it was time for the recitation of *Shema*. And they were raking his flesh with iron combs, and he was** reciting *Shema*, thereby **accepting upon himself the yoke of Heaven. His students said to him: Our teacher, even now,** as you suffer, you recite *Shema*? **He said to them: All my days I have been troubled by the verse: With all your soul,** meaning: **Even if God takes your soul. I said** to myself: **When will the** opportunity **be afforded me to fulfill this** verse? **Now that it has been afforded me, shall I not fulfill it? He prolonged** his uttering of the word: **One, until his soul left** his body as he uttered his final word: **One. A voice descended** from heaven **and said: Happy are you, Rabbi Akiva, that your soul left** your body as you

> uttered: **One. The ministering angels said before the Holy One, Blessed be He: This is Torah and this its reward?** As it is stated: **"From death, by Your hand, O Lord, from death** of the world" (Psalms 17:14); Your hand, God, kills and does not save. God **said** the end of the verse **to** the ministering angels: **"Whose portion is in this life."** And then a **Divine Voice emerged and said: Happy are you, Rabbi Akiva, as you are destined for life in the World-to-Come, as your portion is already in eternal life.**[29]

R. Akiva's martyrdom is, I would suggest, both the denouement of the complex and painful story of the relationship between R. Eliezer and R. Akiva, and the denouement of the conflict over the oven of *akhnai*. R. Eliezer had long predicted this terrible end to R. Akiva's life, and his prediction was finally realized. As we saw in the chapter on the conflict over that oven, the gates of heaven are never closed to the prayers of one whose feelings are hurt by another. R. Eliezer's pain over the ban not only killed Rabban Gamliel, but found its ultimate resolution in the martyrdom of his great student R. Akiva, whose death he had predicted.[30] Of course, that prediction went all the way back to R. Akiva's first words in the study hall, in the debate over the Paschal lamb, which culminated in the debate over the oven. Thus, R. Akiva's martyrdom culminated a very longstanding tension between master and student.

The attentive reader of this passage describing R. Akiva's martyrdom might be struck by a question. Why does a divine voice emerge after R. Akiva's death to announce that he had gained entry into the World to Come? Who would have thought otherwise? R. Akiva was one of the greatest Jews who ever lived, and who suffered a martyr's death. If R. Akiva would not merit the World to Come, then who would? The answer, I would suggest, is that this divine voice meant to announce that the great rift between the two Sages is now healed.

29. Berakhot 61b.

30. If the ban was just, and the intentions of the banner good, why then were they punished? At the end of chapter 2, I suggested two possibilities. According to the second suggestion I made, where there was a lack of empathy for R. Eliezer's situation, one would need to argue that while R. Akiva felt empathy for R. Eliezer, the empathy he felt was not strong enough. See the fuller discussion there.

With the death of R. Akiva, the gates of heaven can now close to the pain R. Eliezer experienced at R. Akiva's hand and at the hands of the Sages. The tragic story has now finally come to a close, the divine voice announces that all is healed, and that R. Akiva may enter the World to Come.

What is the last word R. Akiva utters? It is *eḥad,* "one." Of course, he means to refer to the unity of God. But it is hard to believe that R. Akiva at his death did not recall the devastating predictions of his great master, and the rift between him, and among the whole community of scholars. It is difficult to avoid hearing in R. Akiva's very last word on earth the echo of another unity, the long-shattered unity among the Sages. R. Akiva announces at his death that this unity, too, has finally been restored.

Chapter 4

Who Was Akavya B. Mahalalel?

Mishna Eduyot 5:6–7

INTRODUCTION

Most of the texts we are analyzing in this volume are from the Talmud, but the text which is the subject of this chapter is derived from the Mishna. Overall, the Mishna is largely halakhic, with relatively few aggadic passages, and even fewer passages which tell a story. Among these few is the case of Akavya b. Mahalalel, found in Mishna Eduyot. Eduyot is a compilation of teachings on a variety of subjects, composed in Yavne shortly after the destruction of the Temple. As the Tosefta to Eduyot explains, the rabbis were afraid that in the aftermath of the destruction, the oral traditions of the Torah would be lost, so they assembled numerous testimonies (the meaning of the Hebrew term *eduyot*), beginning with the teachings of Hillel and Shammai, and many of them are about laws governing purity and impurity.[1]

1. Tosefta Eduyot 1:1.

The story of Akavya parallels, in many important respects, that of R. Eliezer b. Hyrcanus, the subject of the last three chapters of this volume. Both were *Tanna'im* who dissented from the majority on a matter of halakha, and both suffered the consequences of their dissent. The similarities and differences between these two stories are illuminating, for which reason I have included it immediately following the chapters dealing with R. Eliezer. What motivated Akavya? What was his jurisprudence? What exactly was his fate? Did he change over the course of his lifetime? What final words of advice did he share with his son before his death?

We possess very few teachings of Akavya, the primary collection of those few being presented in this mishna. A second teaching of a non-halakhic nature is recorded in *Pirkei Avot*:

> Akavya ben Mahalalel said: Reflect on three things and you will avoid transgression: Know where you came from, where you are going, and before whom you will have to give an account and reckoning. "Where you came from" – from a putrid drop. "Where you are going" – to a place of dust, worms, and maggots. "And before whom you will have to give an account and reckoning" – before the Supreme King of kings, the Holy One, blessed be He.[2]

This crucial message appears to have served as the guidepost for Akavya's own tragic life, as we shall see.

Mishna Eduyot 5:6–7

עקביא בן מהללאל העיד ארבעה דברים. אמרו לו, עקביה, חזר בך בארבעה דברים שהיית אומר ונעשך אב בית דין לישראל. אמר להן, מוטב לי להקרא שוטה כל ימי, ולא לעשות שעה אחת רשע לפני המקום, שלא יהיו אומרים, בשביל שררה חזר בו. הוא היה מטמא שער הפקדון ודם הירוק. וחכמים מטהרין. הוא היה מתיר שער בכור בעל מום שנשר והניחו בחלון ואחד כך שחטו, וחכמים אוסרים.

2. *Pirkei Avot* 3:1.

Akavya b. Mahalalel testified to four matters. They said to him, "Akavya! Retract regarding the four things which you say and we will make you the *Av Beit Din* (Chief Justice) of the Jewish people." He said to them, "I prefer to be called a fool all of my days rather than be wicked for a moment before the Almighty, lest they say that he retracted for [the advancement in] political office." He used to declare [a leprous man] ritually impure [as a result of the return of] white hairs and [a menstrual women who saw] yellow blood, but the Sages do not. He would permit using the hair shed by a blemished firstborn, which he set aside [i.e., the hair] and then slaughtered [the animal] but the Sages forbid its use.

הוא היה אומר, אין משקין לא את הגירת ולא את שפחה המשוחררת. וחכמים אומרים, משקין. אמרו לו, מעשה בכרכמית, שפחה משוחררת שהיתה בירושלים, והשקוה שמעיה ואבטליון. אמר להם, דגמא השקוה. ונדוהו, ומת בנדויו, וסקלו בית דין את ארונו. אמר רבי יהודה, חס ושלום שעקביא נתנדה, שאין עזרה ננעלת בפני כל אדם מישראל בחכמה וביראת חטא כעקביא בן מהללאל. ואת מי נדו, אליעזר בן חנוך, שפקפק בטהרת ידים. וכשמת, שלחו בית דין והניחו אבן על ארונו. מלמד שכל המתנדה ומת בנדויו, סוקלין את ארונו.

He used to say that we do not give a convert or freed maidservant [the *sota* waters] to drink but the Sages say that we do. They said to him, "There was an incident with Karkamit the freed maidservant where Shemaya and Avtalyon gave her [*sota* waters] to drink. He said to them, "They only gave to her to drink as an example." And they excommunicated him and he died in a state of excommunication. R. Yehuda said, "God forbid that [one should say that] Akavya was excommunicated, as the Temple courtyard was never closed on a person among the Jews who was as wise and God-fearing as Akavya. Who did they excommunicate? Eliezer b. Hanokh, who cast aspersions on the ritual washing of the hands. And they excommunicated him and he died in a state of excommunication and the court stoned his coffin, which teaches you that whenever someone is excommunicated and dies in that state, they stone his coffin.

בשעת מיתתו אמר לבנו, בני, חזור בך בארבעה דברים שהייתי אומר. אמר לו, ולמה לא חזרת בך. אמר לו, אני שמעתי מפי המרבים, והם שמעו מפי המרבים. אני עמדתי בשמועתי, והם עמדו בשמועתן. אבל אתה שמעת מפי היחיד, ומפי המרבין. מוטב להניח דברי היחיד, ולאחז בדברי המרבין. אמר לו, אבא, פקד עלי לחבריך. אמר לו, איני מפקיד. אמר לו, שמא עילה מצאת בי. אמר לו, לאו. מעשיך יקרבוך ומעשיך ירחקוך.

At the time of his death he said to his son, "My son, retract the four things which I used to say." He said to him, "Why didn't you retract?" He said to him, "I heard [my views] from a majority and they heard from a majority, [and thus] I stood behind my tradition and they stood by their tradition; you, however, have [now] heard [both] from a minority (Akavya) and a majority (the Sages), and it is preferable to set aside the opinions of the minority in favor of the opinions of the majority." He said to him, "Father, please request of your friends [to accept me]." He said to him, "No." [He said to him,] "Perhaps you have found flaws in me." He said to him, "No. But your [own] actions will make you accepted and your [own] actions will cause you to be ostracized."[3]

PART ONE

AKAVYA DISSENTS FROM THE MAJORITY

The mishna starts by reporting that Akavya attested to four laws. The rabbis respond with an offer: If you retract these four testimonies, we will appoint you to be *Av Beit Din*, head of the supreme rabbinical court, a position second only to the *nasi*, the leader of the Jewish community and ultimate chief of the court. Surprisingly, the mishna does not yet tell us the laws about which he testified, nor does it tell us why the rabbis were so insistent that he retract his testimony, questions we shall turn to shortly. No less surprising is the offer the rabbis make, as if they wish

3. Mishna Eduyot 5:6–7, translation from Kenneth Jeremy Wieder, "Mishnah Eduyot: A Literary History of a Unique Tractate" (PhD diss., New York University, 2005), 181–82, with modifications.

to bribe him, seduce him into abandoning his position by promises of great rabbinic prominence.

Akavya's response to their offer is tart indeed. He asserts that he would rather be called a fool his entire life, for rejecting the gain of high office, than be evil before God just for a moment. He then adds that he does not want people to say of him that because of personal gain he retracted his position.

Let us examine each part of his response. The first point he makes is that halakhic truth and personal conscience may never be sacrificed. Even if people think him a fool for abandoning great personal gain, those considerations are irrelevant. As Akavya taught in *Pirkei Avot* cited above, nothing matters but God's righteous judgment. The values of social status, wealth, and prestige, which the rabbis offer, are no more than byproducts of the physical dimension to the human condition, which ends in burial and decay, and thus they are not valuable at all. The only enduring dimension of the human being, the only dimension which possesses absolute value, is that which adheres to God and to the truths of His Torah. The rabbis and he speak different languages, and profess incommensurate values: they equate honor with value, while he does not, and attempt to bribe him with it. Thus, Akavya's teaching in *Pirkei Avot* illuminates the first part of his response to the rabbis' offer.

What, then, are we to make of the second part of Akavya's response? If all that matters is how a person lives before God, then why does Akavya fear public opprobrium? Why does he even care if people say of him that he retracted because of personal gain? If retraction were the right thing to do before God, then retract he must, even if people would think ill of him for so doing. Public opinion should be irrelevant to right and wrong. One possibility is that Akavya means that if he were shamed in public then he would lose his dignity, and loss of human dignity is tantamount to death itself. In other words, while all that matters is how a person lives before God, someone lacking in basic personal dignity is not even a person who can live before God. If someone is publicly shamed their very humanity is undercut. Thus, the Talmud teaches that if someone shames another it is as if he has killed him.[4] Even a man like

4. Bava Metzia 58b.

Akavya, who denies all values but for the value of living authentically before God, must concede that there are certain rudimentary requirements for living a human life, and for him, the basic human dignity destroyed by public shame is apparently one of them.[5] Much like minimum requirements of health or food or water for survival, there are other minimum requirements for living a human life too.

Another possibility is that if Akavya were to retract, people would suspect the entire halakhic system is corrupt, for the position of *Av Beit Din* could be bought by selling one's convictions. If Akavya were a party to this breakdown, surely that would "be wicked before the Almighty." We cannot know for sure what Akavya meant, because the text does not say.

That said, how are we to understand the offer of the rabbis? How could they even attempt to bribe a person by offering him high office, especially a man with such deep and uncompromising principles? While we cannot say for sure, as the text does not explain itself, I would conjecture that the rabbis meant to say this: "You, Akavya, take an isolated position against the majority view. We understand and respect your convictions. However, true human greatness does not lie in isolation. It has been said that humans are by their very nature political animals, that we live and function only within society. You must recognize the essential social context of the human condition. You are a great scholar, and the social context within which you live is the community of scholars. If you accept that reality, and choose to conform to its standards, then because of your knowledge, deep principles, and talents, we will make you a leader." On this account, the offer was not so much a bribe, as it was a means to foster within him the social consciousness which would make his ascension to high office deserved.

The mishna next proceeds to identify the points of halakha in which Akavya opposed the majority. These are in some ways an afterthought to the larger jurisprudential and social issues raised by his stance,

---

5. The Maharal of Prague makes a similar point in explaining this talmudic teaching that shaming another is like murder. He suggests that it destroys his dignity, an expression of the "image of God" with which humans were created. See his *Netivot Olam, Netiv Ahavat Re'a,* ch. 1.

for which reason, I believe, the mishna consciously chose to mention them only after the initial sharp dialogue between Akavya and the Sages. Three of the four laws are complex and highly technical, and not germane to the analysis of this chapter, so we will focus only on the fourth, which is germane indeed.

During Temple times, a woman accused of an adulterous relationship by her husband, under certain well-defined halakhic circumstances, obtains the status of a *sota*, and according to biblical law, she must drink *mei sota*, special waters which are probative of her guilt or innocence. The question at hand is whether or not these laws apply to a female convert[6] as well, or only to a woman born Jewish. Akavya took the view that they do not apply, while the Sages maintained that they did. In support of their position, the Sages recount a tradition, according to which during Temple times Shemaya and Avtalyon, the two leaders of the Sanhedrin then, required a female convert by the name of Karkamit to drink *mei sota*. This demonstrates that the Sages were correct. Akavya responded, somewhat enigmatically, that "they only gave to her to drink as an example." His response, asserts the mishna, led the Sages to excommunicate him, and according to this tradition he died excommunicated, whereupon the court stoned his coffin.

Before we examine the meaning of Akavya's response, and the very harsh response of the Sages, it is first important to observe that the debate at hand could not be resolved on the basis of halakhic argument, which is how halakhic differences are typically adjudicated. This is because the debate between Akavya and the Sages was a debate about which oral tradition was correct. As will be evident later, Akavya maintained that he has an impeccably reliable tradition that the majority position among the ancient Sages was that a convert could not drink *mei sota*, while the Sages maintained with equal certainty that they had an impeccably reliable tradition that a convert could drink *mei sota*. Thus, the debate was not over the substance of the halakha, but only over whose testimony about the tradition is correct. In other words, the debate was about a matter of fact – the empirically verifiable reliability of an oral transmission – rather than a matter of value, as in, what the halakha by virtue of its own inner

6. Or a female gentile slave who when freed becomes Jewish.

logic should require. Therefore, the proof the Sages offer is an empirical one, attesting to the reliability of their tradition by appeal to the historical practice of two great authorities, rather than a halakhic one per se. It is worth noting that this provides an explanation for why Akavya, who lived during Temple times, was not accused of being a rebellious elder, a member of the Sanhedrin who refuses to submit to the majority, a cardinal crime punishable by death. According to one account in the Talmud, the law of a rebellious elder applies only when the majority grounds its position in an oral tradition, while the dissident scholar grounds his position in autonomous human reasoning. This Akavya did not do, since both he and the Sages based their positions on oral traditions.[7]

Interestingly, Akavya does not cast doubt upon the reliability of the Sages' tradition regarding the practice of Shemaya and Avtalyon. He concedes the facts, yet casts doubt on the utility of that precedent for adjudicating the law, by asserting that Shemaya and Avtalyon "gave to her to drink as an example." What is the meaning of this somewhat obscure phrase? The classical commentators offer two interpretations.[8] The first one turns on the personal status of Shemaya and Avtalyon themselves, for according to various rabbinic sources, they were converts.[9] As such, Akavya was arguing that they had a vested interest in regularizing the status of converts, for which reason they treated Karkamit, the female convert, like any other Jewish woman, and they required that she drink *mei sota*. In effect, Akavya was arguing that Shemaya and Avtalyon's position was tainted by personal interest, and their practice could not serve as a basis for adjudicating the law.[10] According to this interpretation, it is not difficult to see why the Sages excommunicated Akavya. First, his curt and acerbic comment cast aspersions on the integrity of the greatest scholars of their generation, heads of the Sanhedrin, and pivotal vehicles for the transmission of the Oral Law to future generations.[11] He suspected

7. See Sanhedrin 88a. The Talmud there offers a second explanation, that Akavya never issued a formal halakhic decision on the basis of his tradition, so there was no schism in practice.
8. See Raavad, Maimonides, and R. Ovadya Bartenura, ad loc.
9. See, for example, Gittin 57b and Sanhedrin 96b.
10. On this interpretation, they themselves are the example in question.
11. See *Pirkei Avot* 1:1, which delineates the great chain of transmission of the Oral Law

them of distorting halakhic truth to serve their own personal interests. Second, such claims undermine the whole of the halakhic system, for if the motives of even the greatest scholars can be suspect, then the halakhic decisions of all scholars may be suspect as well. It would be like arguing that a black male judge must recuse himself from sitting on a case in which the defendant is a black male as well. If this is what Akavya meant, it would be a shocking accusation, outside the pale of standard halakhic discourse. Indeed, it seems fair to ask how he could even make that claim.

The second interpretation is that Akavya meant to say that Shemaya and Avtalyon did not require her to drink true *mei sota*, but only ersatz *mei sota*, that is, water that looked like, but in point of fact was not, the real thing. This was done in order to frighten her, so that she would confess, thereby avoiding the erasure of God's name, required for the standard process.[12] While Akavya's critique of Shemaya and Avtalyon, according to this interpretation, does not seem quite as disrespectful of rabbinic authority or as subversive, one can see still see why the Sages would be troubled. Akavya attributes to Shemaya and Avtalyon deceptive halakhic practices. The *sota* process is a grave one indeed, and Akavya accuses them of subterfuge, of faking it, thereby impugning their halakhic integrity. Moreover, by impugning their integrity, he casts doubt on the integrity of all members of the Sanhedrin, and the halakhic practices they require. This, too, broadly undercuts halakhic authority.

We must ask ourselves how a man like Akavya could make such disturbing accusations. By way of sharpening this question, consider the position of R. Yehuda, cited next in the mishna. R. Yehuda could simply not accept that a man of Akavya's stature was excommunicated. "God forbid," he proclaims, "that [one should say that] Akavya was excommunicated, as the Temple courtyard was never closed on a person among the Jews who was as wise and God-fearing as Akavya." The reference here is to Passover eve, when the Temple courtyard was

from Moses on down through the generations, with key figures taking up that role from generation to generation, as the following paragraphs make clear.

12. Maimonides explains this on grounds of their own convert status, thus siding with the first interpretation as far as the wrong of which Akavya was excused. Above I have followed Raavad and Rabbi Ovadya Bartenura.

jam-packed with worshippers sacrificing their Paschal lambs.[13] Despite the massive crowds, no one exceeded Akavya in wisdom and fear of God. In order to understand R. Yehuda's position, let us first remember that the mishna was composed long after the destruction of the Temple, when Akavya himself lived.[14] With the passage of time, memories may have dimmed about who exactly was excommunicated, and there arose a dispute about whether or not it was Akavya. R. Yehuda maintained that this was just unthinkable, and the oral tradition confused Akavya with another scholar. Akavya, in his view, was unimpeachable.

Now this perspective sharpens one question while answering another. It sharpens the question of how Akavya could have made the comments he did, given his extraordinary stature. However, it helps answer another. Why were the Sages so disturbed about Akavya's dissent on these four laws that they felt compelled to offer him the post of *Av Beit Din*, head of the court, if he retracted his positions? The answer may well be that precisely because of Akavya's stature, his dissent was all the more dangerous. If an average scholar were to dissent, it would not threaten the viability of the system for halakhic adjudication. However, dissent by a man of Akavya's stature could lead to a schism in the community, whose consequences might be its irreparable splintering. The Sages sought to avoid this at all costs. The offer they made preceded the aspersions Akavya cast on Shemaya and Avtalyon, as the sequence in the mishna suggests, and was driven by their legitimate fear of a schism.

But given Akavya's stature, why then did he cast such aspersions on the great Shemaya and Avtalyon? Part of the answer, I would suggest, lies exactly in the praise R. Yehuda offered: Akavya feared sin. His teaching recorded in *Pirkei Avot* stressed the same theme: All that matters in life is how one stands before God in judgment. Akavya lived every moment in the presence of God and in fear of His judgment. He could tolerate not a whiff of deviation from that exacting

13. Rabbi Ovadya Bartenura in his commentary to the Mishna, ad loc.
14. See C. Licht, *Tradition and Innovation: Topics in Rabbinic Literature* (Givat Haviva: 1989), 47–52 (Heb.), for a valuable discussion of this mishna, and summary of the scholarly positions on when Akavya lived, either early or late first century.

standard, not in himself, and not in anyone else, no matter their stature. With this sensibility was the no doubt accurate feeling that not everyone could live up to these standards, and this may have bred a certain skepticism. People are not what they may seem to be, for do even people of stature live by the eternally present fear of sin? How many people can? Yet many people nevertheless achieve high office. Do they really deserve high office? Hardly, by the elevated standards of Akavya. In that respect, all are failures, the question being only to what extent.

This sensibility may have led Akavya to suspect the worst, not because Shemaya and Avtalyon were especially flawed. They were not; indeed, they were great men. But they were men nonetheless, who could never live up to the uncompromising standards of Akavya. Akavya would have suspected the motives of anyone, irrespective of stature, for all motives on the part of people who do not live in exacting fear of God's judgment are mixed. Whose choices reflect no element, even slight, of self-interest? Only those who live in the unremitting presence of God. Those who do not are likely to suffer from a mixture of motives, some altruistic, some self-serving, which undermines their intellectual integrity. Shemaya and Avtalyon may well have been men of great stature, but they could not meet Akavya's relentlessly high standards, and so for him, their motives must have been mixed. Akavya conjectured what their mixed motives might have been, but this conjecture did not mean to imply that they were any worse than other accomplished people. Rather, it emerged from a skepticism grounded in the exacting standards to which he held all human beings. Intellectual integrity, for Akavya, was a paramount value.

However, we might still ask why a suspicion alone would render their decision invalid. Surely Shemaya and Avtalyon's reputations were outstanding, and that should have been enough, suspicions notwithstanding. I would suggest, therefore, that a second factor was at play as well. Akavya possessed an unshakeable commitment to the truth as he saw it. Any halakhic decision which may have been motivated even only slightly by factors unrelated to halakhic truth rendered the decision unreliable. Now, Akavya could not have known with any certainty that the motives of Shemaya and Avtalyon were illicit. Yet he rejected their decision as precedent because of his vigorous commitment to unadulterated halakhic truth. Put differently, a halakhic decision-making process even possibly tainted by bias possesses no halakhic legitimacy, and cannot serve as a basis for the law. This would be especially true when, like here, there is an authoritative tradition standing against the tainted view. Thus, there were two factors at play: first, Akavya's exacting standards for personal intellectual integrity, and second his exacting standards for the processes of halakhic decision making. Taken together, they led Akavya to reject as legal precedent Shamaya and Avtalyon's practice with regard to Karkamit the convert.

We now have an even sharper explanation for why the Sages feared Akavya's dissent. Akavya was such a religious titan, that his dissent really could lead to a schism. Unfortunately, Jewish history has borne out such fears. Charismatic figures over the millennia have fractured the Jewish people, from ancient through medieval into modern times. On this reading, the Sages were right to fear Akavya's dissent.

PART TWO

AKAVYA'S DEATHBED ADVICE TO HIS SON

Time passes, although we don't know how long, and we next meet up with Akavya on his deathbed, in a final conversation with his son. Interestingly, his son remains anonymous. We do not know his name or anything about him; but for this dialogue, he remains lost to the rabbinic tradition, much like the teachings of his father.

In reading this passage, we must ask ourselves whether or not Akavya has changed in any way over the years, whether or not he has softened his views. What advice can a great, if ostracized dissident offer his son as he leaves the world?

"My son," Akavya says, "retract the four things which I used to say." The first point to note is that the phrase "my son" suggests that he addresses his son like a loving father. However acerbic and curt he may have been in addressing the Sages, he does not address his son that way, at least now. Perhaps more importantly, however, the content of what he conveys is astonishing indeed. Akavya sacrificed his social life and religious stature because he was convinced that his oral tradition was correct. If one follows the first view recorded in the mishna, not R. Yehuda's, Akavya spent the remainder of his life excommunicated, after having rejected an offer for one of the highest positions in the land, all because of his uncompromising commitment to the truth. How then could he advise his son to abandon those very halakhic positions for which he had sacrificed so much?

His own son asks him a similar question: If you want me to abandon those positions, why then didn't you? There is only one halakhic truth. Either you were right or you were wrong. If you were right, then we cannot abandon your position, and if you were wrong, then why didn't you yourself recant?

Akavya's response is a fascinating one, and turns on a distinction between halakhic process and halakhic truth.[15] While there may (or may not) be an objective halakhic truth regarding the status of these disputed cases, halakhic practice is always determined by following the formal processes for adjudicating halakhic disputes. One of the cardinal principles for such adjudication is adherence to the majority. Thus, Akavya meant to say to his son: "I am in possession of an impeccably reliable tradition, which I myself heard from a majority of scholars, that the majority took the position I did. Although my colleagues maintain that they are in possession of an equally reliable tradition that the majority sided with their position, I cannot abandon my oral tradition for theirs, because I myself heard it from a majority. Thus, the formal processes for the adjudication of halakha do not permit me to abandon my position."

"However," continues Akavya, "your position is quite different. You heard my oral tradition from me, and you heard the Sages' oral tradition from them. I am a lone advocate of my tradition, while they are not. Therefore, the formal procedure of majority rule requires you to abandon my position, while at the same time requiring me to sustain it."

While this formulation of Akavya's position seems crisp and lucid, it does raise a question. The language Akavya actually uses is, "*It is preferable* to set aside the opinions of the minority in favor of the opinions of the majority" (emphasis mine). Why use the phrase "it is preferable"?

15. Some might use the similar – although not identical – categories of legal positivism vs. legal realism.

Shouldn't he have said "you must"? Two possible explanations suggest themselves. The first is that this is just part of the general softening of Akavya's tone and language at his final conversation with his son. More likely, however, is the explanation of Rabbi Yom-Tov Lipmann Heller, in his commentary to the Mishna, *Tosefot Yom Tov*. He suggests that the obligation to follow the majority strictly speaking obtains only where the majority and minority debate a point of substance in the law. However, that is not the case here. In our mishna, the debate is about what the majority said, and not a debate over substance, and under such circumstances, the procedural rule to follow the majority does not obtain.

While this comment from the *Tosefot Yom Tov* does not explain the reason for this difference, perhaps it follows from the logic behind the majority rule principle. The majority, since they outnumber the minority, are far more likely to see through to all sides of the question, to consider the fullness of the arguments, to better assess all their strengths and weaknesses, and are thereby far more likely to get the halakhic reasoning correct. However, this logic would not apply to a debate over what the majority happened to say, which involves no reasoning at all. In any case, Akavya's son would be under no formal obligation to follow the majority.

Note that the approach of the *Tosefot Yom Tov* would require a slight modification in the words of the formulation I offered above of Akavya's response to his son. Instead of telling him that he must follow the majority, he would be telling him that such would be the better course of action. Nevertheless, the basic point remains the same: "I must follow my conscience," said Akavya, "but you are free to follow yours, and it is best if you follow the majority." No doubt Akavya offered this advice based upon his own suffering under the ban of excommunication. Akavya learned the hard way just how valuable it is to be part of a community of halakhic scholars, and he wanted to share that hard-earned wisdom with his son, before it was too late. This represents a crucial evolution in his thinking and way of looking at the world. Earlier in his life, he chose to risk the loss of his status and his community out of deeply held principles. Later in his life, while he would no doubt do the same, he comes to experience how great a deprivation that is, and insisted that his son spare himself the same fate.

We should note here that there is a curious and tragic consequence to the recommendation Akavya makes to his son, which is that he condemns his own halakhic position to extinction. The very laws for which he staked his life will be lost to future generations, since his son will follow his advice and not adopt his father's view, and therefore no one else will either. From this perspective, Akavya's recommendation is altogether remarkable. For one thing, it demonstrates his ability to live by the distinction between halakhic truth and halakhic process. He had the capacity to fully integrate the conviction that if the halakhic process is a good one, then God's will has been fulfilled, irrespective of halakhic truth, even if it runs contrary to Akavya's own conviction about what is correct. Now it is one thing to understand this distinction, but it is altogether different to fully internalize and live by it. This is especially true when living by it means the extinction of the very halakhic positions for which one has sacrificed so much. How did Akavya manage this almost superhuman feat? I believe it flows from his experience of God articulated in *Pirkei Avot*. All that matters in life is standing before God righteously. Now if God wills that the halakhic process follows the majority, and his son follows the majority, then all is right with God, and Akavya wants no more out of life than that. He had the capacity to completely dissociate himself from his own personal needs, and the feelings he might have had when advising his son, because these needs simply didn't matter to him. All that did matter was standing righteously before God in His judgment. All other values are incommensurate with this overriding value.

Perhaps an example will help get this point across. A three-year-old child may be totally obsessed with acquiring a certain tricycle. However, when the child ages out of its use, he couldn't care less about that old tricycle. It has no value to him or her. Similarly, some people care personally about wealth or social status or prestige. They matter to him or her, while others may place no value on such goods. They simply don't care about them, and the same was true for Akavya. He simply didn't care, not only about his personal prestige, but even about the longevity of his halakhic positions. All he cared about was standing righteously before God. Therefore, he could readily advise his son to abandon the positions for which he had sacrificed so much. In this, he stands in the sharpest contrast with Shemaya and Avtalyon. For Akavya well knew that few people had his capacity to completely reorder their values such that personal interest matters not at all.

The concluding dialogue in the mishna further sharpens this perspective on Akavya. His son finally asks Akavya to commend him to his colleagues. If the father was banned, no doubt the son too suffered the social consequences of his father's ostracism. There is, therefore, considerable pathos to his request for help in easing his way back into the fellowship of scholars. Akavya responds, in his usual curt style, that he cannot. His son then asks him why. Is he unworthy in some way? In the very last words recorded before his death, Akavya responds (when translated literally): "No. But your actions will draw you near and your actions will distance you."

On one level, this is the advice of the old Akavya. Letters of recommendation will do you no good, he tells his son. Your own knowledge of Torah, your integrity, your commitment to the truth, will determine your standing in society. In the language of *Pirkei Avot*, Akavya meant to say that one's standing is shaped by a commitment to living a life of righteousness before the judgment of God. Commendations are superficial. Each individual creates his own destiny by the way he or she lives, and by the critical choices made, for there is no escaping individual responsibility in shaping a life. Akavya meant to say that this conviction, powerfully articulated in *Pirkei Avot*, guided his life, and must guide his son's life as well. While his son should abandon Akavya's positions of law, he must never abandon the principles which made Akavya who he was. Those were Akavya's very last words.

Yet, it is difficult to avoid hearing in these final words another message as well. For if Akavya taught his son a powerful message about life, that very message would apply to his life as well. The words "draw you near" and "distance you" are telling indeed, for Akavya himself was first near the fellowship of scholars, and then distanced from them, all because of his words and actions. If Akavya were to apply to himself the advice he gives to his son, which, to avoid hypocrisy, he must, then Akavya here takes responsibility for the critical choices he made in his own life. Does he regret any of those choices? We have no evidence that he does, and given the portrait we have drawn of him in this chapter, it seems unlikely that he would. Yet we do find in him a softening, a stress on the importance of following the majority for his son, of thereby re-entering the community of Torah scholars. He had learned from personal experience just how painful that segregation can be. Moreover, we must distinguish between his refusal to retract his halakhic positions, and the acerbic comments he made about Shemaya and Avtalyon. While I find it unimaginable that he would regret the decision to remain loyal to his oral tradition, I do wonder about the comments he made regarding Shemaya and Avtalyon. For it was those comments that generated the ban, which likely caused him much pain, and it was that pain he advised his son to avoid. Of course, we can never really know. All we have are his final words, which echo long after we read them.

PART THREE

AKAVYA AND R. ELIEZER

It is altogether apparent that there are important similarities between Akavya and R. Eliezer. As we saw in chapter 2 of this volume, R. Eliezer was banned after he dissented from the majority in the famous dispute over the halakhic status of the oven of *akhnai*, despite a heavenly voice supporting his position. Akavya, too, was banned, likewise after dissenting from the majority, a dissent exacerbated by his caustic accusation against Shemaya and Avtalyon. Both engage in a telling encounter with their sons on their deathbeds, and both emerge as men deeply committed to the principles which governed their lives, tough-minded individualists capable of acerbic comments even about other rabbinic scholars. What can we learn by more deeply reflecting about the similarities and differences between these two great rabbinic dissidents?

One of the most telling differences between them is how each reacted to the ban. R. Eliezer burned with anger, and the pain he felt was destructive. We have no evidence that Akavya reacted this way, and indeed it would surprising if he had. He cared about one thing only, and that was to stand righteously before God in judgment. Nothing else mattered to him, for which reason he would not have been angered by the ban. Either he had made the right or the wrong choices; the ban itself was immaterial. He was, in this respect, stoic-like, and very far removed from the passion of R. Eliezer.

By contrast, it seems fair to say emotions played a powerful role throughout R. Eliezer's life, from his love of Torah, to his repeated crying early in life over the frustration he felt at being unable to learn Torah, to the anger that emerges after the ban and again on his deathbed, to the anguish he expressed during the prayers which almost killed his brother-in-law at sea. No such emotions are expressed in the case of Akavya. While the only evidence we possess is the narrative in these mishnayot, based upon that evidence he emerges as imperturbable, cool, and collected, even at his very death, fully in control of himself, his words and choices. The first words of advice Akavya offers his son, to abandon his father's halakhic positions, reflects a dispassionate assessment of what is best, even at what would appear to be great personal cost to Akavya himself. Not only does he fail to express any anger at his son when asked for a commendation to the Sages, he offers his deep and carefully considered words of wisdom. The personalities of these two great rabbinic dissidents, while alike in some respects, were radically different in others. Surely the individualism, tough-mindedness, and deep commitment to principles common to both made their dissent possible. Nevertheless, their emotional lives seem far apart indeed.

Their jurisprudence differed as well. R. Eliezer maintained that halakhic process should be subservient to divine truth. God Himself, through the heavenly voice, had endorsed his position, and for R. Eliezer, nothing in halakhic decision making matters more than getting God's will right. If God informs the community of scholars that the majority is wrong, then the majority must change its mind. Akavya, on the other hand, maintained that legitimate halakhic process matters more than truth. Although he was convinced that his oral tradition was the authentic one, and correctly captured God's will, he could still advise his son to abandon it, because of the principle of majority rule. I would venture to say that this view requires a certain cerebralism on the part of its advocates, the capacity to dispassionately distance oneself from what one believes to be true merely because legitimate process was followed. If so, this is entirely consistent with the picture of Akavya that emerges here.

Their attitudes toward their predecessors likewise diverged. R. Eliezer prized respect toward the master, and absolute fealty to ancient traditions. For him this was the only reliable path that led back to Moses, and to God's revelation of the Torah at Sinai, with its accompanying Oral Law. God's truth rested in the past, and in the bearers of that ancient tradition. Akavya, on the other hand, was quick to curtly reject the opinions of two of his most respected predecessors. While both could be harsh in their judgment of others, for Akavya, unlike R. Eliezer, that sensibility extended backward in time.

I would suggest that these differences between R. Eliezer and Akavya speak to the fundamentally different ideals that drove their lives. R. Eliezer's overriding passion in life, from his very youth to his deathbed, was the acquisition of true knowledge of God's Torah, mediated by the past. If that passion was frustrated in any way, R. Eliezer felt that frustration acutely, and reacted accordingly, for God's Torah was the passion of his life. Akavya's overriding ideal, however, was to stand in righteous judgment before God. Every choice he made, or any words he uttered, were all measured against that exceedingly high bar. Success in doing so would require a dispassionate and ruthless "account and reckoning" – to borrow Akavya's words from *Pirkei Avot* – a ruthless examination of the sometimes-hidden inner motives that shape our choices. It would require a dispassionate "account and reckoning" of what God truly wants of us, irrespective of our personal needs and our personal feelings. For our personal needs and our personal feelings are products of that dimension of the human condition which "emerges from a putrid drop," and which "returns to worms and maggots."

R. Eliezer was the paradigm of human love of God's truth, while Akavya was the paradigm of human righteousness before God. Yet as different as they were in personality and in theology, each was a remarkable figure, courageously committed to his theological principles no matter the personal cost. Both are therefore enshrined in the classic texts of the mishna. That said, we must conclude with one final observation. The Talmud as we know it would be unrecognizable without the teachings of R. Eliezer, who appears in what seems like almost every page. Moreover, according the talmudic text analyzed in the previous chapter, R. Eliezer after his death is readmitted to the fellowship of scholars, and the ban was lifted. He died uttering the word "pure" and pure he left this world and entered the World to Come.

Such was not the end for Akavya. He very rarely appears in the Talmud and Mishna, and played virtually no role in the enduring conversation about the law which engages Torah scholars the world over to this very day. Was this because his scholarship was simply not as important as his other colleagues of the same era? While possible, that seems unlikely, especially if we accept R. Yehuda's testimony about Akavya's unparalleled wisdom. More likely is that Akavya's ban, unlike R. Eliezer's, endured until his death, for the Mishna nowhere records that it was lifted. Surely it is likely that this ban would have led to a permanent marginalization from rabbinic discourse and tradition. Not eliminated, because the very story of his banning, as well his penetrating teaching recorded in *Pirkei Avot*, are of lasting value, and teach the profound lessons about Torah and about life which have been the subject of this chapter. Yet marginalized he nevertheless remained.

R. Eliezer's last word was "pure," and Akavya's last words were "distance you." The very last words of each bespeak their fate in Jewish history, and echo poignantly in the ears of all who study their lives.

Chapter 5

The Road Not Taken: Torah Study and Friendship in the Lives of R. Yoḥanan and Ilfa

Taanit 21a

INTRODUCTION

Torah study is of preeminent importance in Judaism, yet the practical need to earn a living is difficult to ignore. The problem, of course, is that these two imperatives necessarily conflict, for time is a zero-sum game. Five hours spent at work are five hours not spent in Torah study. There is a very considerable literature about this challenge, within the Talmud, and among halakhic authorities and Jewish thinkers.[1] The aggada we will analyze in this chapter revolves around this tension, as it plays

1. For a comprehensive survey and discussion of these sources, see Yehuda Levi, *Torah Study: A Survey of Classical Sources on Timely Issues*, trans. Raphael Levi (Jerusalem-New York: Feldheim, 2002).

out in the lives of two close friends and study partners, one of whom was perhaps the greatest rabbinic Sage of his generation in *Eretz Yisrael,* R. Yoḥanan, the person most responsible for the Talmud Yerushalmi, and the other one being Ilfa, a relatively unknown scholar. Both were enmeshed in extreme poverty, and were unable to support themselves and their families. Under duress, they both decided together to leave the *beit midrash* to work, yet R. Yoḥanan had a change of heart, returning to the *beit midrash,* while Ilfa chose work. Why did each choose a different path? What became of each? This aggada tells the dramatic story of their different choices, and the impact of their choices on the trajectory of their lives, and on their respective places in Jewish history. The aggada, I will suggest, is richly symbolic, and reflects the complexity of the inner lives of these two great people, and the complexity of the problems they faced.

Taanit 21a

אילפא ור׳ יוחנן הוו גרסי באורייתא דחיקא להו מילתא טובא אמרי ניקום וניזיל וניעבד עיסקא ונקיים בנפשין (דברים טו, ד) אפס כי לא יהיה בך אביון אזלו אותבי תותי גודא רעיעא הוו קא כרכי ריפתא אתו תרי מלאכי השרת שמעיה רבי יוחנן דאמר חד לחבריה נישדי עלייהו האי גודא ונקטלינהו שמניחין חיי עולם הבא ועוסקין בחיי שעה אמר ליה אידך שבקינהו דאיכא בהו חד דקיימא ליה שעתא.

Ilfa and Rabbi Yoḥanan studied Torah together, and as a result **they became very hard-pressed** for money. **They said: Let us get up and go and engage in commerce, and we will fulfill, with regard to ourselves,** the verse: **"Although there should be no needy among you"** (Deuteronomy 15:4), as we will no longer be complete paupers. **They went and sat under a dilapidated wall** and **were eating bread,** when **two ministering angels arrived. Rabbi Yoḥanan heard that one** angel **said to the other: Let us knock this wall down upon them and kill them, as they abandon eternal life** of Torah study **and engage in temporal life** for their own sustenance. **The other** angel **said to him: Leave them, as there is one of them whose time** of achievement **stands before him,** i.e., his time has yet to come.

רבי יוחנן שמע אילפא לא שמע אמר ליה ר׳ יוחנן לאילפא שמע מר מידי אמר ליה לא אמר מדשמעי אנא ואילפא לא שמע ש״מ לדידי קיימא לי שעתא אמר ליה רבי יוחנן איהדר ואוקי בנפשאי (דברים טו, יא) כי לא יחדל אביון מקרב הארץ ר׳ יוחנן הדר אילפא לא הדר עד דאתא אילפא מליך רבי יוחנן אמרו לו אי אתיב מר וגריס לא הוה מליך מר.

Rabbi Yoḥanan heard all this, but **Ilfa did not hear** the angels' conversation. **Rabbi Yoḥanan said to Ilfa: Did the Master hear anything?** Ilfa **said to him: No.** Rabbi Yoḥanan **said** to himself: **Since I heard** the angels **and Ilfa did not hear,** I can **learn from this** that it is **I whose time** of achievement **stands before me. Rabbi Yoḥanan said to Ilfa: I will return** home and **fulfill with regard to myself** the contrary verse: **"For the poor shall never cease out of the land"** (Deuteronomy 15:11). **Rabbi Yoḥanan returned** to the study hall, and **Ilfa did not return,** but went to engage in business instead. **By** the time **that Ilfa came** back from his business travels, **Rabbi Yoḥanan** had been **appointed** head of the academy, and his financial situation had improved. His colleagues **said to** Ilfa: **If the Master had sat and studied,** instead of going off to his business ventures, **wouldn't the Master have** been **appointed** head of the academy?

אזל תלא נפשיה באסקריא דספינתא אמר אי איכא דשאיל לי במתניתא דר׳ חייא ורבי אושעיא ולא פשטינא ליה ממתני׳ נפילנא מאסקריא דספינתא וטבענא אתא ההוא סבא תנא ליה האומר תנו שקל לבניי בשבת והן ראויין לתת לחם סלע נותנין להם סלע ואם אמר אל תתנו להם אלא שקל אין נותנין להם אלא שקל אם אמר מתו ירשו אחרים תחתיהם בין שאמר תנו בין שאמר אל תתנו אין נותנין להם אלא שקל א״ל הא מני ר״מ היא דאמר מצוה לקיים דברי המת.

Ilfa **went and suspended himself from the mast** [*askariya*] **of a ship, saying: If there is anyone who can ask me** a question **concerning a** *baraita* **of Rabbi Ḥiyya and Rabbi Oshaya, and I do not resolve his** problem **from a mishna, I will fall from the mast of this ship and be drowned.** Ilfa sought to demonstrate that despite the time he had spent in business, he still retained his extensive Torah knowledge. **A certain old man came and taught** a *baraita* before **him:** If there is a man **who,** upon his deathbed, **says** in his will: **Give a shekel to my sons** every **week, but** this is a situation **where,** based on their needs, **they are fit** for the **court to give them a *sela*,** i.e., double the amount, **they give them a *sela*.** When the dying man mentioned a shekel, he presumably meant that they should be given a sum in accordance with their actual requirements, not that specific amount. **But if he said: Give them only a shekel,** the court **gives them only a shekel** and no more. The *baraita* further states that **if one said: If** my sons **die, others should inherit** their portion **in their stead,** regardless of **whether he said: Give them** a shekel, or **whether he said: Give them only** a shekel, then the court **gives** his sons **only a shekel** per week, as their father clearly stated that he wishes to give his sons only a specific stipend and that he intends to leave the bulk of his property to others. Ilfa **said to** the old man: In accordance with **whose** opinion **is this** ruling? **It is** in accordance with the opinion of **Rabbi Meir, who said: It is a mitzva to fulfill the statement of the dead.** This entire *baraita* can be explained based on a principle that appears in a mishna: In all cases, one should try to execute the wishes of the deceased.

PART ONE

R. YOḤANAN AND ILFA LEAVE THE STUDY HALL TOGETHER

This striking aggada presents numerous difficulties, which we will raise and seek to address over the course of this chapter. First, it is worth observing that at the outset of the aggada R. Yoḥanan and Ilfa are apparently so close that they are treated as a single unit: "They said, let us get up and go and engage in commerce…" They come to a momentous life decision together, and there are as yet no grounds for distinguishing between the two of them.

The prooftext they provide in support of their decision to leave full-time Torah study is an interesting, and indeed, problematic one: "Although there should be no needy among you…" (Deut. 15:4).

R. Yoḥanan and Ilfa take this to mean that it is right and proper that there be no paupers among the Jewish people, and therefore that they should leave full-time study and engage in commerce. However, the context of that verse is the *Shemitta* year, the seventh year of the crop cycle, during which fields must lay fallow. The Torah there promises that if the Jewish people carefully observe *Shemitta*, then there will be no paupers among them, for God will provide them with sustenance. To apply this verse toward a general obligation of preventing self-poverty is puzzling. Additionally, there is a certain irony here. While the verse there specifically speaks of observing *shemittat kesafim* (the remission of loans at the end of the seven-year cycle), and not the obligation to leave the land fallow, it is very hard to believe that R. Yoḥanan and Ilfa were not cognizant of the agricultural dimension of *Shemitta*, which takes place during the same year, during which, in an agricultural society, there is no work to be done. And Torah scholars would, of course, study Torah during their leisure. Surely there is an irony in citing this prooftext to justify leaving Torah study to work, an irony which was probably not lost on R. Yoḥanan and Ilfa.[2] This leads me to believe that the use of this prooftext may reflect an ambivalence about the choice they made to leave full-time Torah study, an ambivalence which, I would suggest, is almost immediately reinforced, as we shall see.

The staccato string of verbs describing their actions once their fateful decision is made ("Let us get up and go and engage ...") suggests considerable determination and energy, a reading even more apparent in the original Aramaic. Yet the first action they are described as taking once they embark on their journey is to sit under a dilapidated wall to eat. Now it seems fair to ask, first, why the aggada chooses to mention where they ate. Apparently, this is significant. Second, why they would have placed themselves at risk eating under a dilapidated wall, a risk the aggada itself seems to build upon.[3] Is it not likely that this is a further

2. Nahmanides, in his commentary to Deuteronomy 15:4, maintains that the verse explicitly refers to the agricultural dimension of *Shemitta*, and not only its financial dimension. For Nahmanides, the irony would be even more striking.

3. In the halakha, a person may not place himself at risk (see *Shulḥan Arukh, Yoreh De'ah* 116:5, and especially Rabbi Moses Isserles's gloss there on the prohibition of walking under a delapidated wall). One might therefore wonder how they could have even

reflection of the ambivalence they might well have felt upon leaving the sacred and compelling life of pure Torah study? While intellectually they were surely convinced of the propriety of their choice, it seems equally likely that their emotions would not have fallen so easily into line with their beliefs. Perhaps they felt (as opposed to believed) that they in some sense deserved to sit under that dilapidated wall; that *they themselves* were dilapidated, broken down relics of their old sacred selves; that they even deserved whatever gruesome fate that dilapidated wall might have held for them.

While eating their no doubt meager meal, R. Yoḥanan overhears one angel asserting to his fellow angel that they should topple the wall and kill the two of them, for they have abandoned the World to Come in exchange for the transitory satisfactions of this present world. Note that for the first time, R. Yoḥanan and Ilfa are individuated: only R. Yoḥanan hears the angel, not Ilfa. Indeed, R. Yoḥanan asks Ilfa if he had heard the angel, to which Ilfa responds that he had not. This leads R. Yoḥanan to conclude that he is the one who should return to full-time Torah study, and not Ilfa. Thus begins the parting of ways between these two close friends, a journey which will carry them in very different directions. But who are the angels R. Yoḥanan hears? Why does only R. Yoḥanan, and not Ilfa, hear them? Why doesn't R. Yoḥanan share with his close friend what he heard? Would that not have been the loyal thing to do? And finally, why does the accuser take so harsh a stance? Surely there is no obligation to starve, and even if R. Yoḥanan and Ilfa made the wrong choice by angelic standards, their choice had an apparently good prooftext as justification, and should have been perfectly understandable, even if ultimately wrong. At least to this reader, death seems a rather draconian punishment. Of course, more is expected of the gifted, and no doubt their elevated spiritual status may have contributed to the harshness of this angelic judgment. Nevertheless, I can't help but wonder if there is another explanation behind it. This observation leads me in turn to another question. Just who are these ministering angels?

---

sat there in the first place. Of course, the wall may not have been so dilapidated as to count as a violation of the halakha for them, but the aggada itself clearly considers it at least somewhat risky.

The most common interpretation, I expect, is that they are supernatural beings visiting R. Yoḥanan and Ilfa at this critical juncture in their lives. Rabbi Shmuel Eidels, known by his acronym as Maharsha, suggests in his commentary to this passage that these angels are not merely occasional, if remarkable, visitors of R. Yoḥanan and Ilfa, but in fact they are the angels that always accompanied R. Yoḥanan and Ilfa throughout their lives, wherever they went. As the Talmud states,[4] everyone has a personal set of angels who accompany him Friday nights, one (or more) representing good, and one (or more) representing evil. The Maharsha takes this to be true at all times, not only Friday nights, and thus the two angels accompanying R. Yoḥanan and Ilfa are not remarkable at all, but standard for everyone. However, surely this too raises the same question: who are these ubiquitous angels that accompany all of us, at all times?

Instead, there is a different interpretation that I wish to share, which follows from Maimonides. In *Guide for the Perplexed*, II:6, Maimonides discusses the concept of angels at great length, and asserts that "individual natural and psychic forces are called angels."[5] As an example of this thesis, Maimonides cites the teaching of R. Yoḥanan (the very R. Yoḥanan who is a protagonist in our aggada), that when, in Genesis 38:15, Judah saw Tamar at the crossroads and thought she was a prostitute, R. Yoḥanan states that Judah did not actually want to stop and sleep with her, but "the Holy One, blessed be He, caused the angel put in charge of lust…to present himself to him."[6] Maimonides thus calls even physical temptation an angel. Accordingly, angels are natural forces that exist within the human being. The desire to engage in sexual relations is a natural one, and for Maimonides, this is called an "angel" internal to each person, just as the desire to give charity or study Torah would be. Put in other words, we might say that these forces are identical with what is traditionally called the *yetzer tov* and the *yetzer hara*, the inclinations toward good and evil, respectively. Temptation and conscience are embedded within each person, and they are none other

4. Shabbat 119b.
5. Shlomo Pines, trans., *Guide for the Perplexed* (Library of Congress, 1963), 264.
6. Genesis Rabba 85:8.

than the angels of good and bad.[7] Thus, Maimonides has reconceived the standard way of thinking about angels, as natural forces, and in some cases he both internalizes and psychologizes them.[8]

What, then, should we make of the angels overheard by R. Yoḥanan? According to Maimonides, it seems likely that what R. Yoḥanan heard was none other than his own *yetzer tov*, his own conscience beckoning him to return to the study hall. Perhaps this was felt and "heard" during a sleepy post-prandial moment, with R. Yoḥanan exhausted not only from his journey, but from the emotional and spiritual trauma of the decision he made. Now, anyone who has ever felt the pangs of a guilty conscience knows just how harsh and tormenting it can be. R. Yoḥanan had just made a decision to abandon a life of pure Torah study, to which he had devoted himself heretofore at the greatest cost to family and self. Even if he believed the choice to be correct, one can easily imagine how haunted he must have felt by the loss incurred, to himself, and to the whole of the Jewish people, given his extraordinary potential. Would he not have felt as if he, in some sense, deserved to die for making that terrible choice? Hence, the harshness of the accusing angel: sometimes those with great sensitivity and intense aspirations can be tougher on themselves than any prosecutor. Great man that he was, it was R. Yoḥanan's powerful conscience, his *yetzer tov*, which, in the end, drove him back to the study hall. The same internal, less than conscious, impulse to sit under the broken-down wall now harshly accused him of violating his deepest principles.

This Maimonidean approach might explain why R. Yoḥanan did not share with Ilfa the angelic conversation he had overheard. For why, after all, did Ilfa not overhear the "angels" just as his close friend did? Perhaps, R. Yoḥanan reasoned, if Ilfa did not hear the voices, then that must be because he did not feel the same torment. And if he did not feel the same torment, that must be because he had acclimated to the choice, and was ready to leave full-time Torah study and go out into the

7. Rabbi Isaac Arama, the fifteenth-century commentator and philosopher, makes exactly this pont. See *Akedat Yitzhak* (Israel: 1974), *Shaar* 47, in vol. 2, 144.
8. Of course, natural forces are not only internal to human beings, and can also include the separate intelligences.

world. Given their financial duress, R. Yoḥanan would have thought that Ilfa should then indeed continue on the journey they had both begun. But since he, R. Yoḥanan, did feel that torment, did heard the voices, then he must return to the study hall, and not compromise on his ideals. If only one person's "time of achievement [in Torah] is yet to come," thought R. Yoḥanan, that person must be himself, for only he possesses the still burning passion to continue with full-time Torah study despite the sacrifice.

Indeed, R. Yoḥanan cites a verse teaching that poverty will never be eliminated from the human condition. He is ready to bear that burden; Ilfa, who had adjusted to his new life, as evidenced by the absence of a guilty conscience, is not. In this, R. Yoḥanan is a student of the great R. Shimon bar Yoḥai, who taught that there is an irreconcilable conflict between time spent on such mundane ventures as farming, and a life devoted to Torah study.[9] The this-worldly life and the other-worldly life stand in irreconcilable conflict with one another, to paraphrase the angels in our aggada. So, R. Yoḥanan returns to the study hall, but Ilfa does not. The two erstwhile friends and study partners finally part ways.

What makes the parting even sadder, at least for this reader, is that there is no dialogue between them. R. Yoḥanan is not described as making any attempt to explain himself to his friend to account for his change of heart. They had originally come to a mutual understanding, and left the study hall together. Now R. Yoḥanan abruptly reverses himself, and with no recorded explanation, abandons his friend and their carefully laid plans. Why? Was it because once R. Yoḥanan saw that only he was tormented by their fateful choice, and not Ilfa, R. Yoḥanan felt that they no longer had a common discourse, that they could no longer speak the same language? All those years of friendship and Torah study that had bound them together were now, for R. Yoḥanan, severed. The newly formed chasm between their inner lives was too deep to be bridged by

9. Berakhot 35b. See, too, the story of R. Shimon bar Yoḥai in the cave seeking refuge from the Romans, and his troubled departure from it, Shabbat 33b–34a. R. Yoḥanan in Song of Songs Rabba 8:7 describes how he sold all his property to enable his Torah study, leaving him unprovided for in old age. For discussion, see Lau, *The Sages* (Tel Aviv, 2011), vol. 4, 203–10.

language. In any case, this may have been R. Yoḥanan's assessment. But it seems fair to ask if Ilfa agreed with R. Yoḥanan's assessment. Much of the remainder of the aggada seeks to answer that question.

PART TWO

ILFA STAKES HIS LIFE ON THE CHOICE HE MADE

By the time Ilfa returns from his business journey, R. Yoḥanan has been appointed head of the yeshiva. The verb used to describe his ascension to this position is the Aramaic *malikh,* literally, "he was made king." This change in status reflects not only the importance of the position he assumed within the yeshiva (and beyond into the larger Jewish community), but at least according to Rashi,[10] implies material wealth as well. The irony here is that by choosing to remain in full-time Torah study, and accepting poverty upon himself and his family, R. Yoḥanan achieves what he was so sorely lacking – wealth, and great wealth at that. To compound the irony, Ilfa is told by unnamed others that had he chosen to return to the study hall, he, rather than R. Yoḥanan, would have been appointed the head of the yeshiva, and would have become wealthy without engaging in time-consuming commerce. Apparently, for these informants, Ilfa was the superior scholar, and would have acquired the wealth he sought on his business trip by returning to the study hall. One lesson of the aggada, it seems, is that the lesser scholar can achieve superiority, by dint of self-sacrifice and single-minded pursuit of Torah study.

How then does Ilfa react to this turn of events? The answer is nothing short of stunning. From this point on, Ilfa becomes the central figure in the aggada, rather than R. Yoḥanan, and what Ilfa does is climb the mast of a ship, suspend himself from it, and threaten to jump and drown himself if his Torah knowledge fails him. Specifically, he challenges anyone to question him on the mishnaic origin of any teaching of the Oral Law from the teachings not included in the Mishna, the *Baraita.* Remember that this takes place before the Talmud Bavli or Talmud Yerushalmi were compiled. The only written elements of the Oral Law at that time in Jewish history were the Mishna and the more

10. Rashi, Taanit 21a, s.v. *Malakh Rabbi Yoḥanan.*

expansive teachings of the *Baraita* and Tosefta that were not included in the Mishna. These were compiled somewhat later, and traditionally considered the work of R. Ḥiyya and R. Oshaya. Thus, Ilfa is asserting that he has complete mastery of the Oral Law, and can demonstrate its perfect unity, by showing the root of all the Oral Law in the great code of the Mishna. He is so confident of this mastery that he is willing to stake his life on it, and demonstrate that his excursion into the world of commerce did not come at the cost of his knowledge of Torah.

Now several obvious questions beg themselves. Why does Ilfa climb the mast of a ship? Why does he threaten suicide by jumping into the sea and drowning? Of course, suicide is forbidden according to Jewish law, but no doubt so confident was he in his knowledge that he was convinced it would never come to that. But why threaten? And why does he choose this particular test of his Torah knowledge?

The first point to make is that to engage in commerce in ancient times frequently meant to travel by sea for trade.[11] Thus the sea, upon which the ship travels, is a metaphor for the very life Ilfa so fatefully chose. Let us also recall that the sea is often a metaphor for the expansive teachings of the Talmud, traditionally called the *Yam HaTalmud*, "the sea of Talmud." To study Torah is to swim or sail in the vast sea of the Oral Law. Thus, the word "sea" is an ambiguous trope. Now, which sea does Ilfa swim in, the sea of commerce or the sea of the Talmud? Has he abandoned the latter for the former? Is it possible to swim in both seas successfully, to retain mastery of the Talmud while at the same time mastering the sea of commerce as well? R. Yoḥanan's position is that one can swim successfully only in one. The two seas stand in irreconcilable opposition to one another. But Ilfa sought to demonstrate that the position of his erstwhile study partner and friend was wrong, and that one could master both seas simultaneously. The ambiguity of the metaphor is altogether intentional on Ilfa's part, for he means to assert that the two seas must be united in one life.

11. For example, when the Torah describes Zebulun as living on the shore of the sea, the Midrash takes this to refer to his success in trade. See *Midrash Tanḥuma Vayeḥi* 11, and see, for example, the commentaries of Rashi, Radak, and Ḥizkuni on Genesis 49:13, who also make this connection.

From this perspective, I would like to suggest the following reading of this extraordinary passage. To climb up the mast of the ship is to literally stand above the sea, and to thereby figuratively assert mastery of it, to transcend it. To climb the mast of the ship is to look off into the distance, to see what no other person can see, and to understand that the sea of the Talmud and the sea of commerce are ultimately linked, that the supposed tension between the seas is a false one. For what, after all, does one see when one gazes from on high out to the sea? A vast, undifferentiated horizon. Ilfa, standing high above the sea of commerce, also sees a vast, undifferentiated horizon, a unity which includes not only the unity of the two seas of Torah and commerce, but also a unity of all the Oral Law, rooted in the Mishna. For, Ilfa might argue, God is Creator of both seas, the sea of commerce and the sea of Talmud, and if He is one, then there must be unity in all His creation as well. This includes the totality of the Oral Law. For the Oral Law is, in some sense, part and parcel of the real world, the world of commerce, for that is exactly where the Oral Law, which focuses on the myriad details of life, is realized. Ilfa stakes his life on this claim.

It is surely significant that Ilfa's name is also an Aramaic word meaning "ship."[12] Of course, Ilfa would have known the meaning of his own name in the *lingua franca* of his time and place. For Ilfa to stand on the mast of an *ilfa* is for Ilfa to stand above himself. Ilfa transcends his very self, in his vast and encompassing vision, for his life had heretofore been devoted exclusively to Torah study, and was now devoted to trade as well. In this way he transcended his old self. One might even suggest that Ilfa finds his true self, by rising so dramatically above that past, and by living a new life in which Torah and trade are united.

There is, however, a darker side to this "heroic" picture of Ilfa, a darker side which, I will suggest, emerges at the end of the aggada, but which seems adumbrated even here. While no doubt Ilfa was supremely confident in his knowledge of the Oral Law, and never expected that he

12. See *Arukh HaShalem* by R. Nathan of Rome, ed. B. Kohut (Vienna, 1868), 104–5, which suggests that his original name was *Ḥilifi,* or *Ḥilfei,* names which appear more frequenty in the Talmud Yerushalmi, but that the name Ilfa was a nickname, either derived from the story told here, or from his career as a merchant.

would need to transgress the prohibition of suicide, he still threatens it. He is explicit in sharing a graphic and haunting image of himself falling to his death in the sea. Does this disturbing image suggest any self-doubt on Ilfa's part? Did the Torah and material success of his friend lead him to question the choices he made? Is he consciously or unconsciously confronting his own shards of guilt by painting so gruesome a portrait of his demise? Does the bravado of the challenge he poses mask a deeper ambivalence? We cannot know for sure, although the very conclusion of the aggada may lend this reading some credence.

At this point in the aggada, someone rises up to the challenge, and tests Ilfa as he hangs suspended from the top of the mast. The name of this challenger is not given, but he is called a *saba*, an old man, or grandfather. Why is he anonymous, and why is it important for the author of the aggada to mention that he was an elderly man? Is it because his personal identity is not important? Or is it important that as an elderly man he represents ancient wisdom and tradition? This voice from the past is depicted by the author of the aggada as challenging Ilfa's view of the world. The *baraita* he chooses to challenge Ilfa is an interesting one, and relates to the laws of wills and estates. Essentially, the *baraita* teaches that if a man in his will instructs the trustees to provide a weekly shekel to his heirs out of his estate, but the heirs require more than a shekel to live, then they are to be given the greater amount, as that is undoubtedly what the man intended. However, if he stipulates to give them *only* a shekel, they should be given only that amount but no more. Furthermore, if the man in his will stipulates that he wants his estate to provide not only for his children, but for successor heirs (such as grandchildren) should his own children die, then even if he uses more ambiguous language, his children should still be given only the lesser amount. This is because he makes clear that his intent in writing the will was to ensure that there will be sufficient resources for successor heirs such as grandchildren.

Now it seems fair to ask why this anonymous elder chose this specific teaching to challenge Ilfa. There are tens of thousands of teachings he could have chosen. Is there any special significance to this one? My contention throughout this book is that when an aggada contains halakhic discourse embedded in it, then that discourse serves the narrative purposes of the aggada. Specifically, the halakhic dialogue is frequently a code to communicate the deeper themes of the aggada itself. The Sages spoke and thought in halakhic categories, and used those halakhic categories as vehicles to subtly convey, through code and symbol, ideas which they preferred, for reasons specific to each aggada, to cloak in halakhic discourse. How then might this principle be applied to the aggada analyzed in this chapter?

The first point to make is a historical one. R. Yoḥanan and Ilfa lived at the juncture between the tannaitic and amoraic periods in rabbinic history. R. Yoḥanan, as a very young man, studied under R. Yehuda HaNasi, the great compiler of the Mishna. The Mishna was the *magnum opus* of the tannaitic period, which shaped the whole future of rabbinic Judaism, and enabled the Oral Law to survive and flourish, albeit now in written form, to this very day.[13] Yet in his maturity, R. Yoḥanan lived and taught after the conclusion of the tannaitic period, and as such was considered a post-tannaitic figure of the amoraic era. Indeed, as rabbis and teachers living through this transitional period, R. Yoḥanan in *Eretz Yisrael,* and Rav and Shmuel in Babylonia mediated the tannaitic teachings into the amoraic period.[14] In rabbinic jurisprudence, *Amora'im* did not have the stature and authority of the *Tanna'im* who preceded them. But given this decline in generations, surely there was grave danger to the future of Torah. For with the loss of such towering figures as the *Tanna'im,* how would Judaism survive? Could lesser scholars and spiritual leaders ensure the future vitality of halakha and Jewish life? Consider by way of analogy the impact of the Holocaust on Torah scholarship. Thousands of leading scholars were killed by the Nazis. Was there enough Torah scholarship among the surviving scholars, or among those living outside Europe, to ensure Jewish survival, not only the physical

13. Ḥullin 137b.
14. The status of Rav, who was older than R. Yoḥanan and a more senior student of R. Yehuda HaNasi, was more borderline, and he is sometimes treated as a *Tanna* who had the authority to disagree with tannaitic Sages. See, as an example among many, Eiruvin 50b, regarding the phrase *rav tanna hu upalig,* that Rav has the status of a *Tanna* and can contradict other tannaitic statements. It should be noted that according to *Tosafot* on Ketubot 8a, s.v. *rav tanna hu upalig,* R. Yoḥanan himself actually considered Rav an *Amora* and not a *Tanna.*

survival of the Jewish people, but the survival of their halakhic scholarship as well? Could American-educated Torah scholars really replace those who had studied in the great yeshivas of Europe? While the Holocaust was surely unique, it illuminates the challenge every new phase in Jewish history brings to Torah scholarship. So, too, with the decline following the demise of the *Tanna'im*, could Torah scholarship survive and flourish? R. Yoḥanan in *Eretz Yisrael* and Rav and Shmuel in Babylonian were pivotal figures in ensuring the viability of halakhic life and Judaism in new and lesser generations of Torah scholars. They transmitted the teachings of the past, ensuring their survival into an endangered future. While to later generations, the *Amora'im* were towering figures themselves, to a generation that had seen the likes of R. Yehuda HaNasi and R. Meir, they seemed inferior indeed.

From this perspective, the challenge of the *saba* to Ilfa was penetrating. He was telling Ilfa this: "You, Ilfa, like R. Yoḥanan, are a pivotal figure in mediating the Torah of the previous generation into the future. You must ensure the long-term survival of the Jewish people, and you must do so even if it means living with less, even if it means great personal sacrifice. For you are just like that intermediate generation in the *baraita*. The immediate heirs to the dying father must make do with less than they need if the father in his will stipulates that his estate must support even his grandchildren. The great *Tanna'im* of the past generation have provided you with a rich inheritance, for you are the heir to their great traditions. But they are concerned with your heirs too, with the next generation of Torah scholars, and with the long-term future of Jewish life. Where the father stipulates such concern, then the intermediate generation, such as yourself, must make do with less, must sacrifice in order to provide for that great Jewish future. You, Ilfa, refused to make that sacrifice. You chose to abandon the study hall and engage in commerce. I am that elderly man, who is writing his will. I am expressing that concern for my grandchildren, the Torah heirs of tomorrow. You did not adhere to the teachings of this *baraita*. Therefore, you are a failure."

What a disturbing and biting critique of Ilfa, coded in the language of halakha! Can Ilfa defend himself and rise to the challenge? His answer is a simple sentence, which, I would suggest, echoes far beyond its most immediate meaning. He cites the principle of the great *Tanna*

R. Meir of the Mishna that it is a mitzva to fulfill the words of the deceased. At one level, Ilfa is asserting that the *baraita* the *saba* used to challenge him is rooted in the mishna's teaching, in that the teachings of the *baraita* are manifestations of this mishnaic principle, and the various halakhot recorded there are all interpretations of the intent of the deceased. Now this is the literal meaning of Ilfa's retort. However, we must ask ourselves how it is a response to the deeper, encoded, and biting challenge that we suggested the *saba* posed to Ilfa.

One possible answer is that Ilfa does not mean to respond directly to this deeper challenge, in that he disagrees with its very premise. For the premise of that challenge is that Ilfa's departure from the *beit midrash* for commerce was an abandonment of his responsibility to future generations. However, Ilfa maintains that leaving the *beit midrash* did not entail sacrifice of Torah, which can be demonstrated by displaying his encyclopedic knowledge. Moreover, as I suggested above, the metaphor of standing above, overlooking the mixed tropes of the sea, implies that engaging in commerce brings with it an enriched understanding of the unity of God, Torah, and world. This insight is a powerful legacy for future generations, who themselves will need to navigate the seas of Torah and commerce.

A second possibility should at least be mentioned, although it is perhaps a less likely one, since there is no direct hint to it in the text itself. It is possible that Ilfa did indeed mean to respond to the substance of the critique. In this scenario, the deceased, in the critique of the *saba*, is a metaphor for the *Tanna'im*. As is well known by students of Talmud, many *Tanna'im* themselves worked, and indeed praised the value of work, including R. Meir himself, the very author of the teaching Ilfa cites.[15] Thus, the *Tanna'im* whose legacy the critical *saba* was so concerned to preserve, themselves would have supported Ilfa's choice. Ilfa might have meant to respond, then, that the obligation to follow the

15. See *Avot DeRabbi Natan*, version B, 21. R. Meir also endorses work in Mishna Kiddushin 4:14. However, his views on work are complex, as he also teaches in *Pirkei Avot* 4:10 that a person should minimize work and spend more time studying Torah. For a collection of rabbinic sources on the value of work, see David Schnall, *By the Sweat of Your Brow: Reflections on Work and the Workplace in Classic Jewish Thought* (New York: Yeshiva University Press, 2001), 46–59.

teachings of the deceased is the obligation to follow the teachings of the *Tanna'im*, including R. Meir, who taught the value of work.

Finally, I would like to suggest yet a third reading of Ilfa's response, one which seems truest to the pathos of the aggada itself. This reading turns on a different understanding of the identity of the deceased in Ilfa's quotation of R. Meir's teaching. The deceased, on this reading, is none other than Ilfa himself. Observe that the very last word we hear from Ilfa in this dramatic encounter about the very meaning of his life is the word "dead." Remember, too, that despite Ilfa's extraordinary Torah knowledge, his teachings infrequently appear in the Talmud Bavli, especially in comparison to his colleague R. Yoḥanan (although they do appear more frequently in the Talmud Yerushalmi). Relative to his great talent, his presence is hardly felt in the Bavli's *mesora*, a kind of personal death in the great chain of tradition. Ilfa may well have realized that the momentous choice he made to embark upon a life of commerce could lead to a tragic end. Why did this occur? Was it because the commerce in which he chose to engage was so time-consuming in comparison with the vocational activities of the *Tanna'im* who preceded him that he had little time to interact with his colleagues, and so his views were infrequently recorded?[16] Or was it because his potential was so great that, at this critical juncture in Jewish history, for some of his colleagues no vocation could justify abdicating his post as the mediator of Torah to a new generation of Jews? We cannot know for certain, and both these answers may be correct. But to this reader, the word "dead" tragically echoes, long after the passage concludes, as a metaphor for the fate of Ilfa in the great chain of tradition. On this reading Ilfa concedes his failure, concedes his death to the *mesora*, even as he heroically proves his complete mastery of Torah.

But there is another way to read this as well. What does Ilfa actually assert? He cites R. Meir that there is an obligation to follow the

16. The Talmud in Menaḥot 70a refers to notebooks that Ilfa composed of teachings he recorded, referred to by others as a valuable resource. Reuven Margulies, in the introduction to his *Margoliyot HaYam* (Jerusalem, 1977), vol. 1, portrays Ilfa as a successful merchant and Torah scholar, in part on the basis of this text. However, notebooks do not constitute the living dialogue that makes up talmudic literature, in which Ilfa makes only infrequent appearances.

words of the dead. If the dead is a metaphor for Ilfa himself, then Ilfa stubbornly insists that despite what he fears will be his fate, elimination by his colleagues from the chain of tradition, he still must be obeyed. He insists that he teaches a vital lesson to future generations, which is that the seas of Torah and commerce can be united. He knows full well the sacrifice he has made; he knows that with respect to his colleagues he is "dead." Yet he insists that it is a mitzva to obey him. He refuses to concede that he is wrong, refuses to concede that a life of extraordinary Torah achievement is incompatible with a life in the world of commerce.

Which reading of Ilfa are we to favor? The Ilfa whose last word is death, who concedes the failure of his enterprise, or the Ilfa who asserts that he must nevertheless be obeyed? I think the author of the aggada intentionally left the conclusion of this story ambiguous, perhaps because he believed there was no clear answer to the great dilemma it signifies.

We must now, finally, examine one teaching of Ilfa's recorded in the Yerushalmi which may shed light on his great dilemma, and on the life he chose.[17] The context is how *teruma*, the mandatory produce tithe to support the priestly class, is to be measured in the case of olives. Olives are typically used to produce oil. Should *teruma*, then, be measured according to the amount of oil produced by the olives in question, or by the olives themselves, before they are pressed into oil? Ilfa, reflecting his mastery of tannaitic sources, taught that this question was really a debate between two earlier *Tanna'im*. Now, of course, this issue is a purely halakhic one. Nevertheless, I would suggest that the aggada we have analyzed provides this halakhic issue with another layer of meaning. The debate is really about if the religious value of the olive – what is given to the priest – is determined by how it appears on the outside, the whole fruit, or is it determined by what lays hidden within it, the oil which, when burned, gives light? How are we to measure the ultimate religious significance of the olive?

So, how are we to measure the ultimate religious significance of Ilfa? Do we judge him by appearances, by his garb and conduct as a man

17. Y. Terumot 1:9. The passage there uses the name Ḥilfa, which, as we have noted, and the commentary of the *Pnei Moshe* to that passage states explicitly, is to be identified with our Ilfa.

of commerce? Or do we judge him by his inner worth, by the lustrous light of Torah knowledge contained hidden deep within, masked by his outer life? Is Ilfa the olive or the oil, the man of commerce or the sage? Ilfa's own teaching is that the debate goes back to tannaitic times, and it is a debate he does not resolve. This is exactly how the aggada leaves it – unresolved. Who then is the real Ilfa? What did Ilfa really believe about the value of his own life? Was Ilfa right in his choice, or were the *saba* and R. Yoḥanan right? Does the author of the aggada reveal his personal views? Has history made its own judgments? By design, this brilliant aggada leaves the reader much to ponder.

Chapter 6

A Rabbi, a Student, and a Friendship Destroyed: The Life and Death of R. Yoḥanan and Reish Lakish

Bava Metzia 84a

INTRODUCTION

In the previous chapter, we encountered the great R. Yoḥanan at the beginning of his career as a preeminent Torah scholar, willing to live in abject poverty in order to maintain his commitment to a life devoted exclusively to the study of Torah. Here we meet up with him later, already an established figure. This chapter tells the story of his first dramatic encounter with Reish Lakish, another third-century CE Sage from *Eretz Yisrael.* Their teachings, and ever-present debates, are woven into the woof and warp of the Talmud Bavli, and, in fact, R. Yoḥanan himself is traditionally thought to be a prime architect of the Talmud Yerushalmi. They were towering figures of the early amoraic period, and our Talmud would be unrecognizable without them. Not only were they engaged in seemingly incessant talmudic debate as close study partners,[1] but they were also brothers-in-law, as Reish Lakish was married to R. Yoḥanan's sister. Even more striking is that R. Yoḥanan played a pivotal role in Reish Lakish's initiation into Torah study, having helped Reish Lakish emerge as the great scholar he eventually became. Yet, their intimate intellectual and personal relationship was shattered by a tragic misunderstanding, which led to the death of Reish Lakish, and the mental breakdown, then death, of R. Yoḥanan.

The aggada which serves as the subject of this chapter begins with the very first encounter between R. Yoḥanan and Reish Lakish, and continues with R. Yoḥanan's role in Reish Lakish's Torah study and life, the tragic misunderstanding between them, and their ultimate demise. It is an extraordinarily rich story, which touches on such great and enduring themes as: the complex and sometimes conflicted relationship between student and teacher/mentor; the many meanings of beauty and love; the power of the past and its sheer tenacity in shaping and sometimes distorting the present; the essential role of friendship, even of a combative kind, to human flourishing; and the cost to human relationships in upholding deeply held principles.

Bava Metzia 84a

יומא חד הוה קא סחי ר׳ יוחנן בירדנא חזייה ריש לקיש ושוור לירדנא אבתריה אמר ליה חילך לאורייתא אמר ליה שופרך לנשי א״ל אי הדרת בך יהיבנא לך אחותי דשפירא מינאי קביל עליה בעי למיהדר לאתויי מאניה ולא מצי הדר אקרייה ואתנייה ושוייה גברא רבא.

The Gemara relates: **One day, Rabbi Yoḥanan was bathing in the Jordan** River. **Reish Lakish saw him and jumped into the Jordan, pursuing him.** At that time, Reish Lakish was the leader of a band of marauders. Rabbi Yoḥanan **said to** Reish Lakish: **Your strength** is fit **for Torah** study. Reish Lakish **said to him: Your beauty** is fit **for women.** Rabbi Yoḥanan **said to him: If you**

1. Their studies were not limited to halakha. The Talmud (Gittin 60a) reports that the two regularly studied the aggada together every Shabbat.

return to the pursuit of Torah, **I will give you my sister** in marriage, **who is more beautiful than I am.** Reish Lakish **accepted upon himself** to study Torah. Subsequently, Reish Lakish **wanted to jump back** out of the river **to bring** back **his clothes, but he was unable to return,** as he had lost his physical strength as soon as he accepted the responsibility to study Torah upon himself. Rabbi Yoḥanan **taught** Reish Lakish **Bible, and taught him Mishna, and turned him into a great man.**

יומא חד הוו מפלגי בי מדרשא הסייף והסכין והפגיון והרומח ומגל יד ומגל קציר מאימתי מקבלין טומאה משעת גמר מלאכתן ומאימתי גמר מלאכתן רבי יוחנן אמר משיצרפם בכבשן ריש לקיש אמר משיצחצחן במים א״ל לסטאה בלסטיותיה ידע.

Eventually, Reish Lakish became one of the outstanding Torah scholars of his generation. **One day** the Sages **of the study hall were engaging in a dispute** concerning the following *baraita*: With regard to **the sword, the knife, the dagger** [*vehapigyon*], **the spear, a hand sickle, and a harvest sickle, from when are they susceptible to ritual impurity?** The *baraita* answers: It is **from the time of the completion of their manufacture,** which is the *halakha* with regard to metal vessels in general. These Sages inquired: **And when is the completion of their manufacture? Rabbi Yoḥanan says:** It is **from when one fires** these items **in the furnace. Reish Lakish said:** It is **from when one scours them in water,** after they have been fired in the furnace. Rabbi Yoḥanan **said to** Reish Lakish: **A bandit knows about his banditry,** i.e., you are an expert in weaponry because you were a bandit in your youth.

אמר ליה ומאי אהנת לי התם רבי קרו לי הכא רבי קרו לי אמר ליה אהנאי לך דאקרבינך תחת כנפי השכינה חלש דעתיה דרבי יוחנן חלש ריש לקיש אתאי אחתיה קא בכיא אמרה ליה עשה בשביל בני אמר לה (ירמיהו מט, יא) עזבה יתומיך אני אחיה עשה בשביל אלמנותי אמר לה (ירמיהו מט, יא) ואלמנותיך עלי תבטחו.

Reish Lakish **said to** Rabbi Yoḥanan: **What benefit did you provide me** by bringing me close to Torah? **There,** among the bandits, **they called me: Leader** of the bandits, and **here,** too, **they call me: Leader** of the bandits. Rabbi Yoḥanan **said to him: I provided benefit to you, as I brought you close** to God, **under the wings of the Divine Presence.** As a result of the quarrel, **Rabbi Yoḥanan was offended,** which in turn affected **Reish Lakish,** who **fell ill.** Rabbi Yoḥanan's **sister,** who was Reish Lakish's wife, **came crying** to Rabbi Yoḥanan, begging that he pray for Reish Lakish's recovery. **She said to him: Do** this **for the sake of my children,** so that they should have a father. Rabbi Yoḥanan **said to her** the verse: **"Leave your fatherless children, I will rear them"** (Jer. 49:11), i.e., I will take care of them. She said to him: **Do** so **for the sake of my widowhood. He said to her** the rest of the verse: **"And let your widows trust in Me."**

נח נפשיה דר׳ שמעון בן לקיש והוה קא מצטער ר׳ יוחנן בתריה טובא אמרו רבנן מאן ליזיל ליתביה לדעתיה ניזיל רבי אלעזר בן פדת דמחדדין שמעתתיה אזל יתיב קמיה כל מילתא דהוה אמר רבי יוחנן אמר ליה תניא דמסייעא לך אמר את כבר לקישא בר לקישא כי הוה אמינא מילתא הוה מקשי לי עשרין וארבע קושייתא ומפריקנא ליה עשרין וארבעה פרוקי וממילא רווחא שמעתא ואת אמרת תניא דמסייע לך אטו לא ידענא דשפיר קאמינא הוה קא אזיל וקרע מאניה וקא בכי ואמר היכא את בר לקישא היכא את בר לקישא והוה קא צוח עד דשף דעתיה [מיניה] בעו רבנן רחמי עליה ונח נפשיה.

Ultimately, **Rabbi Shimon ben Lakish,** Reish Lakish, **died. Rabbi Yoḥanan was sorely pained over** losing **him. The Rabbis said: Who will go to calm** Rabbi Yoḥanan's **mind** and comfort him over his loss? They said: **Let Rabbi Elazar ben Pedat go, as his statements are sharp,** i.e., he is clever and will be able to serve as a substitute for Reish Lakish. Rabbi Elazar ben Pedat **went and sat before** Rabbi Yoḥanan. With regard to **every matter that Rabbi Yoḥanan would say,** Rabbi Elazar ben Pedat would **say to him:** There is a ruling which **is taught** in a *baraita* **that supports your** opinion. Rabbi Yoḥanan **said** to him: **Are you** comparable **to the son of Lakish?** In my discussions with **the son of Lakish, when I would state a matter, he would raise**

twenty-four difficulties against me in an attempt to disprove my claim, **and I would answer him with twenty-four answers, and the *halakha* by itself would become broadened** and clarified. **And** yet **you say** to me: There is a ruling which **is taught** in a *baraita* **that supports your** opinion. **Do I not know that what I say is good?** Being rebutted by Reish Lakish served a purpose; your bringing proof to my statements does not. Rabbi Yoḥanan **went around, rending his clothing, weeping and saying: Where are you, son of Lakish? Where are you, son of Lakish?** Rabbi Yoḥanan **screamed until his mind was taken from him,** i.e., he went insane. **The Rabbis** prayed and **requested** for God to have **mercy on him** and take his soul, **and** Rabbi Yoḥanan **died.**

PART ONE

FROM BANDIT TO SCHOLAR: THE MAKING OF REISH LAKISH

Before beginning our analysis, I wish to remind the reader of an important point made in the introduction to this volume. My goal is most decidedly not to enter into the minds and hearts of R. Yoḥanan and Reish Lakish by commenting on their actions and personalities directly, for that would be an impossible task. R. Yoḥanan and Reish Lakish were such great men that we can never even presume to understand their inner lives, their motives, their conflicts and feelings. Moreover, we are separated by almost two millennia, and radically different cultures. The goal of this chapter, and others in the book, is a far more modest one, although daunting nevertheless. The author of this aggada himself had a view about R. Yoḥanan and Reish Lakish, and he wrote the aggada, and the compilers of the Talmud included it, because it teaches something that they took to be important, a set of moral, spiritual, theological, or psychological insights and teachings. Our goal is to attempt to understand what the author of the aggada set out to teach in telling this story. Or, put differently and perhaps more simply, our goal is to understand the text as it appears, in all its brilliant complexity and richness. While I will frequently make assertions or suggestions about R. Yoḥanan and

Reish Lakish, the reader of this and other chapters must remember that I write only of the R. Yoḥanan and Reish Lakish who emerge from the text at hand, not of R. Yoḥanan and Reish Lakish themselves. They will always remain shrouded in mystery to us. Who can ever plumb the depths of their extraordinary inner lives?

The context of this aggada is the Talmud's praise for the sheer physical beauty of R. Yoḥanan. Just before our passage, the Talmud relates that whoever wishes to see something resembling the beauty of R. Yoḥanan "should bring a silver goblet from the smithy and fill it with red pomegranate seeds and place a diadem of red roses upon the lip [of the goblet], and position it between the sunlight and shade. That luster is a semblance of R. Yoḥanan's beauty." Moreover, continues the Talmud, R. Yoḥanan would sit by the entrance to the *mikve*, the ritual bath in which women immerse themselves following menstruation and prior to resuming intimate relations with their husbands. He did this, hoping they would see him, and as a result, conceive children as beautiful and learned as he.[2] It is worth observing here, for reasons that will become apparent later in the chapter, that this remarkable concern for the well-being of fellow Jews is of a piece with another of his unusual practices. According to Berakhot 5b, R. Yoḥanan suffered the unimaginable loss of ten sons, who died prematurely. R. Yoḥanan would consistently carry with him a small bone remaining from the last of his children to die. When he met upon another person suffering such loss, R. Yoḥanan would take out and show him that bone, and console him by commiserating with the deepest empathy over their shared tragedy.

In any case, our aggada unfolds amidst this discussion of R. Yoḥanan's physical beauty. R. Yoḥanan goes for a swim in the Jordan River, perhaps to bathe, perhaps to cool off during a hot day. Reish Lakish sees him, and leaps into the river after him. Before we examine just who Reish Lakish was, we might first ask why Reish Lakish leapt

2. Some contemporary readers may find this practice not only surprising, but even troubling. Yet, as will be noted just below, R. Yoḥanan suffered the tragic loss of ten sons to premature deaths. One wonders if those terrible deaths made him hypersensitive to the birth of ever more children who would in some way replace those he lost, by resembling R. Yoḥanan himself. Who would want to judge a person who underwent such unimaginable losses?

into the river. No clear answer emerges from the text. Was it to rob him? That seems unlikely, as R. Yoḥanan probably did not have his possessions with him while swimming. More likely, he thought R. Yoḥanan was a lovely woman swimming in the river to whom he was attracted, an interpretation in fact suggested by his retort to R. Yoḥanan in the next line of the text. Lest one wonder how a bearded rabbi could be mistaken for a beautiful woman, the Talmud, as Rashi understands it, comments just above that R. Yoḥanan was beardless.[3]

The key question is why Reish Lakish would leap into the river in pursuit of a beautiful woman, hardly admirable behavior for a man known for his devotion to Torah. The answer, of course, is that at this phase in Reish Lakish's life he was far from being a Torah scholar. As we shall see, later in our aggada it emerges that Reish Lakish was then a bandit, a marauder, indeed, by Reish Lakish's own account, leader of a pack of bandits.[4] Was Reish Lakish raised that way? We can't know for sure, but the Talmud elsewhere (Shabbat 119b) reports that Reish Lakish shared a Torah teaching from his forebears (though the Talmud also records a different version that he received this teaching from others). Together with evidence from our aggada which we shall soon see, this leads Rabbenu Tam, recorded in *Tosafot*,[5] to conclude that Reish Lakish had studied Torah earlier in his life, but then had abandoned Torah study for a criminal life.[6] On this reading, then, the aggada tells the story not of Reish Lakish's creation as a man of Torah, but of Reish

3. Of course, Reish Lakish may have seen R. Yoḥanan only from behind, but this seems less likely.
4. Gittin 47a reports that Reish Lakish sold himself to the *Ludai*. Rashi (Gittin 46b, and see Rashi, Shabbat 10a, s.v. *Ludim*) interprets *Ludai* to be a cannibalistic nation, but it is hard to understand, then, why or how Reish Lakish could have sold himself to them, even if his economic circumstances had been dire. Another very widespread interpretation is that the term means gladiators. For further discussion, see A. Wasserstein, "Reish Lakish among the Bandits," *Tarbitz* 49 (1980): 197–98 (Heb.). If indeed Reish Lakish had sold himself to the *Ludai* because of economic deprivation, his similarity to R. Yoḥanan and Ilfa, whose poverty was discussed in the previous chapter, is surely of great interest.
5. Bava Metzia 84a, s.v. *ee hadart.*
6. The Yerushalmi appears to offer a different reading of Reish Lakish's background than the Bavli. For a discussion, see Lau, *The Sages*, vol. 4, 239–45.

Lakish's return to his long-lost past, of his repentance, through which he emerges far greater than he ever was before.

R. Yoḥanan responds to Reish Lakish's leap into the Jordan by telling him that the great strength he thereby demonstrated would be better devoted to Torah study than to leaping into rivers for questionable aims. Now why would R. Yoḥanan say that? If Reish Lakish were no more than a mere brigand, why would it even occur to R. Yoḥanan to urge him toward a life of Torah study? Was this just a throwaway comment on R. Yoḥanan's part, or did he intuitively sense something different or unusual about Reish Lakish?[7] Reish Lakish's own response to R. Yoḥanan's comment is sharp indeed: "Your beauty," he says, "is for women." In this exchange, R. Yoḥanan encounters the physical strength of Reish Lakish and seeks its fulfillment in the spiritual, while Reish Lakish encounters the physical beauty of R. Yoḥanan and seeks its fulfillment in the sensual. Ironically, both men were great physical specimens, one of beauty and the other of brawn. Our aggada plays out the unexpected consequences of this deep similarity.

R. Yoḥanan now exploits Reish Lakish's apparent attraction to physical beauty by offering his lovely sister to Reish Lakish in marriage as an incentive for him to "return"[8] from his evil ways, and commit himself to Torah. This gambit is puzzling on a number of grounds. First, how could R. Yoḥanan blithely offer his sister in marriage to a criminal merely on the basis of such a commitment? After all, what R. Yoḥanan observed was a brigand leaping into the water in pursuit of what he mistakenly thought was a beautiful woman. On the face of it, this is hardly a good omen for a suitable marriage for his sister. Moreover, why would Reish Lakish agree to R. Yoḥanan's proposal? Surely there are easier ways of securing a beautiful wife – indeed, a woman he had never even met! – than by committing to a life of Torah study.[9]

7. In general, R. Yoḥanan took a more inclusive view toward those who had left the ways of Torah than some of his colleagues. See Avoda Zara 26a–b.
8. Rabbenu Tam, in the *Tosafot* cited above, argues that the use of the term "returns" here is further evidence that Reish Lakish was well raised and well educated. For otherwise, what is Reish Lakish returning to by committing to a life of Torah?
9. Note that the Talmud (Kiddushin 41a) records a teaching in the name of Rav that a man may not marry until he first sees his prospective bride.

I would suggest that an answer to these questions emerges from an analysis of R. Yoḥanan's beauty. Let us recall that R. Yoḥanan would stand at the edge of the *mikve* so that women emerging therefrom would see him, and as a result would be so inspired that they would conceive children as beautiful and learned in Torah as he. Now whatever the biology behind R. Yoḥanan's hope, or expectation, there is at least a kind of internal logic, if superficial, to the expectation for beauty. The wife witnesses a beautiful man, is elevated by the experience of beauty, and this triggers conception of a beautiful child. But what of the expectation that the child be not only beautiful, but learned in Torah? What does R. Yoḥanan's sheer physical beauty have to do with cerebral talmudic expertise?

The answer, of course, is that physical beauty has many manifestations. Physical beauty may be a consequence of nothing more than perfectly symmetrical and ideally shaped physical features. But it may also reflect much more. In R. Yoḥanan's case, his beauty apparently had what we might call a spiritual dimension. His appearance, which, as we saw, the Talmud describes as possessing a certain luster, must have manifested through his extraordinary spiritual stature.[10] One sometimes encounters people like that, whose very visible aura reflects deep spirituality. For this reason, when women emerging from the *mikve* encountered him, even with no more than a passing glance, they would have felt elevated, inspired, and R. Yoḥanan believed that such an experience would in turn elevate their progeny, soon to be born.[11]

Why then did Reish Lakish leap into the river in pursuit of R. Yoḥanan's beauty, mistaking him for a woman? And why did he agree to R. Yoḥanan's proposal that he devote himself to a life of Torah study in order to secure R. Yoḥanan's beautiful sister as a wife? Because Reish Lakish saw in R. Yoḥanan's beauty a reflection of the divine, a beauty that transcended the merely physical, the same vision all those women saw when they emerged from the *mikve*. Reish Lakish was ineluctably drawn

10. It was R. Yoḥanan himself who taught (Sanhedrin 17a) that members of the Sanhedrin must be good-looking, perhaps a reference to this same idea. However, Rashi on that passage maintains that the purpose of their beauty was to nurture a feeling of reverence toward them.

11. As noted earlier, R. Yoḥanan's loss of ten children may have spurred this practice, but for him, it had a logic all its own.

to that spiritual beauty; he found it simply irresistible. He would leap into the Jordan in its pursuit, and then radically transform his life, from banditry to Torah study, if only he could realize that beauty through marriage, and ultimately, in himself. R. Yoḥanan knew his own powers, for which reason he stood at the entrance of the *mikve*. When he observed Reish Lakish's leap into the river, he immediately sensed that such enormous drive in his pursuit must mask a deep yearning, for a spirituality which, as it happens, Reish Lakish himself once possessed, then lost. "Your power should be for Torah," R. Yoḥanan tells him. The sheer power of Reish Lakish's yearning for R. Yoḥanan's elusive spiritual beauty marked him for religious greatness, and licensed the offer of R. Yoḥanan's sister for his wife.

Many readers of this aggada will assume at the outset a sharp dichotomy between physical beauty and spirituality. Great actors and actresses are not typically known for religious depth, and important strands within all Western religious traditions, Judaism included, assume a sharp dichotomy between body and soul. The soul pulls in the direction of God, while the body pulls away from God, toward the pursuit of sensual pleasure. Our aggada subverts that assumed dichotomy. R. Yoḥanan's beauty is itself not only physical but spiritual, and Reish Lakish's pursuit of that beauty led to a life of extraordinary Torah accomplishment. Now I do not mean to suggest that Reish Lakish leapt only in pursuit of spirituality, for that would be false to the narrative. He was a bandit, attracted to someone he thought to be a woman. Yet physical attraction to a person possessing both physical and spiritual beauty is complex and multi-dimensional, and cannot be reduced either to pure spirituality or pure sensuality. Complex, ambiguous, and even deeply problematic motives can give rise to the heights Reish Lakish achieved, and that is an important insight of our aggada.

Ironically, this very ambiguity is itself undercut in the next stage of the dialogue. Once Reish Lakish accepts this radically new life of Torah, he wishes to retrieve the tools of his banditry, and finds himself unable to leap back from the river to the shore. While the text itself does not explain why, Rashi[12] cites the talmudic teaching[13] that the study

12. Rashi, ad loc.
13. Sanhedrin 26b.

of Torah weakens a person's strength. Although Reish Lakish had not even begun studying Torah, the very commitment to do so sapped his strength. This suggests that the sharp dichotomy between body and soul endures; there is a zero-sum game between the two drives, or, at least, the drive for religious attainment is not compatible with sheer physical strength. This seems to imply that human beings possess a finite and limited quantity of drive, and once expended in pursuit of Torah, little is left for anything else.

At first glance, this claim seems to stand in tension with the insight that the sharp dichotomy between body and soul is a false one. Yet further reflection reveals not only that this is not the case, but that this second teaching is consistent with, and indeed deepens our understanding of the first. For why is it that the drive for Torah study undercuts physical strength? It is because the energy that drives the pursuit of one is the very same energy that drives the pursuit of the other. Just as physical and spiritual beauty can commingle in the same person, so too spiritual and physical drives can be commingled as well. The first portion of the aggada taught that we cannot easily separate out physical from spiritual beauty, and the second portion of the aggada teaches that we cannot easily separate out the sources of physical drive from spiritual drive. What appear to be opposing strands of our humanity are in fact deeply related, contributing to the remarkable complexity of the human condition.

The next few words of the aggada, a concise string of verbs in the original Aramiac, are breathtaking in their compression. R. Yoḥanan taught Reish Lakish the Torah and the Mishna, and thereby made him into a great man. How long did this take? We don't know, but it must have taken years, even decades, of arduous labor, countless hours of unceasing study. No one can acquire mastery of the whole of the seemingly endless tradition, nor become a great person, overnight. Yet our aggada compresses almost a lifetime of effort into a few words. At one level, this is because the subject of the aggada is not all those intermediate years, but only the beginning and end of Reish Lakish's life as a Torah scholar. At another level, though, the compression itself is part of the aggada's very theme. For how did Reish Lakish become the famous Reish Lakish whose teachings are woven into almost every page of the Talmud? This compacted sentence provides one answer: R. Yoḥanan made him. All the years of intense labor on the part of Reish Lakish are elided. Reish Lakish on this accounting is nothing more or less than the product of R. Yoḥanan's teaching and mentoring. It is difficult to avoid wondering how Reish Lakish might have felt about that characterization, for what about the undoubtedly overwhelming effort on Reish Lakish' part to become so great a scholar?

PART TWO

A TRAGIC MISUNDERSTANDING BETWEEN TEACHER AND STUDENT

We next meet R. Yoḥanan and Reish Lakish many years later, in the *beit midrash*, debating a fine point of halakha, as was their wont. The question at hand involves ritual purities and impurities. An object becomes impure only if it has the status of a *keli*, a fully functional vessel. Now when do such objects as daggers, spears, scythes, and similar items achieve the status of a *keli*? The *baraita* teaches that they become fully functional vessels only when they are completely manufactured. But when are they considered completely manufactured? Here, R. Yoḥanan and Reish Lakish disagree. R. Yoḥanan maintains that they become fully functional vessels after they are forged in the furnace, the manufacturing process which makes them the objects they are. Reish Lakish disagrees, however, and maintains that they are complete only after they are scoured in water following removal from the furnace, which gives them their shine. R. Yoḥanan responds *ad personam*: "You, Reish Lakish, do have considerable expertise in daggers and spears, for you once used them, during your days of banditry."

Now did R. Yoḥanan intend to offend Reish Lakish with this comment? Almost certainly not, for such would be classified as the transgression called *onaat devarim*, using language to hurt another person's feelings, especially of their irreligious past.[14] This is a serious offense, and it

14. See Leviticus 25:14, 17. The Mishna in Bava Metzia 4:10 explicitly teaches that reminding a person who had repented about his former misdeeds is forbidden and an instance of *onaat devarim*. Consider R. Yoḥanan's declaration in Bava Metzia 58b that the verbal abuse of *onaat devarim* is worse than other types of interpersonal abuse, such as monetary exploitation. He even goes as far as to say there that it is better for

is highly unlikely that R. Yoḥanan, great as he was, would have violated it intentionally, especially since the object of his remarks was none other than his most intimate friend, colleague, and brother-in-law. Rather, R. Yoḥanan probably meant this as a witticism, as an offhand remark, or possibly even as an observation in support of Reish Lakish's position and against his own, citing Reish Lakish's superior expertise. We cannot know for sure. But we do know how Reish Lakish responded, although the exact meaning of his response is somewhat obscure. I follow here the interpretation of the *Etz Yosef*, a commentary on this passage of the Talmud in the *Ein Yaakov*.[15]

According to this interpretation, Reish Lakish charges R. Yoḥanan with exactly the sin of *onaat devarim*, of hurting his feelings. "Why did you torment me?" he asks. "Even when I was a bandit, I received the respect of my colleagues in crime, just as I receive respect now from my colleagues in the study hall. Do you think I repented and became a great scholar merely for honor, when I received all the honor I needed during my days of crime as well? I repented for the best of motives. Why, then, do you persist in reminding me of my sinful past and hurting me?"

The Aramaic phrase Reish Lakish uses to accuse R. Yoḥanan is *mai ahanat li*. According to this interpretation of their exchange, Reish Lakish uses *ahanat* as meaning "torment," from the same root as *onaa* in *onaat devarim*. However, that same word can have another meaning entirely. It can also mean "provide benefit," with *ahanat* coming from the same root as *hanaa*,[16] and that is exactly the meaning R. Yoḥanan heard. Thus, R. Yoḥanan understood Reish Lakish to be saying: "What benefit have I gained by all these years of Torah study? During my years of banditry, I was also respected as a leader, and I've gained no more respect now than I had then. Thus, the whole enterprise of Torah study into which you inducted me was simply not worth my while."

a man to be with a woman whose marital status is uncertain, and thereby taking the risk of violating one of the cardinal sins of Judaism, rather than publically embarrass his fellow man.

15. For an alternative interpretation, see the commentary of the Maharsha, ad loc. To this reader, at least, the interpretation of the *Etz Yosef* seems the more straightforward, for which reason I adopt it in my exposition of the text.

16. Indeed, this is how the translation, provided above at the outset, renders this word.

To R. Yoḥanan, these words were arch-heresy, and he responded angrily, "What do you mean you derived no benefit from my efforts to teach you Torah? Why, I brought you under the very wings of the Divine Presence!"

This tragic misunderstanding between R. Yoḥanan and Reish Lakish – all turning on the homonymous meanings of the term *ahanat* – sets the stage for the unraveling not only of their close relationship, but of their very lives.

The key question here is, why do both Reish Lakish and R. Yoḥanan interpret each other's remarks in the least charitable way? If, as I suggested above, it was highly unlikely that R. Yoḥanan actually intended to hurt the feelings of Reish Lakish, why then did Reish Lakish react as angrily as he did? Could he not have interpreted R. Yoḥanan's comments exactly as I did above, rendering them innocuous at worst, and even supportive at best? And why did R. Yoḥanan interpret the word *ahanat* in Reish Lakish's comments to mean "benefit," leading to the charge of heresy? Could he not have interpreted the word *ahanat* exactly as Reish Lakish intended, as a statement reflecting the hurt he genuinely felt?

One interpretation of their exchange provides an answer to these questions, that of the *Derekh HaYashar*, by Rabbi Tzvi Pinḥas Lifshitz.[17] According to the *Derekh HaYashar*, the debate between R. Yoḥanan and Reish Lakish was nothing less than a debate about the legitimacy of autonomous human reason in the determination of halakha. R. Yoḥanan recorded the law about impurity as he heard it from his own teachers, while Reish Lakish disagreed with that teaching based on his own experience that weapons are completed only after polishing, when they shine brighter and inspire more fear in the enemy, thus making them more effective in warfare. R. Yoḥanan angrily criticized Reish Lakish's audacious intellectual independence, pointing out that while he might have expertise in weaponry based upon his background as a bandit, not all the items cited in the teaching are even weapons. Some are farm implements, like scythes. Surely Reish Lakish would have no personal expertise with these items. On what basis, then, could he possess the audacity to disagree with the teachings of his great rabbinic predecessors?

17. Vilna, 1864. This is quoted extensively by the *Likkutim* commentary on the page of the standard *Ein Yaakov* to this passage.

To this charge, Reish Lakish responds, "How have you benefited me by teaching me Torah, if I then lose my intellectual independence, and cannot think for myself? What is the point of all my Torah study if I must now close off my mind and my creativity, and merely repeat the teachings of my predecessors? If you think I have gained because now I have the respect of my colleagues, back in my days as a bandit I had my colleagues' respect too." R. Yoḥanan's response is telling: "How can you question the benefit you received? Why, I've enlightened you with the teachings of the Torah! But I did so not to enable you to liberate you own limited intellect to disagree with those far superior to you in wisdom and knowledge." Eventually, according to the *Derekh HaYashar*, R. Yoḥanan comes to regret this blanket condemnation of intellectual freedom, affirms the value of debate, and acknowledges that Reish Lakish's intentions were never to dissent from the teachings of his predecessors in practice, but only to enrich insight via dialogue and debate.

This account of the debate between R. Yoḥanan and Reish Lakish is a fascinating one, and in some ways echoes the famous debate between R. Eliezer and the Sages about the oven of *akhnai*.[18] The theological dilemma about the value of intellectual autonomy versus the weight of traditional authority is a fraught one in Jewish intellectual history, and in Jewish life.[19] According to this interpretation of the aggada, the debate between these two great talmudic authorities speaks directly to this question. Yet I find that as a reading of the text itself, it is somewhat less persuasive. First, no explicit or even implicit distinction is drawn between the different kinds of implements, weapons and non-weapons, a distinction which is crucial to this interpretation to R. Yoḥanan's attack on Reish Lakish. More importantly, the text itself does not allude to the overall theological issue at all that the *Derekh HaYashar* asserts is beneath the surface of the debate. The language used seems to construe

18. Bava Metzia 59b, to be discussed below. Although in that case, the divide is between intellectual autonomy and the divine will, and not the intellect against tradition as it is here, still, they both relate to the question of intellectual autonomy in a religious context.
19. See Moshe Sokol, *Judaism Examined*, 263–304, for an extensive discussion of this issue.

the conflict between R. Yoḥanan and Reish Lakish as a purely interpersonal one, although a conflict with possibly broader implications. Reish Lakish appears to express primarily personal pain at being reminded of his tawdry origins, and R. Yoḥanan takes deep offense at Reish Lakish's comment, and attacks him in return. While these are not grounds for a complete rejection of this reading, which is indeed a powerful one, I would like to offer an alternative one, focusing on the student-teacher relationship, which I believe hews closer to the text itself.[20]

As a beginning point, it is worth reflecting about the power of the past to live in the present. People can change dramatically over time, mature and evolve, yet old experiences and relationships die hard. The impoverished origins of a young man who eventually succeeds even beyond his wildest dreams often continue to shape his experience of the present, driving him obsessively to pursue ever more wealth. One brother may be very successful as a student, the second less so, and although that second brother may eventually succeed in life far more than the first, the dynamic between them remains mired in that past. Much of psychodynamic psychological theory is based upon this insight. One way to read this aggada, then, is that its author presents R. Yoḥanan and Reish Lakish, despite the radical change over time by Reish Lakish, and despite the commensurately radical change in their relationship, as both still at some level tethered to the past. Reish Lakish remained hypersensitive about his early life, although he had become among the greatest of scholars and of men, and R. Yoḥanan still recalled Reish Lakish's sinful past, although that past had long since been transcended, not only by Reish Lakish, but by R. Yoḥanan too, in the transformation of their relationship. Reish Lakish could never really forget the bandit he was, and remained exceptionally sensitive to any allusions thereto. R. Yoḥanan could never forget that it was he who found Reish Lakish in the river, leaping after what he thought was a beautiful woman. As William Faulkner said, "The past is never dead. It's not even past."[21] The

20. For yet another reading, see Yonah Frankel, *Studies in the Spiritual World of the Aggadic Narrative* (*HaKibbutz HaMeuḥad:* 1981), 73–78 (Heb.). That reading is problematic, at least to me, for reasons I cannot go into here.

21. William Faulkner, *Requiem for a Nun* (Random House, 1951), 92.

power of the past to haunt the present is at the root of the unfolding tragedy of their lives.

Yet we must still ask ourselves just why the past did continue to live on in this way into their present. Were there any factors which made it especially difficult for them to move on, to leave the past behind? Two answers to this question, derived from a close reading of our text, suggest themselves. The first emerges from their halakhic debate. One of the interpretive principles of this book is that halakhic debates embedded in aggadic narratives often symbolize and serve to reinforce the themes of the narrative itself. Let us, then, apply this principle to the debate at hand, which is about when certain implements achieve the status of a *keli*, when they are fully complete. For R. Yoḥanan, the implements in question achieve this status when they are fully functional, and can effectively stab, penetrate, or cut down crops. For Reish Lakish they are complete only after the very final step, of polishing them. This enhances their effectiveness, for the gleam of an enemy's weapon in the sun makes it all the more fearsome and therefore effective, not for actually stabbing the enemy, but for frightening him. This is an element of psychological warfare.[22] Appearances matter.

Consider now how this halakhic debate mirrors the relationship between R. Yoḥanan and Reish Lakish. For we might ask ourselves: Who, after all, made Reish Lakish? Was it R. Yoḥanan, who took a brigand, lured him into the study hall with the offer of a beautiful wife, and taught him all the Torah he knew? Or was it Reish Lakish himself, who toiled day and night in the study hall, to master the Torah he was taught? Was it Reish Lakish, who mercilessly interrogated that Torah – and his teacher – by vigorously plumbing its depths, gaining ever greater clarity, for himself, and for his teacher? Every successful student is to some extent fashioned by a teacher. Who makes the student? Better yet, who makes the student into a master? The teacher who imparts knowledge to the student, or the student who must toil to make that knowledge his own? When does the student achieve his or her full realization as a

22. Perhaps by parity of reasoning, the gleam of a scythe swinging in the air while cutting crops make its user feel all the more powerful, and also inspires his fellow reapers to cut quickly and effectively too.

master of the material taught? When the teacher successfully imparts that knowledge to the student, or when the student takes that knowledge and "shines it," makes it his or her own? By struggling to master that knowledge, by relentlessly interrogating it, the student not only acquires knowledge, but grants himself the true, and truly impressive – even fearsome – *appearance* of mastery.[23] Consider, from this perspective, R. Yohanan's own luster, and the shining face of the greatest master of all, Moshe Rabbenu.[24]

R. Yoḥanan took the view that it was he, the fiery forge, who made Reish Lakish the great man he became. But how would Reish Lakish have felt about this characterization, with which he disagreed intellectually? Might he not have felt that his great teacher R. Yoḥanan slighted his own toil, his own contribution to his *bildung*, the countless hours he spent "sharpening" himself so that he could "shine" in the study hall, so that his aggressive, questioning intellect could fiercely wage the war of Torah study? And might R. Yoḥanan have sensed this attitude in Reish Lakish, and resented it?[25] I would suggest that the author of this aggada centered their tragic fallout around this particular debate because he understood the tension it symbolically portrayed to be at the heart of their tragic misunderstanding.[26] Why did their past live on in their present? Because the lives they came to lead, and their evolving relationship, nurtured an ongoing, ever-present tension between them, grounded ultimately in their past.

I believe there is a second factor as well, but to see this we must continue with the aggada as it unfolds. R. Yoḥanan is deeply offended by

23. In Western literature, this tension goes back to the ancient Greek myth of Pygmalion, retold in Ovid's *Metamorphoses,* about the sculptor who falls in love with the image of the lovely woman he sculpted. Centuries later it found a more modern incarnation in the play of that name by George Bernard Shaw, and an even more recent incarnation in the musical *My Fair Lady,* by Alan Jay Lerner.

24. As described in Exodus 34:29.

25. We will explore the reasons for this below.

26. If one takes this aggada to be a literal rendition of the events themselves, then the author of the aggada, who included the debate, probably realized its significance, and would likely have assumed that it was no coincidence that the tragic misunderstanding between R. Yoḥanan and Reish Lakish would have taken place in debate about this particular halakha.

Reish Lakish's comment, as he (mis)understood it. This, in turn, causes Reish Lakish to become ill.[27] This illness is so severe that Reish Lakish's wife – who is R. Yoḥanan's sister – appears crying before her brother, begging him to forgive Reish Lakish, so that her children – his nephews – not be orphaned. R. Yoḥanan refuses, and using biblical language, promises to care for her children himself. She then tries another tack. She begs him to forgive Reish Lakish for her own sake, as his sister, so that she not become a widow. R. Yoḥanan again refuses, and again using biblical language, promises to care for her as well. No appeal helps, and Reish Lakish dies.

Here we must ask why R. Yoḥanan resisted his very own sister's tearful entreaties, and refused to forgive Reish Lakish. Would he not have believed his sister's impassioned plea that failure to do so would result in Reish Lakish's death? His apparent harshness seems difficult to comprehend, especially given what we know of his biography. Let us not forget that he personally suffered the tragic loss of ten sons, and that he would carry a small bone from the youngest with which to console those similarly bereaved. Surely this bespeaks extraordinary compassion on R. Yoḥanan's part, for by carrying that bone he could never completely bury the past, and the suffering that accompanied his unspeakable loss. Perhaps doing so gave meaning and value to his tragedy, even redeemed it. Yet he kept that suffering alive within him, with which to empathize and heal other sufferers. Could he then not have had compassion for his own sister and nephews? Could he not have had compassion for his beloved friend and colleague Reish Lakish, who suffered so deeply after R. Yoḥanan's biting comment that he lay on his deathbed? To compound the question, the Talmud reports that R. Yoḥanan himself was an orphan: His father died while his mother was pregnant, and his mother died at childbirth.[28] Surely he should have wanted to prevent his nephews from a similar devastating fate.

Our text provides no ready answer to these troubling questions,

27. It is interesting to note that in the Aramaic original, the same verb *ḥalash,* which literally means "became weak," is used both for the offense R. Yoḥanan felt, and the illness Reish Lakish experienced. Thus literally, the text would read "R. Yoḥanan became weak, and Reish Lakish became weak."

28. Kiddushin 30b, Moed Katan 17a.

but if we turn to certain teachings of R. Yoḥanan recorded elsewhere in the Talmud, we may gain insight into his behavior. Several in particular seem revealing. In one, Rabba bar bar Ḥana cites R. Yoḥanan saying the following: "What is the meaning of that which is written: 'For the priest's lips should keep knowledge, and they should seek Torah from his mouth; for he is an angel of the Lord of hosts' (Mal. 2:7)? If the rabbi is similar to an angel of the Lord of hosts, they should seek Torah from his mouth; but if not, they should not seek Torah from his mouth."[29] On the basis of R. Yoḥanan's statement, the Talmud questions how the great *Tanna* R. Meir could have studied Torah under the tutelage of infamous scholar Elisha b. Avuya, who had turned heretic.[30] According to R. Yoḥanan, Torah masters must be nothing less than "angels of the Lord of hosts." Even their dress and appearance must be impeccable, declares R. Yoḥanan elsewhere.[31] Of special significance in our context, one passage states: "R. Ḥiyya bar Abba said that R. Yoḥanan said: Whoever issues a halakhic ruling in his teacher's presence is deserving of being bitten by a snake."[32] Students must show absolute respect for their masters, and if a question of law comes up in the presence of both, then even if the student knows its resolution, he must maintain his silence in deference to his teacher. No doubt the immediate reason for that deference is the stature of the teacher, who must be like a very angel of God.

This awe of rabbinic masters and predecessors is reflected in R. Yoḥanan's teaching: "The hearts [i.e., the wisdom] of the early Sages were like the doorway to the Entrance Hall [of the Temple, which was twenty by forty cubits]; the hearts of the later Sages were like the doorway to the Sanctuary [of the Temple, which was ten by twenty cubits]; but our hearts are like the eye of a needle."[33] Likewise, in another pas-

29. Ḥagiga 15b.

30. It is hardly without interest in the context of our present discussion that Reish Lakish is the one there who disagrees with R. Yoḥanan and defends R. Meir's practice, teaching that there is much to learn even from a flawed teacher. His standards were apparently different from those of R. Yoḥanan, perhaps reflecting his own wayward religious journey.

31. Shabbat 114a.

32. Eiruvin 63a.

33. Ibid. 53a.

sage, R. Yoḥanan is quoted as teaching that "the fingernails of the early Sages are preferable to the belly of the later Sages."[34]

One might argue that this awe is fundamental to the survival and flourishing of Torah, for one should recall that the Oral Law for many centuries was exactly that – law transmitted orally from master to student. Even after portions of the Oral Law were committed to writing, circumstances would inevitably arise with no clear precedents. How then could Torah survive a changing world?[35] If a student fails to hold his teacher in awe, fails to accord him absolute respect, how could the Torah emerge unscathed into the future? Only the accumulated wisdom of the past, possessed by great scholars with vast repositories of Torah knowledge, could ensure, to R. Yoḥanan, an authentic Torah for the future.[36]

It was precisely this sensibility that R. Yoḥanan believed Reish Lakish to be questioning. He heard in Reish Lakish's position on the status of a *keli* a critique of the overarching role of the master, and an assertion of the independent achievement of the student, who polishes himself to a fearsome gleam. For R. Yoḥanan, great teachers are the forges who make their students, and for this reason they must be respected absolutely. The metaphor of a forge is brilliantly apt, for, as R. Yoḥanan stated, great teachers are like angels, and angels frequently appear in biblical and rabbinic literature as fiery beings (e.g., seraphim) – the very fire of the forge that makes students. However, for Reish Lakish, students play a pivotal role in their own formation. But might this perspective not undercut the towering role of the master, so essential for the very survival of Torah? This is what worried R. Yoḥanan.

34. Yoma 9b. Again here, Reish Lakish disagress and finds the later Sages more commendable for their Torah study under oppressive conditions.

35. It is worth noting that the formulation of the blessing on Torah study which is according to R. Yoḥanan in Berakhot 11b, makes explicit mention of that future: "Lord our God, make the words of Your Torah sweet in our mouths and in the mouths of Your people, the House of Israel, so that we and our descendants and the descendants of Your people, the House of Israel, may be those who know Your name and engage in Your Torah."

36. See R. Ḥayim Shmulevitz, *Siḥot Mussar* (Jerusalem, 1980), *Maamar* 13, 44–45 (Heb.), where the author stresses the importance for the Jewish future of holding a teacher in the greatest reverence.

The crucial issue here is not intellectual autonomy in the halakhic process, the interpretive thrust of the *Derekh HaYashar*, but the relative role of teacher and master in the formation of the student, which speaks more to the personal tension between R. Yoḥanan and Reish Lakish evident in the aggada, and provides a strong reading of the symbolic significance of their debate.

R. Yoḥanan, as a matter of the deepest principle, could not retract his position and reconcile with Reish Lakish. As compassionate a man as he was, as much as he might have loved his sister and nephews, he held firm to his conviction about the towering importance of absolute respect for a Torah master. He knew Reish Lakish's influence, and the respect Reish Lakish was accorded by his colleagues, who themselves called him a master. R. Yoḥanan's yeshiva in Tiberias was the very center of Torah study in *Eretz Yisrael* at that time. If he were to forgive Reish Lakish and compromise on his ironclad commitment to respect for Torah masters, the very future of Torah would be threatened. R. Yoḥanan was thus caught on the horns of a tragic dilemma. What takes precedence? His love of his family and intimate friendship with Reish Lakish, the great fruit of his years of teaching Torah? Or his commitment to the principle of absolute respect for a Torah teacher? R. Yoḥanan fatefully chose principle over family and friendship. As the aggada unfolds, it becomes apparent that the cost of this choice was not only the death of Reish Lakish, the widowing of R. Yoḥanan's sister, and the orphaning of R. Yoḥanan's nephews. The cost of that choice was the madness, then death, of R. Yoḥanan himself.

Immediately after the failed entreaties of R. Yoḥanan's sister, Reish Lakish dies, and R. Yoḥanan begins to feel the terrible personal consequences of his decision. "R. Yoḥanan was sorely pained over him." Who could replace Reish Lakish? R. Yoḥanan's colleagues and students sought to console him by sending R. Elazar b. Pedat, a very accomplished scholar, to serve as R. Yoḥanan's study partner. Instead of debating him, R. Elazar b. Pedat would support every teaching that R. Yoḥanan shared by citing an earlier tannaitic source as precedent.[37] To this well-intended but failed attempt at consolation, R. Yoḥanan responds to

37. Note the similarity here to Ilfa, in chapter 5 of this volume, who insists he can find

R. Elazar b. Pedat in despair: "Are you like the son of Lakish? With the son of Lakish, when I would state a matter, he would raise twenty-four difficulties against me, and I would answer him with twenty-four answers, and the halakha by itself would become broadened. And yet you say: It is taught in a *baraita* a support for you. Do I not know that what I say is good?"

This anguished comment is illuminating in many ways. First, it sheds light on the mature relationship between R. Yoḥanan and Reish Lakish. In a word, it was combative. Reish Lakish, the erstwhile brigand, sublimated the aggressiveness displayed during his criminal past toward the service of Torah study. He exploited the very negative character trait that led him to crime into a tool for the advancement of Torah knowledge, a remarkable and impressive feat indeed. This combativeness made him a perfect foil to R. Yoḥanan, who possessed vast Torah learning. Reish Lakish's pugilistic style of Torah dialogue – twenty-four questions about a single teaching – forced R. Yoḥanan to reflect more deeply and analytically about the very Torah he taught. This in turn clarified and broadened that Torah for him, for all his students, and for the millennia of Torah scholars who lived and taught in his wake. Where would the Talmud, and the whole halakhic tradition, be without the myriad controversies between R. Yoḥanan and Reish Lakish? No other colleague or student could replace Reish Lakish's penetrating intellect and aggressive interrogation of every halakha. The absence of that clash of ideas was devastating for R. Yoḥanan, its fullest significance tragically realized only after it was permanently lost to him, and indeed lost to him by his very own portentous choice.

I would suggest that this characterization of their relationship sheds further light on the question of why Reish Lakish's past continued to live on and haunt both R. Yoḥanan and Reish Lakish, that despite Reish Lakish's radical change from criminal to towering scholar, both remained tragically tethered to that past. No doubt R. Yoḥanan knew the intellectual value of their incessant give-and-take, which brought

support for later halakhic positions from early mishnaic sources. Ilfa took pride in this accomplishment. R. Yoḥanan, ironically, sought something very different from Reish Lakish.

so much Torah to light. Yet emotions don't always ineluctably follow in the wake of knowledge. Is it not possible that R. Yoḥanan felt that Reish Lakish's aggressive questioning may sometimes have crossed the border between respect for him and disrespect, especially in light of the importance R. Yoḥanan placed on absolute respect for Torah masters, as we have seen? And might Reish Lakish not have sensed that R. Yoḥanan sometimes felt ambivalent about his aggressive mode of questioning? For R. Yoḥanan, fending off yet another aggressive round of questioning by Reish Lakish would have recalled just how aggressive Reish Lakish once was. And Reish Lakish, sensing that, may have remained sensitive about that unfortunate period in his life. Thus, the very combative nature of their relationship may have sustained a tension which made it extraordinarily difficult to escape the past.[38]

This characterization of their relationship also sheds further light on the dilemma R. Yoḥanan faced over whether or not to reconcile with Reish Lakish when his own sister came to appeal to him. While R. Yoḥanan may not have realized, to the fullest extent possible, the value of Reish Lakish to his own Torah learning, it is hard to believe that he was not cognizant of it at all. After all, his life in Torah was characterized by this incessant debate. He undoubtedly knew that with the death of Reish Lakish, this would cease, and with it would end the brilliant productivity of their intellectual combat. The tragic dilemma he suffered when making the decision not to heed his sister's entreaties was not only a clash between the value of absolute respect for teachers of Torah, and his love of family and of Reish Lakish himself. It was no less a clash of deeply held principles, between the value of respect for Torah teachers, and the value of ascertaining the truth about Torah, the very meaning of God's will. For if he reconciles with Reish Lakish, Torah will proliferate for him, and all his students throughout the ages will be heirs to that clarity and breadth. What could be more important than that? Yet if he reconciles with Reish Lakish, and thereby undercuts his commitment to the importance of respect for Torah teachers, he would endanger the very future of Torah as an institution capable of

38. For important parallels to this, see chapter 7 of this volume, which discusses the relationship between R. Yoḥanan and R. Kahana described in Bava Kamma 117a–b.

guiding Jews throughout the ages. How, then, does one weigh the value of Torah truth against the value of the institutional structure that makes the future of Torah possible?

R. Yoḥanan chose to valorize respect for Torah's masters over his own search for Torah truth, and perhaps this was the theologically correct choice.[39] But if so, that heroic choice devastated him emotionally, for R. Yoḥanan discovered that his passion for and love of Torah knowledge were so intense that he simply could not bear to live with its consequences, even if the choice had been right. Great man that he was, his love of Torah truth was just unquenchable, and its frustration drove him mad. The Talmud states: "He went around, rending his clothing, weeping and saying: Where are you, son of Lakish? Where are you, son of Lakish?" Was he ripping his clothing over Reish Lakish's death, or over the loss of Torah knowledge consequent upon his death, or both? We cannot know. But "he screamed until he went insane." The rabbis prayed for him, and asked God to have mercy and take his soul. God heard their prayers, and R. Yoḥanan died.

It seems worth wondering why the rabbis prayed for R. Yoḥanan's death, and did not pray for his healing. Perhaps the answer is that there could be no healing for the pain R. Yoḥanan felt. R. Yoḥanan loved Torah truth too passionately for that love to be requited with anyone other than a man like Reish Lakish, and he loved the future of Torah so intensely that he could never place it in any danger. There could be no reconciliation of those two great loves in R. Yoḥanan's life. The rabbis understood this too well, and they did all they could for him – they prayed for his death.

39. While it is certainly possible that R. Yoḥanan realized he made the wrong choice and regretted it, is seems more likely that a man who had devoted his entire life to upholding a set of deeply held principles would be unlikely ever to have given them up.

Chapter 7

R. Kahana Dies and R. Yoḥanan Seeks Forgiveness: The Conflict between Teacher and Student, and a Mysterious Encounter at the Grave

Bava Kamma 117a–b

INTRODUCTION

All close human relationships are complex, and the relationship between student and teacher is no exception. This aggada explores the relationship between R. Kahana, a third-century *Amora,* first with the great Babylonian master Rav, who was the head of the yeshiva in Sura, and second, and most importantly, with R. Yoḥanan, the leading master of his generation in *Eretz Yisrael.* The story it tells is a remarkable one, and ends in R. Kahana's death, and R. Yoḥanan's attempt to atone for his role in that death through a mysterious encounter with the dead R. Kahana in his grave. The aggada provides a vivid picture of life inside the yeshiva of R. Yoḥanan, and is a study in the personalities of each of these great figures, their approach to Torah study, to human relationships, and to how they resolved failures and conflicts. Our discussion will be divided into two parts, the first focusing on R. Kahana's experiences in Babylonia and then in the yeshiva of R. Yoḥanan in *Eretz Yisrael*, and the second on R. Yoḥanan's encounter with R. Kahana in the grave. I wish to remind the reader that, as discussed in the introduction to this volume, those of us living in the twenty-first century can have no access to the inner lives of such towering figures as R. Yoḥanan, Rav, and R. Kahana. What we can attempt to do, at best, is to understand what the *author of the particular aggeda seeks to convey* in the story he tells, or, put differently, what the text's moral, religious, or psychological lessons are. While I will make numerous suggestions about the motives and behavior of the three protagonists in this aggada, they are intended to be no more than suggestions about *what the text might convey* regarding these great Torah personalities, not about the men themselves. The true inner lives of R. Yoḥanan, Rav, and R. Kahana must always remain, for us, shrouded in enigma.

Bava Kamma 117a–b

ההוא גברא דהוה בעי אחוויי אתיבנא דחבריה אתא לקמיה דרב א"ל לא תחוי ולא תחוי א"ל מחוינא ומחוינא יתיב רב כהנא קמיה דרב שמטיה לקועיה מיניה קרי רב עילויה (ישעיהו נא, כ) בניך עולפו שכבו בראש כל חוצות כתוא מכמר מה תוא זה כיון שנפל במכמר אין מרחמין עליו אף ממון של ישראל כיון שנפל ביד עובדי כוכבים אין מרחמין עליו א"ל רב כהנא עד האידנא הוו פרסאי דלא קפדי אשפיכות דמים והשתא איכא יוונאי דקפדו אשפיכות דמים ואמרי מרדין מרדין קום סק לארעא דישראל וקביל עלך דלא תקשי לרבי יוחנן שבע שנין.

The Gemara relates another incident: There was **a certain man who desired to show another** individual's **straw** to the gentile authorities, who would seize it. **He came before Rav,** who **said to him: Do not show** it **and do not show** it, i.e., you are absolutely prohibited from showing it. The man **said to him: I will show** it

and I will show it, i.e., I will certainly show it. **Rav Kahana was sitting before Rav,** and, hearing the man's disrespectful response, **he dislodged** the man's **neck from him,** i.e., he broke his neck and killed him. Seeing Rav Kahana's action, **Rav read** the following verse **about him: "Your sons have fainted, they lie at the head of all the streets, as an antelope in a net"** (Isaiah 51:20). **Just as** with regard to **this antelope, once it falls into the net,** the hunter **does not have mercy upon it, so too** with regard to **the money of a Jew, once it falls into the hand of gentiles, they do not have mercy upon him,** i.e., the Jew. Since gentiles who seek a Jew's money will kill him in order to seize the property, Rav Kahana acted appropriately when he broke the miscreant's neck, as he protected the Jew's property and, by extension, the Jew himself. **Rav** then **said to** Rav Kahana: **Kahana, until now there were Persian** rulers **who were not particular about bloodshed. But now there are Greeks who are particular about bloodshed, and they** will **say: Murder** [*meradin*], **murder,** and they will press charges against you. Therefore, **get up** and **ascend to Eretz Yisrael** to study there under Rabbi Yoḥanan, **and accept upon yourself that you will not raise** any **difficulties to** the statements of **Rabbi Yoḥanan** for **seven years.**

אזיל אשכחיה לריש לקיש דיתיב וקא מסיים מתיבתא דיומא לרבנן אמר להו ריש לקיש היכא אמרו ליה אמאי אמר להו האי קושיא והאי קושיא והאי פירוקא והאי פירוקא אמרו ליה לריש לקיש אזל ריש לקיש א״ל לרבי יוחנן ארי עלה מבבל לעיין מר במתיבתא דלמחר למחר אותבוה בדרא קמא קמיה דר׳ יוחנן אמר שמעתתא ולא אקשי שמעתתא ולא אקשי אנחתיה אחורי שבע דרי עד דאותביה בדרא בתרא א״ל רבי יוחנן לר״ש בן לקיש ארי שאמרת נעשה שועל.

Rav Kahana **went** to Eretz Yisrael and **found Reish Lakish, who was sitting and reviewing** Rabbi Yoḥanan's **daily** lecture in the **academy for the Rabbis,** i.e., the students in the academy. When he finished, Rav Kahana **said to** the students: **Where is Reish Lakish? They said to him: Why** do you wish to see him? Rav Kahana **said to them:** I have **this difficulty and that difficulty** with his review of Rabbi Yoḥanan's lecture, **and this resolution and that resolution** to the questions he raised. **They told** this to **Reish Lakish. Reish Lakish** then **went and said to Rabbi Yoḥanan: A lion has ascended from Babylonia,** and **the Master** ought **to examine** the discourse he will deliver **in the academy tomorrow,** as Rav Kahana may raise difficult questions about the material. **The next day, they seated** Rav Kahana **in the first row, in front of Rabbi Yoḥanan.** Rabbi Yoḥanan **stated a *halakha* and** Rav Kahana **did not raise a difficulty,** in accordance with Rav's instruction. Rabbi Yoḥanan stated another ***halakha* and** again, Rav Kahana **did not raise a difficulty.** As a result, **they placed** Rav Kahana further **back** by one row. This occurred until he had been moved back **seven rows, until he was seated in the last row. Rabbi Yoḥanan said to Rabbi Shimon ben Lakish: The lion you mentioned has become a fox,** i.e., he is not knowledgeable.

אמר יהא רעוא דהני שבע דרי להוו חילוף שבע שנין דאמר לי רב קם אכרעיה א"ל נהדר מר ברישא אמר שמעתתא ואקשי אוקמיה בדרא קמא אמר שמעתתא ואקשי ר' יוחנן הוה יתיב אשבע בסתרקי שלפי ליה חדא בסתרקא מתותיה אמר שמעתתא ואקשי ליה עד דשלפי ליה כולהו בסתרקי מתותיה עד דיתיב על ארעא רבי יוחנן גברא סבא הוה ומסרחי גביניה אמר להו דלו לי עיני ואחזייה דלו ליה במכחלתא דכספא חזא דפרטיה שפוותיה סבר אחוך קמחייך ביה חלש דעתיה ונח נפשיה למחר אמר להו רבי יוחנן לרבנן חזיתו לבבלאה היכי עביד אמרו ליה דרכיה הכי.

Rav Kahana **said** to himself: **May it be** God's **will that these seven rows** I have been moved **should replace the seven years that Rav told me** to wait before raising difficulties to the statements of Rabbi Yoḥanan. **He stood up on his feet and said to** Rabbi Yoḥanan: Let the **Master go back to the beginning** of the discourse and repeat what he said. Rabbi Yoḥanan **stated a *halakha* and** Rav Kahana **raised a difficulty.** Therefore, **they placed him in the first row,** and again, Rav Yoḥanan **stated a *halakha*, and he raised a difficulty. Rabbi Yoḥanan was sitting upon seven cushions** [***bistarkei***] so that he could be seen by all the students, **and** since he could not answer Rav Kahana's questions,

he removed one cushion from under himself to demonstrate that he was lowering himself out of respect for Rav Kahana. He then **stated** another ***halakha*** **and** Rav Kahana **raised** another **difficulty.** This happened repeatedly **until** Rabbi Yoḥanan **removed all the cushions from underneath himself until he was sitting on the ground. Rabbi Yoḥanan was an old man and his eyebrows drooped** over his eyes. **He said to** his students: **Uncover my eyes for me and I will see** Rav Kahana, so **they uncovered** his eyes **for him with a silver eye brush.** Once his eyes were uncovered, Rabbi Yoḥanan **saw that** Rav Kahana's **lips were split** and **thought** that Rav Kahana **was smirking at him.** As a result, Rabbi Yoḥanan **was offended, and** Rav Kahana **died** as punishment for the fact that he offended Rabbi Yoḥanan. **The next day, Rabbi Yoḥanan said to the Rabbis,** his students: **Did you see how that Babylonian,** Rav Kahana, **behaved** in such a disrespectful manner? **They said to him: His** usual **manner** of appearance **is such,** and he was not mocking you.

על לגבי מערתא חזא דהוה הדרא ליה עכנא א״ל עכנא עכנא פתח פומיך ויכנס הרב אצל תלמיד ולא פתח יכנס חבר אצל חבר ולא פתח יכנס תלמיד אצל הרב פתח ליה בעא רחמי ואוקמיה א״ל אי הוה ידענא דדרכיה דמר הכי לא חלשא דעתי השתא ליתי מר בהדן א״ל אי מצית למיבעי רחמי דתו לא שכיבנא אזילנא ואי לא לא אזילנא הואיל וחליף שעתא חליף תיירי‍ה אוקמיה שייליה כל ספיקא דהוה ליה ופשטינהו ניהליה היינו דאמר ר׳ יוחנן דילכון אמרי דילהון היא.

Hearing this, Rabbi Yoḥanan **went up to** Rav Kahana's burial **cave** and **saw** that it was **encircled by a serpent** [*akhna*], which had placed its tail in its mouth, completely encircling the cave and blocking the entrance. Rabbi Yoḥanan **said to it: Serpent, serpent, open your mouth and** allow **the teacher** to **enter** and be **near the disciple, but** the serpent **did not open** its mouth to allow him entry. He then said: Allow **a colleague** to **enter** and be **near** his **colleague, but** still the serpent **did not open** its mouth. Rabbi Yoḥanan said: Allow the **disciple** to **enter** and be **near the teacher,** referring to Rav Kahana as his own teacher.

The snake then **opened** its mouth **for him** to allow him entry. Rabbi Yoḥanan **requested** divine **mercy** from God and **raised** Rav Kahana from the dead. Rabbi Yoḥanan **said to** Rav Kahana: **Had I known that this was the Master's manner** of appearance, **I would not have been offended. Now** let **the Master come with me** to the study hall. Rav Kahana **said to him: If you are able to request** divine **mercy** so **that I will not die again, I will go** with you, **and if not, I will not go** with you. The Gemara comments: **Since the time** decreed for his death **had passed, it had passed.** Rabbi Yoḥanan then completely **awakened him** and **stood him up.** Thereafter, **he asked him** about **every uncertainty that he had, and** Rav Kahana **resolved** each of **them for him. And this is** the background to **that which Rabbi Yoḥanan says** to his students on several occasions: What **I said was yours is** in fact **theirs,** i.e., I thought that the Torah scholars in Eretz Yisrael were the most advanced, but in fact the scholars of Babylonia are the most advanced, as evidenced by Rav Kahana's knowledge.

PART ONE

R. KAHANA LEAVES BABYLONIA TO STUDY UNDER THE GREAT MASTER R. YOḤANAN, AND WHAT TRANSPIRES IN R. YOḤANAN'S YESHIVA

The aggada begins with a striking encounter between three individuals: a man who walked into Rav's study hall, Rav himself, and R. Kahana, Rav's student. The man seeks Rav's permission to report a fellow Jew's straw to the gentile authorities, who would likely seize it. This Rav objects to vehemently, repeating his opposition twice. Using language almost mimicking Rav, the questioner proceeds to twice affirm that he will go ahead and do exactly what Rav forbade. Rav's student, R. Kahana, overhears the conversation, and is so enraged by the questioner's response that he proceeds to break the man's neck.

Was this the right or wrong thing to do? Rav supports his student's action, apparently on grounds that the man was putting the life of a fellow Jew in danger by reporting him to the authorities, since the straw owner would be at the mercy of the barbaric gentile government, which often killed without compunction. In halakhic terms, the reporter is called a *moser*, a Jew who reports another Jew to otherwise lawless authorities, and therefore in this case a *rodef*, in effect "pursuing" the owner of the straw to the point of death, and thus forfeiting his own right to life.[1] R. Kahana thus was saving the straw owner's life. R. Kahana may also have been incensed at the disrespect shown to his revered master, but this alone would hardly have warranted murder. However, the matter does not end there, for while Rav supports R. Kahana's choice, he points out to him that his life is in danger, as the authorities may now prosecute him for murder,[2] and he tells R. Kahana to leave Babylonia immediately for *Eretz Yisrael*, to study under the great master R. Yoḥanan. Now had Rav left it at that, we would have taken his words to be no more than prudent advice for an endangered student. However, Rav adds a very intriguing demand. He instructs R. Kahana to ask no questions of his new master, R. Yoḥanan, for a total of seven years (a very long time indeed). Surely this suggests that Rav's instruction to leave Babylonia was not only for the purpose of securing R. Kahana's safety. But then why exactly would Rav have so instructed R. Kahana? The text itself provides no explicit answer to this question.

Several explanations are offered by the classic commentaries on this passage, and their suggestions seem confirmed by the story itself as it unfolds. The Maharsha here proposes that Rav was upset with R. Kahana not because he thought the choice he made was wrong, but because on a matter of such great import – killing another human being – R. Kahana should have consulted with the master himself, Rav, who was of course present, before "executing" the questioner. Halakha stipulates that it is wrong for a student to decide a matter of Jewish law in the presence of his master, even going so far as to declare this student worthy of the death penalty,[3] since he has implied disrespect for the master's authority. To

1. See *Teshuvot HaRosh* 17:1 and *Arukh HaShulḥan, Ḥoshen Mishpat* 388:7. For an extensive discussion of these laws, see Michael Broyde, "Informing on Others for Violating American Law: A Jewish Law View," *Journal of Halakha and Contemporary Society* 41 (2002): 5–49.
2. Once again double language is used in the original text, a literary characteristic of this aggada.
3. Eiruvin 63a. See chapter 6 of this book regarding this passage and R. Yoḥanan's emphasis on the importance of these matters.

atone for this failure of respect, he must accept the teachings of his new master, R. Yoḥanan, in respectful silence, raising no objections. Rabbi Yosef Ḥayyim,[4] in his commentary *Ben Yehoyada* here, stresses that while R. Kahana was not culpable for murder, Rav held R. Kahana to a very high standard of piety, and recommended that R. Kahana exile himself from home and country, and journey to a new land as atonement for killing a man, even when technically justified, and accept upon himself a kind of vow of silence as part of the atonement. Both commentators thus see in Rav's instructions a call to repentance, although repentance for different wrongs.[5]

Further reflection suggests an even deeper link between the approaches of these two commentators. For what personal trait or traits might lead both to homicide and to deciding a matter of law in the presence of a great master? Two traits come to mind: aggressiveness and brashness. Surely homicide is aggressive, as is leaping to take action in the presence of a great teacher, and both are brash as well. R. Kahana was indeed a very great man, but the author of this aggada depicts R. Kahana, like all human beings, as struggling with weaknesses too. Following the cogent interpretations of the two commentators cited above, the aggada has Rav sending his gifted but brash student into exile to learn to tame these temptations.[6] It is worth noting that in Berakhot 62a, there is another episode about R. Kahana and Rav which provides further confirmation of this picture. There, the Talmud reports that R. Kahana hid under the bed of Rav while Rav was engaged in intimate relations with his wife, and even criticized Rav, while this was taking place, from under the bed. Not surprisingly, Rav objected

---

4. Popularly known and nicknamed for his halakhic work, *Ben Ish Ḥai.*
5. The Maharasha explains the seven-year period as reflecting one-tenth the average human lifespan. Ben Yehoyada notes that the number seven is used frequently in classical Jewish sources, e.g., the years of *Shemitta.*
6. As the *Iyun Yaakov* notes in his commentary to this passage, which appears in the standard *Ein Yaakov,* and as we will see later in this chapter, there were differences in the styles of Torah study between Babylonia, which was more aggressive and combative, and *Eretz Yisrael*, which was more tranquil and tolerant, and it is therefore likely that Rav's intent in sending R. Kahana to *Eretz Yisrael* was also to learn from their more tolerant and less aggressive style.

strenuously, to which R. Kahana retorted that intimate relations between husband and wife are Torah, and must be studied like any other portion of Torah. The behavior described in this episode might also be characterized as aggressive and brash – at least by Rav – and, of course, it was Rav who sent R. Kahana into exile in our aggada, perhaps recalling this episode and the character traits it revealed.[7]

In any case, the story told in our aggada as it unfolds will provide ample confirmation of this analysis. Consider what R. Kahana does immediately upon arrival in *Eretz Yisrael*, in the renowned yeshiva of R. Yoḥanan in Tiberias. Reish Lakish, the great student turned colleague of R. Yoḥanan, has just finished repeating and explaining to the assembled students the day's lecture delivered earlier by R. Yoḥanan. R. Kahana, apparently sitting unobtrusively in the back or just outside, overhears Reish Lakish's review. R. Kahana then abruptly appears and asks the students still present where Reish Lakish might be, as Reish Lakish by then had left the room. They respond, somewhat suspiciously (for who, after all, is this newcomer from abroad raising questions?), and in good Jewish fashion, with a question of their own: "Why do you want to know?" R. Kahana proceeds to raise a whole series of objections to the review lecture Reish Lakish had delivered,[8] and also proceeds to offer a whole series of answers to the very questions he himself had raised. This feat of talmudic pyrotechnics clearly impressed the students, who later report it to Reish Lakish. Reish Lakish, in turn, apparently out of concern for the dignity of his senior colleague and close friend, goes to R. Yoḥanan and says, "A lion has come up from Babylonia. The master should prepare his lecture for tomorrow very well indeed." Note the use of the term "lion," which is also generally a metaphor for "king." This might suggest that based upon R. Kahana's brilliant performance

7. Medieval authorities discuss the identity of R. Kahana who appears in *Eretz Yisrael*, with some maintaining that there were two R. Kahanas, and others believing that R. Kahana made two trips to *Eretz Yisrael*. See *Tosafot*, Kiddushin 8a, s.v. *Rav Kahana*, and *Piskei HaRosh*, Kiddushin 4:24. Since our focus here is on the story this aggada tells, this historical question is moot.
8. Once again, the author of the text uses the double language so characteristic of this aggada.

in the study hall, Reish Lakish feared that R. Kahana could threaten R. Yoḥanan's stature as "king," or head of his own yeshiva.[9] Note that R. Kahana acts in his new yeshiva with exactly the same character traits he demonstrated in Babylonia, traits which led to his exile. Surely it is both brash and aggressive for a student, making his first appearance at the doorsteps of a new yeshiva, to pummel one of its leading scholars with a series of questions and answers. As we shall see, this same theme is reinforced as the aggada continues to unfold.

The next day R. Yoḥanan appears in the study hall to deliver his customary lecture, no doubt very well prepared. Where do we find R. Kahana, now a student in the yeshiva? Sitting in the very front row. In yeshivas of that period, students were seated according to their rank. The very best students would be seated in the front row, and the weakest, usually the youngest or newest, would be seated in the back row, with other students seated variously according to their abilities. Thus, there was a formal hierarchy within each yeshiva, much like the earlier Sanhedrin, with seating a measure of rank.[10] Of course, this is different from the practice in most contemporary yeshivas, and quite interesting in its own way. In any case, R. Kahana, the newest student, is now seated with the very best, based upon his performance the day before. The reader almost feels the tension prevailing then in the study hall. Will R. Kahana recapitulate his extraordinary performance of the day before, and batter R. Yoḥanan with questions? Will their great teacher R. Yoḥanan manage to answer those questions satisfactorily? Will R. Yoḥanan's preeminence, his very authority, survive the challenge presented by this brilliant young scholar, newly arrived from Babylonia?

R. Yoḥanan proceeds with his lecture. He discusses one teaching. R. Kahana remains silent, just as Rav had instructed. R. Yoḥanan

9. As we shall see, this is consistent with the overarching theme of the relative authority of Torah centers in *Eretz Yisrael* and Babylonia.

10. See Y. Gafni, "The Babylonian Yeshiva in the Light of Bava Kamma 117a," *Tarbitz* 49 (1980): 292–301 (Heb.). Some scholars see in the description of R. Yoḥanan's yeshiva certain reflections of Babylonian practices. See also Sh. Friedman, "The Further Adventures of Rav Kahana: Between Babylonia and Palestine," in *The Talmud Yerushalmi and Graeco-Roman Culture*, ed. P. Schafer (Tubingen: 1998), and the sources cited therein.

offers another teaching. Again, R. Kahana remains silent, just as Rav had instructed. This continues, as R. Yoḥanan offers seven teachings, and R. Kahana remains silent after each. One can only begin to imagine the intense inner struggle R. Kahana must have felt. Could he control his brilliance, his brashness, and remain silent? He was surely tempted beyond words to blurt out the questions he had, and their answers. Torah was his life. How could he contain himself? Yet his great master Rav had decreed silence. This intense inner struggle was no doubt exacerbated by another striking feature of the practice in R. Yoḥanan's yeshiva. Rank was fluid. For every teaching during which R. Kahana remained silent, he was demoted a row, and by the end of R. Yoḥanan's seven teachings, R. Kahana was now demoted to the very last row, with the weakest of the students. Brilliant R. Kahana! Imagine how difficult this must have been for him to tolerate. Of course, all this was exactly Rav's point, for Rav believed that his brash and brilliant young student R. Kahana must learn self-control.

Before proceeding with the story, it is worth pointing out that the fluidity of rank in R. Yoḥanan's yeshiva likely bore with it certain educational and social consequences. The tension in the room must remain high, for the standing of each student shifts constantly, depending upon what transpires in the study hall. Did you ask a good question? You are promoted to a better seat. Did you ask a bad question, or offer a poor answer to a question asked? Then you are demoted to a worse seat. Performance was constantly assessed and acted upon, publicly. There was no hiding the day's successes or failures, for they would immediately be apparent for all to see, in the new seating assignment.[11] On the one hand, this is a highly competitive environment, which is a powerful impetus for success in Torah. It is thus no wonder that R. Yoḥanan's students, and students in other yeshivas which followed this pattern, were the outstanding scholars who have shaped Torah teachings to this very day. On the other hand, one also wonders if it came at a certain psychological cost to some of those students as well, whose names were lost to Jewish history. We cannot know for sure. But the success of some of

11. It is not made clear who makes these seating assignments, quite a source of power in the study hall. If the student himself chose to alter his seat according to his successes or failures, then R. Kahana would surely have felt intensely frustrated.

the greatest Torah scholars of all time may be, at least in part, attributable to this method.

In any case, R. Yoḥanan is surprised by the turn of events. He had been expecting fierce attack and was instead met by silence. He comments to Reish Lakish, probably *sotto voce*, "The lion you said arrived has turned out to be a fox." The shift in animal metaphors is interesting. Lions are regal, and reflect authority, and Reish Lakish had feared that R. Yoḥanan's authority was under threat. Foxes in the popular imagination and in folklore are wily, tricky, and very far from regal. They sneak in to steal the chicken, and do not roar with the awesome power of a frontal attack.[12] R. Yoḥanan was implying not only that R. Kahana lacked the Torah authority to be a threat, but that he was tricky, lacked true Torah substance, and that his performance the day before was no more than deceptive. Did the author of the aggada believe that these comments were a bit harsh? That remains to be seen.

In any case, we must now ask how R. Kahana reacted to this string of demotions, and to his no doubt painful struggle to fulfill his master's request and remain silent. He says, "May it be your will that these seven rows of my demotion replace the seven years Rav requested that I remain silent."[13] R. Kahana simply cannot keep quiet when he possesses talmudic insight. For R. Kahana, the restraint he exercised in remaining silent for a single demotion was the equivalent of an entire year of silence! Imagine, then, the intensity of R. Kahana's internal struggle during R. Yoḥanan's lecture, how difficult it must have been to control himself. Following his prayer, if we can call it that, R. Kahana gets up – a symbolic as well as literal change in his space – and asks R. Yoḥanan to repeat the lecture, which R. Yoḥanan obligingly does. Following each portion of the lecture, R. Kahana, true to form, poses his provocative questions. Following each successful battery of questions, he is in turn promoted, one row after the other, until he finds himself back in the

12. For an example of this in rabbinic literature, see Berakhot 61b, where in a famous parable about the importance of Torah study to Jews, a wily fox attempts to convince a fish to come to dry land.

13. While the more straightforward reading of the text is that R. Kahana beseeches God for this dispensation, it is also possible that he means to appeal to Rav himself.

very first row. Clearly, R. Kahana so far is an unchanged man. The same aggressive traits which characterized his behavior in Babylonia, and his first appearance at the yeshiva in *Eretz Yisrael*, remain. Rav's plan to send his student into exile, and to discipline him through silence, has yet to succeed, despite the trials R. Kahana had undergone.

How does R. Yoḥanan fare after this onslaught of questions? Remarkably enough, with every round of questions R. Kahana lobs at him to which he does not respond, R. Yoḥanan is himself demoted, commensurate with each of R. Kahana's promotions. R. Yoḥanan, by virtue of his stature as head of the yeshiva (and perhaps also his advanced age) had been sitting atop a pile of seven pillows. For each failure to respond to R. Kahana, he loses one pillow, and by the end of the round of questioning, he is seated on the floor, while R. Kahana is promoted to the first of seven rows. In effect, there seems to be a zero-sum game between the two, and their respective statures in the study hall are inversely related. The author of this aggada portrays these two great men, at this stage in their relationship, as in diametric opposition to one another. I will suggest later in this analysis that the issue dividing them may be far more than the merely personal.

It does seem fair to ask how literally we are to take this portion of the story. Is it really possible that someone removed a pillow from under R. Yoḥanan after each encounter with R. Kahana, and that he would be left on the floor?[14] Who would deign to do so to a scholar of R. Yoḥanan's stature and advanced age? Rabbi Judah Leow, the Maharal of Prague, in his commentary to this passage,[15] suggests that the spatial shifts both R. Kahana and R. Yoḥanan undergo are not literal, but rather figurative ways of expressing the shifts in the esteem in which they were held by students in the yeshiva.[16] R. Yoḥanan doesn't literally sink to the floor, but sinks to the floor in the estimation of his students, who now see him as vulnerable. And R. Kahana's movements from first row to

14. While it is possible that R. Yoḥanan removed the pillow himself, that seems far from likely given the esteem in which R. Yoḥanan held himself and his position as head of the yeshiva in particular.
15. *Ḥiddushei Aggadot*, ad loc.
16. This reading is consistent with the Maharal's interpretation of the whole of this aggada, and with his overall approach to aggadic texts.

last row, then back, likewise reflect shifts in the respect other students felt toward him. A figurative reading of the text, at least with respect to R. Yoḥanan, seems to this reader very plausible indeed.

The aggada next informs us of something we did not know. At this stage in R. Yoḥanan's life he was an elderly man, whose eyebrows had grown so long that he was unable to see clearly through them. Thus, he had never even seen this new student from Babylonia who had so effectively humbled him with his penetrating questions. R. Yoḥanan, now sitting on the floor (either literally or figuratively), asks his students to push his eyebrows aside so he can get a better look at his nemesis. The students bring a silver comb for that purpose. What R. Yoḥanan now sees disturbs him greatly, for R. Kahana appears to him with a grin on his face. R. Yoḥanan takes this to be a smirk of mockery, and is deeply offended. This offense in turn causes R. Kahana's death. R. Kahana who killed is now killed himself. The circle closes.

The next morning R. Yoḥanan appears in the study hall and comments to the students about how R. Kahana had mocked him with a smirk. The students respond that this was a misunderstanding. R. Kahana was not smirking, they reported, but rather possessed a split lip,[17] which gave the appearance of a grin.[18] Interestingly, both R. Yoḥanan and R. Kahana are portrayed here as possessing a physical disability: R. Yoḥanan's eyes were occluded, and R. Kahana's mouth was deformed. It has been observed that there may be a deeper, symbolic significance to these disabilities.[19] R. Kahana's challenge has been verbal. Did he possess the ability to keep his mouth closed when such would have been the better choice? R. Yoḥanan's challenge was visual. Was he capable of

17. Rashi suggests here that the split lip was the product of an injury. One wonders if R. Kahana had been involved in other physical altercations like the one described at the beginning of our text.
18. The parallels to the aggada about R. Yoḥanan and Reish Lakish, discussed in chapter 6 of this volume, are striking. In both texts, R. Yoḥanan misunderstands a fellow scholar, and as a result takes great offense, which causes the death of his misunderstood colleague. The same verb to describe R. Yoḥanan's feelings of offense, *ḥalash,* appears in both texts. I argue that in both aggadot the issue at stake is not merely personal affront, but much larger and deeper principles which divide R. Yoḥanan and his interlocutors.
19. Shmuel Faust, *Aggadeta* (Or Yehuda, 2011), 257–58 (Heb.).

seeing through to the true value of R. Kahana and the method of Torah study he so vigorously embodied? Note that the aggada specifies that the students used a silver comb to brush aside R. Yoḥanan's eyebrows. Why mention the silver comb? Is this a further symbol of distance between R. Yoḥanan, who stood at the height of wealth and prestige in the Torah heartland of *Eretz Yisrael*, and an outsider from Babylonia like R. Kahana?

In any case, R. Yoḥanan must confront the devastating truth that he misinterpreted the appearance of R. Kahana's mouth, and therefore was responsible for R. Kahana's death. R. Yoḥanan leaves, immediately it seems, to find the grave of R. Kahana, apparently to seek forgiveness. Thus begins the last and in many ways most enigmatic portion of the aggada.

PART TWO

R. YOḤANAN SEEKS FORGIVENESS AT THE GRAVE OF R. KAHANA

When R. Yoḥanan arrives at R. Kahana's grave, a burial cave, he finds a snake coiled around the entrance, with its tail in its mouth,[20] blocking the way. What is R. Yoḥanan to do? He decides to speak directly with the snake, and asks it to open its mouth and allow the "master to enter and meet his student." The snake does not budge. R. Yoḥanan now reformulates his request, and asks the snake to allow a "colleague to meet a colleague." R. Yoḥanan no longer characterizes his relationship with R. Kahana as master to student, but rather as colleague to colleague, thereby diminishing his own stature and elevating the stature of R. Kahana This too is of no avail. Finally, R. Yoḥanan reformulates the request yet again, this time completely inverting his relationship with R. Kahana: He asks the snake to allow the student to enter and meet his master. R. Yoḥanan is now not R. Kahana's teacher, but his student. The snake accedes to this formulation of the request, and allows R. Yoḥanan to enter. The inversion of their relationship we encountered with R. Kahana's eleva-

20. This follows Rashi's interpretation. The motif of the snake guarding the entrance to a burial cave appears elsewhere in the Talmud, such as in Bava Metzia 84b, in the long and fascinating tale about R. Elazar b. R. Shimon.

tion by seven rows, and R. Yoḥanan's descent to the ground with the loss of seven pillows, is recapitulated at the entrance to the grave. Crucially, at the grave R. Yoḥanan himself articulates and indeed lives that inversion.

The aggada thus suggests that atonement for R. Yoḥanan is conditioned upon his acceptance of his own limitations, and his acknowledgement of the superiority of R. Kahana. Did the author of the aggada mean to take R. Yoḥanan to task for characterizing R. Kahana too harshly as a fox, just a day ago? Who now is the lion and who the fox, who now is the true king of Torah and who the mere fox? This reversal seems to be exactly the point. Interestingly, yet another animal makes a pivotal appearance in the aggada, a snake. The snake forces R. Yoḥanan to revise his estimation of the relative worth of himself and of R. Kahana, to revise his estimation of who the true lion is, and who is the true fox. More specifically, the snake reverses for R. Yoḥanan the symbolic referents of the first two animals, for the snake reveals to R. Yoḥanan that R. Kahana, and not he, is the true lion, and that he, R. Yoḥanan, and not R. Kahana, is the true fox.

It is difficult to avoid recalling the image of the snake in Genesis, who lures Eve into eating of the Tree of Knowledge. The snake in this aggada, too, forced R. Yoḥanan to eat of the Tree of Knowledge – self-knowledge, perhaps the most difficult form of knowledge to acquire. In a sense, this snake too lures, but the power of its seduction derives not from within the snake itself, like the snake in Genesis, but rather from within the snake's interlocutor, R. Yoḥanan. For it was R. Yoḥanan's conscience which drove him to seek entrée into the cave in order to find forgiveness, and thus it was R. Yoḥanan's own conscience which ultimately forced him to concede his limitations. Acknowledgment of those limitations gained him entrée into the inner sanctum of truth and reconciliation. In an ironic twist, the biblical snake seduces into forbidden knowledge, whereas R. Yoḥanan's snake seduces into necessary – if elusive – knowledge, true knowledge of the self.

After R. Yoḥanan enters the cave, he proceeds to resurrect R. Kahana, no mean feat. R. Yoḥanan then tells R. Kahana that had he known of his deformed mouth, he never would have taken offense, and then invites R. Kahana to rejoin him back in the yeshiva for more Torah study. While R. Yoḥanan's ability to resurrect R. Kahana is remarkable enough, perhaps even more remarkable is the invitation he extends to R. Kahana to rejoin him in the study hall. For R. Kahana clearly represents a threat to R. Yoḥanan's authority, and nevertheless R. Yoḥanan seeks his presence. Why would R. Yoḥanan invite the newly crowned lion, the new master, into the study hall that had heretofore been his own domain? Why would he risk once again a dramatic loss of stature, symbolized by the disappearing pillows? Two interrelated reasons suggest themselves. First, to invite R. Kahana back to the study hall is to right the wrong of R. Kahana's mistaken banishment therefrom, by his death. Atonement requires a return to the *status quo ante,* for that is the very meaning of the term *teshuva,* repentance, a return to the sinless past. Second, and this becomes even clearer as the aggada unfolds, R. Yoḥanan came to recognize that he had much to learn from R. Kahana, and earnestly sought his knowledge and insight back in the study hall. This is testimony to R. Yoḥanan's passionate love of Torah, for he was willing to sacrifice his very dignity and station to gain more knowledge. How many of us would be willing to make such sacrifices, and submit to public shame, in order to acquire more knowledge of the Torah?[21]

How does R. Kahana respond to R. Yoḥanan? Unfortunately, the language of the response as recorded in the aggada is somewhat obscure, and Rashi here offers two plausible, if very different interpretations. According to Rashi's first interpretation, which he favors based on evidence from other talmudic sources, R. Kahana refuses to rejoin R. Yoḥanan in the study hall, because he is afraid that he will offend R. Yoḥanan yet again, and be subject, yet again, to death. Rather, following his resurrection, he chooses to return alive not to the study hall, but to his home, where he can live out his years in safety. According to Rashi's second interpretation, R. Kahana refuses resurrection entirely. He has already experienced the pains of death once, and that is more than enough for him, even if his second death were to come at the ripe old age of 120. Thus, R. Kahana chooses death over life. Let us explore the implications of each of these interpretations separately, and for ease

21. This same extraordinary commitment to Torah knowledge and truth emerges in the aggada about R. Yoḥanan and Reish Lakish's death, analyzed in chapter 6 of this volume.

of reference call the first interpretation, "R. Kahana Lives," and the second, "R. Kahana Dies."

According to the first "R. Kahana Lives" interpretation, why does R. Kahana fear returning to the study hall? Because he does not want to take even the slightest risk that he might offend R. Yoḥanan again. This speaks to his apparent conviction that R. Yoḥanan was very sensitive to affronts to his dignity, a theme which emerges in R. Yoḥanan's attitude toward Reish Lakish as well, analyzed and explained in chapter 6 of this volume. Yet it also speaks to R. Kahana's self-knowledge. For he recognizes that given the kind of person he is, and the character traits he possesses, he of all people is unlikely to escape offending R. Yoḥanan. On the one hand, this suggests a certain self-awareness on R. Kahana's part of his own limitations. This may be a sign of moral maturity, as he is not blind to his own flaws. Perhaps this is one of the great lessons R. Kahana takes from this whole unfortunate turn of events. He now knows himself, knows he cannot reform satisfactorily, despite Rav's explicit instructions to him back in Babylonia after he kills the miscreant man, and abandons hope of reentering R. Yoḥanan's study hall.

On the other hand, why can't R. Kahana change? Why can't he undergo the moral reform necessary to be a productive member of the great R. Yoḥanan's yeshiva? Contrast his status with that of R. Yoḥanan. R. Yoḥanan undergoes a deep moral change. He accepts his failure, seeks atonement, acknowledges R. Kahana's superiority, and, at great potential personal cost, invites R. Kahana back into the study hall. This is deeply impressive, and no doubt part of the lesson the author of the aggada wished to convey to his readers. R. Kahana, on the other hand, finds himself to be incapable of making the requisite changes necessary to accommodate R. Yoḥanan's sensitivities. In the end, despite Rav's best efforts in sending R. Kahana on a mission of self-reform, complete reform was not attained, even if greater self-knowledge was.

Rashi's second interpretation, "R. Kahana Dies," is more difficult to understand. Why exactly does R. Kahana choose to remain in his grave? This is even more puzzling if we take the aggada at its word, that R. Kahana was resurrected. For does R. Kahana mean to remain in the grave alive? How would he survive? Moreover, if he is alive, then at some point he will die, so how then is he avoiding a second death? And if he is dead, then what is the meaning of the aggada's statement that R. Yoḥanan awakened him? If he is dead, how then does R. Yoḥanan speak with him? Is R. Kahana in some liminal state, between death and life? Later in this chapter I will attempt to answer some of these questions, but for now it is worth observing that R. Kahana on this second interpretation of Rashi appears resigned to his death. This seems unlike the combative, aggressive R. Kahana of yore. Does this mean that R. Kahana has, in fact, evolved as result of his recent experiences, that he is more willing to accept his circumstances, to remain quiet forevermore in the grave? After all, in choosing to remain alone in the burial cave, he will never again be able to engage in the fertile combat of Torah study. Does he thus recognize the great cost of his aggressive style, for which reason he chooses to stay in the grave? It is difficult to say with any certainty. Rashi himself writes that R. Kahana was afraid of the pain of a second death. This may mean the pain of his behavior, whose repercussions led to his death, or the pain of the dying process itself.

However we are to understand R. Kahana's opaque response to R. Yoḥanan's offer, what happens next is fascinating. R. Yoḥanan awakens R. Kahana,[22] and proceeds to barrage him with a battery of questions, representing every uncertainty he possessed about Torah. R. Kahana in turn proceeds to answer each and every question. This is a brilliant inversion of their original roles. Just a day ago it was R. Kahana the student who had assaulted R. Yoḥanan the master with a battery of questions. In the space of a day their roles are wholly reversed, and now it is R. Yoḥanan the student who assaults R. Kahana the master with a battery of questions. R. Yoḥanan indeed meant what he said when, seeking admission to the cave, he asked the snake to allow the student – himself – to meet the master – R. Kahana. R. Yoḥanan thus fully accepts his status as student, asks all his questions of R. Kahana, and is a changed man with respect to his relationship with his erstwhile student and now master, R. Kahana. Of course, a key difference between the two episodes is that R. Yoḥanan failed to answer R. Kahana's questions, while R. Kahana succeeds in answering R. Yoḥanan's questions. The turnabout is complete.

22. Why would R. Kahana need awakening, if he has already been resuscitated? I shall return to this question below.

R. Kahana, even in a state of quasi-death, remains a source of knowledge to his now student and erstwhile master, R. Yoḥanan, although R. Yoḥanan remains very much alive.

This, then, is a tragic end to R. Kahana's life, on the second interpretation of Rashi, the "R. Kahana Dies" interpretation. Except for those precious moments when R. Yoḥanan asks R. Kahana every question he has, R. Kahana's formidable mastery of Torah remains lost for all time, interred with him in the cave. Ironically, R. Kahana is the great master, yet his Torah is lost in the death that he himself chose. R. Yoḥanan is the humbled student, yet he continues to teach even after R. Kahana's death, his Torah alive to the many students who flock to study under his wings. Perhaps the author of this aggada meant to teach that Torah brilliance alone does not bequeath to its possessor a living Torah. What then does? Apart from sheer mastery, what yields a living Torah are the virtues R. Yoḥanan embodied at the end of this story: humility, the capacity to evolve and grow, to change and improve, to admit the truth and, despite great personal cost, seek reconciliation and atonement.

Following the telling of this tale, the aggada concludes with an epigrammatic comment: "This is what R. Yoḥanan said, 'You think the Torah I taught was yours, residents of *Eretz Yisrael*? Well it was not. It was the Torah of Babylonia.'" I shall return to the significance of this addendum to the story at the conclusion of the chapter, but before doing so I wish to consider the broader contours of the enigmatic concluding portion of the aggada which we have just analyzed. Did R. Yoḥanan really resurrect R. Kahana? Was R. Kahana really dead, or was he alive? According to Rashi's second interpretation, "R. Kahana Dies," he seems to live in some liminal state between life and death. What is that? Was there really a living, breathing snake, who literally understood R. Yoḥanan's speech? Why would the snake know what was necessary for R. Yoḥanan's atonement? Overall, I think it is fair to say there is a surreal quality to the story.

Of course, some may nevertheless wish to interpret this aggada literally, and that is a time-honored tradition in the reading of aggadic materials.[23] However, Maimonides argues in his commentary to the

23. See Saperstein, *Decoding the Rabbis*, 1–21, for a survey of post-talmudic attitudes toward aggada.

Mishna, in his "Introduction to *Perek Ḥelek*," introducing the tenth chapter of Sanhedrin, that those who interpret the parables of the Talmud literally when they are inconsistent with what we know to be true of the world are foolish, since some aggadic texts "seem so fantastic and irrational that if one were to repeat them literally, even to the uneducated, let alone to sophisticated scholars, their amazement would prompt them to ask how anyone in the world could believe such things true, let alone edifying."[24] Literal readers of such aggadic sources "destroy the glory of the Torah and extinguish its light."[25] He goes on to argue that this literalist approach leads the more sophisticated reader to question the value of rabbinic teachings, and the intelligence of the rabbis themselves. Thus, for example, a contemporary reader might suggest that some aggadic narratives are no more than charming folk tales. This overall approach Maimonides found untenable, and he chose to read many aggadic teachings as parables of deeper philosophic truths.

The Maharal, in his commentary here, applies the same allegorical method of reading aggada that we saw previously (which is the hallmark of his approach to aggada generally). The reading I shall suggest – and it is no more than a suggestion – is, like the Maharal's, a non-literal one, but, unlike the Maharal's, is not allegorical. Rather, it has its hermeneutic origins in one geonic approach to the aggada, and several great medieval rabbinic authorities who follow in the footsteps of Maimonides himself.[26] The earliest source is Rav Hai Gaon, living in Babylonia in the tenth to eleventh centuries, followed by Rabbi Abraham, the son of Maimonides, of the twelfth to thirteenth centuries and later, the Ritva (Rabbi Yom Tov Asevilli), the Spanish thirteenth- to fourteenth-century commentator on the Talmud and student of the Rashba (Rabbi Shlomo ben Aderet). All three reflect a more rationalist reading of aggadic sources.

Beginning with the latest of the three sources, the Ritva was confronted with a long string of aggadot in Bava Batra 73a describing the remarkable experiences of various talmudic Sages while traveling in the

24. See Isidore Twersky, *A Maimonides Reader* (New Jersey, 1972), 407–10.

25. Ibid.

26. We already saw one source from the medieval era apply this approach in chapter 2.

sea, including frogs the size of a fort, antelopes the size of a mountain, a bird tall enough to reach the sky, and so on. What is one to make of these tales? Various classical sources have struggled with their meaning. The Ritva writes: "In the episodes of this chapter, there are many things strange to people with which they are unfamiliar, but are better understood (lit., "nearer") to those with more knowledge.... There are also in these stories allusions, and the events described as what they saw did not actually appear to their eyes, but appeared to them in a dream. This is because when the Sages traveled in the great sea they saw the wonders of God. When they were there [at sea] they sat alone and thought about the awesome sights they saw, and when they went to sleep there appeared to them like thoughts about wondrous things which teach about the matter."[27] Thus the Ritva takes at least some of these tales to be dreams which "are allusions," which possess a deeper meaning, "which teach about the matter."

Likewise, Rabbi Abraham, the son of Maimonides, in an extensive discussion of aggada which offers an important hermeneutic methodology for interpreting such texts, writes about some of the aggada: "There are episodes described that appeared [to the Sage in question] in a dream. They are written in a clear and simple fashion [i.e., as if they describe events that took place in the real world] because it is impossible that any person with intelligence and understanding would take them as literally having taken place [and therefore no person with intelligence and understanding would ever interpret them literally].... Someone whose heart is not with him will think that these things took place in the world as described, and he will come to think and believe that something which is impossible must be accepted as true. But all this occurs because of the preponderance of his foolishness, and his minimal understanding of the natural world."[28]

Here Rabbi Abraham may have been drawing on the views of his own father, who wrote in his *Commentary to the Mishna* that he planned to write a future work in which he would explicate the puzzling teachings of the Sages, in which he would "explain which are to be taken literally,

27. This is quoted extensively by the *HaKotev* commentary to the *Ein Yaakov*. The translation here is mine.

28. "Essay on the *Derashot* of the Rabbis," published in the beginning of *Ein Yaakov* (Jerusalem, 2008), 29. The translation here is mine.

which are parables, and which occurred in a dream, but were recounted straightforwardly, as if they took place while awake."[29]

Finally, the earliest of the sources is Rav Hai Gaon, who struggled to interpret an aggada which describes a dialogue between R. Bibi b. Abaye and the Angel of Death, in which R. Bibi b. Abaye challenges the behavior of the Angel of Death, who brought death to an undeserving person.[30] Rav Hai Gaon offers a number of possible interpretations of this aggada, among them: "It is possible that this episode appeared to R. Bibi b. Abaye in a dream, like many people relate what they saw in their dreams."[31]

All these medieval authorities are thus willing to interpret at least some fantastical events described in the Talmud as occurring in dreams. As I argued above, the concluding portion of our own aggada surely possesses fantastical elements. In the footsteps of these authorities, then, I would like to suggest that at least one way to read this last phase of our aggada is that it occurred in a dream, or, more precisely, that the *author of the aggada may have wished the reader interpret the story he tells as occurring to R. Yoḥanan in a dream*. Did R. Yoḥanan actually dream what the story tells? The medieval commentators cited above, if they were to apply their method to this text (which is, of course, an open question) would have said yes. Alternatively, the author of the aggada may have chosen to portray events as if they took place in a dream, whether or not R. Yoḥanan actually dreamt them. On this more literary reading, the author was not writing what he took to be a literally true rendition of events in the lives of R. Yoḥanan and R. Kahana, at least with respect to this part of the aggada.[32] In any case, the text does not announce that the events took place in a dream. However, the author,

29. Y. Shilat, *Introductions to Maimonides's Commentaries to the Mishnah* (Jerusalem, 2006), 140 (Heb.). Translation here is mine.

30. Ḥagiga 4b. See also Z. H. Chayes, *Mevo HaTalmud: The Student's Guide to the Talmud*, trans. Jacob Schachter (London: East and West Library, 1952), ch. 28, for a fuller discussion of these sources.

31. *Teshuvot HaGeonim*, ed. Abraham Harkavy (Berlin, 1887), 122, no. 245.

32. See chapter 8, on Ḥoni the miracle worker, for a similar analysis and discussion. Throughout the remainder of the chapter I will write as if R. Yoḥanan did actually dream, but my analysis would apply to both possibilities, which I leave to the reader to choose between.

like many throughout literary history, may have chosen to communicate by allusion and indirection, to provoke the reader to tease out the many deeper meanings of the text.

Now, I do not mean to argue that this is the only way to read the concluding enigmatic portion of this aggada, but that it is one way to read it, a reading which, I would argue, has considerable merit, for three reasons. First, it responds to Maimonides's overall argument about the value of reading difficult aggadas as teaching deeper truths, enabling the more rationalist reader to plumb its depths. Second, as we shall see, it provides a fertile framework for explaining some of the nuances, difficulties, and richness found in the text. Third and finally, it is a reading which makes good psychological sense. Would a person responsible for the death of an innocent man not be troubled enough to dream about it?

This last point explains why R. Yoḥanan would have been depicted as having such a dream, and what its deeper significance, its "allusion" – the *remez*, in the words of the Ritva – might be. At one level, as noted, it would not be surprising if R. Yoḥanan did dream about seeking atonement from the man for whose death he was wrongly responsible. What moral person would not be acutely troubled by his role in the death of an innocent person, and especially the death of a great Torah scholar at that, troubled to the point that it disturbs his dreams? Death, after all, is (at least typically) irreversible. Thus, R. Yoḥanan desperately seeks out R. Kahana in a dream to beg for reconciliation and atonement. In his dream, he encounters a snake, that great symbol of primal sin, who forces him to confront his own failures, and accept the true value of R. Kahana's Torah. Only in his dream, unlike while fully awake, could he confront the true superiority of R. Kahana, and face the true scope of his personal limitations.

However, R. Yoḥanan does not fully succeed in achieving reconciliation in his dream, because in it R. Kahana refuses to leave the grave, or even if he agrees to leave it (depending upon which interpretation of Rashi one follows), he will not return to R. Yoḥanan's yeshiva. This at least partial failure reflects R. Yoḥanan's most acute inner fear, that forgiveness and reconciliation would forever elude his grasp. On this reading of the aggada, the puzzling inner logic of R. Kahana's status in the cave that so troubles the reader is just a feature of dreams in which mundane logic of course rarely holds, as is the very opacity of R. Kahana's response with which Rashi struggled. In the end, R. Yoḥanan dreams that he draws as much Torah knowledge as he possibly can from R. Kahana, asking him all the Torah questions he has. Even though in the dream R. Kahana refuses fully to reconcile with R. Yoḥanan and rejoin his yeshiva or return to life, R. Yoḥanan dreams that he can still attempt to make amends. How? He can still acknowledge the Torah greatness of R. Kahana, and thereby invest R. Kahana with eternal life – in R. Yoḥanan's own lived world of Torah.

Thus, we might say that in his dream, R. Yoḥanan ultimately succeeds in "resurrecting" R. Kahana, by seeking the dead man's Torah, which now illuminates the life of the living. This dream-like quasi-resurrection embodies the success, even if only partial, of R. Yoḥanan's deepest inner desire to repent and reconcile. Likewise, the meaning of R. Kahana's refusal to return to R. Yoḥanan's yeshiva, discussed at length above, may be an expression of an aspect of R. Yoḥanan's complex inner struggles. For, from R. Yoḥanan's perspective, might not R. Kahana have himself been at least partially at fault in this whole episode? How much self-knowledge did R. Kahana ultimately achieve? R. Yoḥanan dreams of his own inner transformations, but what does R. Yoḥanan think about R. Kahana? Did R. Kahana bear any responsibility for the aggressiveness with which he questioned Reish Lakish and then R. Yoḥanan? And did R. Kahana recognize his own limitations and failures, or did he simply deny them, never evolving beyond his initial persona? As we saw, Rashi wasn't certain, nor, in our analysis above, were we. That too may reflect the ambiguity which characterizes the very dream state itself.

On this reading, utilizing the hermeneutic framework of a dream provides a compelling explanation of so many of the puzzling, fantastical features of the aggada, and speaks to R. Yoḥanan's powerful conscience, and to his determination to make amends.

I would like to suggest, however, that here is yet another dimension to the cave sequence of this aggada, which extends beyond the interpersonal conflict between R. Yoḥanan and R. Kahana and echoes onto the broad canvas of Jewish history. Let us recall the concluding epigraph to this aggada, the quote from R. Yoḥanan: "What I said was yours was in fact theirs." The Torah that I taught you, he means to say, ultimately derives from the Torah not of *Eretz Yisrael*, but of Babylonia. In other words, R. Yoḥanan was saying, "I always thought that the Torah of *Eretz Yisrael* was superior, but I learned so much from R. Kahana, who was educated in Babylonia, that I now see that Torah authority resides there, not in *Eretz Yisrael*."

Consider that Rav, the teacher of R. Kahana, was a student of R. Yehuda HaNasi, the compiler of the Mishna, when he was in *Eretz Yisrael* before relocating to Babylonia. R. Yoḥanan likewise was R. Yehuda HaNasi's student, although far junior to Rav (he died some twenty-five years after Rav did), but he remained in *Eretz Yisrael*. Following R. Yehuda HaNasi's death, R. Yoḥanan eventually became his heir to Torah leadership in *Eretz Yisrael* as head of its leading yeshiva in Tiberias. Rav, upon his arrival in Babylonia, established a preeminent Torah center in the southern Babylonian city of Sura. His colleague, the great Babylonian Sage Shmuel, who was based in the northern Babylonian city of Neharde'a, was a second leading Torah scholar in Babylonia, and heir to the Torah scholarship in Babylonia that preceded him. Rav, Shmuel, and R. Yoḥanan were the three towering teachers of Torah in their generation. In effect, then, there were two competing centers of Torah during that time period, *Eretz Yisrael*, led by R. Yoḥanan, and Babylonia, led by Rav and Shmuel. Which center would become preeminent? Where would the best students choose to study? Who had the authority to issue halakhic rulings for Jews wherever they lived? Who would determine when the new moon arrived, thereby controlling the calendar and the timing of the Jewish holidays?[33] For economic reasons, Jewish life was under great

33. See Berakhot 63a–b for the story of Ḥananya, who left *Eretz Yisrael* for Babylonia, then attempted to control the calendar for Babylonian Jews from Babylonia, wresting universal authority over the calendar from the authorities in *Eretz Yisrael*. The reaction of the authorities in *Eretz Yisrael* to Ḥananya was harsh indeed. This tension is a theme in the epistle of Pirkoi ben Baboi, discussed in B. Brody, *The Geonim of Babylonia and the Shaping of Medieval Jewish Culture* (New Haven and London, 1998), 113ff.

stress then in *Eretz Yisrael,* while Babylonia flourished economically, and in Torah scholarship, under the leadership of Rav and Shmuel. Recall that *Eretz Yisrael* had always been the preeminent source of Torah authority, going back to the Sanhedrin which sat in Jerusalem. "For Torah will emerge from Zion," from Israel, goes the biblical verse.[34] Yet powerhouse Babylonia emerged as a threat to this hegemony, a threat not only to R. Yoḥanan's yeshiva, and to R. Yoḥanan's personal authority, but to the time-hallowed centrality of *Eretz Yisrael* in Jewish life, which all Jews held dear, and especially those resident in the Holy Land itself.[35] Could *Eretz Yisrael* hold as the universal center of Torah study, or would it lose its power to Babylonia?

Among the differences between Torah scholarship in Babylonia and *Eretz Yisrael* was the style of study. The Talmud records this teaching from R. Oshaya, a slightly older colleague of Rav's:

> This demonstrates what **Rabbi Oshaya says: What** is the meaning of that **which is written: "And I took for myself two staves; the one I called Graciousness, and the other I called Binders"** (Zechariah 11:7)? **"Graciousness"; these are** the **Torah scholars in *Eretz Yisrael,* who are gracious to one another in** discussions of *halakha.* They treat each other with honor and love, as demonstrated in the statements of Reish Lakish and Rabbi Yehuda HaNasi. **"Binders [*ḥovelim*]"; these are** the **Torah scholars in Babylonia, who injure [*meḥabbelim*] each other in** discussions of *halakha,* i.e., they speak harshly to each other when they disagree. Similarly, it is stated: **"Then he said to me: These are the two anointed ones, that stand** by the Lord of the whole earth" (Zechariah 4:14), and it is stated: **"And two olive trees by it,** one upon the right side of the bowl, and the other upon its left side" (Zechariah 4:3). With regard to the expression **"anointed ones," Rabbi Yitzḥak says: These are** the **Torah scholars in *Eretz Yisrael,* who are pleasant to each other in** discussions of *halakha* **like**

34. Isaiah 2:3, Micah 4:2.

35. See Lau, *The Sages,* vol. 4, 123–239, for a review of the intellectual history of this period and the differences between Rav, Shmuel, and R. Yoḥanan.

> **olive oil,** which is not bitter. The verse **"and two olive trees by it"** should be interpreted as follows: **These are** the **Torah scholars in Babylonia, who are bitter to each other in** discussions of *halakha* **like an olive.**[36]

Both these teachings, apparently authored by scholars from *Eretz Yisrael*,[37] contrast the style of Torah study between *Eretz Yisrael* and Babylonia, and favor the former while implicitly criticizing the latter. The scholars of *Eretz Yisrael* are portrayed as collegial, friendly, and mutually supportive, even in their own use of the dialectical style of talmudic study. They cooperate to ascertain matters of halakha, without attacking one another even when they disagree. The scholars of Babylonia, on the other hand, are portrayed as aggressive, attacking one another when they disagree, bitter as olives in their combat. R. Kahana exemplifies this Babylonian style brilliantly when he arrives in *Eretz Yisrael*, with his relentless attack on both Reish Lakish and R. Yoḥanan, preeminent leaders of the *Eretz Yisrael* style of Torah study.[38]

It would hardly be surprising if R. Yoḥanan affirmed this way of looking at the Babylonians,[39] and saw in R. Kahana not merely a personal threat to his authority as head of the yeshiva, but as an avatar of the ascendancy of the Babylonian style of Torah study, and the consequent

---

36. Sanhedrin 24a.
37. R. Oshaya lived and taught in *Eretz Yisrael*. It is not altogether clear which R. Yitzḥak the Talmud here cites, one being a member of R. Yoḥanan's circle in *Eretz Yisrael* (the more probable identification), the other a slightly earlier figure who may have been born in Babylonia, but then moved to *Eretz Yisrael* to study Torah, where his allegiance lay. See M. Margoliyot, *Encyclopedia of the Sages of the Talmud and Gaonim* (Tel Aviv, 1962), vol. 2, 577–79 (Heb.).
38. Interestingly, as we saw in chapter 6, Reish Lakish himself was somewhat combative in his Torah study, not unlike the Babylonians, although in his case that likely reflected his own personality.
39. For example, the Talmud (Menaḥot 100a) cites a teaching of R. Yoḥanan, that Jews from *Eretz Yisrael* actually hated the Babylonians. *Tosafot* there, s.v. *shesonim*, explain that this is because they did not move to *Eretz Yisrael* as followers of Ezra, although another explanation suggests itself too, as emerges in our discussion. R. Yoḥanan also remarked derogatorily to a Babylonian that "while you were eating berries in Babylonia we explained [a particular verse] based upon the latter clause of the Mishna" (Bekhorot 18a).

ascendancy of Babylonia as a competing center of Torah authority. Note the phrase "A lion ascended from Babylonia" in describing R. Kahana's arrival. Why stress R. Kahana's origins? And when he explains R. Kahana's death to his students, why does he not mention his name? R. Yoḥanan asks, "Did you see how that Babylonian behaved?" For R. Yoḥanan, R. Kahana once again was no more than his Babylonian origins. Why? Perhaps because his origins are crucial to understanding the broader challenge R. Kahana represented to R. Yoḥanan and his yeshiva: the shift in Torah authority – the "lion" – from *Eretz Yisrael* to Babylonia. R. Yoḥanan, deeply loyal to the ancient traditions of *Eretz Yisrael* Torah centrality, going back to the Holy Temple and Sanhedrin, would have been disturbed by this potential Babylonian displacement. R. Yehuda HaNasi, great codifier of the Mishna and leader of the Jewish community in *Eretz Yisrael*, had bequeathed all Jewry with a canon of Oral Law, and it was up to his successors in *Eretz Yisrael* to apply and interpret it. Allowing Torah authority to slip from the sacred land, from the home of the Sanhedrin, the home of R. Yehuda HaNasi, would have been acutely troubling, if not utterly sacrilegious, to R. Yehuda HaNasi's successor, R. Yoḥanan. And to allow it to slip into the hands of relative newcomers to serious Torah scholarship, the combative, argumentative, "bitter" Babylonians – powerfully exemplified by none other than R. Kahana – would have been even more disturbing. Is it at all surprising, then, that the author of the aggada would have R. Yoḥanan dream about this fear, especially given the personal background described above? Thus, if we are to interpret the grave sequence as a dream, it reflects two layers of anxiety on the part of R. Yoḥanan. The first is purely personal, deriving from R. Yoḥanan's role in R. Kahana's untimely death. The second layer of anxiety is about the ascension of Babylonia as the center of Torah authority over *Eretz Yisrael*, R. Yoḥanan's home and the location of his yeshiva. Each level of anxiety reinforced and intensified the other.

As disturbing as the ascension of Babylonia might have been to R. Yoḥanan, in fact Jewish history bore out his worst fears. R. Yoḥanan was prescient. Torah authority did eventually come to rest with the Babylonians, for all the remainder of Jewish history. It is the Babylonian Talmud, not the Jerusalem Talmud, that shaped Jewish life for over one and a half millennia, the Babylonian Talmud and not the Jerusalem

Talmud which drove the development of halakha, the Babylonian Talmud and not the Jerusalem Talmud which is studied to this day with utmost diligence in yeshivos around the world. The Babylonian Talmud, with its fiery debates and extensive detail, contrasts with the much shorter, more irenic Jerusalem Talmud, reflecting those ancient differences between the Babylonian and *Eretz Yisrael* styles of Torah study.

But is it fair to ask if there was any merit to the Babylonian style? Is it not possible that their combative, argumentative approach to Torah study clarified ideas, and illuminated otherwise obscure issues? The give-and-take, the constant repartee and parrying of arguments, the intense criticism and dialectic, may well have sharpened wits and ideas, and contributed to the flourishing of Torah knowledge. I would suggest that this is the deeper meaning to the concluding statement of the aggada, in which R. Yoḥanan is quoted as saying that Torah is not the province of those from *Eretz Yisrael*, but of those from Babylonia. R. Yoḥanan poses to R. Kahana all the Torah questions he has, because he has come to recognize, in the dream, that it is the brilliance of the Babylonian dialectical style, not that of *Eretz Yisrael*, which will provide for the future of Torah in a world changing under their very eyes.[40] *Eretz Yisrael* scholars, exemplified by R. Yoḥanan himself, are the students seeking entrée into the study hall of the Babylonian masters, the mystery of the cave, entrée into the hidden, complex, sinuous, controverted, and ever-argued universe of Babylonian Torah. In the end, R. Yoḥanan can never truly kill R. Kahana, can never kill the Babylonian method, for it would live on forever, a source of Torah for all time to come.[41]

40. This realization late in life by R. Yoḥanan of the value of Babylonian-style dialectics is likely reflected in the torment R. Yoḥanan feels over the death of Reish Lakish discussed in chapter 6 of this volume. Reish Lakish apparently had a Babylonian-style combativeness in his relationship with R. Yoḥanan, which R. Yoḥanan only fully appreciates after Reish Lakish's tragic death. In both aggadas, R. Yoḥanan must come to terms with an approach to Torah study which he finds distasteful, but whose merits he must come to acknowledge.

41. It is worth observing that this account of the deserved rise of Torah scholarship and authority in Babylonia over *Eretz Yisrael* is told in the Babylonian, but not Jerusalem, Talmud.

Chapter 8

Ḥoni Sleeps: Carob Trees, Dreams, and the Passage of Time

Taanit 23a

INTRODUCTION

This aggada, now popularized far outside the circle of those who study Talmud, tells the fantastical story of a great miracle worker by the name of Ḥoni[1] who meets a man planting a carob tree which takes seventy years to bear fruit. This puzzles Ḥoni, who cannot understand why anyone would invest so much time and effort on a project from which he will not personally benefit, a perspective sharply rejected by the farmer himself. While this is the most famous part of the story, in reality it is

1. He is often called in the Talmud by his full title, Ḥoni HaMe'aggel. The most common translation of "HaMe'aggel" is "Circle Maker," after the story recorded in Mishna Taanit 3:4, according to which Ḥoni draws a circle in the ground around himself and threatens never to leave it unless God brings rain. Other possibilities include that it was the name of the town he came from, or that it derived from his profession as a wheel maker.

embedded in a longer, very rich and complex tale whose theme is sleep and the passage of time, which in turn is itself embedded in another series of tales about Ḥoni. Just who was Ḥoni the miracle worker, and why does he sleep for seventy years? Why does no one recognize him after he awakens, or take him in, even his own grandchildren? Why does he fail to understand the value of planting trees for future generations? Finally, why at the end of the story does Ḥoni pray – successfully – for his own death? The story, or at least the first part of it, is told several centuries after the events it describes took place, by R. Yoḥanan, one of the great talmudic rabbis whose life and times were the subject of the first three chapters of this book. The theme of loss so resonant in the chapter on the death of Reish Lakish and R. Yoḥanan emerges in this chapter as well. Just as R. Yoḥanan could not survive the loss of Reish Lakish, so too Ḥoni could not survive the loss of relationships that mattered deeply to him. In this respect the theme of the story echoes into the tragic life of its very author, R. Yoḥanan.

Taanit 23a

אמר ר׳ יוחנן כל ימיו של אותו צדיק היה מצטער על מקרא זה (תהלים קכו, א) שיר המעלות בשוב ה׳ את שיבת ציון היינו כחולמים אמר מי איכא דניים שבעין שנין בחלמא.

The Gemara relates another story about Ḥoni HaMe'aggel. **Rabbi Yoḥanan said: All the days** of the life **of that righteous man,** Ḥoni, **he was distressed over** the meaning of **this verse: "A song of Ascents: When the Lord brought back those who returned to Zion, we were like those who dream"** (Psalms 126:1). **He said** to himself: **Is there** really a person **who can sleep and dream for seventy years?** How is it possible to compare the seventy-year exile in Babylonia to a dream?

יומא חד הוה אזל באורחא חזייה להוא גברא דהוה נטע חרובא אמר ליה האי עד כמה שנין טעין אמר ליה עד שבעין שנין אמר ליה פשיטא לך דחיית שבעין שנין אמר ליה האי [גברא] עלמא בחרובא אשכחתיה כי היכי דשתלי לי אבהתי שתלי נמי לבראי.

One day, he was walking along the road when **he saw a certain man planting a carob tree.** Ḥoni **said to him: This** tree, **after how many years** will it **bear** fruit? The man **said to him:** It will not produce fruit **until seventy years** have passed. Ḥoni **said to him: Is it obvious to you that you will live seventy years,** that you expect to benefit from this tree? **He said to him: That man** himself **found a world** full **of carob trees. Just as my ancestors planted for me, I too am planting for my descendants.**

יתיב קא כריך ריפתא אתא ליה שינתא נים אהדרא ליה משוניתא איכסי מעינא ונים שבעין שנין כי קם חזייה לההוא גברא דהוה קא מלקט מינייהו אמר ליה את הוא דשתלתיה א"ל בר בריה אנא אמר ליה שמע מינה דניימי שבעין שנין חזא לחמריה דאתיילידא ליה רמכי רמכי.

Ḥoni **sat and ate bread. Sleep overcame him and he slept. A cliff formed around him, and he disappeared from sight and slept for seventy years. When he awoke, he saw a certain man gathering** carobs from that tree. Ḥoni **said to him:** Are **you the one who planted** this tree? The man **said to him: I am his son's son.** Ḥoni **said to him:** I can **learn from this that I** have **slept for seventy years,** and indeed **he saw that his donkey had sired several herds** during those many years.

אזל לביתיה אמר להו בריה דחוני המעגל מי קיים אמרו ליה בריה ליתא בר בריה איתא אמר להו אנא חוני המעגל לא הימנוהו אזל לבית המדרש שמעינהו לרבנן דקאמרי נהירן שמעתתין כבשני חוני המעגל דכי הוי עייל לבית מדרשא כל קושיא דהוו להו לרבנן הוה מפרק להו אמר להו אנא ניהו לא הימנוהו ולא עבדי ליה יקרא כדמבעי ליה חלש דעתיה בעי רחמי ומית אמר רבא היינו דאמרי אינשי או חברותא או מיתותא.

Ḥoni **went home and said to** the members of the household: **Is the son of Ḥoni HaMe'aggel alive? They said to him: His son is no** longer with us, but **his son's son is** alive. **He said to them: I am Ḥoni HaMe'aggel. They did not believe him. He went to the study hall,** where he **heard the Sages say** about one scholar: **His *halakhot* are as enlightening** and as clear **as in the years of**

Ḥoni HaMe'aggel, for when Ḥoni HaMe'aggel **would enter the study hall he would resolve for the Sages any difficulty they had.** Ḥoni **said to them: I am he, but they did not believe him and did not pay him proper respect.** Ḥoni **became very upset, prayed for mercy, and died. Rava said: This** explains the folk saying **that people say: Either friendship or death,** as one who has no friends is better off dead.

PART ONE

ḤONI SLEEPS FOR SEVENTY YEARS

R. Yoḥanan reports that Ḥoni, whom he describes as a righteous man, was troubled all his life by a verse in Psalms, which reads, "A song of ascents: When God brought back those that returned to Zion, we were like those that dream" (Ps. 126:1). Now this is a reference to the return of the Jews to Israel seventy years following the destruction of the First Temple and the sacking of Jerusalem. The author of this chapter of Psalms asserts that those seventy years of exile were like a dream, an assertion which troubled Ḥoni. Dreams take place only while sleeping, and, he wondered, how can one sleep for seventy years? To him, the verse made little sense.

The question, of course, is what is Ḥoni's question? The verse itself reads that exile was not a dream proper, requiring sleep, but "like a dream." The dream state is thus a simile, and the text means to say that exile may be compared to a dream-like existence, lacking the reality of life itself. Surely this is the simple reading of the text. Why then does Ḥoni insist on reading the text not as a simile, but as an assertion that during the seventy years of exile Jews were literally sleeping and dreaming? It is a reading which renders the text nonsensical. After all, can people sleep for seventy years? Before attempting to answer this question, let us follow the narrative along.

Ḥoni is traveling down a road one day when he encounters a man planting a carob tree, whereupon he asks him how long it takes for a carob tree to bear fruit. The man responds that it takes a full seventy years. Ḥoni then asks the man if he expects to live another seventy years, the minimum necessary for him to benefit personally from the arduous labors of planting and tending to the tree. The man responds that just as he found a world graced with fruit-bearing carob trees because his ancestors planted them for future generations, so too he would plant a tree for his own children and their descendants.

On the face of it, this is a charming tale expressing the principle that each generation must look after not only its own selfish interests, but also after the interests of future generations as well. The significance of that message has not been lost on Jewish environmentalists, for example, who have contributed much to the popularization of this tale, nor has it been lost on those who encourage or engage in philanthropic endeavors. Yet this reading, while not wrong, is also not complete, for it fails to take into account what I think is an important question: Just what was Ḥoni himself thinking? Let us remember that Ḥoni lived in an agricultural society, and in a region where carob trees were common. It is highly improbable that he did not know how long it took for a carob tree to bear fruit. Analogously, how many homeowners today do not know how long it takes for a typical mortgage to mature? Rather, his question was likely rhetorical, and what he really meant to do was challenge the planter of the tree, as if to say: "Why would you even consider planting a carob tree, since you know you will not live to see its fruits?"

This interpretation makes Ḥoni's position even more puzzling, perhaps even troubling. Why would it not even occur to Ḥoni that it might be a good thing to care for future generations? Was Ḥoni so self-centered that he couldn't imagine a person providing for his children? Do not parents frequently sacrifice much to enable their children to succeed? As we shall see, Ḥoni is depicted by the Talmud as a holy man. Is holiness consistent with such egotism?

The story continues, and eventually seems to lose its grip on reality. After Ḥoni hears the man's response to his question (or challenge), Ḥoni eats a meal, and promptly falls asleep. That in itself is not remarkable, but what follows is remarkable indeed. First, an outcropping of rocks rises up and hides him from view, and then he sleeps for a total of seventy years. This is hardly the typical post-prandial nap. Why the miracle of the metastasizing rocks? When he awakens, he observes a man who looks like the planter of the tree eating of its fruit. When he asks the man if he planted the tree, he is told that it was not he but his grandfather who planted the tree. From this comment, Ḥoni deduces that he has miraculously slept for seventy years! He then observes that people can indeed sleep for seventy years, and, the author of the aggada implies, the verse that so troubled him in Psalms should now not trouble him at all. Thus, Ḥoni's miraculous sleep is adduced to resolve for him the verse in Psalms. But how does it? Just because Ḥoni slept a miraculous seventy years, does that mean that the whole of the Jewish people fell into a miraculous sleep of seventy years? The author of the aggada seems to take Ḥoni's sleep literally, and then applies it to Ḥoni's puzzle about the Jewish people. But does it make sense to apply it literally to the whole of the Jewish people? How has Ḥoni's problem with his willfully literal reading of the verse been solved by the lesson taken from this literal reading of his sleep? Moreover, why doesn't Ḥoni comment on what appears to be the central moral of the story? The farmer's lesson to Ḥoni turns out to be valid, for the farmer's own grandchild eats from the fruit of his labors.[2]

Before attempting to answer these many questions, let us continue its storyline. We have seen that following his awakening, Ḥoni encounters a man eating the fruits of the carob tree. That is the first of four encounters which take place following his sleep. He next meets up with his donkey who, it turns out, has sired several herds of donkeys during the seventy years of his sleep. Several questions emerge: How could his donkey have lived for seventy years, well more than twice the lifespan of a typical donkey? In addition, why does the author of the aggada point out the fecundity of the donkey? How is it germane to the tale and its message? Of course, it is possible that this fact reinforces the reality of

2. This question is central to Jeffrey Rubenstein's source-critical analysis of this aggada, in *Stories of the Babylonian Talmud* (Baltimore, 2010), 64ff. Yonah Frankel attempts to read the text in a unitary fashion, in "Paronomasia in Aggadic Narratives," *Scripta Hierosolymitana* 27 (1978): 27–51. I follow Frankel here in a unitary reading, but veer sharply from his analysis. The reading he proposes envisions Ḥoni as self-centered and selfish, which is, at least *prima facie*, inconsistent with the mishna's description of Ḥoni, cited below, as a holy man in an intimate relationship with God. As will be seen, my interpretation of the text, rather than stand in tension with that mishna, grows directly from it, and is also responsive to the arguments raised by Rubenstein.

the story. The more detail, the more real a story appears to the reader. But is there more meaning to it?

The third encounter is with Ḥoni's family. He visits them at the family home, and inquires if his son is still alive. Ḥoni is told that while his son is no longer alive, his grandson is. Ḥoni then proclaims, no doubt with anticipation and excitement, "I am Ḥoni HaMe'aggel!" Sadly, he is met with stark disbelief, and departs abruptly, probably deeply dejected. Now it seems fair to ask why Ḥoni made no reported attempt to prove his bona fides. After they pronounced their disbelief, why didn't he retell some old family stories, reveal family secrets no one outside the family knew? And why didn't his family make any attempt to inquire further? While seventy years had elapsed, surely they knew of Ḥoni's reputation as a miracle worker. Why didn't they invite him in for the proverbial cup of tea, to ascertain if Ḥoni had miraculously been resurrected, or whether he was some long-lost family member? And even if he was not, what happened to the mitzva of caring for the traveler, *hakhnasat orḥim*? Perhaps this old man was in need. How could they so abruptly and harshly dismiss him from their home and lives? The encounter with his family is puzzling indeed.

Things do not improve with his fourth and final post-sleep encounter, which takes place in the study hall. Upon his arrival, he overhears the rabbis in the study hall comment about the day's study, to the effect that the Torah taught was as clear as if it had been taught by Ḥoni HaMe'aggel. He overhears them say whenever Ḥoni entered the study hall, he answered all questions and clarified all doubt. What a perfect opportunity to announce himself! Ḥoni enters the study hall and exclaims, no doubt proudly and boldly, "I am he!" Yet in the study hall too, just like in his home, he is met with disbelief. And not only did they not believe him but, the author of the aggada reports, they did not treat him with the respect Ḥoni thought he deserved.

Before examining Ḥoni's reaction to this unfortunate encounter, we must first note just how puzzling it is. Much as we asked about his encounter at home, why did Ḥoni make no attempt to prove his bona fides? Why didn't he interject himself into the Torah discussion that day with some insightful comments of his own? And why didn't the rabbis even make the most basic effort to inquire as to who this stranger was?

Why didn't they ask him some questions about the Torah they had been studying? Or even invited him in and inquired after his welfare, as obligated by the mitzva of *hakhnasat orḥim*? Moreover, why did they not show Ḥoni respect? While Ḥoni's expectations for respect may have been unrealistic, exceeding their obligations, in deference to an old man, why didn't they do more?

Ḥoni became so upset by his treatment that he beseeched God for death. Ḥoni's prayer was answered and he died, a tragic end to the tale. However, the Talmud adds a coda, a kind of commentary on the story: Rava is reported to have said that Ḥoni's despair and death were an instance of the folk saying, "Either friendship or death." Ḥoni possessed no friends, so he sought death. But why was Ḥoni so disturbed by the lack of respect showed him by the rabbis in the study hall that he committed suicide by prayer? Was respect so important to him that when treated without respect he chose death instead? Perhaps Rava's comment is meant to answer that question. For Rava, what so disturbed Ḥoni was not so much the lack of respect as the lack of friends evidenced by the disrespect shown. Yet one wonders if that explanation is complete. There are many people who feel alone, yet do not turn to suicide, even through prayer. Is Rava saying Ḥoni is correct or understandable for his actions here?

PART TWO

WHO WAS ḤONI?

As we have seen, the story told about Ḥoni is charming but tragic, with numerous unanswered questions. To resolve these questions, we need a better understanding of Ḥoni the man. As noted in the introduction to this chapter, this tale about Ḥoni is embedded in a longer narrative about him, based upon a story told in the mishna, which reads as follows:

> The mishna relates: **An incident** occurred in **which** the people said **to Ḥoni HaMe'aggel: Pray that rain should fall. He said to them: Go out and bring in** the clay **ovens** used to roast the Paschal lambs, **so that they will not dissolve** in the water, as torrential rains are certain to fall. **He prayed, and no rain fell** at all.

What did he do? He drew a circle on the ground **and stood inside it and said before** God: **Master of the Universe, Your children have turned their faces toward me, as I am like a member of Your household.** Therefore, **I take an oath by Your great name that I will not move from here until You have mercy upon Your children** and answer their prayers for rain. **Rain began to trickle** down, but only in small droplets. **He said: I did not ask for this, but** for **rain to** fill the **cisterns, ditches, and caves** with enough water to last the entire year. Rain **began to fall furiously. He said: I did not ask for this** damaging rain either, **but** for **rain of benevolence, blessing, and generosity.**

Subsequently, the rains **fell in their standard manner** but continued unabated, filling the city with water **until all of the Jews exited** the residential areas of **Jerusalem** and went **to the Temple Mount due to the rain. They came and said to him: Just as you prayed over** the rains **that they should fall, so too, pray that they should stop. He said to them: Go out and see if the Claimants' Stone,** a large stone located in the city, upon which proclamations would be posted with regard to lost and found articles, **has been washed away.** In other words, if the water has not obliterated the Claimants' Stone, it is not yet appropriate to pray for the rain to cease.

Shimon ben Shetaḥ, the *Nasi* of the Sanhedrin at the time, **relayed to** Ḥoni HaMe'aggel: **Were you not Ḥoni, I would have decreed that you be ostracized, but what can I do to you? You nag [*mitḥatei*] God and He does your bidding, like a son who nags his father and** his father **does his bidding** without reprimand. After all, rain fell as you requested. **About you, the verse states: "Let your father and your mother be glad, and let her who bore you rejoice"** (Proverbs 23:25).[3]

This fascinating story requires its own analysis, but suffice it to say, for our purposes, that Ḥoni demonstrates what might be called a brazen attitude toward God. He threatens that he will not leave the circle he

3. Mishna Taanit 3:4.

has drawn in the ground until God immediately responds to his prayers, in exactly the way he wants things. In fact, he is so confident that God will grant his wishes that he tells everyone in advance to remove their Passover ovens, which would get ruined in the rain. While God apparently is not all that pleased with Ḥoni's demands, as He chooses initially not to grant the right kind of rain, nevertheless He eventually succumbs to Ḥoni's wishes. Ḥoni here describes himself as a member of God's household.

Shimon ben Shetaḥ, the leading rabbinic scholar of the era, expresses great displeasure with Ḥoni's behavior, and would even ban him, but for the intimacy of Ḥoni's relationship to God. Shimon ben Shetaḥ compares his relationship to that of a favored son who, while sinning against his father,[4] is nevertheless forgiven and indulged. The metaphor of the favored son is extended even further in a *baraita* quoted in the Talmud immediately preceding the passage which is the subject of this chapter. Shimon ben Shetaḥ there compares Ḥoni to a son who sins against his father, but one who also makes the following requests:

> Father, take me to be bathed in hot water; wash me with cold water; give me nuts, almonds, peaches and pomegranates. And his father gives him. About you the verse states "Your father and mother will be glad, and she who bore you will rejoice" (Proverbs 23:25).

The image here is of the spoiled child whose every whim is indulged by his father, who cannot say no to him, even if he is undeserving.

Left unexplained is exactly why Ḥoni has the status of a favored son, but clearly God is very fond of him, and these texts depict a remarkable intimacy between them. Whatever the theology behind this, for our purposes we need reflect about its implications for Ḥoni's experience of time.[5] As anyone who has been blessed with children knows, they

4. The Hebrew word used by Shimon ben Shetaḥ, *mitḥatei,* is ambiguous, and may be translated as "sinned," or "nagged."
5. The issue here is not the reality of time, its metaphysics, but rather how time is experienced, its phenomenology.

demand immediate gratification. If a child wants his mother's attention, he cannot wait for her to finish the task at hand. As children age, they learn the art of patience – one hopes! – but the younger the child, typically the more the need for immediate gratification. Every passing second is intolerable, for every passing second feels to the child like an eternity. A child's experience of time, when in need, is compressed. He or she wants a response now, not in five minutes, or in three minutes, or in one minute, but right now. This is likely related to the spontaneity of young children, who cannot plan ahead with the foresight of adults, but live in the moment, and therefore experience their needs with such intensity. If one cannot project oneself into the future, then the experience of the present prevails in all its force. The future is beyond the horizon of their experience, which can therefore be filled only with the present.

Ḥoni is described in these passages as similar to a child in his relationship with God, who demands an immediate response to his prayers, drawing a circle around himself, much like a child demands an immediate response to his or her needs. Perhaps we might explain this as follows: Ḥoni experienced God with such present intensity that for him there was no past or future. Consider any sublime experience, such as witnessing the Niagara Falls for the first time. For some, that experience may be so powerful that it drives out any thoughts of the past or future. Or consider the powerful intimacy of spousal love. For some, that too may drive out thoughts of past or future. Ḥoni's intimate relationship with God may have been similar. He demanded rain immediately because in the overwhelming immediacy of his experience of God there was for him no past or future. All his experience was compacted into the moment of his encounter with God. Ḥoni's experiential space was flooded with the divine, and it was in that space that he prayed. How could he wait into the future for a response, if his entire world collapsed into the present lived encounter with God? Like a child, for Ḥoni there was no past or future.

This account may help explain why Ḥoni was so puzzled about that verse in Psalms, which compares Jewish life in exile to a dream. He could not understand how Jews survived for seventy years waiting for redemption. Of course, Ḥoni knew that the Jews did not sleep literally for seventy years. But he could not understand how they could sleep for seventy years figuratively. For to sleep means to wait, to take no action, to accept reality as it is, while sleeping through its travails. For Ḥoni there could be no waiting into the future, no accepting reality as it was. Nor, for Ḥoni, could there be a dream, for to dream about a better future, to wait patiently for redemption, is to project oneself out of the present and into that future. For Ḥoni, who lived with God in an eternal present, this would have been impossible. Just as a child cannot wait for a parent's attention, so too the Jews, whose relationship with God was alive in all its intensity, could not wait as well. Perhaps with the naivete of a child, Ḥoni refused to accept that the body of the Jewish people could live outside the intensity of the encounter with God.

For this reason, too, Ḥoni could not understand the labors of the farmer who planted the carob tree whose fruit he would never see. What mattered to Ḥoni more than anything was his present, lived experience of God. How could a farmer worry about the long-term future, when his experience of God should explode those concerns out of his consciousness? For Ḥoni there was only the present, and he could imagine no other way of being in the world. This is not to say that Ḥoni was a bad father, or that he did not provide for his children. If Ḥoni was a righteous man (to use R. Yoḥanan's phrase), surely he was not so self-centered as to focus only on his own selfish needs. Yet to provide for his family in the present, a mitzva whose force we have no reason to believe Ḥoni ignored, is not the equivalent of planning for them long term into the future. Let God worry about the future, Ḥoni might have thought, as he lived in the momentous divine encounter of the present, fulfilling its obligations in the present, but no more. In short, Ḥoni's experience of time was not the experience of time of so many of us, and therefore his behavior may be puzzling to us, but could not have been otherwise for him.

Following Ḥoni's encounter with the farmer, the story takes a surreal turn. Ḥoni falls into a deep sleep, rocks magically grow up around him, and the aggada reports that he awoke after sleeping for seventy years. He first meets up with the grandson of the farmer, then his own donkey, who it turns out has sired many foals, after which he is rejected by his family and by his colleagues in the study hall. As we have seen, each of these four encounters is more fraught with questions than the next. What are we to make of all this?[6]

I would suggest that the historical background to Ḥoni's life and times are crucial to understanding this aggada. Let us first recall Shimon ben Shetaḥ's extreme displeasure with Ḥoni's behavior. He would have placed Ḥoni under a ban, but for the obvious intimacy which prevailed between Ḥoni and God. Why exactly was Shimon ben Shetaḥ so upset, and why exactly did Ḥoni persist in his ways? Binyamin Lau has suggested that Ḥoni and Shimon ben Shetaḥ represent two polar opposites in how best to best secure Jewish well-being in that era.[7] In times past, when Jews were in need of divine guidance or assistance, prophets would mediate between them and God. Thus, Shimon ben Shetaḥ, in the *baraita* partially quoted above, observes that the prophet Elijah possessed the keys to rain. If the Jews needed rain, Elijah would pray, and rain would come. But the era of prophecy had come to a close. How then were Jews to secure their needs?

One answer to that question is embodied in the very tractate, Taanit, from which our chapter's text is drawn. The rabbis devised a series of complex ritual practices, including public prayer and fasting, to bring rain in times of drought, and these are laid out in great detail in this tractate, which all Jews were encouraged to study and learn. Many of these practices required considerable effort on the part of the Jewish community as a whole. First, the rituals had to be learned, and this required time for study. Second, regular fasting (the meaning of the title of the tractate, and a key part of the ritual) is hardly a pleasant undertaking. This approach empowered each member of the Jewish community to take religious and spiritual responsibility for the fate of the community as a whole, and the fate of each of its members. It required hard work and much spiritual effort.

An alternative approach was to find replacements for the prophets, holy men whose prayers God answered. Tractate Taanit tells tale after tale of great men whose prayers for rain were (and sometimes were

6. Rubenstein again sees all this in a source-critical context. As noted, I aim here for a unitary reading.
7. Lau, *The Sages*, vol. 1, 62–71.

not) answered. Ḥoni represented the epitome of this model. It required very limited spiritual labors on the part of the community, who delegated prayer, and their own well-being, to the holy men in their midst. These holy men, miracle workers, had the power to make things right with God, and they undertook to use their powers for the good of the Jewish community. Shimon ben Shetaḥ compares Ḥoni to Elijah, in that both possessed power over rain, but he nevertheless rejected Ḥoni's model. This is because Shimon ben Shetaḥ, and the rabbinic establishment he led, believed that in a world devoid of prophets, each Jew must take responsibility for his destiny and for the destiny of the community through Torah study and through elaborate spiritual exercises. Ḥoni may have been a holy miracle worker, but he was not a prophet, and in the post-prophetic world Jews must not seek miracle workers but rather must be empowered to take responsibility for their own well-being and religious life. Ḥoni, however, knew well the extent of his own powers, and sought to exercise them for the good of the whole.

Shimon ben Shetaḥ led the rabbinic establishment of his day, and their model prevailed over time. The whole of the evolving rabbinic tradition reflects that shift, and Jews today are heirs to the model advocated by Shimon ben Shetaḥ and his colleagues. The study, development and observance of Jewish law, and the importance of prayer, became the foundations of traditional Jewish life. This is not to say that over the millennia Jews did not appeal to holy miracle workers. They most certainly did. Given the travails of Jewish history and of people's personal lives, and given the natural tendency for many religious believers to seek help from holy miracle workers, it would have been astonishing if they had not. Most recently this was (and is) exemplified in the hasidic world. Nevertheless, the overall thrust of rabbinic Judaism prevailed. Ḥoni lived during a transitional period in history, when post-prophetic Jewish life was on the cusp of change to the dominance of the rabbinic religious model, and Ḥoni found himself on the wrong side of history.[8]

8. The hasidic world, over time, has also come to adopt more elements of the classic rabbinic model, and even in its early years there were, and continue to be, great hasidic leaders who were also distinguished Torah scholars.

How might Ḥoni have felt about his waning, vestigial role in the new religious order? It would hardly be surprising if he felt deeply alienated. His world of highly respected, almost-worshipped miracle workers, who lived in intense personal relationship with God, was being displaced by the world of scholars and the laws they elaborated upon or instituted to cope with the new challenges of post-prophetic Jewish life. While the aggada as we have it attributes to Ḥoni great scholarship, Ḥoni's halakhic teachings are nowhere cited in the vast corpus of rabbinic literature. Why is that? The likely explanation is that while Ḥoni may (or indeed may not) have been very knowledgeable, his primary accomplishment, his fame, authority, and public role were those of the holy miracle workers. And the fame, role, and authority of holy miracle workers were in decline. Ḥoni no doubt knew of the sharp criticism leveled against him by Shimon ben Shetaḥ, that his role was under attack. He no doubt knew that the new world in which he found himself had an ever-shrinking place for a man like himself.

With this background, we can return to the aggada itself. Recall how Ḥoni could not understand how the Jews lived seventy exiled years in a dream, could not understand how a farmer could look to the future rather than live in the intense present with God at his side. Both phenomena were at odds with his own relationship with God, and his commensurate experience of time. Disturbed by the verse and by the encounter with the farmer, he then eats and falls into a deep sleep, a dream that lasts for seventy years. How is it possible to sleep for seventy years? But consider this: What happens when people sleep? They typically dream. My suggestion is that the seventy-year sleep, and the surreal events that follow, are puzzling only if they had taken place in the real world. But if they were events that took place in a dream, they make very good sense indeed, for they follow the serpentine logic of dreams, and possess exactly their surreal quality. If the events seem like a dream, perhaps they really are. Now, of course, the text itself does not announce that the events it described took place in a dream. But the author of the aggada, like many great authors throughout literary history, may have chosen to communicate by allusion and indirection, to provoke the reader to tease out the many deeper meanings of the text. Alternatively, the author of the aggada may have chosen to portray events *as if* they had taken place in a dream, whether or not Ḥoni actually dreamed them himself. On this more literary reading, the author of the aggada was not writing what he took to be a literally true biography of Ḥoni's experiences.

But even if the author of the aggada had been writing the literal truth as he understood it, we saw in chapter 7 that many medieval commentators to the Talmud maintained that episodes recorded in the Talmud which are inconsistent with what we know to be true of the world took place in dreams. Surely sleeping for seventy years in the natural order of things is impossible. Of at least equal importance, however, is my suggestion that if we interpret all of Ḥoni's post-prandial experiences as part of a dream, or depicted as dream-like, we may gain a much richer, deeper and more nuanced understanding of the text as we have it. What made so little sense to the reader at first, begins to make very good sense indeed.

Ḥoni falls asleep immediately after his encounter with the farmer, and he dreams. What would a man like Ḥoni dream about? He feels profoundly alienated from his changing Jewish world, and that alienation would manifest itself in the magical rocks that grow up around him, probably in the dream itself, hiding him from view. They are a physical embodiment of the barrier between Ḥoni and the rapidly evolving world in which he struggles to remain relevant. His dream is triggered by the troubling conversation he has with the farmer, since the farmer represents an alternative to Ḥoni's model of life. For Ḥoni, life is lived in the moment's powerful encounter with God. The farmer, on the other hand, is rational and practical, looks into the future and plans for it. Not only that, the farmer works hard toward that future, slowly and methodically, planting, watering, and daily tending to his trees. He takes responsibility not only for himself, but for future generations. Indeed, in an important sense, carob tree farmers are very much like the rabbis themselves, and the life the rabbis promote. For the rabbis maintain that Jews in the post-prophetic era must take responsibility for their own lives and the lives of their descendants, through the laborious study of Torah and the ritual practices they mandate. In Hebrew, a farmer is an *oved adama*, a person who works or serves the land, and the rabbinic Jew, in that same sense, calls himself an *oved Hashem*, a person who serves God. Both toil according to extensive and demanding prescribed rituals, laboring toward the future. Ḥoni, the "righteous man," of course served God as well, and no doubt kept all the same rituals, but for him the ecstatic experience of the moment defined his religious life, unlike the toilers in the orchards of the farm, or the toilers in the fields of the ritual and intellectual service of God.

For all these reasons, Ḥoni would have been especially troubled by his encounter with the farmer, and that would have triggered his dream, a dream which enacted his deepest anxieties and feelings of alienation. He dreams[9] that he slept for seventy years, and was transposed into a future to which he does not belong, *a future which Ḥoni fears has already arrived in his lived present.* In that dream he awakens to meet up with the grandson of the farmer eating the fruits of the tree. He infers that it is possible to sleep for seventy years, since it takes seventy years for a carob tree to bear fruit, and he had fallen asleep when the carob tree was being planted. From this he further infers that the verse in Psalms that Jews dreamt for seventy years while in exile makes good sense after all. Now if we take this as a depiction of events transpiring in the real world, these inferences are puzzling indeed, but if we take them as transpiring in a dream, their logic is perfectly cogent.

What Ḥoni saw, and came to understand, in his dream, was that the slow-moving, rational rabbinic world that was superseding his own possessed considerable religious worth. Trees were planted and bore fruit; descendants survived into the future and ate of the painstakingly grown fruit of the past. Jews could live in exile for seventy years as if in a dream, because the ecstatic, eternally present model of Jewish life Ḥoni embodied was not the only, or not even the best, mode of living with God. There were other ways to survive and flourish in changing times. Shimon ben Shetaḥ and his colleagues, and the whole of the evolving rabbinic tradition, made that clear to Ḥoni, at least in the hidden recesses of his dreams. Read backward into Jewish history, even

9. Throughout this exposition I shall write as if Ḥoni actually dreamt what is described in the text. The more literary reading, noted above, is that the author of the aggada was not writing Ḥoni's literal biography, and that the dream did not take place in reality, but is the product of the author's attempt to understand and convey what he took to be the hidden inner life of Ḥoni. Both these readings equally provide the framework for my analysis.

before that tradition had fully taken root, Ḥoni came to understand that keeping the mitzvot, struggling to live the best Jewish life one can under dire circumstances, makes survival in exile possible too. Why does Ḥoni comment on the verse in Psalms, rather than directly on the lesson the farmer taught him? Because the lesson the farmer taught him was literally about farming. The figurative, deeper, and more important lesson, about how to live a Jewish life, is best expressed exegetically, on the verse in Psalms.

Ḥoni next encounters his donkey and its many descendants. How can a donkey live for seventy years? Well, it can't in reality, but it can in a dream. Why does Ḥoni dream about his donkey? Probably because his donkey figuratively embodies the Shimon ben Shetaḥ model of Jewish life. Consider the verse in Genesis (49:14): "Issachar is a strong-boned donkey, crouching among the sheepfolds." Donkeys work, and they work very hard indeed. They toil, drag people or burdens from place to place over the many years of their life. They do not understand why they do what they do, but good donkeys unquestioningly carry out their tasks. They experience no flashing insights, no extraordinary encounters with the divine. They go about their business, slowly and methodically, accomplishing their many unfathomable tasks. Such donkeys, and the people like them in these respects, bear fruit long into the future. People who are like Ḥoni do not. Let us recall that in the rabbinic tradition, cited by Rashi in his commentary to that verse in Genesis 49, Issachar represents the rabbinic scholar, who "bore the yoke of Torah study." It would hardly be surprising, then, if the author of this aggada chose the image of a donkey to embody the rising world of Shimon ben Shetaḥ and rabbinic scholarship, against the setting world of men like Ḥoni, and given this background, it is hardly surprising that Ḥoni's symbol-filled dream would contain an image of a donkey.

Ḥoni's encounter with his still living donkey and its many descendants is a perfect counterpoint to his next encounter, with his family. The donkey had many foals, and many, many descendants. Ḥoni only asks to see his son, in the singular, his one son, not many, and that son, it turns out, is no longer alive. Ḥoni's most immediate family no longer exists, unlike the donkey, which is surrounded by his foals and descendants. Ḥoni's legacy is barren. He cannot even meet his one and only grandson, for the family refuses to believe that he is Ḥoni, their *paterfamilias*. In Ḥoni's frightening dream, his own religious legacy is barren, in contrast to the legacy of those who toil, the planters of carob trees, the learned rabbis who, like the donkey in Genesis, "bore the yoke of Torah study." Ḥoni's suppressed feelings of deep alienation and anxiety come alive in his disturbing dream, a dream in which Ḥoni becomes exactly what he feared.

Perhaps the most troubling encounter of all is Ḥoni's final one, with the denizens of the study hall. In his dream, he overhears them attribute great scholarship to Ḥoni, yet when Ḥoni identifies himself, they refuse to believe him. Was Ḥoni a great scholar? While we cannot say for sure, there is no evidence in all the vast rabbinic literature we possess that he was, for his halakhic positions are never quoted. But in Ḥoni's dream world he was a great scholar indeed, yet even so the world of scholarship had passed him by. For the world of the study hall had been Shimon ben Shetaḥ-ized, was evolving evermore toward the rabbinic mode of rigorous scholarship that came to dominate religious life for millennia. Whatever Ḥoni's level of knowledge, it was likely rooted in the simpler biblical, and less characteristically rabbinic, modes of the past. Ḥoni dreamed what he feared, that he could no longer visit the study hall of the Jewish present and future. It was no longer his study hall, the scholars therein no longer his partners in the quest to know God.

Surely the two most important elements in the social life of a deeply religious person would be religious colleagues and family. But here too Ḥoni dreamed what he feared, a growing, unbridgeable estrangement from both. Rava's final coda, on this analysis, is brilliantly revealing: "Either friends or death." Rava did not mean to teach that suicide is an appropriate course of action for someone lacking friends. Rather, Rava meant to illuminate the central dilemma of Ḥoni's life: In the radically changing world of Jewish life and values, Ḥoni could find no place for himself; he became a vestigial figure in Jewish history. He felt this alienation, perhaps partially repressed, and dreamed vividly of its frightening implications. Rava's comment, either friendship or death, thus takes on a rich resonance: Either adjust to the new rabbinic model of the present and future, or die a historical death.

It is important to note at this point that the reading I have proposed in this chapter provides a unitary account of Ḥoni's life. His rainmaking prowess, his inability to understand the verse in Psalms, and his mysterious sleep and enigmatic encounters with donkey, family, and colleagues, all flow from the kind of person Ḥoni was and his relationship with God. In the end, there are not many Ḥonis, but one.[10]

In conclusion, we must ask ourselves if Ḥoni actually prayed for death, and thereby committed suicide by prayer. More precisely, did Ḥoni actually pray for his death in real life, then die, or did he only dream that he prayed for his death, and then die only in his dream? The standard interpretation is the former, namely, that Ḥoni actually prayed for his death and died thereafter as a result of his prayers. Of course, that may very well be true. According to this interpretation, it is surely fascinating that Ḥoni's death would echo the experience of R. Yoḥanan's death – the author of at least the first part of this aggada. Recall how in chapter 6 of this volume, we saw that the death of R. Yoḥanan's student, and eventual close friend, study partner, and brother-in-law, Reish Lakish, so disturbed R. Yoḥanan that he lost his mind, and his colleagues prayed successfully for his death. Rava's apothegm would surely apply to R. Yoḥanan as well: "Either friendship or death." The two stories eerily echo one another.[11]

That said, there is the second alternative, according to which Ḥoni only dreamed of his death, an alternative made possible by my analysis, which opens up another plausible reading. We also possess a different account of Ḥoni's death than that described here, found in Josephus's *Antiquities*, and scholars assume that these are two irreconcilable traditions. Of course, that may very well be the case. However, if Ḥoni prays for death and dies only in his dream, and not in real life, then these two traditions are entirely consistent. Moreover, the Josephus account deepens our understanding of Ḥoni's desperate alienation. According to Josephus, Ḥoni lived during the civil war between Hyrcanus and Aris-

10. Likewise, there are not many textual variants to the Ḥoni story, as suggested by some scholars, but one.

11. Interestingly Elijah the Prophet, to whom Ḥoni is compared, also prayed for his death. Might Ḥoni have so identified with Elijah, that he recapitulated this in his dream?

tobulus, which took place during the first century BCE. Hyrcanus's followers, knowing of Ḥoni's prowess in prayer, captured and compelled him to pray on their behalf, and against their nemesis Aristobulus. This Ḥoni refused to do, whereupon he was stoned to death by the mob supporting Hyrcanus. What follows is the text from Josephus:

> Now there was one, whose name was Onias [the Greek version of Ḥoni], a righteous man he was, and beloved of God, who in a certain drought, had prayed to God to put an end to the intense heat, and whose prayers God had heard, and had sent them rain. This man had hid himself, because he saw that this sedition would last a great while. However, they brought him to the Jewish camp, and desired, that as by his prayers he had once put an end to the drought, so he would in like manner make imprecations on Aristobulus and those of his faction. And when, upon his refusal, and the excuses that he made, he was still by the multitude compelled to speak, he stood up in the midst of them, and said, "O God, the King of the whole world! Since those that stand now with me are thy people, and those that are besieged are also thy priests, I beseech thee, that thou wilt neither hearken to the prayer so those against these, nor bring to effect what these pray against those." Whereupon such wicked Jews as stood about him, as soon as he had made this prayer, stoned him to death.[12]

Ḥoni loved all the Jewish people. How could he pray for one faction and against another? The prayer he did utter, which no doubt he knew put his life at risk, was both eloquent and poignant: He prayed that God heed the prayers of neither side, for to heed the prayers of one side was to cause irreparable harm to the other. Ḥoni simply could not comprehend fratricidal warfare among the Jews. Is this because his own intimate relationship with the ultimate Father of all Jews, God Himself, was that of a beloved son to his father? The explosive intimacy of Ḥoni's childlike bond with God was such as to frame for him the whole of the relationship between Jews and God as familial. In Ḥoni's experience, the Jews

12. Josephus Flavius, *Antiquities*, trans. W. Whiston (Philadelphia, 1905), 14:2, 409–10.

are not primarily a nation, but rather primarily a large family. Ḥoni, the favored son of God, felt more powerfully than most the force of those family bonds, and therefore more than most could not fathom or tolerate internecine civil war.

The political background to the latter part of Ḥoni's life sheds even more light on the alienation Ḥoni would have felt from the world around him. The people he loved, his very brothers and sisters, were enmeshed in a bitter battle, while his understanding of religious life was under threat both literal (from Shimon ben Shetaḥ, who almost banned him) and figurative. Now, of course, estrangement caused by changing modes of religious life is hardly identical with estrangement from the chaos of fratricidal warfare. Nevertheless, the feelings of estrangement from the one would have reinforced the feelings of estrangement from the other. For example, consider someone who loses his job and becomes depressed. Later, he is divorced by his wife. Each negative event, while different, intensifies the feelings of depression caused by the other. The same pattern would be true for Ḥoni's feelings of estrangement. His whole world was disintegrating around him, and out of that painful emotional background his encounter with the farmer triggered the specifics of the dream.

In light of the Josephus account, the phrase "Either friendship or death," with which our aggada concludes, takes on more meaning than ever. We have analyzed the multiple causes and consequences of Ḥoni's anguished feelings of alienation. On this analysis, could the result have been anything but death? Ḥoni's personality, his unique experience of God, his feelings of estrangement from a world rapidly changing around him, gave rise to his richly symbolic dream, through which he vividly experienced his greatest fears. In his dream, Ḥoni came to understand that the future was not his, that it would rest in the hands of the great rabbinic scholars of the future, and in the hands of those who diligently studied and lived by their works. In this insight Ḥoni was right, as over two thousand years of Jewish history so eloquently attest.

Supplementary Readings

The best place to begin the study of the Talmud is with its classic commentaries. In the case of the aggada, many of these appear in the compendium *Ein Yaakov*, by the fifteenth-century Spanish scholar R. Jacob ibn Ḥabib, whose commentaries have not yet been translated into English. A recent edition, published in Jerusalem in 2008, includes citations to additional and also more recent rabbinic commentary. Binyamin Lau's multi-volume work *The Sages* (Tel Aviv, 2007–2017), some of which has been translated into English and published by Maggid Books, provides invaluable historical and intellectual context to the lives and teachings of the talmudic Sages. Y. D. Gilat's *R. Eliezer ben Hyrcanus: A Scholar Outcast* (Ramat Gan, 1984), provides important background for the trilogy of chapters on R. Eliezer.

I have benefited as well from numerous additional secondary sources, which themselves contain references to yet more sources, some of which are cited below, by chapter. While I found myself disagreeing with some of the assumptions of these authors, many of their readings and insights into certain passages in the texts proved valuable, which I am happy to acknowledge. Many of these sources appear only in the Hebrew.

Chapter 1

Binyamin Lau, *The Sages* (Tel Aviv, 2008), vol. 2, 38–46.

Anat Shapira-Lavi, *Talmud Now: A Journey into Stories of Talmudic Narrative* (Haifa, 2017), 101–20 (Heb.).

Chapter 2

Y. Brandes, *Practical Aggada: Man in Society* (Jerusalem, 2011), vol. 2, 72–88 (Heb.).

Y. Englard, "Majority Decisions versus Individual Truth," *Tradition* 15 (1975): 137–52.

J. Rubenstein, *Talmudic Stories* (Baltimore, 1999), 34–63.

Chapter 3

Azarya Beitner, *Tales of Yavne: Visiting the Sick and Comforting Mourners* (Ramat Gan, 2011), 58–100 (Heb.).

Y. Frankel, *Aggadic Narrative: Harmony of Form and Content* (Tel Aviv, 2001), 156–62 (Heb.).

Chapter 4

C. Licht, *Tradition and Novelty: Subjects in Rabbinic Literature* (Givat Haviva, 1989), 47–62 (Heb.).

A. Saldarini, "The Adoption of a Dissident: Akabya ben Mehlalel in Rabbinic Tradition," *Journal of Jewish Studies* 33:1–2 (1982): 547–56.

Chapter 5

Y. Frankel, *Studies in the Spiritual World of the Aggadic Narrative* (Jerusalem, 1981), 87–91 (Heb.).

J. Rubenstein, *Stories of the Babylonian Talmud* (Baltimore, 2010), 41–61.

Chapter 6

Y. Frankel, *Studies in the Spiritual World of the Aggadic Narrative* (Jerusalem, 1981), 74–78.

A. Kosman, *Man's Tractate: On Manhood, Love and Authentic Life* (Jerusalem, 2002), 34–51 (Heb.).

Chapter 7

Sh. Faust, *Aggadeta* (Or Yehuda, 2011), 254–59 (Heb.).

Anat Shapira-Lavi, *Talmud Now: A Journey into Stories of Talmudic Narrative* (Haifa, 2017), 47–69 (Heb.).

Chapter 8

Y. Frankel, "Paronomasia in Aggadic Narratives," *Scripta Hierosolymitana* 27 (1978): 27–51. A Hebrew version of this article appears in Frankel's *Aggadic Narrative: Harmony of Form and Content,* 61–62, 183–89.

J. Rubenstein, *Stories of the Babylonian Talmud* (Baltimore, 2010), 62–76.

Binyamin Lau, *The Sages* (Tel Aviv, 2007), vol. 1, 62–85.

Index of Biblical and Rabbinic Sources

TOSAFOT

Subject Index

Maggid Books
The best of contemporary Jewish thought from
Koren Publishers Jerusalem Ltd.

Garden and Metaphor

Edited by
Ana Kučan and *Mateja Kurir*

GARDEN AND METAPHOR

Essays on the Essence of the Garden

With photographs by
Anne Schwalbe

Birkhäuser

Contents

In tribute to Professor Dušan Ogrin
(1929–2019)

Prolegomena

First There Was the Garden

Ana Kučan

In the film version of the story *Alice in Wonderland,*[1] Alice does not spot the White Rabbit in a meadow but beside the meticulously trimmed hedge of a garden maze. The creature strikes Alice as somewhat unusual, somewhat adventurous, and her boundless curiosity lures her down the rabbit hole, where she lands in a place called Under Ground. The Under Ground is presented as an enchanted, mysteriously beautiful, but slightly frightening garden, both strange and miraculous, and it eventually leads her to the realm of the absurd.

First, there was the garden. And this is true of both of the garden's most extreme forms. In the first of these, the images of the carefully cultivated garden in the film present a metaphor of an orderly, socially rigid, refined world, a cosmos in which, despite unanswerable riddles, it is possible to understand this world precisely because of its order. Not only understand it, but master it. In the second of these forms, a wild place is revealed, teeming with unusual, unearthly flora and fauna, not least the strange Cheshire Cat. It is a world of endless possibilities, untameable and unpredictable, intangible and inexplicable, full of surprises: an infinitely attractive world of wonders. Thus, the garden is cultivated *and* untameable, even both at the same time: anything, to put it simply, can happen in the garden.

The fact that there was a garden from the very beginning is also thematized by the essays in this book, which range from presentations of in-depth studies about the meaning and role of the garden, accompanied by lucid insights born of keen

1 *Alice in Wonderland* (USA), 2010. Director Tim Burton, screenplay Linda Woolverton, based on the works of Lewis Carroll's *Alice's Adventures in Wonderland* and *Through the Looking Glass.*

Rioan-ji, Kyoto, presumably late 15th century; the enclosure is carefully premeditated to help meditation.

Shoden-ji, Kyoto, is an example of an enclosed garden. It adopts the principle of *shakkei* (borrowed scenery), as Hiei, a mountain in the background, is drawn into its visual composition. First half of the 17th century, renovated by Mirei Shigemori in 1953.

observations, to poetic and artistic contributions that combine views on both the function and infinite allure of the world of designed nature.

Why write about the garden?

This book about the contemporary role of the garden as a concept and as an emerging reality started to materialize in 2019. One reason was the necessity to reflect on present conditions; the other was the need to invent new concepts and artistic expressions which could help us to cope with complex social and environmental problems. The Biotechnical Faculty at the University of Ljubljana and the Museum of Architecture and Design have combined their efforts to publish a series of reflections on how we are involved – through the garden – with nature. There is no doubt that with the increasing extent of human interventions on the surface of the planet, the discipline of landscape architecture has acquired a more important role and a greater level of responsibility. "We are constantly questioning what our contact with nature means to us, how we are involved with nature, how we need it, how we arrange for it to meet our needs, how we attempt to preserve it, while at the same time exploiting, subordinating, and destroying it. We are a part of nature, but also change it, invade it, transform its space. This forces us to constantly evaluate these actions, to assess and criticize, and also to engage in self-reflection and poetic thought. The discussion presented in *Garden and Metaphor* occurs in a context that is particularly fraught. We live in a moment when we have become witnesses to the gradual climatic and environmental breakdown for which we are ourselves responsible, and the responses we muster are too few and too modest to prevent it", wrote the director of the Museum of Architecture and Design at the time (2010–2020), Matevž Čelik, in the introduction to the Slovenian edition, *Vrt in prispodoba*,[2] which was published in 2021. The second, no less important reason was the intention to pay tribute to Dušan Ogrin (1929–2019), the founder of landscape architecture in Slovenia. Thus, besides being a collection presenting the breadth of reflection about our possible future in the professional, social and philosophical sense, this volume about the garden is also a dedication.

The garden as dedication

Of course, the question arises as to why we choose to honour Dušan Ogrin with this collection of reflections that do not directly address either him or his work. Indeed, the essays in this book do not specifically celebrate or evaluate Ogrin's oeuvre of contributions to landscape architecture which have made a deep impression on both Slovenian and international spatial planning.[3] Likewise, they do not address his most important

2 Matevž Čelik, Foreword, *Vrt in prispodoba*, Ljubljana: Biotechnical Faculty of the University Ljubljana and Museum for Architecture and Design, 2021, p. 13.

André Le Nôtre, Versailles, 1663–1693, Grand Canal cross axis.

professional achievement: the foundation of a school of landscape architecture in Ljubljana. He imbued this school with unique principles, in particular a cosmopolitan outlook, an interdisciplinary approach, international connection, and social engagement (developed with the help of his colleague Janez Marušič). Equally seminal were his many books, articles, landscape architecture designs, projects, lectures, and not least the many students who continue to co-create our spatial reality to this day, around Europe and beyond. The Department of Landscape Architecture at the Biotechnical Faculty of the University of Ljubljana has become one of the leading institutions of landscape architecture and is recognized as an outstanding educational institution both inside Slovenia and in academic and professional circles abroad.

This book deviated from the more predictable format for two reasons. The first is rooted in Ogrin's personality: regardless of what his attention was called to at any given instant, the garden was always at the centre of his interest. As he understood it, the garden was both the essence and the beginning of man's ordering of the world, and represented his most intimate preoccupation. This could be seen in both his own garden and in the studies and writings that he dedicated to the garden. The second reason is general: we now face challenges in spatial planning and design that demand reflection on points of departures, goals, and values, and also the conceptualization of a new imaginary that will suit our emerging reality.

Ogrin spent an extensive part of his long years of research work on the garden and the world heritage of garden architecture. In 1993, drawing on those years, he wrote *The World Heritage of Gardens*, which was published by Thames & Hudson in English (in her contribution, Barbara Habič Pregl writes about how this book came into the world), and was simultaneously

3 In 1972, Dušan Ogrin organized one of the first symposia in the world about landscape planning, which the international expert public still view as a great service to the field. The symposium, entitled *Krajinsko planiranje / Landscape Planning / Landschaftsplanung*, took place in Ljubljana, 29–31 August 1972. Twelve invited speakers from Yugoslavia, Europe, the U.S., and Israel participated, among them Carl Steinitz, Ruth Enis, Sven Ingvar Andersson, and Meto Vroom. Carl Steinitz is still affiliated with the Ljubljana school.

released in Slovenian under the title *Vrtna umetnost sveta* and soon afterwards was also translated into Italian.[4] This book not only established a suitable vocabulary of Slovenian professional terms,[5] but also attempted to understand the garden in all of its functional aspects and subtleties of meaning. Yes, in all of them, because he was relentless. Like André Le Nôtre, the creator of the Gardens of Versailles, Ogrin was a "gardener" immersed in the creation of gardens[6] and also a passionate connoisseur of plants and natural processes. As such, he was able to see the garden beyond the usual art-historical or horticultural context. It is no doubt because of this unique approach that Ogrin received the 1995 Friedrich Ludwig von Sckell Ring of Honour,[7] an award granted by the Bavarian Academy of Art, for his contribution in the field of history of the garden arts and theory of landscape architecture. At the award ceremony, Ogrin, in his lecture "Are the Garden Arts Actually Art?" ("Ist Gartenkunst tatsächlich Kunst?"), placed the garden at the centre of the developing field of landscape architecture. The garden interested him not only as a tangible object, but also as an idea, the idea that stands at the very beginning of the long journey of landscape planning and design as the central focus of landscape architecture. In this context, he could not cease asking what indeed was the contemporary role of landscape architects and what their – our – contribution could be to the resolution of current problems in the spatial and social restructuring of the world. For millennia, the creation of gardens has taught us to merge nature and culture. What's more, it has taught us to skilfully navigate the current of dynamics between development and conservation. It is for this reason that this collection of reflections about the garden seemed the most appropriate way to pay tribute to the memory of Ogrin and his work.

4 Dušan Ogrin, *The World Heritage of Gardens*, London: Thames & Hudson, 1993; *Giardini del mondo*, Milano: Fenice 2000, 1995.

5 Ogrin negotiated with Thames & Hudson for the book to be printed in Slovenia (by Gorenjski tisk). This allowed for the simultaneous publication of the book in Slovenian, which he considered an obligation. A book of the print quality demanded by the photographic material Ogrin provided would have otherwise been far too expensive for such a small community of readers.

6 We find an exhaustive illustration of the gardener in Érik Orsenna's biography of Le Nôtre. Using the most magnificent example of the garden arts, the Gardens of Versailles, Orsenna presents the complexity of the knowledge and skills embedded in the emerging art of landscape design in relation to natural limitations and the sociocultural context. See Érik Orsenna, *Portrait d'un Homme Heureux: André Le Nôtre, 1613–1700*, Paris: Folio, 2000. The English translation was published under the title *André Le Nôtre: Gardener to the Sun King*, translated by Moishe Black, New York: George Braziller, 2001.

7 The award is named after Friedrich Ludwig von Sckell, the renowned landscape designer who brought English landscape gardens to southern Germany in the 18th century.

Cultivating nature as an existential means to preserve one's own humanness: Prospect Cottage Garden, Dungeness, England, Derek Jarman, 1985–1991.

The basis for the second, more general reason for our approach to this book also emerges from the desire to explore possible methods of solving today's environmental and social problems (which will require a reassessment of our values), as well as appropriate ways to design our physical space. A look around the world quickly reveals that human beings have inscribed themselves into the physical environment with incredible inventiveness and force, and in both the symbolic and pragmatic realms. People have arranged and adapted their living environment; they have conjured up amazing creations that exhibit a high level of mastery of natural processes and – especially – the ability to coexist with them in a fragile balance. Today this balance has been all but destroyed, and thus it has become necessary to re-examine the origins and foundations of our relationship to nature and to our fellow human beings. At the very centre of this relationship stands the garden as its metaphor and also as a multi-faceted reality.

For the authors who contributed to this book, the garden was an inspiration, the starting point for engaging in the kind of reflection that will help us understand not only landscape architecture, but much more than that. Thus, the book is intended not only for landscape architects but for all curious readers. "After all", wrote the vice-dean of the Biotechnical faculty, Mojca Golobič in her short dedication to Ogrin in the Slovenian version, "the garden, like the house and the family, is almost universal in giving meaning to the human microcosmos. And it is even more intimate than that. First, there was the garden, yes – as you know: Adam and Eve. And the garden is at the end."[8]

Garden, landscape, nature

With its varied perspectives, the book *Garden and Metaphor* unveils the multi-layered contextual essence of the garden and explores more contemporary concepts of (re)designing nature in both public and private life. Renowned experts in the fields of landscape architecture, architecture, art, literature, philosophy, and sociology place the garden in the context of contemporary ways of life and the social questions we face. Thus, the book compiles a unique collection of essays about the meaning and role of the garden for the quality of life on this planet, where mankind and nature are still inextricably linked. In this sense, the book is an interdisciplinary exploration of what has been called the heart of landscape architecture: the meaning of the garden in our time.

The English edition of *Garden and Metaphor* is divided into six chapters that frame ideas about the meaning of the garden. The contributions in the *Garden as Essence* section present views on the existential role of the garden, its inherent

8 Mojca Golobič, Foreword, *Vrt in prispodoba*, Ljubljana: Biotechnical Faculty and Museum for Architecture and Design, 2021, p. 15.

contradictions and potential. The part *Garden as Future* opens up possible future scenarios, while *Garden as Community* presents the complexities of current practice, emphasizing the multiple potential of the garden. The chapter *Garden as Enchantment* digs into the sensual and spiritual aspect, as well as into the joy gardens offer us in both the public and private realms. *Garden as Art* exposes the somewhat unfathomable dimension of human involvement with nature, and *Garden as Reflection* offers some philosophical insights in the past and present aspects of this relationship.

In some ways, the arrangement is an artificial one: the garden is characterized precisely by its capacity to belong to many worlds simultaneously. It can be all of the above. Indeed, it is because the garden is connected to two worlds, the world of man and the world of nature, that Michel Foucault located it at the centre of his concept of heterotopia.[9] The garden is and is not nature. It is not nature but nevertheless is still part of nature, and it is thus also not entirely human. The garden is a space of transition between two worlds; it belongs to both worlds and to neither at the same time. It is a construction of reality and also its embodiment. The garden is both nature and culture, and not entirely one or the other. Anyone can make their own garden, if nowhere else, in their imagination.

Clearly, the garden is not pristine, wild nature. The natural processes that are allowed to flow in the garden are invisible during many phases of its development. What separates it from the landscape is the fact that it is enclosed. It is an enclosed piece of land, separated from the rest of the world. Well, at least at the beginning that was what it was. Even if new forms of the garden are no longer fenced in, they still have at their centre someone who cultivates them.[10] On the other

9 Michel Foucault, "Des espaces autres: Hétérotopies", March 1967. English edition: "Of Other Spaces: Utopias and Heterotopias", translated by Jay Miskowiec, *Diacritics*, 16 (1986) 1, pp. 22–27, John Hopkins University Press. https://doi.org/10.2307/464648, https://www.jstor.org/stable/464648

10 In this context, the garden of the British film director Derek Jarman is particularly interesting. He created it in defiance of the unfavourable weather conditions on the windy Dungeness coast. His garden is a metaphor of the will to live and a manifestation of the *open* garden, the garden that is made without plans and is never finished. See Derek Jarman, *Modern Nature: Journals, 1989–1990,* foreword Olivia Laing, London: Penguin Books, 2018; Derek Jarman and Howard Sooley, *Derek Jarman's Garden,* New York: Overlook Press, 1995.

hand, the term *landscape,* though in essence referring to cultural phenomena, is not connected to a specific terrain, at least not in the same way as *countryside* or *region*; its primary definition – although there are others – resides in the vista. In the Renaissance, when the concept was invented, *landscape* turned the countryside, hitherto a socioproductive category, into an object of aesthetic contemplation. The only boundaries of *landscape* became those to which the gaze could reach. And, of course, landscape, not only as an idea but also as a physis, was – and still is – no longer nature. The design of landscape, whether for practical or aesthetic purposes, involves the search for and establishment of control over natural processes, which are the necessary ingredients for all interventions in the landscape. However, natural processes often run counter to the boundaries established by people. They also do so in the garden, but in the garden they are easier to master. The garden, as Marušič writes in his contribution: "is a response to the complexity and uncertainty of the world in which we must live". The garden is our environment, but, at the same time, it is more than that: it is our world.[11]

Here we encounter the concept of *Umwelt* (literally: around world), the self-centred world, as conceived by Jakob von Uexküll.[12] Every living being has an environment, a space of living, but only man (who, according to Uexküll, has his own environment just like other living beings have theirs) does not live in an environment that is closed. Man's environment is composed of both culture and nature, and this is unique to humanity. Only for man does knowledge become a crucial element. If we simplify the conclusion of Giorgio Agamben, it is

11 Ivan Marušič provides a detailed presentation of the discursive division between nature and landscape, as well as the division between nature and the environment, in his book *Landscape: Creative Protection of the World*, Ljubljana: Biotehniška fakulteta, 2022.

12 The German biologist Jakob von Uexküll (1864–1944) explains how each living creature establishes a relationship with its environment and thus also co-creates it. The relationship to the environment is crucial for the survival of each organism. The Italian philosopher Giorgio Agamben presents Uexküll's ideas at the beginning of an ingenious essay in which he lays the groundwork for a new biopolitics and establishes definitions of the differences between man and animal, as well as a new relationship between man and the world. Giorgio Agamben, *L'aperto: L'uomo e l'animale,* Torino: Bollati Boringhieri, 2002. English edition: *The Open: Man and Animal*, translated by Kevin Attell, Stanford: Stanford University Press, 2003.

Alan Sonfist, *Time Landscape*, proposed 1965, completed 1978, 45×200 feet, a reconstruction of the precolonial forest that once existed within New York City, around the time of project completion.

precisely man's retreat from nature, from his animality, that allows him to create the world.[13] Just as man is not only a natural being, the human world is not composed only of nature. But now, it seems, we have come to a point in history when if we do not conserve nature as such, for its own sake, the quality of the environment as our living space will radically decrease. Nature, as we have also seen during the recent pandemic, defends itself (if we can use that word) forcefully and unpredictably. The human environment is very complex: not because we are at the top of the hierarchy of living beings, but because man is so far the only living being capable of being aware of and understanding the environments of other living beings. Maybe it is time to finally make a shift from anthropocentric to biocentric ethics. The Anthropocene has pushed us in this direction; it seems it is either this or we will not survive.

The necessity to save the planet has become urgent. Is it possible (because there is no division in the garden between nature, on the one hand, and culture on the other, because the garden *is* both from the very beginning) that the garden could provide a model for future behaviour? Could the complexity, and the union of nature and culture, which is at the heart of landscape architecture, offer plausible solutions? Sitting on the fence while advocating the rights of nature will lead nowhere, just as thoughtless exploitation of natural resources will not. And just as it is impossible to entirely separate human activity from nature, it is also clear that the human race is distinguished by its ability to transcend the rule of instinct.

From the perspective of the intricate involvement of man and nature in the

13 Ibid.

Alan Sonfist, *Time Landscape*. The photographs (2015 and 2016) show the development of the project since its completion.

Anthropocene it is pointless, as Pavel Gantar argues in his contribution, to make a division between native and foreign plants because ecosystems are in constant motion, and nature itself is chaotic and unpredictable. The assumption that native is good and foreign bad is a rigid equivalence that has entered the social discourse. What meaning, looking at this duality, can be acquired by the idea of the garden, which today appears to be one of the only possible images of harmonious balance? Which forms of the garden are accepted today and which marginalized? Is there, juxtaposed with the tendency to tame nature in cities, also a place where wild and untamed nature can exist? Where nature serves nobody and nothing? Some time ago, Robert Smithson and Alan Sonfist asked this question from a somewhat reversed perspective, pointing to a "lost past". In 1970, Smithson sketched out an idea of a *Floating Island*, a barge landscaped with soil, rock, and trees, towed by a tugboat around the island of Manhattan, which would only be realized posthumously in 2005. In 1965, Sonfist conceived and in 1978 created a project called *Time Landscape*, a plot of land in the middle of Manhattan, covered with indigenous trees. In both of these projects, the artists used native plant species that allegedly had grown in the area of present-day Manhattan before the arrival of the colonialists. But what is native today? What "nature" will we protect? And how are we going to avoid falling into the trap of making ecology an ideology, hostile to people, something that Luc Ferry warned us about as much as thirty years ago?[14]

14 Luc Ferry, *Le Nouvel Ordre écologique: l'arbre, l'animal et l'homme,* Paris: Éditions Grasset, 1992. English edition: *The New Ecological Order*, translated by Carol Volk, Chicago: University of Chicago Press, 1995.

Robert Smithson, *Floating Island*, Holt/Smithson Foundation, New York, 2005.

Humanity has become the primary geological factor. Pristine or unspoilt nature no longer exists. The little that still remains is enclosed in carefully fenced and protected nature reserves. If the garden is a demonstration of our attitude towards nature, or our idea of what pure nature is like, then we could also classify nature reserves among new gardens. It could even be said that the nature reserve has taken on the role of the garden of paradise, the garden as it was before man ate from the tree of knowledge, the garden from which man was expelled. Necessary not only for the conservation of threatened species of animals and plants, but for entire ecosystems, nature reserves function as a sort of new arcadia without man. Human beings protect the nature reserve from themselves, thereby purchasing indulgences that will allow them to lumber around outside of it, also closing their eyes to social differences: the social effects of environmental changes are profound, and the most vulnerable groups pay the price for mankind's arrogant relationship to the planet. For this reason, interrogating the meaning of the garden, which also stands as a metaphor for cultivation and care, is not only a question connected to the preservation of nature but also touches on the very essence of humanity.

The garden is a space in which man orders his world. The garden is a space of freedom, a space of wonder. And yet, today, despite social progress, not everyone can afford a garden. From the beginning, the garden has been (and often still is) a sign of privilege and wealth. The global Covid pandemic revealed the garden not only as a privilege, but as a metaphor for selfishness. Access to gardens in the form of various urban green areas once again raised important questions about social justice. Thus, reflections about the garden as a point of departure for spatial planning as well as a foundation for our relation to nature not only touches on the urgent need to conserve nature and protect the environment, but also on issues related to climate change. These reflections also touch on questions of equal access to "gardens" and encompass all the integrated meanings of the garden as a concept and as an emblem of spatial interdependence: a place where people have active contact with nature and which thus becomes a constituent element of their living environment, an environment that they co-create.

The dual nature of the garden and the garden as creative gesture

The collection of essays in this book offers a perspective beyond the self-evident everyday reality of the garden and reopens questions about what the garden actually is and what it represents. It asks whether the garden today, in a time when we no longer think in terms of metaphors, can even be a metaphor. Can the garden, as a place of nature *and* culture, body *and* spirit, continue to function as a metaphor, and, if so, of what? Or, are our circumstances such that the garden has become solely the terrain for our direct engagement? For example, are the community gardens that have en masse appeared in our cities merely spaces for satisfying our current life needs? What is their message? Are they perhaps a metaphor for the desire to form communities? Or merely the expression of this desire? The idea of the garden as the totality of the world[15] is long obsolete: our understanding of the world has changed so much that new forms of the garden are appearing. And yet – either despite or perhaps because of it – is it possible to conceive of the garden today in a way that would encompass the entire world? Perhaps the new language of garden design, the language of relaxed disorder that we encounter in community

15 The Gardens of Versailles, otherwise the apex of a long period of development, are considered the canonical example of the garden as totality of the world. The gardens, which cover some eight hundred hectares, appear to extend into infinity with their mirroring pools, the monumental flow of the trees, the refined tectonic structure. They are the single most famous and brilliant spatial incarnation of man's will to power.

gardens and also in the "redesigns" of our streets (regardless of whether these are the ad hoc interventions of inhabitants or are generated by city planners) referred to by thinkers such as Urška Jurman, Martin Rein-Cano, and Lilli Lička is a language of hospitality, which may be the garden's new potentiality. Yet, even if the garden as a space of meaningful structure is less frequent today than the garden as an everyday practice, the later may just *seem* to be casually disarrayed. After all, such casualness is virtually always the result of a sequence of agreed-upon rules for the careful selection and arrangement of plant and animal life.

The question then is: what is the goal of this endeavour? Perhaps we need nothing else but to transcend the dualistic conception of nature and culture and begin to create a non-dualistic unified philosophy of nature that will fundamentally change our behaviour. This is what Martin Prominski challenges us to do. And again, precisely the garden, which has long functioned as a unifying force, is the space and place in which the world of man and the world of nature, regardless of what form they take, are the most interconnected.

Marc Treib asks if the garden must be a metaphor at all. Addressing the question of what we acquire when we attribute to the garden cognitive associations that transcend our direct experience, he answers that it is precisely the fragmentation of meaning and the multitude of cultural codes that makes it necessary to focus first on the garden as a space of enjoyment. And yet, perhaps precisely because of its power as a space of coexistence, the garden remains a utopia that guides our behaviour: that is its most powerful metaphor. Even Treib recognizes that the garden emerged from the necessity to create a more beautiful and fertile world than the one in which we live.[16] Which is why, in our search for a path into the future, the garden remains

16 Marc Treib, *Austere Gardens,* Novato, CA: ORO editions, 2016. On Treib's initiative, Jane Gillette's book *The Most Beautiful Gardens Ever Written*, was published by Gordon Goff, the publisher of ORO editions, in 2016. The book is a guidebook that takes us across the world and through the periods of human history in order to reveal the function, sensuality, and meaning of the most beautiful imagined gardens from the literature of Murasaki Shikibu to Gustave Flaubert.

a metaphor that will continue to produce new knowledge and insights.

Thus, this book does not offer perspectives into history, but confronts the question of how to understand the garden and what to do in order to create a better and more beautiful world than the one in which we live. The fact is that man exerts such a powerful influence on nature that man and nature can no longer be separated.[17] How can we accept the reality of such a connection? If the whole world is our garden, how should we behave in it? How should we order it, make use of it, and also conserve and protect it?

In 2012, Carl Steinitz, a global authority in the field of landscape planning, published the book *A Framework for Geodesign,*[18] in which he presents key concepts, history, and methodology, and, from this framework, derives methods for ordering the planet. This, he believes, is the scale that must guide our thinking. Before deciding, each intervention should be reflected upon from the perspective of the wider spatial and social context and its long-term consequences. But above all, it is necessary to balance and harmonize (political) interests. Steinitz emphasizes that most key decisions about how our future world will look like are made outside of the professional circles of landscape architecture – namely in the fields of politics, law, and economy. A broader awareness is necessary of the connection and co-dependence of nature and culture mirrored in our actions.

Yet regardless of how necessary the systemic change in thought and action is, Foucault's concept of heterotopia – an authentically embedded place that in the middle of our world opens into another – a place of communication and tension between the real and the miraculous, resides in the anti-utilitarian nature of the garden. We can look upon it as a space that

17 Agamben writes about the interconnection of all living things in his book *Il regno e il giardino,* Vicenza: Neri Pozza Editore, 2019. English edition: *The Kingdom and the Garden,* translated by Adam Kotsko, Calcutta: Seagull Books, 2020. With his reinterpretation of Christian traditions, Agamben shows how the Garden of Eden has long been a symbol of Man's true nature. Our future resides in this garden, where there is no division between nature and culture. *Earthly paradise* is presented as a political project, because, Agamben claims, paradise has become alien to us and we must win it back.

18 Carl Steinitz, *A Framework for Geodesign: Changing Geography by Design,* Redlands: Esri Press, 2012.

escapes the logic of commodification and financial valuation because, as Marušič claims, the garden is a place to which symbolic meaning, emotions, and identity are deeply connected. At the same time, the garden is nature (Martin Prominski, Saskia de Wit, Nadja Zgonik), is art (Lev Kreft, Miklavž Komelj, Olaf Nicolai, Erika Bordon), and is also a political project that creates new methods of cooperation and collectivization (Urška Jurman, Lisa Diedrich, Lilli Lička).

The political nature of the garden is nothing new, the ultimate example being the Gardens of Versailles. This arrogant show of authority displayed by perpendicularly subordinated nature governed by axial symmetry saw its antipode in England: there the social change of the 18th century demanded the invention of the new space, which in the formal sense, in its image and intent, and even in its method of use, insisted on demonstrating the inextricable link between nature and culture.[19] Currently, it seems, a similarly profound change is occurring in the language of landscape design, giving priority to biodiversity and micro-climate mitigation over other dimensions of "the garden". By contrast, Martin Rein-Cano supports his reflections about the contemporary implications of the development of English landscape garden with an example which, despite his perhaps peripheral point of departure, awakens the memory of the stylistic eclecticism that was present in the design of parks in the late 18th century and throughout the 19th century, and the enchantment with fragments from history and "exotic lands" of which the most celebrated are Désert de Retz and Parc des Buttes-Chaumont,[20] but uses it to enhance a more democratic use of urban space in a multi-cultural society.

Relying on familiar imaginaries is understandable, as we have yet to create new ones. In addition, we also witness the repetition of certain practices that continue to pop up in

19 The garden as an expression of a certain social-cultural situation is per se a political statement. The political is revealed in the structure as well as in the formal language of the garden. The Versailles Gardens with their visual language of axial symmetry, the illusion of infinity, and the convergence of vistas, embody absolutism. In contrast, in the 18th century, both as a form of rebellion and as a need of the Enlightenment nobility and the new liberal bourgeoisie for their own spatial expression, the English landscape garden emerged. This school of design, inventing a space of undulating lawns and scattered clumps of trees, saw perpendicularity as reactionary and rejected it "with disgust", as Christian Cay Lorenz Hirschfeld claims in *Theorie der Gartenkunst* from 1779.

20 Jurgis Baltrušaitis, *Aberrations: Quatre essais sur la legende des formes,* Paris: Perrin, 1957. English edition: *Aberrations: An Essay on The Legend of Form,* translated by Richard Miller, Cambridge, MA: MIT Press, 1989.

related forms, even though, as a result of their fragmentation and lack of systemization, they are still not compelling or efficient enough to change the way we function in the world. Activism still takes place in the same basic format as it did in the 1960s and 1970s. Even calls to care for the planet as our greatest garden were already loud throughout the second half of the 20th century, which was also a period during which tools and methods were developed that, given sufficient political will, would have allowed us to coordinate economic progress and environmental conservation.[21]

And still, the garden, regardless of its explicit purpose – cultivation, indulgence, meditation, or representation – remains the juncture and intersection of two worlds, the world of man and the world of nature, the reality of the senses and the reality of thought – both actually and in representation. A series of metaphors emerges from this. For Dean Komel, the garden is comprised of multiple realities and multiple metaphors that he draws on from his own experience. Aleš Vodopivec sees the garden as a shelter in an uncertain world, and offers some examples of poetic dialogue between architecture and nature, and Mateja Kurir muses about the garden as the intersection of the physical and the spiritual, the sensual and the rational drawing on the example of the Garden of Epicurus.

The garden is a liminal space in which the two worlds meet, two worlds that are otherwise separated by the eternal and unchanging order of the universe. It is also always a space of the fabulous, the unknown, the unexpected. Thus, the individual and society, the personal and the cultural, the instinctive and the spiritual, the real and the imaginary, the seen and the unseen, the possible and the impossible meet in the garden. The garden is the space of all types of conversations and all possible meetings. In the stories from *One Thousand and One*

21 Rachel Carson, *Silent Spring*, Boston: Houghton Mifflin, 1962; Ian L. McHarg, *Design with Nature*, Garden City, NY: Natural History Press (for the American Museum of Natural History), 1969.

Nights, as Dževad Karahasan explains in *Knjiga vrtova* (Book of Gardens),[22] the garden is a pool of possible encounters. In Scheherazade's stories, everything that is taboo in society or seems impossible can take place in the garden and only in the garden. The dichotomies that emerged during the Enlightenment do not apply in the garden. For Karahasan, therefore, the garden is not only a metaphor of multi-culturalism, but also an actual space of the flourishing of a multitude of cultures, not only in the horticultural sense. In his contribution to this publication, he speaks about the complexity and the principles of inclusion. The garden is Alice's Wonderland.

Andrew Benjamin and Gerard Reinmuth also refer to the complexity of the garden. They discuss the borderline, liminal nature of the garden with the legendary story of the expulsion from paradise, in which the border as a method of determining and/or rearranging the territory is placed in a clear political context. Benjamin and Reinmuth describe this delineation as an expanded intermediate space which represents both the original characteristic of the garden and the possibility of modernizing our perception of it. Such a modernization would break with the logic of the garden as seen through the eyes of the Enlightenment, i.e. as a setting for human leisure, and instead define it as a place of biodiversity, a place that would (at last) also include animals; at the same time, it would clearly separate the garden from the wilderness because such a biodiversity is the result of human interventions.

Sven-Olov Wallenstein also problematizes the Enlightenment canons that emerged from the conception of nature as it was then, which is very different from our contemporary conception. Wallenstein introduces the issue of understanding the garden through the aspect of nature with the help of the discourse developed by the Italian historian of architecture

22 In *Knjiga vrtova* (Sarajevo: Connectum, 2008), Dževad Karahasan establishes the garden as a metaphor of language and analyses the role of the garden in the stories from *One Thousand and One Nights*, revealing the garden as a fateful compositional node that crucially influences the destinies of the protagonists. Only in the garden are the (fateful) encounters of two worlds possible: the seen and unseen, the living and dead (the world of people and the world of souls and deities), the real and the imaginary.

Manfredo Tafuri, who took the change of the Enlightenment position as the point of departure for the critique of modernist architecture and its attitude towards nature.

The garden is once again a topic of interest. We live in an era when, regardless of cultural and geographical differences, the intricate engagement of man and nature is so all-encompassing as to be finally inextricable. For this reason, it is urgently necessary to rethink and re-examine our relationship to the world, to define new concepts of nature, and to work for the good of our planet (Lisa Diedrich, Saskia de Wit, Miloš Kosec, Janez Marušič, Martin Prominski, Carl Steinitz, Udo Weilacher). Steinitz is critical of making the garden the signifier of landscape architecture because so many who work in the field understand the garden as a luxury for a few selected people. He believes that the garden is understood in this way within the Eurocentric cultural model, which, given today's challenges, is far too narrow a perspective. Nevertheless, his call for the design of the world in which, to one degree or another, we would all participate, can be read as a metaphor of concern for the environment and for our fellow human beings, something that both Kinga Szilágyi and Davorin Gazvoda address in their contributions. Today, the garden is not only a metaphor of leisurely life, but increasingly a metaphor of respect for people and nature in the time to come, which can also be read in Mladen Dolar's contribution about Candide. As Dolar emphasizes, Candide's legendary and repetitive summons to cultivate our own garden is not a call to withdraw into privacy, into a sublime shelter, but rather a call for engagement, for change. In this spirit, we could say that if the world is our garden, we must cultivate it. To cultivate means to have respect for what is cultivated. To think ahead. To plan. Such an effort is by definition collective.

If for Steinitz the garden as a metaphor of luxury and exclusivity is not worth considering when reflecting on a model for future actions, for Lev Kreft, the garden, as we know it, gives no hope for other reasons: if the garden is a metaphor or image, it is of powerlessness and limitation. Creation, Kreft claims,

The Parc de Buttes-Chaumont, Paris, 1867, designed by Jean-Charles Adolphe Alphand and built in a former quarry and refuse dump, is a prime example of the enchantment with fragments from history and "exotic lands". Its famous feature Temple de la Sibylle was inspired by Roman ruins and is located on a bluff fifty metres above an artificial lake.

is beyond the scope of humanity. Similarly, Nadja Zgonik explores the development of the language of garden design, and places processes in nature in the foreground as opposed to form that emerges from human intervention into nature. She sees the latter as an increasingly obvious manifestation of our changed relation to nature. The symbolic potential of the enclosed garden as paradise, claims Zgonik, has increasingly changed into its de-idealized opposite. At the same time, we also are witness to the consumption of the garden as an image.

Jure Mikuž addresses this phenomenon, describing the culture of selfies that generalizes and flattens our relation to the world.

In all of the essays in this collection, we see the dual nature of the garden as, on the one hand, a tendency to situate man in the world, a tendency for order and control, and, on the other hand, a space of unpredictability, wildness, the miraculous, and the tendency towards all that is other, all that is different. With its reflections on the garden, the book as a whole advocates a necessary change in our perspectives on the relation between humanity and nature. Many of the essays suggest that we must rethink our way of dealing with nature and ourselves. We find a frequent equation of social justice with "justice towards nature". Ideas about the usefulness and usability of the garden as fundamental infrastructure are increasingly emphasized in our contemporary practice and in our struggle for such practice, in response to questions of access to "our own garden" even if in alternative urban forms and to questions of the necessity of "the garden" for quality of life. After all, green spaces in our cities are systems, just as any other infrastructure that makes cities work; they are a public good and serve the public interest, which may be the one true sense of the garden as a contemporary metaphor. Catharine Ward Thompson emphasizes how important it is for the health of people of all ages living in cities to have access to urban nature, from formal to informal gardens, even places where nature springs up spontaneously. But the garden is not only characterized by the principles of *utilitas* and *firmitas* – both enabled by our knowledge of nature and natural processes as well as by technical advancement – demanding an ongoing interplay of human involvement

"La colonne détruite" at Désert de Retz, Chambourcy, France, François Racine de Monville, 1777–1782.

and withdrawal; there is, of course, also the principle of *venustas* – the mysterious, ambiguous illusion of the world, which, despite its resistance to time captured in the circle of life, reveals the uncertain quality of our existence and the transitory nature of our moment.

In our search for a new relation to nature, in the formation of metaphors and their realization, we do not want to lose the testimonial, mythological, and cultural integrity of the garden as a symbol of the ultimate human intervention into nature. Both usefulness and usability emerge from what this world already has to offer, and so in our search for a contemporary paradise, for a garden that will help us to survive, we need imagination, because only imagination can open new worlds beyond the one we already have.

Most of the contributions in the book do not describe human intervention into nature as a threat, but rather as a creative gesture. The time has come to create an *open* garden. As human beings, we not only take from nature but also give back precisely when we create and this is what continues to place our greatest hope in the hands of humanity.

After what has already occurred in the 21st century, we can be certain: the future will not be easy. But we have no choice: we must summon our knowledge, curiosity, and imagination, and jump down the rabbit hole. G&M

Olmsted's Long Meadow, Prospect Park, Brooklyn, New York, Olmsted, Vaux & Co., 1871.

Japanese Gardens

34

Photographs by *Anne Schwalbe*

Garden as Essence

A Renaissance "wilderness": *Très Riches Heures (The Very Rich Hours)*, April, Frères de Limbourg, c. 1412–1416.

The Garden of Life: From Birth to Death, Where Else but a Garden?

Catharine Ward Thompson

The garden as a concept continues to hold meaning as it has done across many cultures, over many thousands of years. It has always been in some way an expression of a "heavenly place", whether the Paradise of ancient Persia, the Garden of Eden in which Adam and Eve roamed, the Buddhist "pure land" of Amida or the Elysian Fields of classical Greek and Roman literature.[1] Culturally laden in terms of design and detail, it nonetheless expresses a universal desire for a version of the natural world in which nature is bountiful and non-threatening: a delightful, multi-sensory experience offering refreshment for body and soul.

In my brief discourse here, I distinguish the garden from the public park. The public park, as developed in an increasingly urbanized world from the 19th century onwards, is conventionally a place designed to serve society and (at least potentially) open to all users. In practice, the legitimacy of uses and users, and the freedom of access to all members of society, has been a contested issue, much challenged in park provision. The public park continues to be a place where the democratic process is worked out, quite literally, on the ground[2] but its principles are founded in a desire to provide a place of recreation for the whole community.

By contrast, the garden is a place where we reveal our private desires and aspirations, our images of a personal, heavenly

1 Catharine Ward Thompson, "Linking Landscape and Health: the Recurring Theme", *Landscape and Urban Planning*, 99 (3), 2011, pp. 187–195; M. P. Keane, *Japanese Garden Design*, N. Clarendon, VT: Tuttle Publishing, 2012.

2 Catharine Ward Thompson, "Urban Open Space in the 21st Century", *Landscape and Urban Planning*, 60 (2), 2002, pp. 59–72; Catharine Ward Thompson, "Historic American Parks and Contemporary Needs", *Landscape Journal*, 17 (1), 1998, pp. 1–25.

place to be and to cultivate, or perhaps just an attractive place, "heavenly enough", that is easy to maintain. And images of idealized "nature" are very much part of the garden, whether as a contrast to the wilderness or desert beyond, or as somehow capturing that very wildness, in a particular way, within the garden. The "wilderness" of Renaissance garden illustrations seems an ordered array of trees and shrubs to contemporary eyes but, for all that, may have contained far more biodiversity of life, especially insects and animals, than any wild place experienced in most people's urbanized life today. Even when we go to nature reserves or wilder landscapes now, we are experientially unaware of the reduction in biodiversity compared to a century ago, and our habituation to it. We don't miss what we have never experienced, goes the argument, so as each generation grows up with a more impoverished experience of wildlife and its diversity, our imagined "bountiful nature" is not rich in species but increasingly limited, despite the abundance of colourful and exotic-looking plant cultivars produced by the horticulture industry. And the desert beyond the garden's boundary is as likely, in the 21st century, to be the urban desert of a paved and impermeable built environment or the green desert of intensive monocultural agricultural production.

Feel Good Garden by Matt Keightley, for Chelsea Flower Show, London, 2018.

A replication of wilderness

So, in studying gardens in recent decades as exclusive places set apart for particular groups or individuals, we continue to get insights into the aspirations and tastes at the heart of different members of society. They reflect their users' sociocultural contexts, set against broader global fashions and concerns in this internet age. If we look back over the last century in the UK, for example, we can see the changing priorities (for those with wealth and resource enough) illustrated in the award-winning gardens designed for the annual Chelsea Flower Show in London. We can see celebrations of plant diversity in: the massed groups of propagated cultivars with their huge range of colours (early 1900s); in the elaborately constructed rockeries that emulated an idealized form of wild mountain nature (1930s); in the supposedly "naturalistic" herbaceous border of the "English country garden", with plants from all parts of the world that actually require very high levels of maintenance (1950s); in enthusiasm for the exotic "otherness" (to British eyes) of orchids (1960s); in the desire for order, neatness, and ease of maintenance in households with small gardens and no time to spare, covering their garden with timber decking and

Irish Sky Garden by Diarmuid Gavin, Chelsea Flower Show, London, 2011.

river pebbles (1970s and 1980s); in the prominence of the celebrity garden designer (1990s) and in the 21st century enthusiasm for pollinator-friendly gardens, reflecting our concern over their loss in the wild. Commentary on the 2016 Chelsea Flower Show, for example, notes "For most of the top designers, the overall theme remains extreme naturalism ... entire regions are evoked by designers ... who seek to replicate wilderness."[3]

It would be a wonderful time-travel experiment to be able to compare the biodiversity of, say, a mediaeval "flowery mede" or a pleasance with that of a 21st century "wildflower meadow" designed to encourage pollinators and wildlife in the garden.

3 Joanna Fortnam and Gordon Rayner, "Chelsea Flower Show 2016: The Telegraph Garden Wins Best in Show", *The Telegraph*, 26 May 2016.

Mediaeval flowery mede/pleasaunce: illustration from *Roman de la Rose* (*The Romance of the Rose*), Master of the Prayer Books, Bruges, c. 1490–1500.

One suspects the former would be far richer in species, flora, and fauna, than the latter, whatever the intentions of the gardeners in trying to control or encourage biodiversity. And while we now recognize the vital importance of paying attention to species extinction and its prevention, wherever possible, we remain aware of the many hazards that nature still presents for human well-being. Climate change, global travel, and mass transport of goods brings the prospect of a return to Europe of diseases once eradicated, such as malaria, and the increasing spread of others into new territory, e.g. Lyme (borreliosis) disease, into northern Europe. We find that our enthusiasm for wild grasslands or natural water bodies bring new health hazards (or rediscovered ones) alongside biodiversity. As T. S. Eliot said, "humankind cannot bear very much reality"[4] and our gardens reflect our desire for only as much reality as we can cope with.

A multi-sensory experience

Yet recent research on the human microbiome suggests we need more contact with nature than many are comfortable with in today's sanitized lifestyles. The very first days, weeks, and months of a baby's life are times when its immune system is at crucial stages of development, supported by its contact with a diverse microbiota in the external environment. Growing up in microbe-rich environments can support good health in children, especially in guarding against allergic disease, but changes in human lifestyles, diet, and

4 T. S. Eliot, "Burnt Norton" in *Four Quartets*, London: Faber & Faber, 1941.

Child and parent in allotment, Edinburgh, 2003.

Child with spade and stick in a puddle, 2015.

living environment as a result of urbanization seem to have threatened this.[5] Many children now grow up with very limited exposure to soil, vegetation, and animal biodiversity. If we add these understandings to those now well-established arguments for the importance of access to natural places for a child's healthy development in all its dimensions, physical, mental, social, educational, and emotional,[6] it seems that the garden is potentially an ideal environment for this, offering a non-threatening, multi-sensory, and biodiverse experience.

We thus find ourselves returning to the writings of Patrick Geddes, among others, who a century ago promoted the importance of embodied, outdoor learning as part of a healthy education for children and who was instrumental in his native Scotland in developing small garden plots for school children to enjoy in the densely-packed, hard urban environment of Edinburgh's Old Town: "by leaves we live".[7] As we confirm the importance of the garden as the ideal place for a healthy childhood, so we also remember its importance in old age. Whether we're following Voltaire's Candide in his encouragement to cultivate one's garden as a peaceful end to a turbulent life, or considering recent evidence on the virtues of access to a garden for healthy ageing,[8] the garden, or at least access to it, may be the best place for our declining years – an important message in an ageing society. G&M

5 Nishat Tasnim, Nijiati Abulizi, Jason Pither, Miranda M. Hart, Deanna L. Gibson, "Linking the Gut Microbial Ecosystem with the Environment: Does Gut Health Depend on Where We Live?", *Frontiers in Microbiology*, 8 (1935), 2017. doi:10.3389/fmicb.2017.01935

6 Sarah MacQuarrie, Clare Nugent, Claire Warden, "Learning with Nature and Learning from Others: Nature as Setting and Resource for Early Childhood Education", *Journal of Adventure Education and Outdoor Learning*, 15 (1), 2015, pp. 1–23; Andrey I. Egorov, Pierpaolo Mudu, Matthias Braubach, Marco Martuzzi, *Urban Green Spaces and Health*, Copenhagen: World Health Organization Regional Office for Europe, 2016; Elizabeth A. Richardson, Jamie Pearce, Niamh K. Shortt, Richard Mitchell, "The Role of Public and Private Natural Space in Children's Social, Emotional and Behavioural Development in Scotland: A Longitudinal Study", *Environmental Research*, 158, 2017, pp. 729–736.

7 Catharine Ward Thompson, "Patrick Geddes and the Edinburgh Zoological Garden: Expressing Universal Processes through Local Place", *Landscape Journal*, 25 (1), 2006, pp. 80–93.

8 Theresa L. Scott, Barbara M. Masser, Nancy A. Pachana, "Exploring the Health and Well-Being Benefits of Gardening for Older Adults", *Ageing & Society*, 35 (10), 2015, pp. 2176–2200.

The Garden as the Experience of a Promised World

Janez Marušič

It is difficult to limit discussions of the garden and its symbolism to reflections about a plot of land we love so much that we place a fence around it because of that love. The garden is an important symbol of controlling and enclosing space, not only because of the territorialism to which we are inclined as a biological species, but – and perhaps above all – as a response to the complexity and uncertainty of the world in which we live. To fence in uncertainty softens it a bit. And yet despite fences, we have not managed to separate the world from the garden. The garden remains the world. And that indeed is its crucial feature.

As the philosopher Paolo Virno observed, the experience of the world is that which is most human, that which separates humans from all other beings. Living beings, all of them, are destined to exist within their own particular environments.[1] The human environment is a dynamic structure that is constantly being reshaped within the world, transformed to human needs and humanity's growing capacity to read and understand the world.

The landscape is also a world. Like the human environment, it is a dynamic composition of useful or in some way important components. Like the world, it is a region of unpredictability, and, for this reason, is an object of ceaseless exploration, discovery, evaluation, and also of corrections and additions, and above all newly discovered uncertainty. Thus, the garden is a

1 "Man does not have an environment, if by this term we mean a circumscribed vital sphere, rigidly fixed and not subject to transformation, each part of which corresponds to an operational task of a specific organism." Paolo Virno, *Scienze sociali e "natura umana". Facoltà di linguaggio, invariante biologico, rapporti di produzione*, Soveria Mannelli: Rubbettino Editore, 2002, p. 32. Translation into English by Erica Johnson Debeljak.

landscape around which we put a fencc and where we impose order to at least somewhat reduce our uncertainty. The garden is an artefact that does not want to be an artefact. For this reason, unnecessary artifice in the garden and landscape results

Gustave Doré's illustration to Dante's *Inferno*, 1857. Canto I begins with the famous line "I found myself within a forest dark".

in its negation. The garden is a narrative that does not want to, and must not tell all that can be told.[2]

The meanings of the garden are various, from survivalist utilitarianism to human spirituality. We speak of the utilitarian garden that can be a vegetable garden, an herbal garden, an orchard, or other forms of gardens where we cultivate what we need, and yet it can also be a decorative garden. Even the latter type of garden when it is planted beside a house acquires two conceptual forms: both the garden as an outdoor living room and the garden of a plant lover.

Of course, both of these meanings of the garden represent "violence" against the real role of the garden. The garden can be defined either as decorative or as utilitarian, but in fact it always performs both "tasks" at the same time. We may ascribe to the cultivation and growing of plants an emotionally based culture and a form of inspiration, and not only or merely utilitarianism. And even the residential garden is not just an extension of the living room into plants. "Living among plants" is itself an expression of human susceptibility to the spiritual inspiration of nature and to nature as a material resource.

If it perhaps seems that the utilitarian perspective of the garden is primordial because spiritual needs should follow utilitarian needs, many expressions of the past relation of man to the world in which he lives suggest that these two perspectives exist side by side and are deeply connected. This cohabitation reaches far back to the beginnings of human culture, and maybe is even biologically conditioned. The garden is man's environment, it is "the world remade", recalling the world "there outside". It is both here and familiar: "my favourite environment" which is not only an environment but also the world. As a metaphor, the garden symbolizes the transition of man from an observer of the world and a gatherer of fruits to an active

2 This is the dividing line between architecture, which produces artefacts and strives for its products to be permanent and to not change with time, and landscape architecture, which takes into account the changing nature of its results.

creator of the environment and a cultivator of nature, one who strives to tame its spontaneity.

One could say that the experience of the landscape involves a series of steps: from the perception and then understanding of the environment, the recognition of the relation between the components of the world, to an awareness of the possibilities for continued existence and activities within that environment. If the sequence of events between the beginning and end of this process is compressed, it starts with the recognition of what is seen and the experiencing of the landscape as a space of future activities and living and it ends with the "planning of survival" within that landscape. The beginning includes the current condition of the environment and also its past. The end of the experience means the end of interrogating our own situation, our possibilities of continuous existence and activities in the space, a suitable life within the environment and what everything we experience in the environment means for the future. This series of steps is not necessarily linear. It can be enriched by feedback loops and improved interpretations. It is also not always perfect.

It is common knowledge that many things captured by the retina of the human eye are only truly seen after we understand the relation between these objects, and, moreover, that many details in the environment are only truly perceived when we create explanations for what we have seen. This description

The "Casa Pendente" at Giardino degli mostri in Bomarzo. This leaning house marked the entrance to the garden during Vicino's time and the tilted floors and walls set the tone of disorientation and mystery for the garden visit.

of reality is sufficiently fundamental that it is also treated in philosophical texts. For example, it has been argued that "in experiencing reality while looking at the landscape, sensory perception unites with the deep intellect that gazes at objects".[3] But the deep intellect does not necessarily stand for the human soul. Hence we can also understand perception as the process by which information that in the previous experience of the environment was already "uploaded" into the memory "storage" of the brain (or was acquired through evolution) is interactively linked with data that the senses send to the brain.

Ludvik Bartelj argues that "The experience of reality is quotidian, untheoretical. It is typical for all living beings. It is the condition for survival, for satisfying the fundamental needs of the organism, and the human objective field of experience is complemented with realities such as culture, civilization, ethics, and religion."[4]

Biological research of organisms other than humans reveals the nature of their "orientation towards the external pre-theoretical world". This orientation expresses itself as "an evaluative response" to objects in the organism's environment. The evaluative response serves it as a sort of road map. The organism is otherwise guided by instincts, but the diversity of the environment is so great that adaptation is necessary for survival. With the help of feelings, the organism chooses the best possible responses for survival, the best possible environment,

3 Bojan Žalec, "Filozofija Franceta Vebra: kontekst, pomen in vrednost", *Anthropos* 2011, 43(3/4), pp. 105–127, here p. 113.

Giardino degli mostri in Bomarzo. The inscription above the entrance reads "Ogni pensiero vola" (every thought flies).

and in this way searches for ways to adapt to the world.[5] This is actually the organism's "gaze" into the future. Both contemporary biological research and philosophical debates rely on the writings of the ecologist Jakob von Uexküll (1864–1944) who concluded that "... all living beings, from the simplest to the most complex ... are placed in the environment with a certain level of perfection".[6] The philosopher Giorgio Agamben adds: "Where classical science saw a single world encompassing all living species, hierarchically arranged from the most basic forms to higher-level organisms, Uexküll placed an infinite variety of perceptual worlds, all as perfect and interconnected as in some sort of an extensive musical score. [...] There does not exist a forest as an objectively fixed environment: there exists a forest-for-the-park-ranger, a forest-for-the-hunter, a forest-for-the-botanist, a forest-for-the-wayfarer, a forest-for-the-nature-lover, a forest-for-the-carpenter, and finally a fable forest in which Little Red Riding Hood loses her way."[7] The perception of the forest, its particularities, are defined by interests. And these are derived from the needs of the subject defining the environment. The perception, evaluation, and experience of the environment are all connected with the needs of action and existence, with the need to live in the world.

It is possible to conclude that admiration of the landscape, the emotional response to a given landscape scene, is therefore an expression of needs, an expression of an interested (as opposed to disinterested) evaluation of the world into which we emerge. Evaluation can also be described as an interactive process, in which the reality that is perceived by our senses and recognized by our brain is juxtaposed with "sediments" of past observations and with the experience of how successfully perceived components of reality contributed to the quality of how we act in the world.

4 This quotation comes from Matjaž Potrč's review of Dr. Ludvik Bartelj's book *Ontofilozofija*. See Matjaž Potrč, "Dr. Ludvik Bartelj: Ontofilozofija", *Anthropos*, 1994, 1–3, p. 258.

5 Andreas Weber, *Alles fühlt: Mensch, Natur und die Revolution der Lebenswissenschaften*, Berlin: Berlin Verlag, 2007. English edition: *The Biology of Wonder: Aliveness, Feeling and the Metamorphosis of Science*, Gabriola Island, BC: New Society Publishers, 2016. Slovenian edition: *Čuteča narava: Človek, narava in revolucija znanosti o življenju*, Ljubljana: Modrijan, 2011, p. 69.

Evaluation means the judgement of possibilities that the individual defines as potential variants of his or her future life, existence, and activities within the space. It is the path to the creation of the individual's environment in the way that Jakob von Uexküll described different experiences of the forest depending on the interests of each individual. Certain features are attributed greater meaning, more value, while others are endowed with little value or none at all. Evaluations emerge from assumptions and norms, including ethical, ideological, or religious convictions. Of course, evaluations also depend on the particular goals that the individual wants to achieve.

Expectations are implicit in evaluative judgement. Evaluations include the future. This claim may seem unusual. That to which we attribute value is already here. The space or certain components of the space are here. They exist now, within reach, and for that reason are the objects of our evaluative interpretation. They are a part of the reality that surrounds us. But their value is not directly ascertainable. Rather it resides in a physically non-existent quality that is only revealed in the evaluation of their usefulness. Value is created in context. Usefulness or non-usefulness can only be located in possible future use. Values are not objective facts and are always an expression of perceptions of the future.

Satisfaction with the landscape

Satisfaction with the landscape could also be described as an integrated response to the possibilities of living there, existence, surveying the space, relaxation, and enjoyment of the environment. It could be said that satisfaction is a synthesis of all evaluations. The experience of the landscape is a presentation

6 Jakob von Uexküll, *Streifzüge durch die Umwelten von Tieren und Menschen: Ein Bilderbuch unsichtbarer Welten. Bedeutungslehre,* Reinbek: Rowohlt, 1956. English edition: *A Foray into the Worlds of Animals and Humans; with a Theory of Meaning*, translated by J. D. O'Neil; Introduction by D. Sagan; afterword by G. Winthrop-Young, Posthumanities series; vol. 12, Minneapolis: 1st Minnesota Press, 2016, p. 206.

7 Giorgio Agamben, *L'aperto: L'uomo e l'animale,* Torino: Bollati Boringhieri, 2002. English edition: *The Open: Man and Animal*, translated by Kevin Attell, Stanford: Stanford University Press, 2003, pp. 46–48.

of possibilities that the individual defines as variations of his or her future functioning in the space.

Satisfaction or dissatisfaction with the landscape inevitably derives from our idea of how we will act in the landscape in the next instant. The possibilities of choice determine satisfaction or dissatisfaction, "happiness" or "unhappiness" in the experience of the landscape. The sense of satisfaction in the landscape is the final step in the interactive process, which includes the evaluation of possibilities in order to realize the observer's goals and expectations. The experience of reality and the sense of satisfaction is a process that always includes, in addition to the present (perception) and the past (experience), the future (evaluation).

The Swiss historian Jacob Burckhardt, an expert on the Renaissance, wrote that the landscape was discovered by the Renaissance Italian and elaborated as follows: "But the significance of nature for a receptive spirit is fully and clearly displayed by Petrarch – one of the first truly modern men. ... The enjoyment of nature is, for him, the favourite accompaniment of intellectual pursuits."[8] Burckhardt considers Petrarch's ascent of Mont Ventoux in Provence the decisive event in this discovery. However, we can also understand Burckhardt not in the sense of the discovery of the landscape itself, but indicative of a change in how we experience landscape. Dante, only around forty years older than Petrarch, also knew about landscape. He offers a description right at the beginning of *The Divine Comedy*. But this description of the landscape is not a demonstration of the deeper effect that natural beauty has on human beings, although, as Burckhardt notes, we also encounter this in Dante. The poet finds himself in the middle of a dark wood. He experiences the landscape as a place from which he cannot

8 Jacob Burckhardt, *Die Cultur der Renaissance in Italien*, Basel: Schweighauser'sche Verlagsbuchhandlung, 1860. First English translation by S. G. C. Middlemore, *The Civilization of the Renaissance in Italy*, London: Albert & Charles Boni, 1878. English edition: *The Civilization of the Renaissance in Italy*, translated by S. G. C. Middlemore, with a new introduction by Peter Burke and notes by Peter Murray, London: Penguin Books, 1990, chapter 3–4.

Monumental perspective devoured by fog, from the series *Versailles: L'espace infini* by Ana Kučan, 2015.

Captured uncertainty, from the series *Versailles: L'espace infini* by Ana Kučan, 2015.

escape and that fills him with horror. He has no plan for the next step.

Thus, for Dante, nature is not only full of beauty. It can also be a dark pathlessness, dangerous and terrifying. Of course, Dante's predicament in the landscape is a metaphor. And yet it seems significant that Dante chose precisely the relationship to the landscape to illustrate a crisis in life.

The deeper effect that natural beauty has on the observer depends not only on her or his ability to recognize the possibilities and make a plan for the next step but also on the multiple chances embedded in the very landscape itself. This is obviously an everyday experience.

We become aware of the natural beauty of the landscape when we can endow the perceived contents of the environment with high and positive values, when we co-create potential with the landscape in order to achieve certain useful goals, satisfy our needs, fulfil our desires and mission in the world – in the landscape.

The garden as a safe world

The garden is reality. It is a world that offers human beings a safe and suitable next step. It is a world that is safe (enclosed). It is a world that enables in the most direct possible way "the next step" (the garden path). It is a world that provides spatial clarity (order – arrangement of the elements of the garden) and temporal clarity (plants that allow us to recognize the seasons, an open sky that tells the time with its light and sunbeams and heavenly bodies).

The garden can be a display of the idealized end of the process of experiencing the world. It is a landscape in which the next step is not unknown: it is a remade world in which we recognize many things and we can read their narratives. We feel safe in the garden. Although we are in the world and there is much that is unknown around us, we feel at home in the garden, in our own environment.

Perhaps the image of such a garden can be best seen in its opposite, its antithesis: the Giardino degli mostri (the Park of the Monsters) at Bomarzo. The creators of the garden, Vicino Orsini (1523–1585) and Pirro Ligorio (1514–1583), were in their own way following the spirit of the times or not (their reasons are not entirely known to us), but their garden is the antithesis of the accepted symbolism of the garden described above. It appears to be a protest against the enclosure of a human environment within the world, a protest against the idealized experience of the world as an earthly paradise. In reality, the world is cruel and unforgiving. All possible monsters attack man: earthquakes, plagues, beasts, wars, invading Hannibals with their elephants. And merciless time reigns over all, burying beneath the soil magnificent antique temples of which we can only catch a glimpse of a cornerstone here and there.

Is the symbolism of the garden that we receive from history still relevant at all? What is the symbolism of the garden in the time of information abundance and artificial intelligence? Indeed, what is uncertainty anymore? Can the metaphors used by Dante and also by the Slovenian Romantic poet France Prešeren,[9] still be understood? Can the symbolism of the garden persist – home, certainty, reconciliation with time – when the dangers of wilderness have subsided or been mitigated by modern technology, at least in many affluent countries?

Uncertainty is timeless. This is beautifully evident in the series of photographs of the gardens of Versailles submerged in fog.[10] The photographs reveal the universality of the uncertainty

9 France Prešeren, "Mid Wastes of Africa a Wanderer Sped", *Sonnets of Unhappiness and Other Poems*, translated by Paul Server, Ljubljana: Založba Sanje. https://cangura.com/knjigarna/knjige/sonnets-of-unhappiness-and-other-poems-f-preseren/. Slovenian edition: *Poezije*, Ljubljana: Joshef Blasnik, 1833. France Prešeren (1800–1849) wrote the first Slovene ballad and the first Slovene epic. After his death, he became the leading name of the Slovene literary canon.

10 These photographs, taken by Ana Kučan, were used to illustrate the Slovenian translation of Érik Orsenna's *Portrait d'un homme heureux: André Le Nôtre, 1613–1700,* Paris: Folio, 2000. Slovenian edition: *Portret srečnega človeka: André Le Nôtre, 1613–1700*, translated by Zoja Skušek, Ljubljana: Založba /*cf., 2016.

Sennedjem and Iynerferti in Aaru, the "field of reeds", wall painting in their crypt, Thebes, Deir el-Medina, Egypt, c. 1295–1213 BCE, documented by Charles K. Wilkinson, 1922, tempera on paper.

of the world, and this with the well-chosen and apt metaphor of denying the most outstanding message of the Versailles gardens: their monumental perspective.

It is difficult to judge whether the obsessive use of balconies, terraces, and roofs in multi-unit apartment houses for the utilitarian purpose of growing plants and urban beekeeping is a long-term trend. Miniature gardens are perhaps a response to lives lived mostly in enclosed spaces (cars, buildings etc.).[11] They also are a – somewhat naïve – reaction to the fact that the supply of food may become a primary concern in the time to come. Of course, miniature balconies and roof gardens are rather a symbolic gesture than a serious contribution to food security. But even as a form of relaxation in cultivating plants and small animals, these little gardens speak above all to our anxieties which are expressed as a return to earlier forms of humanity's survival practices.

It should not be overlooked that such a return does not necessarily emerge from the actual need for survival, but from a symbolic escape to a time when supposedly work was pleasant and life calm and predictable. The grave paintings on the tomb of the ancient Egyptian artisan Sennedjem and his wife, Iynerferti, in Deir el-Medina, a settlement close to the royal tombs in the Valley of Kings, speak eloquently to this point.

11 The cultural historian Rebecca Solnit describes how the life of many people is spent in a series of interiors that are disconnected from each other and talks about the "sense of place that can only be gained on foot. ... On foot, everything stays connected...". Rebecca Solnit, *Wanderlust: A History of Walking*, New York: Verso, 2001, p. 9 (editor's note).

The paintings on the tombs depict the couple dressed in festive pleated cotton robes, farming, ploughing, harvesting wheat, and pulling flax from the field of Aaru – the "field of reeds" that was heavenly paradise in ancient Egypt. It seemed that eternal life could be found in these fields, placid and lovely, a reward for honourable behaviour during earthly life.[12]

Sennedjem was a craftsman-artist during his earthly life. His work certainly granted him with a decent livelihood if he was able to afford such a beautifully decorated tomb for himself and his wife. Was farming Sennedjem's and his wife's favourite activity in their free time?[13] Could farming in the afterlife be understood as a longing for something in the past? Can we conclude that for the artisan engaged in the construction of royal tombs, and a member of the social class to which Sennedjem and Iynerferti belonged, the rural landscape and farming represented a tranquil life without stress that they longed to continue enjoying in the field of reeds?

We might conclude this journey through the symbolism of the garden with the notion that the garden is man's environment that wants to be a landscape – that wants to be a world – at least in the manifestations that are open to or include natural growth and uncontrolled variation. This is the garden's basic frame, within which are gathered the cultural uniqueness of gardens in each era, the unique cultural environment in which they are generated, and the particular technologies that are essential for their arrangement and maintenance. Gardens are always an expression of the predicament or the specificities of the relationship of man to the world with its traditions and historical memory, with the situations that this relationship triggers, and also with the concerns that arise from the many uncertainties in the connection between people and their environment, and also their future. G&M

12 Hany Farid and Samir Farid, "Unfolding Sennedjem's Tomb", *KMT: A Modern Journal of Ancient Egypt*, Spring 2001, pp. 1-8, http://www.cs.dartmouth.edu/farid/downloads/publications/kmt01.pdf

13 During the excavation of the Valley of Kings at Deir-el-Medina, archaeologists discovered many details about the lives of craftsmen and the builders of the tombs, and also about how they spent their free time while working on the tombs. Deir-el-Medina was created literally in the middle of the desert so that its occupants would be separated from the rest of the population, as described in the *Ancient History Encyclopedia*. Water was carried from a source a half-hour's walk away. Food was also carried to the site. See Joshua J. Mark, "Deir-el-Medina", *Ancient History Encyclopedia*, 21 September 2016, https://www.ancient.eu/article/933/daily-life-in-ancient-egypt/

On Mistaking Garden for Nature

Pavel Gantar

I shall begin this casual sociological reflection about the garden with a surprising example from Singapore: "Today, depending on the type of plant or animal, 35 to 90 per cent of the original species are gone, or survive only under strict husbandry in Singapore Zoo or the Singapore Botanic Gardens."[1] Despite this fact, Schilthuizen concludes that Singapore has a high level of biotic diversity and a rich animal and plant life in an otherwise "fragmented ecology", where little pieces and patches of greenery and water surfaces are woven into the densely constructed urban area. Indeed, he contends that what is characteristic of the urban ecology is not the endemic flora but plants that have either entered Singapore by ways of natural plant migration or been introduced to it.

Why is this surprising? Above all because the conviction generally prevails that the nature that surrounds us and in which we live is native, or even primaeval, while in fact it is a product of ecological succession, processes that began a long time ago, and have been sometimes initiated by humans. At the same time, it is considered entirely normal and legitimate to keep plants, and even animals, that do not belong to our ecosystem in a garden (as in a zoo, an arboretum, a botanical garden, or the like). It is quite common for gardens to function as a display window for exotic plants and animals that one can't otherwise find in the local context. Perhaps what is happening in Singapore (and Schilthuizen believes that this applies to more or less

1 Menno Schilthuizen, *Darwin Comes to Town: How the Urban Jungle Drives Evolution*, London: Quercus Editions, 2018, p. 39.

all big cities) is in fact the opposite: namely, what is indigenous to our surrounding local ecosystem is in the city only maintained in carefully protected gardens, and what came from the outside (being foreign to the surrounding local ecosystem) has in fact formed what we consider the natural environment (the "nature") of the city.

I will leave aside the metaphorical and even symbolic dimensions of the garden. What seems more important is the possible implications of the reverse relationship between the garden and nature pointed out by Schilthuizen. Much has changed in our understanding of nature in the last twenty or thirty years. Very little has remained of the concept of nature that is "not human and distinguished from the work of humanity. Thus 'nature' is opposed to culture, to history, to convention, to what is artificially worked or produced, in short, to everything that is defining of the order of humanity."[2] Soper emphasizes that such a concept of nature "refers to that part of the environment which we have had no hand in creating."[3] And yet, where can we find today, even in what might be called pristine nature, a place where there has been no human influence, a place where no human foot has ever stepped? At the same time, "nature" still functions as something alien and other, encompassing all of the animal and plant species that man has not yet discovered but that he has probably indirectly influenced.

2 Kate Soper, *What is Nature? Culture, Politics and the Non-Human*, Oxford: Blackwell, 1995, p. 15.

3 Ibid., p. 16.

The foreign and the native

One of the numerous threads of debate about the alien and other quality of nature (in comparison to the homeliness of the garden) raises the question about the

View from Ljubljana Castle in the direction of Ižanska Street.

foreign and the domestic in our natural environment, meaning the question about the autochthonous nature of the ecosystems in which we live. Pearce contends that the difference between native and foreign species in a certain ecosystem, and in ecosystems in general, is actually a question of the time horizon. The longer the time frame, the more the difference between native and foreign fades. He says that "the spread of invasive species today is merely a continuation of a natural process of the colonization begun when the ice retreated."[4] He continues: "All lodgings are temporary and all ecosystems in a constant flux, the victims of circumstance and geological accident."[5] Therefore, when we consider longer time periods, the borders between native and migrant (foreign) species disappear, and with it also the concept of the climax as a true natural condition that it is necessary to preserve. This makes me think of the fate of the spruce forests that have been attacked by the bark beetle in recent years. We must not forget that spruce is artificially cultivated on many sites, even though most people believe them to be native. Is this not an indicator of Pearce's argument about "temporary lodgings" that shift before our eyes as a result of external influences such as climate change?

Supposedly, as Worster points out, "the most natural state of nature is balance".[6] He adds: "Throughout the modern era the scientific community had assumed that nature, despite a few appearances to the contrary, was a perfectly manageable system of simple, linear, rational order."[7] However, the conviction about a delicately balanced ecosystem, the functioning of which can be rationally explained, and about mankind being nature's only adversary, has been refuted since the 1960s. Natural processes are more non-linear and very small changes can cause important shifts (the butterfly effect). In short, nature is extremely chaotic, wild, and unpredictable and often is a threat

4 Fred Pearce, *The New Wild: Why Invasive Species Will Be Nature's Salvation*, London: Icon Books, 2015, p. 68.

5 Ibid., p. 70.

6 Donald Worster, *Nature's Economy: A History of Ecological Ideas*, Cambridge: Cambridge University Press, 1997, p. 389.

7 Ibid., p. 406.

to humanity, regardless of the fact that the hand of man is often behind the wildest acts of nature.

The city as a natural phenomenon

If nature threatens us again (as it always has in the past) with natural catastrophes and non-linear changes that usher in an unpredictable and open future, it is time to ask the question: what does a garden have to do with all of this? If nature is far from balanced and predictable, and indeed is becoming increasingly unstable, the idea of a garden (in all of its conceptual forms) acquires new meanings and dimensions: the image of harmonious nature is today only possible in a garden. The garden is, it seems, a demonstration of nature as we imagine it, as it should be, not the nature that actually surrounds us, wilderness on one side of the continuum and the mono-cultural agro-industrial desert on the other side. But not only the garden. Kaika says that with the ending of the modern project that had as its goal the taming of nature, the dualism between the city and nature has also ended and this has led to the discovery of nature in the city itself.[8] Schilthuizen makes a similar argument, interpreting the human city "as fully natural phenomenon, on a par with the mega-structures that other ecosystem engineers build for their societies."[9] Although the author, a biologist, overlooks some of the specifically human social characteristics of the city and its construction, and this carries the risk of "naturalizing" specifically social power relations, he is certainly correct when he warns that: "Compared to such sterile, geometric landscapes, the messiness of the urban centre, a varied mix of backyards, green roofs, old stone walls, overgrown drains, and city parks, is a haven for a lot of wildlife."[10]

8 Maria Kaika, *City of Flows: Modernity, Nature and the City*, London/New York: Routledge, 2005, p. 13.

9 Schilthuizen, *Darwin Comes to Town*, op. cit., p. 26.

10 Ibid., p. 56.

In recent decades, this changed perspective on the relationship between the city and nature has, in addition to the already traditional gardens and conventional "green areas of the city" (parks, lawns, tree-lined streets, botanic gardens, zoos ...), triggered new forms of urban gardening. As Certomà and Tornaghi point out: "These initiatives unfold in a variety of forms: the spontaneous appropriation and rehabilitation of marginal and neglected spaces at the city periphery, new bilateral agreements for sharing private land, community stewardship of urban greens and parks in well-maintained city centres are just a few of the arrangements through which gardening in both public and private spaces is taking place in various urban settings."[11] If we look at cities in Slovenia, above all Ljubljana (where I live), there are a number of initiatives of this type: I need only mention the activities of the groups ProstoRož (FreeFlowers), the community garden Onkraj gradbišča (Beyond a Construction Site), the Vodnikova initiative, the renaissance of community life in the Savsko housing settlement and Tabor. The key point of all these stories, however much they differ from each other, is in how they expand and build on the concept of urban culture, and do not limit it to mere artefacts, such as squares, streets, bars, and other public and semi-public spaces, but actually bring nature into it. Certomà and Tornaghi observe that new forms of political activism are also developing in the city that are no longer directed towards discursive forms of demands, recommendations, and initiatives in connection with the public space, but "on practices whose main appeal resides in the power of doing a state of things rather than merely talking about it."[12] Gardening has moved from the shelter of domestic gardens to also include public and semi-public spaces, and has become more urban. The site of urban gardening can be anything: skyscrapers, roofs, abandoned

11 Chiara Certomà and Chiara Tornaghi, "Political Gardening. Transforming Cities and Political Agency", *Local Environment*, vol. 20 (10), 2015, p. 1.

building sites, dilapidated buildings, abandoned streets ... The difference between "culture" and "nature" fades, and the skyscraper, for example, is not any more an emblem of architectural perfection, but can also be a productive force of nature that creates goods, from shade to aesthetic comfort to lettuce, tomatoes, and honey, and at the same time organizes people in smaller and larger communities.

Urban gardening reliably changes the experience of the city. Despite all the positive effects of gardening, it is necessary to point out the paradox with which I started this essay. Urban gardening as a political practice is directed towards changing the city, but it leaves out the question of autonomous and "wild" nature in the city, which is often characterized by non-native species. (In many European countries, a particularly blatant example for such an invasive plant is the Japanese knotweed, *Fallopia japonica*.) The difficulty is apparent in the case of "wild gardens", that is gardens in which we should not intervene through cultivation; however, these gardens are supposedly disliked both by users and planners.[13] People like nature but only if it is not too "natural". If therefore the idea of the urban garden combines nature and human artefacts into a unit that is part of the social, aesthetic, and life experience of the city, then we recognize that we have domesticated nature into a metaphor of the garden: what is wild and untamed remains somewhere else. G&M

12 Ibid, p. 2.

13 Barbara Goličnik, "Model naravnega vrta v načrtovalski praksi druge polovice 20. stoletja", *Urbani izziv*, vol. 11, p. 1, Urbane mreže/Urban Networks (June 2000), Ljubljana: Urbanistični inštitut Republike Slovenije, 2000, p. 87.

Taking Responsibility for Landscape

Kinga Szilágyi

Man has been building gardens since ancient times, as reflected in the ancient Persian word *pairi-daeza,* etymologically related to "paradise", describing a walled or fenced and thus sheltered open space. Later on, in Christian culture, the new term of paradise arose from the tradition and spatial structure of Persian gardens. Paradise or paradise garden both refer to the lost Eden, where there is a heavenly harmony of nature and the world. Therefore, and despite the narrowness of the literal definition, the garden has always been about nature and creative imagination of humankind. So it is also a metaphor for an infinite and life-giving landscape.

Perhaps neither creators nor people who use the gardens are conscious of this essential meaning. For millennia, only a few privileged individuals enjoyed the harmony and pleasure and satisfaction of private gardens, until the English landscape garden movement and the economic and social changes of the 18th century opened the gates for all members of society to access personal or public gardens, albeit with only a small crumb of garden culture, the blessing of well-being provided by the garden. And when, if not now, amid the global crisis and the threat of climate change,

Balatongyörök Garden, Hungary, by Mihály Mőcsényi: a landscape in an abandoned quarry waiting for healing, 1972.

Balatongyörök Garden: early interventions, 1972.

is there a greater need for recognition: the garden is the microcosmos of the landscape, and to sustain it in this role, we must understand its evolution and operation, accept its limitations, and improve its ecological supply; however, the "ecosystem service" provided by the landscape should not move towards ecological exploitation but towards a harmonious balance.

Redeeming landscape

The 20th century has brought recognition to the regional and global effects of environmental damage caused by economic and urban development. The realization of ecological problems went in parallel with the birth and growth of schools of landscape architecture. For some of these schools, garden design and garden art were their cradles, for others, horticulture or landscape management, or architecture and design. Still, in the second half of the century, landscape architecture strengthened and widened its competencies and foundations by developing wide-scale scientific research and knowledge of its own; it became a complex environmental science everywhere, a principle and a form of behaviour in creation, design, and architecture of open space and landscape. In dynamically developing cities, more and more people are turning to the pleasures provided by private or community gardens, with urban green systems offering a variety of planted areas, public parks, and open spaces for recreation. What is their motivation, if not the search for roots, the wish to rebuild the connection with nature, lost in the noise of urbanization and development? As a landscape architect, I deeply believe in the benefits of urban green infrastructure. A garden can awaken a sense of responsibility for nature and the landscape.

The Balatongyörök Garden

A good example of assuming responsibility for landscape is the outstanding oeuvre of Mihály Mőcsényi (1919–2017), Hungarian professor of landscape architecture. Once upon a time, in the late 1960s, Mőcsényi and his wife stopped by chance at Balatongyörök on the north-west coast of Lake Balaton. They had to give their old Trabant car a rest and set out for a walk to a nearby hill at Szépkilátó (Belvedere), where a dolomite quarry gaped like an open mouth, like a massive wound in the landscape crying out in pain. Leaving behind the abandoned quarry pit, they climbed along the barren hilltop where a breathtaking view opened up with the Lake Balaton landscape and the surrounding Tapolca Basin and the basalt mountains. From the top of the hill, the quarry showed an entirely different perspective; the pit appeared no longer a prolonged destruction of the harmony of the landscape, but rather an injury, waiting for rehabilitation and healing. Imagination smoothed out the steep quarry faces, built the necessary retaining walls, created inviting spaces, and vibrant, prosperous biotopes for green walls, rock gardens, pergolas, and comfortable resting areas.

The soaring imagination and the commitment of the landscape architect meant a task for decades and provided the opportunity to create a home. In the exploited, ugly, abandoned mining landscape Mőcsényi had seen a miraculous, exceptional endowment. For him, the garden in Balatongyörök was the incarnation of his landscape architecture philosophy.

"Once we had the 'wound in the landscape', we healed it to make it useful and beautiful. What are the previews, according to the principles? Reviving ancient, atavistic *engrams*,[1] displaying their originators should be mentioned first. In the

The path at Balatongyörök Garden from the courtyard to the top of the hill, 1978.

View of the retaining walls stabilizing Balatongyörök Garden, c. 1987.

'collecting' era of *Homo sapiens*, safety could be found in a cave or a forest clearing. On the edge of the clearing, leaning against a tree, with a protected back, the caveman could see the grassy, flowery meadow, the space bordered by shrubs and trees. There he could not be attacked unexpectedly. It was a benefit and a joy to have a stream or a small lake in the clearing, to have drinking water or to realize and recognize himself in the water mirror. We are 'at home' in a receptive space form bordered by natural elements, perennials, shrubs, trees, or earthworks. Being at home, being 'inside' is good. The love of concave space form, the reminiscent of an open arm is an ancient feeling, deeply fixed in the *engram*."[2]

A good three decades of intensive building devoted to the healing of landscape resulted in the unique Mőcsényi Garden. The design of the much-coveted concave walls involved substantial earthworks. First, the task was to settle the crumbling, dolomite-crushed walls of the quarry. By the 1970s, already several retaining walls stabilized the dolomite face. The motto "forge virtue out of necessity" became a reality here. Step by step, level by level, the quarry face, with its snow-white arches and walls, tamed the destroyed landscape, almost evoking Greek rock towns. But landscape healing would not have been complete if it had not involved the creation of new biotopes and habitats, and the greening of the dolomite face. In the cassettes formed between the retaining walls and in the baskets "glued" to the pit wall on the levels of tiny recreation houses, a carefully composed perennial and annual ensemble, several solid cypresses, and wild vine dressed in purple in the autumn, have settled. Here, the design diligence also preserved the double-stemmed black pine that had stood here from the very beginning of landscape restoration and thus could be considered a witness to the construction. On the rock face in its

1 In 1904, Richard Semon (1859–1918) introduced the term "engram" to describe the neural substrate responsible for storing and recalling memories. The engram is the entity that reflects the neural substrate of stored information resulting from past experience and bestowing upon organisms the ability to express memory in their behaviour. The concept of a physical memory trace likely originated in ancient Greece. Richard Semon, "Der Engrammschatz des Gedächtnisses" [1904], in Uwe Fleckner (ed.), *Schatzkammern der Mnemosyne*, Dresden: Verlag der Kunst, 1995, pp. 206–212.

2 Mihály Mőcsényi, Essays, 2012. *Balatongyörök – Mőcsényi esszék* 10, https://epiteszforum.hu/balatongyorok-mocsenyi-esszek-10

natural state, nature could also work in peace. The planned, planted vegetation on the plateaus and the vertical space walls became settled by plants of the dolomite slopes, blending into the landscape.

Professor Mőcsényi was a full-blooded teacher. Not only family, friends, and relatives participated in the work on the quarry landscape, the construction of the retaining walls, and the planting of vegetation, but also colleagues and students who – many of them – returned year after year to contribute to the healing of the landscape. The Mőcsényi Garden has become a place of pilgrimage, a sanctuary of Hungarian landscape architects.

The early 1980s were an excellent time for the landscape architecture profession in Hungary. Professor Mőcsényi's international reputation made it possible for Hungary to host the IFLA XXII World Congress in Siófok on Lake Balaton. The

The house in the former quarry, overlooking Lake Balaton, 2018.

3 Among them was Dušan Ogrin, to whom this volume is dedicated. He was the colleague and friend of Mőcsényi, whom he met for the first time in 1971 when both were among the fifteen invited landscape architects in the international competition for the Karlsplatz, Vienna.

participants[3] visited the Belvedere of Balatongyörök and were welcomed in the former quarry with a gravel slope planted with drought-tolerant perennials and shrubs. Mőcsényi presented quarry recultivation, which had been mostly realized by manual labour. In the 1990s, the interventions reached the upper edge of the original quarry, the Belvedere site that inspired Mőcsényi's first plans. In September 2017, then at the age of 98, he started his final journey from here.

The Mőcsényi Garden in Balatongyörök is a dream engraved in stone. Even though luxurious holiday houses have sprung up around it, the garden is still, and perhaps even more today, the embodiment of a dialogue between nature, the landscape, and the person who acts responsibly. Reckless development that exceeds the carrying capacity of the landscape results in wastelands that cry for healing and renewal. There is a need for a change of attitude in the search for ecological balance. Only an elementary responsibility of humankind may provide healing to our exploited world. We all have to contribute towards redressing our environment, even if only in small steps. In this respect, it may be easier to turn to the garden, the Garden of Eden, embodiment of heavenly harmony. Based on the revelation of Classicism and the liberal philosophy that resulted in the English landscape gardens, and on the natural philosophy of Romanticism, the in-depth knowledge of our landscape might offer guidance towards a noble goal and perhaps a pledge to our future. G&M

Landscape architect Mihály Mőcsényi at the Belvedere, c. 2010.

The Garden as a Spatial Idea

João Gomes da Silva

The garden is a detached space: detached from the immediate area, from the surrounding context, both social and spatial. That is why we seek to approach it, pass through its gates, and submerge ourselves into its material and sensorial density. Then we feel detached, isolated, sharing our presence with other(s), or just with ourselves. This means a decisive suspension of the surrounding hubbub of life, a kind of alienation from the immediate. It does not necessarily imply loneliness or isolation, but rather a separation from one part of our life and an encounter with another: the one which we carry inside of us, less pragmatic but ultimately more intense. Ribeiro Telles was referring to precisely this when he defined recreation as an act, a more or less extended moment, in which we are capable of creating the self again by relating to nature, matter, and space.[1] Comprising a space whose qualities can vary from density to openness, from shadow to light, from mineral to vegetal or aquatic, the garden's limitations are also its foundations. If located in a yard, a cloister, or a court, architecture becomes its limitation and its dimensional confinement. Our measure of space deals with the architectural dimension, with proportions generated between our body, the volume of trees, the extent of water surfaces. Our confinement deals with the sky as scape, with the sense that the depth of water eludes our senses, with the more or less permeable character of the architecture that holds the garden. But if the garden is open to the landscape, to the immense and extensive space made up of city, fields,

1 Ribeiro G. Telles, "O Homem e o Lugar" (Man and Place), in Ribeiro G. Telles, *Textos escolhidos,* Lisbon: Argumentum, 2016.

woods, or sea, then our detachment becomes oriented and our gaze relies on the near or distant context.

The garden, with its origins in Mesopotamia and Persia, corresponds to the idea of resilient permanence in situ, to the creation of a specific space made of ground and water and plants as architectural phenomena. Agriculture and architecture were the fields of knowledge behind the creation of landscape spaces, including the garden. Since its genesis, the meaning and metaphorical sense of the garden have been inextricably related to the idea of the garden expressed through its spatial conditions. The idea and meaning of the garden have acquired different spatial expressions during different eras and in various geographical circumstances. In a way, the garden has always represented the idea of landscape as metaphor. In an abstract sense, the meaning of fertility is expressed through the cultivation of fruit plants between walls where they benefit from the flow and accumulation of water, where spaces of production are generated, and where plants and animals are protected. This spatial configuration is the dwelling of man. This recalls the *pairi-daeza* idea from the Persian culture and other garden forms cultivated at the same latitudes on a range

The archaeological garden by João Luis Carrilho da Graça and João Gomes da Silva at Castelo São Jorge in Lisbon, 2009. The garden highlights and preserves the excavation site.

of longitudes from the mid-Orient to the Iberian Peninsula, including the north and south shores of the Mediterranean Sea. It calls to mind the mediaeval expression *hortus conclusus* when the garden was created between walls, arcades, or porticoes as a fertile reminiscence of the landscape, as a secluded space, a different entity. But was it all that different from the classic form of the garden enclosed within the peristyle, where the external landscape appeared inside the walls of a villa as in Pompeii? Or when the interiority of the Patio de los leones at the Alhambra expanded through the throne room and contemplated the distant landscape?

The garden as a reinvented space

Many forms, meanings, and symbolic expressions have entered the spatial character of the garden and produced a wide range of meanings. But what makes the idea of the garden timeless is not the language, not the symbolic system expressed through iconography or the structural system involved. It is the architectonic and landscape idea expressed by the space itself. In this sense, the garden is a space that must be reinvented each time it is created. As Telles proposed, the idea of the garden is precisely to be re-created each time, and will always emerge as a new and a timeless idea.[2] By analogy, we can absorb Olgiati's notion of the "absolute architectonic idea" into the conceptual discussion when we refer to the garden as a timeless spatial idea, independent of meaning, symbol, or language.[3] In its abstraction, the garden differs from landscape and from natural space, because as a spatial idea it cannot be confused with, but only opposed to, the spatial ideas of landscape and other natural spaces. A garden is a space detached from the landscape by

2 "How will Man continue to re-create himself and be a gardener?", in Telles, "O Homem e o Lugar", op. cit., p. 168. English translation by the author.

3 Valerio Olgiati, Marcus Breitschmid, *Non referential Architecture,* Zurich: Park Books, 2019, p. 50: "...if buildings are studied by means of their ordering systems, the architect gains an absolute architectonic understanding of how a building is ordered."

its precise limits, matter, and scale. Being a delimited space, the notion of the border becomes fundamental and is expressed through a secluded limit (such as a wall or a hedge), an interrupted one (such as a window or a gate), or a merging limit (a topographic or rhythmic effect). The spatial idea of the garden is defined precisely by its limits, and thus the garden exists in antagonism with the idea of the park, the forest, or the beach.

The material character of the garden provides another aspect of differentiation. When inserted into the landscape, the topics of *exotic* and *autochthonous* become a fundamental factor of differentiation. Biodiversity becomes the denial of the absolute mineral character of a specific urban context, which differentiates the garden in the urban context. Scale is the last significant criterion of identification. It exists in contrast to context and is necessary to any spatial idea. The scale of a natural phenomenon, such as a river, a valley, a peak, identifies the space more with the idea of park than with the idea of a garden. Although natural phenomena and matter do occur in the garden, the garden is always identified as a *natural artifice*, never to be confused with a *natural space*. Soil, mineral, water, plants, and animals are the normal material of the garden, just as wind and water circulation, biotope, and light distribution

The enclosed cloister garden, *hortus conclusus*, of the Convent of Jesus in Sétubal, founded in 1490. It was one of the first bulidings in Portuguese Manueline Gothic. The whole complex was restored in 2020.

are natural processes in the garden. In this sense, the garden can be considered a constantly re-created spatial idea, independent of meaning, symbolic structure, or programmatic character, created from aspects derived from the landscape and architectonic ideas, and this is what makes the garden a timeless cultural creation. G&M

Patio de los leones, Alhambra, Granada, c. 1362–1391.

Garden as Future

The Wasserkrater Garden in Bad Oeynhausen, Germany, by Agence Ter, 1998, provides a multi-sensory expression of supernature.

The Garden as an Expression of Supernature

Saskia de Wit

Gardens can be conceived in many ways, from many angles and through many lenses: as a social space, a place for activities or relaxation, an outdoor room, a catalogue of plants, an ecological safe haven, an exhibit of its owner's wealth or creativity, an expression of culture, a place of joy, a gardener's cause for eternal worries, or a representation of the cosmos. Underlying all of these, the garden has always been a reflection of the relationship of man and nature, a relationship that changes over time, and is as much a reflection of its time, and thus a cultural expression.

Understandings of nature

Over time, the understanding of our relationship to nature developed from that of fragile creatures in a fearsome entity to the heroic story where man is conquering nature, which in Western culture culminated in the Baroque garden. In the Romantic period nature was idealized as the source of all good, the mirror of the human soul. In the 20th century, the concept of nature oscillated between an ancient sense of nature as a cosmic order, full of symbolic potential, and a rather simplistic expanse of undefined greenery, and the idea arose that whereas nature is necessary for the human well-being, mankind can only corrupt nature or, if they tried hard, preserve what remains. So it is best left alone, as a benign background. Consequently, the view on nature shifted away from a human focus to a predominantly ecological view, in which nature came to be seen as a combination of complex systems and processes. Nature as an autonomous force (not contaminated by human intervention) was reflected in the garden as a collection of naturalistic images, as opposed to the humanized spaces of previous times. Although the idea of nature as a system of processes still holds strong, at present a subtle change seems to be taking place. The premise that we somehow stand outside (or apart from) nature no longer holds true. With the natural processes of growth and decline still at the core, we can see a shift from abstract biological systems to the realm of human perception.

I would like to define this contemporary interpretation of the relationship of man and nature as "supernature", which might be represented in gardens as a force of abundance, beautiful and dramatic, showing existence to its full extent in which humans are only a small part, and at the same as something close to home, part of our daily environment. Nature is not only to be found "out there", in unattainable wilderness areas untainted by man, but also "in here", in the small, intimate space of the garden. Here, the space and its inhabitants can have such

In the outer ring of the Wasserkrater, the dappled sunlight that falls through the canopy evokes the image of a natural forest glade.

a close connection that they can seem to be in symbiosis, and the boundary between man and nature can dissolve. It is about the body's immersion in the world, guided by emotions, interaction, performance, technology, experience, and the feeling that a place can evoke, augmented by sensory qualities.

This integral connection between nature and bodily experience is related to the concept of the spirit of place, the *genius loci*: as a "ghost" that is rooted in a place but is not physically present. Let me take a little sidestep here: the notion of ghosts, of the *supernatural*, is originally a Romantic notion, and in an essay called *Faustus and Helena: Notes on the Supernatural in Art* the Romantic author of supernatural fiction Vernon Lee described ghosts as:

> the damp, the darkness, the silence, the solitude; a ghost is the sound of our steps through a ruined cloister, where the ivy-berries and convolvulus growing in the fissures sway up and down among the sculptured foliage of the windows, it is the scent of mouldering plaster ... Each and all of these things, and a hundred others besides, according to our nature, is a ghost, a vague feeling we can scarcely describe, something pleasing and terrible which invades our whole consciousness.[1]

Here Lee described the ghost as the landscape itself; there exists no separation between ghost and place. This substrate of potential bodily responses that resides in a location connects the physical reality of the natural to the ephemeral plane of the supernatural, collapsing the boundary between what is out there and in here.

1 Lee Vernon, *Faustus and Helena: Notes on the Supernatural in Art*, London: Smith, Elder & Co., 1898. Reprint in Catherine Maxwell and Patricia Pulham (eds.), *Hauntings and Other Fantastic Tales*, Peterborough, ON: Broadview Press, 2006, p. 310.

The garden in the metropolitan landscape

Interestingly enough, this notion of the supernatural (combining the whimsicality and irregularity of the picturesque, the spirit of the place, and embodied experience) remained in the realm of ruins and shadows until Rem Koolhaas re-introduced the supernatural as an integral component of the metropolitan landscape, making a direct connection between artificial nature and metropolitan conditions. He qualified the supernatural as intensified, theatrical nature for the metropolitan realm but also as artificial nature replacing the original nature, mimicking the natural processes. In *Delirious New York,* he made this direct connection between artificial nature and metropolitan conditions by announcing supernature as a golf course in the "bastion of the anti-natural", the Downtown Athletic Club:

> Having been extirpated by the Metropolis, nature is now resurrected inside the Skyscraper as merely one of its infinite layers, a technical service that sustains and refreshes the Metropolitanites in their exhausting existence. The Skyscraper has transformed Nature into Super-Nature.[2]

In his double coding supernature implied both larger-than-life nature and fake, plastic nature. Koolhaas used the prefix "super" ironically, suggesting a promise of the possibility to transcend late-modern dreariness without lapsing into nostalgia or conservatism. The image he presented nonetheless strongly reminds us of the modernistic, architectural vision of a generic, shapeless landscape (flowing and park-like) of un-manipulated nature, an image light-years away from the ecological view that

2 Rem Koolhaas, *Delirious New York, A Retroactive Manifesto for Manhattan*, New York: The Monacelli Press, 1978, p. 130.

In the centre of the Wasserkrater, a water column erupts at irregular intervals, gradually building up to a dramatic climax and then subsiding into nothing, only to start over again in an apparently endless cycle. The thundering sound of the fountain is echoed by the hard materials of the crater (rock-filled gabions and metal) and is so loud it prevents people from talking and allows them to retreat into themselves. When the water jet falls away suddenly, everything is wrapped in a dense mist. This articulation of sound, light, humidity, texture, height differences, and smell creates a multi-sensory experience of nature, challenging the visual image of a man-made construction.

lived among landscape architects in the same period. So, although Koolhaas had reduced supernature to one of the many inventions to make life more comfortable the notion struck a chord, and outlived its ironic connotation. In 2010, landscape architect Malene Hauxner[3] presented a more mature and landscape architectonic version of supernature: as an intensified version of nature that is deeply embedded in history, culture, and technology and brings together the architectural and the ecological view of the 20th century. The abundance of nature and natural processes determines its own architectural language.

The garden that has always been an artificial (artistic) reflection of nature has now evolved into an artificial reflection of a version of nature that in itself has become as much artificial as natural. This entanglement of natural and artificial seems to express the contemporary understanding of what geologist Paul Crutzen coined as the Anthropocene, the "age of man": the current era after the Holocene, in which humanity intervenes as a force of nature, and nature no longer exists without human influences.[4]

Without the distinction between what is natural and what is man-made, the contemporary garden can expose wilderness not in opposition of, but as an integral part of the metropolitan realm and our daily environment, evoking an immersive encounter with nature: an embodied experience. Something close to the skin, so nature as the object of appreciation dissolves as a separate and distant entity and becomes inextricably intermingled with the perceiver. To be fully engaged with nature means to come into a visceral and immediate contact with it. An articulation of sound, light, humidity, colour, texture, or height differences can create such a multi-sensory experience, which emphasizes the exposure of nature and involves a feeling

3 Malene Hauxner, *Fra naturlig natur til supernatur, Europæisk landskabsarkitektur 1967–2007 set fra Danmark*, Aarhus: Ikaros Academic Press, 2010.

4 Dirk Sijmons, "Wakker worden in het Antropoceen", in G. Brugmans and J. Strien (eds.), *Urban by Nature*, Rotterdam: IABR, 2014 (catalogue of the International Architecture Biennale Rotterdam), p. 13.

of being infused with an enveloping, engaging tactility. The emphasis in these gardens shifts from representing identifiable natural territories to exposing spatial and temporal natural dynamics, and from representation to engagement, underlining the necessity of an attentive interaction with, and care for, the living environment, which is not an abstract and inexhaustible force but interwoven with everything we do. G&M

Placed outside existing urban structures, the quality of the Wasserkrater as a marginal space is celebrated: the whimsicality of this spatial configuration escapes normative expectations as far as function and meaning are concerned. Set apart from daily life, the intensified nature experience induces the visitors not so much to contemplate the space as to actively engage in it, moving and playing.

Thinking About the Future of Landscape Architecture

Carl Steinitz

A few years ago, I was one of many people asked to participate in a publication about the future of landscape architecture.[1] I thought – and still think – that there are four reasonably clear possibilities.

The first possibility is simply a continuation of where I think we are today, and perhaps garden as a metaphor can be persuasive in this respect.

The second possibility assumes increasing competition for what has become "hot property" – the landscape. Architects may increasingly design landscapes as part of what they consider to be architecture; urban designers may increasingly and effectively design landscapes of middle scale; geographers, engineers, and ecologists (and politicians, bankers, and lawyers) may increasingly make the significant design decisions at the larger landscape scales. These trends will increasingly impinge upon education in and the practice of landscape architecture. External competition will likely produce a narrower landscape architecture profession, far different from that imagined over a hundred years ago by its founders.

The third possibility is perhaps the most likely, and at the same time the most wrongheaded. It is very possible the artificial division between "planning" and "design" will continue and even be reinforced, and that landscape architecture will *itself* choose to focus on the design of smaller projects, both

1 Carl Steinitz, "On The Future of Landscape Architecture", in The Landscape Foundation (ed.), *The New Landscape Declaration*, Los Angeles: Rare Bird Books, 2017, pp. 105–110.

private and public. In part, this may result from successful competition on larger studies from other professions which consider such issues as food and water supply, biodiversity, cultural heritage, population increase, and climate change to be important shapers of landscape. Mainly, however, it will result from two factors: society's unfortunate but common caricature of landscape architecture as closely related to gardening, and the landscape architecture profession's own professional and academic choices.

The fourth possibility relies on recognizing the wisdom of the founders of the profession. First, we must know something that other professions do not. In our case this must be rooted in the landscape itself and at every scale: in its climate, geology, hydrology, ecology, vegetation, history, perception etc. Second, we must learn to understand that almost everything we do to change (design) the landscape requires collaboration, whether with architects on the smaller scale, urban designers on the middle scale, geographers on the larger scale, and with engineers on all scales, and lawyers and bankers and government officials, yet with no one losing his/her professional identity. This was the vision of my department at the Graduate School of Design, Harvard University, when I joined the faculty and it is a perspective which I hold to this day.

We cannot argue that we are the sole bearers of wisdom as it pertains to the land and we cannot argue that we have some self-defined right to be its stewards, to be in charge or even to coordinate. Sometimes we will lead, and sometimes we will not. But if we are to work on society's most important needs, both specialist knowledge and collaborative skills *in designing* are essential. We must not allow the profession to become limited by the scales and scope of its competences. I am strongly in favour of this last prospective future, and I hope that it shapes a significant part of the education and practice of future landscape architects.

In my opinion, the idea that the garden should be a metaphor for landscape architecture and a guide to general principles for its diverse activities is insufficient and not compelling. Gardens have normally been conceived in very personal ways by a combination of users and designers, and most often for pleasure. I cannot believe that this "bottom-up" perspective is a sufficient metaphor for our times, when we must also be thinking about dealing with overpopulation, starvation, loss of biodiversity, pollution on a global scale, and all under conditions of climate change. Gardens mean looking at the global problem and the needs of society in the wrong direction. Decisions that will shape humanity and its supportive landscapes are more likely to be effective if they arise from the orientation from global survival to the garden, from the sciences to the arts, from politics to individuals, and from policy collaboration among scientists and designers to an individual designer's often idiosyncratic inspiration.

These two perspectives – i.e. top-down and bottom-up – will have to interact with each other on the scales at which they best operate, and this will profoundly influence how design is accomplished, and how it is likely to be taught. The alternative for the future of landscape architecture is increasing irrelevance, except to serve a special few. We should consider seeing the whole world as a metaphor for landscape architecture. G&M

Garden Thinking and Garden Action

Udo Weilacher

"In the garden we learn how to deal with nature without having to deny the creative power within us. And thus, it becomes a model and a test case with regard to how we deal with the entire natural and built environment."[1]

In the early 1990s, the Swiss landscape architect Dieter Kienast (1945–1998) underlined the fundamental significance of garden thinking today and stated that the garden is the last luxury of our time. It demands those things that have become the rarest and most precious in our society, for example time, focused attention and free space. "It is a true reflection of nature in which, once again, we require spirit, knowledge, and craftsmanship in the careful handling of the world and its microcosmos, the garden. Changing social values are causing a garden renaissance."[2] In the light of current tendencies such as "urban gardening", one can truly speak of a garden renaissance. For landscape architecture, this is highly welcome because many people (re-)discover important aspects of life that will be crucial for the protection and development of future environmental qualities. Real sustainability can only be achieved if people's social awareness and their sensitivity to the quality of their living environment increases around the world. Six aspects in particular make gardens and gardening so interesting for landscape architecture today:

1 Dieter Kienast, "Zwischen Poesie und Geschwätzigkeit", *Garten + Landschaft*, 1, 1994, pp. 13–17. English translation by the author.

2 Dieter Kienast, "Sehnsucht nach dem Paradies", *Hochparterre*, 7, 1990, p. 50. English translation by the author.

Acknowledging the interrelationships of life

A garden without nature – even in the metaphorical sense – cannot exist. Whether as an idealized image of pristine nature or a cultivated manifestation of domesticated nature: in every garden, change is inevitably one of the most important inherent properties of nature. Whoever works with soil, cultivates plants, waters, fertilizes, maintains the vegetation, and in the end harvests fruits will begin to understand the most fundamental principles of all ecosystems, also the urban versions. This type of thinking is not only important for the understanding of today's landscape architecture and the role it plays in the shaping of the environment. For landscape architects' garden thinking, the understanding of complex interrelationships is so crucial because the landscape itself is ultimately complex.

Teaching patience

Faith in rapid success and the demand for quick results dominate today's life style, even in landscape architecture and landscape planning. A huge, mostly computer-controlled arsenal of technology is available in these professional fields. This technology allows planners and designers to increasingly accelerate the processes of design-making and decision-taking. But this speed no longer has an adequate relationship to the slow passage of time in living environments. Nature does not "function" like a machine, but instead has only one permanent

Bejing is growing fast, producing a highly complex system of spaces, a metropolitan landscape, challenging the current understanding of "garden".

View of industrial plant in Beijing with fishpond and greenery.

feature: the permanency of its change. This change, however, does not normally become apparent during a sudden eruption of natural forces, but rather takes place in an extremely slow and subtle manner. Gardening teaches the gardener to patiently observe and sensitively guide the process of change, admitting that the results of gardening will not always meet the initial expectations.

Promoting personal responsibility

People who create and maintain a garden get physically involved. Personal responsibility and civic engagement are important issues for landscape architecture in the face of increasingly insistent and globally expanding consumerism. For many people, especially in urban contexts and industrialized societies, it is a matter of course that they live in a well-designed and well-maintained environment, built according to their wishes and needs. Those who are actively involved in gardening directly experience in the best sense of the word what it means to assume responsibility for the flourishing of nature and for the preservation of an environment they have personally helped to shape.

The Mountain Garden in Graz, designed by Dieter Kienast in 2000, was a manifesto for contemporary landscape architecture inspired by visual arts.

With this small garden in Zurich from 1996, Dieter Kienast shattered the stereotype image of ecological garden design by integrating natural processes in modern landscape architecture.

Stimulating the senses and raising awareness

With time, the practical exploration of gardening methods and natural processes leads to a greater awareness of the environment and to a good sense of the fascinating interaction between nature and the artificial, tranquillity and vitality, form and function, space and time. A garden communicates these relationships in very direct and educational ways. This will eventually lead to a sharpening of the senses. In the future, landscape architects can only expect broad public acceptance for their work if they meet with a public that has the ability to appreciate high-quality environmental design. This appreciation would ideally be cultivated through the personal creative experience of all.

Inventing and experimenting

"The garden is the place of inventions of our age", the French garden artist Bernard Lassus stated in 1996.[3] He was referring particularly to the gardens of the Renaissance, which were inspiring places of invention in their time. From the ha-ha to the water organ – the inventiveness of all gardens in history has always been almost unlimited. In all facets of today's urban gardens there is an amazing love of invention and experimentation, be it the organization of water supply, the development of new types of planters, or the horticultural use and design of unusual urban spaces. Garden pioneers regularly discover new garden niches in their city. Landscape architecture can and must profit from this inventiveness, as it has to discover, develop and qualify new living environments in today's ever-denser cities.

3 Bernard Lassus, quoted in Udo Weilacher, *Between Landscape Architecture and Land Art,* Basel: Birkhäuser, 1996, p. 109.

Recognizing the need for maintenance

The increased sense of responsibility for the environment, trained through actual gardening, is a good foundation as well as an important context for the creation of new open spaces in cities and the preservation of existing parks and gardens. Since public resources for the maintenance of open urban spaces are becoming increasingly scarce, this aspect is becoming more and more important. If urban dwellers lose their sense of belonging, the urban public spaces will inevitably be threatened with utter neglect. Today's landscape architectural projects in many cases only have a chance to survive for a longer period of time if residents from the neighbourhood are willing to take on a particular degree of responsibility for the maintenance of these areas.

In 1983, the German zoologist and behavioural scientist Hubert Markl (1938–2015) warned that all life on Earth is based on an intact symbiosis of nature and culture: "Our responsibility for life must prove itself on the success of this symbiosis of nature and culture. An example of such a symbiosis that we are all familiar with is the garden, which is a form of land use that is more than mere harvest-maximized biotechnology. With regard to our use of the earth, we need this thinking about gardens as a humanizing addendum to the calculating rationality of economic planning. Garden thinking means more than just squeezing everything we can out of the land."[4]

4 Hubert Markl, "Die Verantwortung für den Bestand des Lebens – Evolution und ökologische Krise", *Mitteilungen der Deutschen Akademie für Städtebau und Landesplanung*, 3 (27), 1983, pp. 25–35. English translation by the author.

Even in European cities, such as Lisbon, gardening is often not a fashionable leisure activity but a mode of survival for those of low social status and minimum income.

Gardeners directly experience what it means to assume personal responsibility for the flourishing of nature and the preservation of an intact urban environment – here in Lisbon.

In the Anthropocene, the current age of man, gardens have a new importance as testing grounds for art and culture, as interim activation concepts on unused sites, or as catalysts for new urban development concepts, driven by the eternal longing for paradise and the desire to transform an image of Arcadia into a vibrant and sensually perceptive space. Landscape architecture today is not gardening, but if it is completely decoupled from garden thinking, it runs the risk of not being able to establish an intact symbiosis of nature and culture. "If we take responsibility for the existence of life seriously, then we must also want to have garden thinking and garden action ... as the basic principle for all land use and design of the land."[5] G&M

5 Ibid.

In the metropolitan landscape of Munich, the garden is only one of many components that cannot exist when disconnected from the life-supporting network of landscape structures.

Becoming World Gardeners in the Anthropocene

Martin Prominski

In May 2019, in the month when Dušan Ogrin (to whom this book is dedicated) sadly passed away, the thirty-four members of the Anthropocene[1] Working Group within the International Commission on Stratigraphy voted positively to declare a new geological epoch – the Anthropocene. This was an important step – one which took the group many years of discussion. Once a definitive geological marker has been identified to formalize the process, geography books all over the world will have to be revised to include the new epoch. What does this have to do with the garden? Well, the Anthropocene calls for a rethinking of the Western concept of nature,[2] and in this process the garden could be a fertile metaphor for showing a path for human survival. We need a new relationship to what was formerly known as nature and culture.

The emergence of the term

The term "Anthropocene" was coined by Paul Crutzen and Eugene Stoermer in 2000[3] and designates a completely new geological situation, in which humanity now influences every square metre on the earth's surface, as well as its atmosphere, for example through carbon or nitrogen emissions. Geology is able to trace human impact in the earth's sediments, and the influence is so strong that a return to the Holocene seems to be

1 Meera Subramanian, "Anthropocene Now: Influential Panel Votes to Recognize Earth's New Epoch", *Nature*, 21 May 2019, www.nature.com/articles/d41586-019-01641-5

2 Bernd Scherer and Katrin Klingan, *Introduction to The 'Anthropocene' Project: An Opening*, 10–13 January 2013, Berlin: HKW – Haus der Kulturen der Welt, pp. 2–6, www.hkw.de/media/en/texte/pdf/2013_2/programm_6/anthropozaen/booklet_anthropozaen_eine_eroeffnung.pdf

3 Paul Crutzen and Eugene Stoermer, "The 'Anthropocene'", *Global Change Newsletter*, 41, 2000, pp. 17–18. www.igbp.net/download/18.316f18321323470177580001401/1376383088452/NL41.pdf

impossible. Consequently, there is no nature left in the classical philosophical sense. According to this notion there is a dichotomy between nature and human culture, and nature is a powerful agent in its own right with its own inherent value, independent of human influence – a concept that has dominated the Western world for centuries. Acknowledging the Anthropocene amounts to an unmistakable call to transcend the West's dualistic concept of nature versus culture towards a non-dualistic, unitary philosophy of nature.[4] This means that there is also no longer any hope of protecting "good nature" from "bad human influence" in order to survive, as the Half Earth hypothesis proposes (e.g. Edward Wilson)[5] by conserving fifty per cent of the earth's surface for non-human species. Instead, we have to address one hundred per cent of the earth as a complex entanglement of natural, social, and technological forces and need to take care of it responsibly. Currently, we are falling short of accepting this responsibility, and are facing mass extinction and a hothouse earth on which human societies as we know them might not survive.[6] In the Anthropocene we should become "World Gardeners".

In this situation, the German geologist Reinhold Leinfelder, who is a member of the Anthropocene Working Group, sees the garden as an appropriate metaphor for addressing the challenges of the new geological era. For him, "knowledge-based sustainable 'gardening' must supersede the prevailing over-exploitation of nature".[7] He calls for gardeners to design the world because a gardener is able to steer the complex relationship between human and non-human forces. This remarkable statement by a major proponent of the Anthropocene already had a precedent in Germany, set by someone who probably came too early to be followed. Hubert Markl (1938–2015), an eminent German biologist, who served as the president of the

4 Martin Prominski, "Andscapes: Concepts of Nature and Culture for Landscape Architecture in the 'Anthropocene'", *Journal of Landscape Architecture* 9 (1), 2014.

5 Edward O. Wilson, *Half-Earth: Our Planet's Fight for Life*, New York: Liveright Publishing Company, 2016.

6 Will Steffen et al. "Trajectories of the Earth System in the Anthropocene", *Proceedings of the National Academy of Sciences*, 115 (33), 2018, pp. 8252–8259.

7 Reinhold Leinfelder, "Assuming Responsibility for the Anthropocene: Challenges and Opportunities in Education", *RCC Perspectives Issue*, 3, 2013, p. 26; doi.org/10.5282/rcc/6211

German Research Foundation (1986–1991) and the Max Planck Society (1996–2002), coined the word "Anthropozoikum" as early as the 1980s as a completely new geological age, in which nature is determined and dominated by humans and should be designed and preserved responsibly by humans.[8] To achieve this, he could not think of a better metaphor than the garden because it resembles a successful nature-culture symbiosis:

> The symbol and example of such symbiosis familiar to all of us is the garden as a form of using land that is more than yield-maximizing biotechnology. With regard to the earth we use, we need garden thinking as a complement, in the hands of responsible humans, to the calculating rationality of economic planning. Garden thinking means more than getting the last out of the land. A garden is anything but unproductive; useful crop plants characterize it and hold sway. But it is never just a place of productive efficiency. It is always also a place of organic beauty and harmonious comfort, which require incessant care and tending, which, however, can only be prepared, not produced, let alone produced forcibly. A beautiful garden lives from the wealth of its self-realization, from its order as well as from its derailments, from interference as well as from wilfulness, from planning as well as from self-organization. It is not only order and thus more than a plantation; it is not only wilderness and thus also usable. A real garden is when nature and culture harmonize. If we take responsibility for the existence of life seriously, then we must want garden thinking, garden behaving ... to be the basic principle of every use and shaping of the land.[9]

8 Hubert Markl, *Natur als Kulturaufgabe*, Stuttgart: DVA, 1986, p. 324. English translation by the author.

9 Ibid., pp. 372–373. English translation by the author.

The garden as a simile for a new geological era

Both Leinfelder and Markl make it clear that the garden is perhaps *the* metaphor for a geological era in which humanity has become the dominating factor of the earth's system and is in need of a new concept of responsibility. The garden metaphor is very powerful for several reasons. First, it shows the entanglement of humans and non-humans, and second, it emphasizes complex relationships instead of simple, mono-functional approaches. Third, a garden needs anticipatory thinking, a gardener has to reflect the future effects of current actions, which in effect teaches humility because the results are not predictable. Fourth, a garden combines utility and beauty, thus, finally, implying that a garden depends on creative, subjective ideas and cannot rely purely on rationality.

The two latter aspects of beauty and creativity are the most challenging in striving to achieve a true world garden. The technical solutions for Leinfelder's "knowledge-based sustainable gardening" are largely there, for example by reducing carbon dioxide or increasing biodiversity. Yet rationality and technology are not enough to motivate people to make the necessary changes in their lifestyles, it is probably even more important to trigger emotions. Thus, we need ideas to synthesize the spectrum of solutions in beautiful projections – for example, as ideas for gardens that we long for. No discipline is more capable of addressing this complex challenge than landscape architecture – so, landscape architects, please enter the stage for world gardening! G&M

The Garden's Complex Instrumentality

Andrew Benjamin and *Gerard Reinmuth*

From one perspective the garden has a continuous history.[1] It might be conjectured, for example, that its presence as a *hortus conclusus* was clear in Renaissance works of art, for instance Fra Angelico's *Annunciation* (c. 1440–1445) and architectural treatises of that period.[2] Works of architecture have continued to incorporate the garden as part of the overall design motif. In 2011, Peter Zumthor referred to the concept of *hortus conclusus* with his design for the Serpentine Pavilion in London. In all such cases, the garden appears as a separated and enclosed space within which a specific combination of plant and animal occupants is arranged. However, the presence of the garden, even in this form, is more complex. The garden has a certain reality within architectural history and thus within the history of thought more generally. That difference involves a reconfiguration of the relationship between spatiality and instrumentality.

In broad terms there are two ways in which the garden can be approached. The first involves the contention that the presence of the garden within the history of thought is linked to what any one garden stages. The second, and this at the beginning is a theoretical claim, is that, while drawing on history, the presence of the garden as a designation within design need not be determined by that history. This allows for the transformation of a given ground condition such that it can be considered a garden. These two positions will be addressed in turn.

1 This essay draws on an architectural design studio taught by Gerard Reinmuth and Andrew Benjamin at the University of Technology, Sydney, between August and November 2020. The site investigated was the Korean Demilitarized Zone (DMZ) and one of the possibilities was to think of the DMZ as a garden. For a different approach to the DMZ in terms of a park that draws on the possible coalescence between garden and park, see Iain Watson, "Affirming Conflict and Identity in the Korean Peace Park (DMZ) Proposals", *Inter-Asia Cultural Studies*, 16 (4), 2015, pp. 631–647.

2 For both the history and contemporaneity of the *hortus conclusus* see Rob Aben and Saskia de Wit, *The Enclosed Garden,* Rotterdam: 010 Editions, 1999.

Garden staging

Staging necessitates recourse to the position of the garden within a network or relations and thus to the conditions that allow the garden to emerge from within them. The garden here is a purely discursive event. Those conditions create the setting in which the garden's staging attains centrality. Saint-Preux's description of Julie's garden in *La nouvelle Héloïse* commits Rousseau to a position in which nature's cultivation must reach a point where any sign of the garden having been cultivated has vanished.[3] The argument is that nature reaches perfection through artifice. Nature and artifice collide. Staged here is a way in which the relationship between nature and culture is to be played out. The garden is not just a *locus* activity. More emphatically, in the case of its presence in *La nouvelle Héloïse*, it becomes the setting where a series of conceptual oppositions unfold. Giving room to forms of development means that the conceptual pairings that constitute those oppositions are then able to be examined. Julie's control over nature produces nature. As such, nature's posited originality is called into question. Undecidability prevails. At the same time, the impossible possibility of originality that haunts Julie's garden comes to have greater extension. The opposition between appearance and reality that has a determining force in relation to both the work of language and the structures of emotional life is also challenged. The literary text becomes the site in which the surety of the philosophical is brought into question. This is part of what the presence of the garden within it stages. While the garden in Rousseau's *La nouvelle Héloïse* is a single instance, if it is allowed a sense of generality then what is clear is that gardens are not metaphors. They are locales of activity. As noted they are structured by the types of activities they are taken to stage.

3 For a more developed discussion of the interpretive issues raised by the presence of gardens in *La nouvelle Héloïse* see Mary Ellen Birkett, "Gardening and Poetry: The Languages of Love in *La nouvelle Héloïse*", IV, II *Romance Notes*, 26 (2), Winter 1985, pp. 115–119.

The Serpentine Gallery Pavilion of 2011, by Peter Zumthor and the garden designer Piet Oudolf, referred to the concept of *hortus conclusus*.

There is a necessary and constituting reciprocity therefore between the created garden and the activity that it creates. Here the garden – while conceptually rich – nonetheless remains a closed discursive site.

Moving from word to line introduces the possibility of a profound alteration. As a result of which it becomes possible to locate an edge condition, one in which the garden's staging exceeds what it presents. In the Western tradition, the garden that continues to set the measure is the one from which Adam and Eve were expelled.[4] While that particular garden warrants detailed investigation in its own right insofar as the expulsion allows human beings to be interpreted in terms of either sin or finitude, the presence of these two possibilities constitutes a setting. There are many paintings and images of Eden as an already defined place. However, what is of much greater interest is how threshold conditions are presented within drawings (and by extension here engraving). For there to have been an expulsion there needs to be a border. (On one level the border is both that which is presupposed and constituted by the act of expulsion.) More is involved within this setting than the simple presence of a line of separation. According to the account of the expulsion presented in Genesis 1:24, they were "driven out". As part of that process an armed angel guards the threshold between the Garden of Eden and the land to which Adam and Eve were returned. The angel at the border reinforces that position as a site of separation. That reinforcing demands continuity. The separation of good from the potentiality for evil is not an act that only occurs once. The cherubim with the flaming sword is ever vigilant. Policing has therefore its own form of constancy. The act of expulsion and the presence of a policed threshold entails that here the border condition demands a form of radical division. As a result, it is not difficult to extend this position

4 For a recent investigation of the role of this garden in the construction of the political choices available today see Giorgio Agamben, *Il regno e il giardino,* Vicenza: Neri Pozza Editore, 2019. English edition: *The Kingdom and the Garden,* translated by Adam Kotsko, Calcutta: Seagull Books, 2020.

and argue that here the border condition stages a fundamental division.[5] The expelled are the enemy insofar as they stand opposed to the presence of absolute good. That distinction necessitates the presence of a policed border. Gardens and borders are thought and presented together. That presentation is as much conceptual as it will be an outcome of drawing.

Expulsion from the Garden of Eden

What is at stake is the policed border. The expulsion from the Garden of Eden ties policing and the border together. Expulsion assumes that there is no way back. This complex set of concerns is clear from one of the engravings published in 1694 by Nicolas Chaperon of the frescoes by Raphael in the loggias at the Vatican. The engraving in question is, of course, of the expulsion of Adam and Eve. The engraving both in its drawn detail and in the Latin description repeats Genesis 1:24. The significant point for these concerns however is the way in which the separation – the expulsion – is staged. Adam and Eve have already descended. They have crossed the threshold. Their emotional response is mixed. They have stepped from the Garden. At the end of the stairs there is an extended step functioning almost as a plinth insofar as it reinforces the distinction between the Garden of Eden and the ground. The angel is elevated. The angel stands in this now liminal space. Adam and Eve are already walking away. The stairs and the plinth as well as the final step, when taken

5 That division is inscribed within a conception of the political that identifies the latter with the friend/enemy distinction, thus recalling the political thinking of Carl Schmitt; see, for instance, Ellen Kennedy, *Constitutional Failure: Carl Schmitt in Weimar,* Durham, NC: Duke University Press, 2004, p. 182, and John Agnew, *Globalization and Sovereignty: Beyond the Territorial Trap*, Lanham, MD: Rowman & Littlefield Publishers, 2017, p. 75.

Nicolas Chaperon, *The Expulsion from the Garden of Eden*, 1694.

together, comprise the border to be policed. While it may be possible to identify the border with an absolute line, the line for example created by the presence of the final extended step on the ground, there is a fundamental precondition that needs to be introduced if that claim is to hold. Namely, that such a possibility only really works if the line is policed. The engraved line contains. It limits and restricts. And yet, it does not contain absolutely. There is already a form of instability. Adam's shadow is still on that final step. Light shines from the Garden of Eden. It is not just that there are relations. They provide a possible opening. Rather than the conceptual openings that emerge in *La nouvelle Héloïse*; here there is the possibility of other spatial registers. Here there is drawing. If the relations and points of literal imbrication are privileged, then there is the possibility of reconceiving – reconceiving by redrawing – the border as a thickened condition that cannot then be reduced to the presence of the single line. However, a degree of caution is necessary here.

The line as a point of absolute separation works to the extent that the border is policed. Were that aspect to be suspended – not just conceptually but equally as an act of drawing – then there are two immediate consequences. The first is that the politics based on the opposition friend/enemy and the line as the site of absolute separation would themselves have been suspended. The second is that once that line and its attendant policing no longer define the way in which the border is at work, then the border or threshold takes on the quality of a thickened condition. In the case of Chaperon's engraving that possibility is underscored, at the outset, by the light shining from the stairs, the outstretched arm of the angel, and Adam's cast shadow. Viewed as creating a form of network, they elide the line of absolute separation. When these are taken as elements staging relations the thickened condition which constitutes the space between the Garden of Eden and "the ground" (*haadamah*)[6] outside the Garden where Adam has to work henceforth, becomes a site withdrawn from all instrumental logics. The line of absolute separation is absorbed within it without it deterring the overall quality of the space as such. (Indeed, it is possible to go further and say that this thickened condition no longer has an overall determining quality.) It is as though the line of separation has been reterritorialized. As such, it becomes the garden's other possibility. In other words, if the opposition between the Garden of Eden and the "ground" – thus an opposition maintained by the work of differential logics whose differences have a sustaining interdependence – are defined in terms of modes of instrumentality then the suspension of those modes occasions the opening of another space. It would be a space created by the suspension of instrumental logics. It would have a relation to instrumentalized spaces but would not be determined by them. The created spaces would be neither spaces of leisure nor spaces of work. They would be created spaces. Spaces for the activity of design. Spaces to be designed. If such a space had a name it would be possible to begin with *garden*. It would be a garden that while it was able to draw on the history of gardens can only have that engagement as a result of the suspension of the logics in which the history of gardens is already positioned. Indeed, the further argument is that the possibility of such a conception of the garden can only be actualized and thus can only be part of the history of the garden as a result of the suspension of the logics that organize and position gardens historically.

A moment of recapitulation is necessary here. While the presentation of the garden in Rousseau's *La nouvelle Héloïse* troubles a set of organizing oppositions, if not the primacy of

6 Also spelled *adamah* (Biblical Hebrew: המדא), the term is used in the Genesis creation narrative and can be translated as "ground" or "earth". The etymological connection between *adamah* and *adam* points to the teleological link between humankind and the ground.

philosophy's relation to truth, that site remains closed. However, Chaperon's engraving gives rise to a possible productive abstraction. Located within it is therefore another possibility. Emphasizing what might be described as imbricated relationality allows the line of absolute separation to be noted and absorbed. Precisely because it can be attributed the status of drawing, Chaperon's engraving allows for its own reconfiguration. This is the power of the abstracting move in which primacy is no longer attributed to figures and thus to their symbolic presence. Rather it is given either to existent or to just established modes of relationality. These modes have their own qualities. They create spaces that refuse the determinations of already assumed conceptions of instrumentality. What is created therefore is an opening within an already determined setting. In regard to Chaperon's engraving what can be drawn in is a possible *third space* between the Garden of Eden and "the ground".[7] There is another *garden*.

The border between North and South Korea as a garden

Catapulting forwards to a contemporary condition – the Demilitarized Zone (DMZ) between North Korea and the Republic of Korea – provides an example of this instrumentality at work. There are two reasons for approaching the site as a garden. In the first instance the DMZ recalls the logic of friend and enemy. It is a site which – while created by that logic – opens up the possibility of design-based interventions that take the suspension of that logic as their point of departure. To explain, the level of contestation symbolized by the DMZ has also had material consequences. The clarity of the Armistice Agreement

7 On the concept of "third space" see Andrew Benjamin, John Hong and Gerard Reinmuth, *Terroir: Third Spaces*, Melbourne: Uro Publishers, 2019.

View of the Demilitarized Zone (DMZ) between North Korea and the Republic of Korea from the Cheorwon Peace Observatory.

The Demilitarized Zone (DMZ) on the east coast.

is absent on the ground. Despite the clear establishment of a four kilometre wide zone for the DMZ, both sides have moved their line over the past decades such that at some points the total width of the DMZ is as low as two kilometres. The critical Military Demarcation Line (MDL) that marks the absolute border between the two Koreas is marked by 1292 posts but with a lack of clarity that makes it possible to encounter enemy units around the MDL despite the fact that it is forbidden to cross it. While the Republic of Korea's (ROK) bases are located on hilltops resembling a series of mediaeval fortifications, the North Korean posts are less visible and are connected by an access tunnel that forms an "underground great wall" two hundred kilometres in length. Four additional (known) tunnels traverse under the DMZ to the ROK side, monuments to failed plans of surprise invasion, reconfigured as tourist attractions. The coastline adjacent to the DMZ is also ambiguous, with a project of artificial reefs claiming both territory and access to valuable fish stocks. A "bridge of no return" that connects to the two sides is so named due to the impossibility of coming back once one chooses to be expatriated to the other. On the southern side, General Outposts exist just beyond the DMZ forming another line occupied by regiments forming a front line of defence, or attack, as the occasion may be. Behind this lies a Civilian Control Zone consisting of small villages, occupation of which still invites the risk of death or disablement from an encounter with an unidentified land mine, while in the northern equivalent are a series of theatre-set villages, one of which includes a constant broadcast of the achievements of the North and boasts of the world's tallest flagpole adjacent, on which flies a huge North Korean flag. If this multiplicity of fragmented and adjusted lines, fuzzy edges, and tunnels was not enough, the military personnel that patrol both sides of the MDL do so in open contravention of the armistice through participation in another piece of theatre whereby they are costumed and thus rebadged as "police" who are allowed to be in the zone. Police as a named presence and policing as an activity play an essential role with the way the DMZ as it is currently territorialized. Policing is already a measure.

The importance of this account of current conditions is that site creation – the transformation of the ground into a locale of design – necessitates that already present modes of territorialization be understood. In turn, the development of countermeasures can only occur with an understanding of the differing way modes of territorialization have occurred. Mapping and remapping are an essential part of this project. Mapping, analysis, and the emergence of a site presuppose and create knowledge. To the extent that such a possibility attains actuality – and here "actuality" refers to the design process – what can be undone are already present forms of instrumentality and thus what might be created can be described as third spaces that take on the quality of the *garden*. These third spaces, precisely because they assume the suspension of already present modes of instrumentality, cannot have already determined preconfigured forms. Staged here are therefore interventions that result from a dynamic relationship between mapping projects, site creation, and the emergence of form. In the second instance, the recourse to the *garden* allows for the reconfiguration of a site in non-anthropocentric terms. The creation of the DMZ has resulted in a "garden" created by the hardening of the boundary. But rather than a garden formed from a particular curation of plant and animal species, the DMZ is host to a range of (often endangered) animals that have been able to sustain life in the DMZ precisely due to its non-curation by humans.[8] As has been noted by a range of commentators paradoxically,

8 In a similar way, the border zone between the former West (Federal Republic of Germany) and East Germany (German Democratic Republic) forms today the Grünes Band Deutschland (Green Ribbon Germany). It is 1393 kilometres long and fifty to two-hundred metres wide and has mostly the status of a protected biotope, providing a habitat for more than 1200 endangered animal and plant species (editor's note).

a condition of peace and free movement between the two Koreas would be the end for many of the animals that rely on their bordered garden for existence.[9] These animals now have almost mythic presence in contemporary Korean cultural production – for example, in Tae-Sok Oh's musical *My Love DMZ* (2002–2010) various animals that now populate the DMZ play pivotal roles. In Catherine Diamond's terms:

> The play proposes how the two Koreas might resolve their infamous border – protecting its sanctuary status in perpetuity. Oh allows the animals and soldiers to tell their stories and plead with the spectators, especially young people who know little of the war, not to forget them. He resorts to staging ancient ritual to find a solution, and insists that the voice of artistic imagination be considered in determining the DMZ's fate, suggesting its transformation from an unintentional to an intentional sanctuary.[10]

The presence of the border as sanctuary within the play is not just the precondition for peace, and thus the provision of a place for non-human animals, a place holding the human and the non-human in place, thus, in reterritorializing their relation, recalls the possibility of the Garden of Eden, but where the garden becomes a place of negotiation. It is a place in which differences are not resolved; on the contrary, they are lived out. To go further, the argument is that the possibility of coexistence between the Koreas is almost predicated on what could be termed a peaceful coexistence between human and non-human animals. At work here is of course an emphatic reworking of the border that separates human and non-human animals – transformed in the process is what is meant by the

9 See the report on NPR (National Public Radio): https://www.npr.org/2019/04/20/710054899/in-korean-dmz-wildlife-thrives-some-conservationists-worry-peace-could-disrupt-i

10 Catherine Diamond, "Human No-Go Zones: Theatricalizing Unintentional and Intentional Wildlife Sanctuaries", *Theatre Research International,* 45 (2), 2020, p. 169.

forms of life proper to each. The reworking of the border, the occasioning of other lives, is what allows it to become a sanctuary. It is, moreover, an instantiation of the *border condition* that suspends the role of policing and thus it stands counter to policing and thus an architecture of wire, border posts, and militarization. The suspending of that border and its architecture is the precondition for the emergence of an architecture of negotiation.

What is left out of consideration is the need to recognize that any one configuration of the *border condition* is already a mode of territorialization. In the case of the DMZ, in its actual configuration, this is the mode of territorialization that sustains the politics of friend/enemy and thus which necessitates the architecture of militarization. What has to occur is a reterritorialization of the ground and thus another transformation such that it is a different locale of design. Such a move would enjoin both another politics and another architecture.

That presence allows us to consider analysis and design – the further elaboration of this garden – as centred around the diversity of animal life. The presence of animal life breaks with the logic of the garden if the latter is understood simply in terms of a setting for human leisure activities. Equally, it undoes an insistence on wilderness by recognizing that the DMZ is populated by animal life as the result of human interventions. And yet, because those interventions have their own form of instrumentality what becomes necessary is maintaining animal life while suspending already present forms of instrumentality. What is gestured to by all these positions is the reconfiguration of the DMZ as the other *garden*. This is an essential part of its continuity as a locale of design. A locale in which animals will continue to predominate. Such is the now complex instrumentality of the DMZ as *garden*. G&M

Winterscapes

Photographs by *Anne Schwalbe*

Garden as Community

Parc aux Angéliques, Bordeaux: the post-industrial park encompasses phytoremediation areas on the brownfields of the Garonne riverbank, which are gradually transformed into a green public spine, under the auspices of MDP – Michel Desvigne Paysagistes.

Quai des Antilles, Nantes: this former quay of an abandoned wharf forms part of the Île de Nantes urban transformation project, where an evolutionary "plan guide" introduced in 2000 by Atelier de l'île and Alexandre Chemetoff ensures the radicantity of the design.

Radical Gardens

Lisa Diedrich

In these turbulent times, the garden sometimes seems an irrelevant issue for landscape designers and design researchers, or at least not worth referring to in their efforts to face the greater environmental problems. Is the garden really so irrelevant? Environment, said French landscape architect Gilles Clément in his inauguration speech at the Collège de France in 2011,[1] is just the way of naming nature by those who think they can master it. For him, this means to reduce nature's biological complexities and sensorial qualities into a scientific system of objective, measurable elements that can be understood by everybody always in the same way. The acidity of a soil can be measured with the same instruments and expressed through the same parameters in Europe, Africa, and Asia; the acoustic value of a site, the radiation emission of a rock, the CO_2 charge of the atmosphere, the pollution of a water course are captured the same way all over the globe and communicated in what Clément calls a "scientific Esperanto", an engineered language that does not touch anybody's emotions. Landscape, however, says Clément, is equally nature, but grasped another way, through the senses. It is what expands around oneself and what the view embraces, or, for the blind, what all the other senses embrace. Landscape is also what remains in memory when one's body has left the space in which the senses were actively capturing impressions. Impressions are of course intangible, ephemeral, subjective – hence suspect to those who ask for objectivity to master the world.

For Clément, there is a third category beyond the "environment" and the "landscape" – the garden. It unites and

1 Gilles Clément, "Jardins, paysage et génie naturel", Paris, Collège de France, coll. "Leçons inaugurales", 222, 2012, http://lecons-cdf.revues.org/510, doi: 10.4000/lecons-cdf.496

transgresses both as it is shaped as a landscape and maintained through technical and environmental skills, while all being about life and survival. Clément explains that in all cultures the garden has been understood as an enclosure, until ecological thinking burst its borders – to eventually embrace the whole planet as a vast garden, confined by the limits of outer space. The "planetary garden" is the figure of thought Clément has cultivated during his entire career, building prototypes, drawing synthetic sketches, writing books, and shaping exhibitions.[2] He wants to engage broader audiences into the creation of the planetary garden: professionals, politicians, people should act as gardeners and take care of life and the survival of the planet, with all of their knowledge, skills, and inspiration but also with the ages-old wisdom of the gardener, working with biological complexities as much as with sensorial qualities.

The garden is a place where everyone can live and care for on a daily basis, be it the smallest balcony in an inner-city condominium or an entire stretch of land somewhere under the sky. For people living under the contemporary condition of ongoing urbanization,[3] with effects on the most remote areas of the planet, the garden is perhaps the nexus between sustainability science and feelings of beauty. In her seminal essay "Sustaining Beauty – the Performance of Appearance"[4] landscape scholar Elizabeth Meyer called for reinserting the aesthetic dimension into the sustainability triad of environment, culture, economy. She posited it would not be enough to provide functionally correct spaces that counteract environmental problems but that there was a need to create wider public awareness for, acceptance of, and engagement in tackling the threatening ecological, social, and political problems of today. In her keynote speech at the conference "Beyond Ism: The Landscape of Landscape Urbanism" at SLU Alnarp in Malmö,[5]

2 Gilles Clément, *Le jardin planétaire: Reconcilier l'homme et la nature*, Paris: Éditions Albin Michel, 1999. English edition: *"The Planetary Garden" and Other Writings*, translated by Sandra Morris, foreword by Gilles A. Tiberghien, Philadelphia: University of Pennsylvania Press, 2015; Alessandro Rocca (ed.), *Gilles Clément. Nove giardini planetari,* Milan: 22publishing, 2007. English edition: *Planetary Gardens: The Landscape Architecture of Gilles Clément*, Basel: Birkhäuser, 2008.

3 Neil Brenner, *Critique of Urbanization. Selected Essays*, Basel: Birkhäuser, 2016 (Bauwelt Fundamente series 156).

4 Elizabeth Meyer, "Sustaining Beauty – the Performance of Appearance", *Journal of Landscape Architecture*, 2008.

5 Elizabeth Meyer, lecture at the conference "Beyond Ism: The Landscape of Landscape Urbanism", Alnarp, Malmö, October 2016.

Meyer referred to contemporary social scientists to claim that changes in behaviour and policies require more than data analysis and rational thought. She suggested that aesthetic experiences of landscape could help involve larger publics in caring for the spaces in which they live. Affective encounters, she argued, could establish the missing link between the overwhelming planetary problems and the everyday personal trajectory, and result in new imaginaries, engagement, and activism.

Designing the planetary garden

To complement the assumed objectivity of scientific and technological investigations into the environment, understood by everybody in always the same way, landscape architects have the responsibility to design gardens, and design researchers to sharpen its conceptualization. There is a need today for conceiving and understanding site- and time-specific interactions between human and non-human life within singular sites. This designerly engagement with site and time cannot be reduced to generic scientific rules, it is not objective. But neither is it arbitrary, whimsical, or purely subjective – there are grades in between, there is always a game played between designer, garden, user, society. To understand design beyond scientific analyses and emotional reactions, it is important to ask what designers "read" on a site understood as a garden (and what not), how they then "edit" it upon their readings, and which personal, cultural, societal backgrounds motivated the reading and the editing.[6] Designers design more or less consciously, and this is where design researchers can add a layer of transparency when unpacking the many strands of reflection and sensation

6 Lisa Diedrich, "Translating Sites: A Plea for Radicant Design", in Carol Burns and Andrea Kuhn (eds.), *Site Matters. Concepts, Histories and Strategies*, 2nd ed., London/New York: Routledge, 2019.

around the design work. These interpretations, as much as the design works themselves, do not aim at scientific truth, they provide for affective encounters, which is a powerful way of enticing people to become the gardeners of this planet, and to join the great project of sustainable living, or, in Clément's words, the planetary garden.

A garden never starts from scratch but is rooted on existing ground, and it is never finished but continues to evolve, its plants grow or decay and produce seeds, seedlings, new roots, eventually expanding over the site and beyond, and in time. Designing a garden does not mean to design a static object in a confined area for a moment in time. Researching design work does not mean to interpret a fixed state of form. It is interesting to notice that the contemporary French art critic Nicolas Bourriaud draws on dynamic concepts from botany to distinguish between two ways of creating works of art since the turn of the century, one called "radical" and the other "radicant". He proposes to replace the idea of the single root, "radix" (a noun, static) by the one of continuous enrootings (a verb in gerund, dynamic):

> One might say that the individual of these early years of the 21st century resembles those plants that do not depend on a single root for their growth but advance in all directions on whatever surfaces present themselves by attaching multiple hooks to them, as ivy does.
> Ivy belongs to the botanical family of the *radicants*, which develop their roots as they advance, unlike the *radicals*, whose development is determined by their being anchored in a particular soil.[7]

7 Nicolas Bourriaud, *Radicant: Pour une esthétique de la globalisation*, Paris: Éditions Denoël, 2009. English edition: *The Radicant*, translated by James Gussen and Lili Porten, London: Sternberg Press, 2009, p. 51.

On radicant design

In this sense, radicantity is the opposite of radicality, it is dynamic. This observation resonates with the understanding of sites as dynamic relational constructs, continuously undergoing transformation. Radicantity invites to focus on transient aspects of site, and the garden epitomizes this understanding. Consequently, radicant design profiles as an activity of creating ever ongoing enrootings – this is what designers do when conceiving a garden. Radicant design offers an alternative to the idea of design as starting from scratch and aiming at finished work. Because of its evolutionary nature, radicant design stretches form over time into what Bourriaud calls a "journey-form" – and the garden might serve as a synthetic image of what such a design work resembles in material terms in landscape architecture.

If we upscale this idea to Clément's concept of the planetary garden while involving Meyer's plea for the design of landscapes as places of affective encounter kick-starting active individual engagement, then the garden is a very timely concept, completely oriented towards 21st century perspectives, and landscape architects can make a powerful contribution in offering radicant design. G&M

Naturpark Südgelände, Berlin: here, a former railyard had been colonized by pioneer vegetation over decades before being turned into a park informally by local groups. Eventually, municipal services, researchers, and landscape architects established it as an official park which continues to be shaped by processes of nature and human interventions.

The Community Garden as a Metaphor of Coexistence

Urška Jurman

In his *Manifeste du Tiers paysage* (Manifesto for the third landscape),[1] Gilles Clément, renowned French gardener and botanist, defines the uncultivated landscape as an invaluable sanctuary for biological diversity, the genetic reservoir of the planet, and as a biological necessity, the space of the future. This third landscape includes protected natural reserves and "primary nature" zones not (yet) used by people, as well as abandoned or marginal areas removed from functional use. In the urban context, the third landscape is generally comprised of abandoned, transient locations that are (temporarily) exempt from human control and management. As Clément points out, plant species tend to thrive in the third landscape that succeed poorly, if at all, in cultivated areas and especially in soil that is used for industrial agricultural and other high-yield production. Various spatial, social, and cultural practices and communities, which cannot or do not want to participate in the processes of creating added value (profit) that propel not only capitalist dynamics but urbanization as such, also find refuge in abandoned urban areas. As David Harvey,[2] the British-born Marxist economic geographer, argues, these practices and communities are unable to exist in an increasingly regulated and controlled public space.

1 Gilles Clément, *Manifeste du Tiers paysage*, Paris: Sujet Objet, 2003; see an English excerpt here: http://www.gillesclement.com/cat-tierspaysage-tit-le-Tiers-Paysage

2 David Harvey, *The Right to the City*, https://davidharvey.org/media/righttothecity.pdf

A long dormant construction site on Resljeva Street in Ljubljana, close to both the railway station and the city centre, represented one such "non-functional space". The site, which during its long years of dormancy had become overgrown with willows, birches, invasive plants, and other wild vegetation, became the inspiration for the project "Onkraj gradbišča" (Beyond a Construction Site). The project was launched in 2010 with the support of Bunker, a non-profit organization for cultural events, as part of their programme "Vrt mimo grede" (Garden by the way), which set its gaze on the surrounding neighbourhood of Tabor with the goal of unearthing green parts of the city, encouraging urban gardening, and supporting social urban spaces that are not subordinate to commercial consumerism. The dormant construction site in the middle of an otherwise residential neighbourhood on Resljeva Street, a symptom of an era of real estate speculation and the capitalist production of the urban space, struck us as the ideal location for an initiative in which space becomes the constitutive dimension for social action.

The project's initiators (Obrat Association) had the primary goal of making the fenced area accessible and converting it into a sort of community green space, specifically a space that would be planned, designed, and managed by the people who were involved in the project. A secondary goal was to encourage a more active role for residents in co-designing their own city, which in turn would demonstrate the power and potential of community actions in the space, and test where this kind of tactical urbanism, a form of activism that responds more quickly to actual social and spatial needs than typical long-term planning, might lead.

An urban garden as a relational space

The qualities of the specific location (an enclosed overgrown property) and its immediate surroundings (characterized by the lack of green spaces and in particular of allotments)[3] combined with the feedback collected from the residents[4] ultimately transformed the abstract idea of the creation of a green community space into a tangible urban community garden project. The owner of the property, the Municipality of Ljubljana, supported the project with a contract for the temporary unpaid use of the property.

The first months of the project were mostly spent cleaning up the abandoned construction site and setting up the first beds from scrap wood found at the location and soil that we brought there. Only a very small number of people from the neighbourhood participated in this phase of the project. "Beyond a Construction Site" would have to wait until the spring of 2011 for the first real interest in the project to be aroused by a summons entitled "Make Your Own Garden" that we distributed to residents in the neighbourhood. Many responded to the summons because they recognized the advantages of having a garden near their homes where they could grow vegetables, herbs, flowers, and medicinal plants. A smaller number responded because of the community-oriented nature of the project that promised, in addition to the cultivation of a garden, the cultivation of social ties. In the years that followed, during which the original group of nearly thirty participants almost tripled, these initial motivational proportions slightly changed. Nevertheless, the desire to garden and have contact with the soil remained the primary motivation both for participants who had experience with gardening and those who did not. From the beginning, "Beyond a Construction Site" has

3 "Beyond a Construction Site" also was a form of criticism and an alternative to the then municipal policy for the management and renting-out of allotments in Ljubljana that began to be implemented in 2010 with the first prototype gardens. The measures taken for the management of gardens served as a negative reference: specifically, they reflected a rigid and overly formalized approach, including criteria for the rental of gardens (almost exclusively to older people with low income) that transformed the city's allotments into homogenous social areas, and mostly relegated them to the outskirts of the city. Not surprisingly, these measures triggered anxieties that the surface area in the city dedicated to gardens would be drastically reduced. With the global financial crisis that hit Slovenia in 2010, the high expenses of establishing municipal (prototype) gardens, and the removal during the previous years of a large number of illegal gardens by the municipal authorities, it became clear that the city administration would not be providing the funding needed for gardens to the level and at the pace that had originally been planned. It was partially in response to this set of circumstances that we tried, through the project and its related activities (round tables, initiatives to change municipal spatial plans, collaboration with Mreža za prostor, a Slovenian network of NGOs for sustainable and inclusive urban development, etc.), to rethink municipal policies and propose alternatives that are more inclined towards the temporary use of space and the encouragement of gardening in densely populated urban neighbourhoods.

4 During informal conversations with people living and working near the location, and especially at the first meeting with interested parties, we confirmed that our plan to open the dormant construction site for temporary use and transform it into a green community space was both feasible and desirable. During the meeting, the participants discussed the need for more greenery, gardens, and places to socialize. Similar findings were also revealed in a sociological and anthropological study about the Tabor neighbourhood that had been carried out by Bunker in 2010.

The evolution of "Beyond a Construction Site", a community garden on a dormant lot in the city centre of Ljubljana, over time, 2010–2019.

been an intensive classroom not only about gardening but also about coexistence – between participants, between people and other living species, and between a community garden and the neighbourhood and the city.

The community garden "Beyond a Construction Site" is above all a "relational space" that defines the community as a form of relations but does not attempt to eliminate differences or contradictions, or for that matter (creative) dissonances and (productive) conflicts that are necessarily connected to the sharing of the space, water, tasks, activities, and time. This is an important aspect: namely, that the project has more to do with the negotiated relations of differences than with the confirmation of commonalities that emerge from similarities. In contrast to a concept of community based on homogeneity, and ideas of identity and belonging ("being in") that can be quickly transformed into the exclusion of the other/the outside, "Beyond a Construction Site" strives to create a community that promotes more open and fluid relations and thus encourages the feeling of "being with". Just as the gardens in "Beyond a Construction Site" do not have a uniform image,[5] the community developed through and within the project is also composed of fragments. Just as gardening is an activity, so too is the community an activity and a process for the creation of relations and connections[6] both among the participants of "Beyond a Construction Site" and beyond it.

The question of coexistence among people and other living species immediately became apparent when we first entered the third landscape of the dormant construction site. We began by getting acquainted with the plants that were already growing on the property,[7] and searching for a balance between the natural elements that had emerged on their own and the spaces for planned gardens – both individual and collective

5 In addition to organic gardening and cooperation in the maintenance of the community space, one of the three basic rules established by the project's initiators at the outset was that people would make their own garden beds. The spatial planning and design of "Beyond a Construction Site" was the outcome of a negotiating process.

6 Vijay Devadas and Jane Mummery, "Introduction – Community Without Community", *Borderlands* e-journal, vol. 6, no. 1, 2007. In the article, the authors refer to the idea of community as defined by Jean-Luc Nancy and Giorgio Agamben, http://www.borderlands.net.au/issues/vol6no1.html

7 One of the first things we did when we entered the dormant construction site was to simply walk through the location guided by Zlatko Zajec, an amateur herbalist. He showed us the plants that were already growing on the location, explained their properties and uses, and we later used samples of them to create an herbarium.

beds and smaller plantings. As temporary guests, we intuitively followed the concept of the *garden in motion*[8] as articulated by Gilles Clément. Clément places the garden in motion on a neglected parcel of land where plants are allowed to develop on their own, not influenced by cultural principles such as geometry, order, etc. The principle is for the gardener to make the best use of this found dynamic without excessively intervening in it. "Trying to work with nature as much as possible, rather than against it."[9] This is how Clément summarizes the garden in motion, the goal being to maintain and increase biological diversity. This approach calls more for observation than for actual gardening; it requires us to become acquainted with plant species and their characteristics in order to make the best use of their natural potential. And this, similar to listening to and negotiating with participants in a community garden, requires time, attention, sensitivity, and openness.

According to Clément, one of the most important aspects of managing the dynamics of the garden in motion is the movement of life on the ground, the physical migration of plants within a specific area. This is where the name of this type of garden comes from. Flowers sometimes grow on organized paths, for example, because of the movement of seeds carried by the wind, people, or animals, and gardeners are then confronted with the decision of whether to remove them or allow them to grow there. The garden in motion has the principal of maintaining all species of plants in the locations where they grow spontaneously.

In "Beyond a Construction Site", we generally made the decision to keep the trees that were already growing on the property, some of which had in time gotten so large that they blocked the sun on the beds. We mowed relatively rarely, though with time, we learned that it is necessary to remove the

8 Gilles Clément, *Le jardin en mouvement,* Paris: Pandora Éditions, 1991.

9 Zygmunt Borawski, "In Hope of a Garden: An Interview with Gilles Clément", https://przekroj.pl/en/society/in-hope-of-a-garden

saplings of the invasive *Ailanthus* tree, to prune a branch here or there, and sometimes leave a dead tree where it lay, making use of it, for example, as support for a dog rose or as a shelter for various insects.

Temporary spatial practices in motion

"Beyond a Construction Site" is not a traditional garden for cultivating produce or satisfying the aesthetic need for beauty. It is also not a true example of a garden in motion as Clément defined it, although the principles of the garden in motion guided us in our search for balance between the dynamics of nature and human activities. The coexistence of diversity and looking for balance between what grows spontaneously and what is planned is also one of the key questions and challenges posed by the contemporary city. As Clément asserts, the garden should not be subordinate to the (architectural) plan but, in its ceaseless transformation, is dependent on the watchful eye of the custodian and caretaker. Similarly, contemporary urbanism should be more about enabling, among other things, the third landscape and temporary spatial practices in motion to which the urban garden certainly belongs. In this regard, it is important to reconsider the category of the beautiful, which is a frequent reproach against self-grown green and self-designed garden areas, and to open ourselves to new concepts of community and public green spaces that favour living (life?) over form. G&M

Architect Polonca Lovšin during her intervention "A Plan with a Goat" (2010). For an entire day she followed a goat through the overgrown land of "Beyond a Construction Site" and recorded its movements. This experiment questioned rational planning and was also intended as a tribute to our ancestors, who often relied on animals for choosing land, setting up pathways, and building houses.

The City as a Garden

Dževad Karahasan

I spoke about my city to a group of young people from various European countries who were attending the summer school of architecture in Sarajevo. My lecture was limited to the Turkish and Austro-Hungarian, which is to say the Oriental and Central European, parts of the city, and, in limiting it in this way, I provoked a small revolt among my listeners. First, one young woman from Sarajevo reproached me for not talking about the new parts of the city, and the basis for her reproach was that she had been born and lived part of her life in the large housing estate of Alipašino Polje that was built in the 1980s. I attempted to apologize with the statement that I didn't have much to say about these modern settlements, and this drew the objections of other listeners to the lecture. I recall that a student from Ukraine protested vociferously, claiming that her city was one big modern housing estate, and there were many things that could be said about it.

I realized that I had hurt the feelings of these young people with my imprecise formulation. They had concluded from my remarks that because I had nothing to say about modern housing estates that I also undervalued them, that I viewed them as unworthy of conversation and less worthy in general; they were defending their childhood, the ambience in which they grew up, their homes and memories, and that is why they spoke so emotionally; and because they misunderstood my imprecise statement, they attributed to me a contempt for the neighbourhoods in which they grew up. I clarified that I had not intended to express condescension for the cities, neighbourhoods, and buildings in which they grew up. Then I told them how a friend who had got an apartment in one of the new housing estates had once rung the bell at the wrong door because he had mixed up the buildings. How could he not become confused if ten or fifteen buildings all looked exactly the same, and were arranged in a geometric pattern? How many car owners recognize their vehicle from the licence plate? And yet how else would they recognize it if ten or more identical models were parked in the same lot? The identical appearance of items and the inability to distinguish between them is the foundational logic of industrial standards, which, by their nature, require total unification or the uniformity of the products. This logic has its advantages. Staying with the example of automobiles, a car owner can buy reserve parts any place in the world and be certain that they will fit. But the system also has its downside: one's city and house are transformed into an industrial product. Modern cities and modern houses – as if they had emerged in a laboratory – often completely ignore the requirements of the climate, configuration of the terrain, the vegetation and lifestyles of people in the place where they were built. So they may look completely the same in the Mediterranean and in Scandinavia. What kind of city declines any connection to the real world in the place where it exists? It is an industrial city built according to the logic of industrial standards. That is why there is not much to say about these cities, neighbourhoods, and buildings – because they have no characteristics except for one – that they function as "residential spaces". My point is that people can only remember something and gain orientation if they can contextualize a location.

On sameness and difference

If we compare a housing estate from the 1960s or 1970s and its sameness with a garden, we immediately understand a fundamental aspect: the garden is based on difference. Even if the garden is nothing more than the translation of the gardener's concept into reality, it remains part of the real world because it is composed of elements from the real world (trees and flowers, streams and meadows, sand and stones), but also because the garden, as a whole, is composed of the relations between these elements, and thus of the interplay of similarities and differences between them. The garden speaks in a kind of language with its own morphology, syntax, and semantics. Each segment of the garden has its own form, and the individual segments relate to each other, which visibly constructs a syntactic whole. There is an interplay of similarities and differences between individual forms, types, syntactic units. A feeling of lostness will not overwhelm a person who can see the border between the flower beds and the meadow, who can recognize and differentiate individual parts of the garden by the trees that grow in it, who can find the path that crosses the meadow and leads to the fishpond.

Similarly, a traditional city is a response to the configuration of the terrain, the climate and vegetation of its location. That is why the streets rise and fall and make their turns following the natural morphology of the land. A traditional city (such as the Turkish part of Sarajevo, dating back to the Ottoman Empire), like a garden, has an ambience of clear identities, an ambience in which individual elements are not interchangeable.

Nothing is taken away from the elements when they are part of the composition of the traditional city or the garden: a hyacinth remains a hyacinth even when it is an element in a garden.

It looks and smells the same, it grows and withers in the same way whether it is in the wild or in a flower bed that is part of a garden. However, in the flower bed, it becomes part of a complex game that respects what hyacinths and marigolds, carnations and calendula have in common (all are flowers), and at the same time reveals the differences between them (the various scents and colours), and these differences form the whole of the flowering garden. The garden becomes a syntactic whole by placing side by side samples of a various type (of flower) and employing the differences in colours, scents, shapes, and forms of blossoms included in that type of flower.

In this interplay, individual flowers acquire entirely new, even borrowed attributes that they do not possess outside of this whole. They gain new characteristics in the totality of the higher order that is created through the interaction of similarities and differences in flowering gardens and other elements of the garden such as the lawn, decorative bushes and fountains, gravel paths and arrangements of stones. Thus, the garden constantly adds new properties to its material elements and constructs an increasingly more complex whole, while not taking away any of the elementary properties that each of the components has on its own. Similar processes inform a traditional city. The bakery smells of bread, the streams and rivers run in their beds, and the squares are located in the places where the ground is the flattest. But the street as a part of the totality of the city acquires completely new (borrowed) properties in relation to other streets, which it crosses or runs parallel to, with the buildings that line them, and the squares to which it leads.

Both systems – that of a garden and a traditional city – are based on the principle of inclusion, not the principle of exclusion. They preserve the fundamental nature of the material elements, these elements function in a more complex manner, acquiring new properties, which in turn leads to an even more complex and extensive whole. In this way, the garden and the traditional city are essentially different from the modern city and the plantation in commercial farming that are guided by the reductionist principle because of which the material elements of the whole (the system) are reduced to one property.

Shaping and preserving time

Both the garden and the old city are irreplaceable. Thus, the garden and the traditional city are as much essential forms of culture as they are a way of shaping and preserving time. The term "culture" is derived from the Latin word "cultus", which means the "cultivation of the earth" or more precisely "to cultivate the earth". Was the first form of cultivation of the earth the burying of the dead or the creation of the garden? We cannot know this, but do not need to, as they are not mutually exclusive. Perhaps our ancestors planted the first garden (in memory of the one from which their own ancestors had been expelled?) when they began to bury their dead. G&M

Map of Sarajevo, 1912, showing the old city centre.

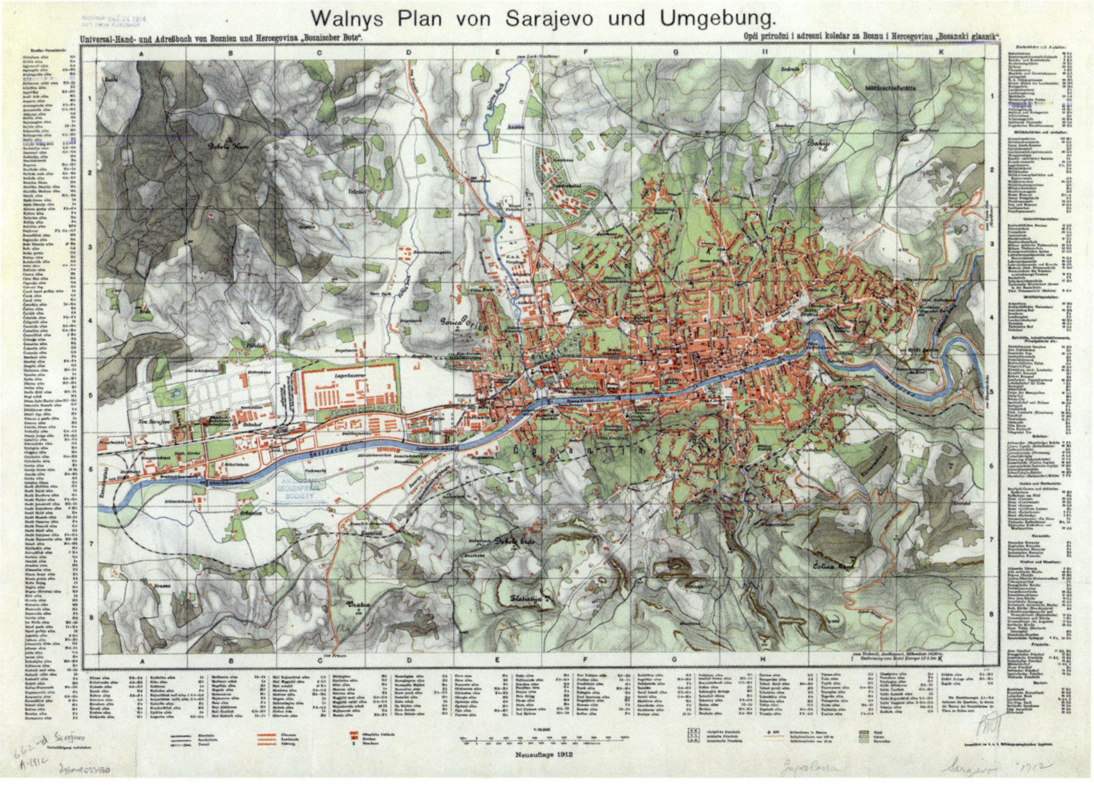

Overgrown Plans

Miloš Kosec

When I first heard about the cherry and apple trees deep in the Kočevsko forest, trees that had once been cultivated and have since been absorbed into the wild, my previously unquestioned ideas about architecture began to waver, perhaps for the first time. There was a time when the Kočevsko region was a considerably less forested and much more populated landscape than it is today. From the 14th century onwards, the region of southern Carniola was populated in clustered settlements by the descendants of Eastern Tyrolian colonists who became known as Gottscheers. Upon their arrival, the colonists cut down the forests, organized the land for agricultural purposes, and created a unique cultural landscape out of what was previously wilderness. They spoke a quaint southern Bavarian dialect and settled in about 180 hamlets and villages. The region around Kočevje was poor, and, except for the churches and the ducal mansion in the town of Kočevje, did not have many old or well-constructed buildings. Most adult men, because of poverty, peddled goods throughout the Holy Roman Empire, returning to their homesteads, their wives and children, their fenced

Landscape in the region of Kočevje in southern Slovenia, which was home to a German-speaking community from c. 1330 until 1941.

Cherry tree in the forests near Kočevje.

Dilapidated and overgrown mill in the Kočevsko region.

gardens and orchards in this God-forsaken border region, only to spend the winter. The area, between 1869 and 1878 once home to around 26,000 people, had already been depleted by waves of emigration to America when it was almost completely devastated during the Second World War by the catastrophic decision of the community leadership to support Nazi settlement policies, convincing almost all of the twelve thousand Gottscheers in the Kočevsko region to move to the belt beside the Sotla River, the new "defensive line" of the German Reich, and occupy the homesteads from which Slovenians had been expelled. The Gottscheers left as suddenly as they arrived seven hundred years earlier, leaving behind empty houses and barns that were soon burned down by Italian soldiers in their battles with local partisan forces. In the absence of land management, the woods began to grow over the pastures and fields until they approached the orchards and gardens and soon invaded the ruined walls of the homesteads and farm buildings. The roofs collapsed into the chambers and rooms, the remaining wood rotted, the mortar between the bricks mouldered, the walls crumbled. Today, here and there, the ruins of a more solidly built belfry can be glimpsed among the treetops. The partial remains of certain graveyards have been preserved and maintained. Only eighty years have passed since the departure of the Gottscheers, the length of a single human life, but enough time to almost completely erase the traces of the previous seven hundred years of settlement. The land beneath the powerful trees now lies silent and peaceful. The last traces of the daily rhythmical work – cutting, clearing, digging, and building walls – have been almost entirely subsumed by the damp soil and ground cover.

Remnants of forgotten orchards

Except for the fruit trees that is. If you happen to wander into the old forests in these parts, you will probably encounter some of them here or there, the illegitimate progeny of a past, carefully cultivated orchard. These fruit trees are the first and, in many places, the only remnant of the human settlements. In contrast with the notion of many architects that human lives are transitory and built structures are permanent, buildings that are no longer warmed by caring hands, repaired, renewed, and occupied, turn out to be extraordinarily transitory, often having a shorter life span than a human being. They leave behind building material in the terrain that, except to the archaeological eye, is indistinguishable from the natural relief. The ruins of the Kočevsko region are not brick walls or letters engraved in stone, but the growing descendants of fruit trees that are the memories of a past cultural landscape brought into the present. They no longer contradict the forests that have overgrown the homesteads and gardens but intermingle with the woods in a sort of post-catastrophic survivalist symbiosis. It is not the moss-covered traces of a stonemason's chisel or a bricklayer's trowel that preserves the memory of past homes and hearths; it is rather this living, adapting, self-generating, and growing natural-cultural system.

Wooden shed in abandoned hamlet in the Kočevsko region.

Limits of architecture

When I heard about these remnants of past orchards, I was not only captivated by the encounter with the transitory quality of bricks and stones, but also by the realization of the limitations of architectural ideas about building and planning. A single conviction runs like a red thread through the centuries of professional presentations of the masters of building and their descendants in modern architecture: that construction is the realization of a previously defined idea. The curve of architecture, with the help of the drawn line, ascends to its fulfilment and achieves its apex when the building is completed. But everyday use smoothly travels towards obsolescence until there is nothing else but for the curve to slowly slide down towards its starting point. When it encounters the horizontal, it is finally defeated. This is the everyday heroic and tragic experience of the architect's profession, a battle lost in advance, although the architect is certain of victory until the instant he or she stumbles onto a cherry tree in the woods. At that moment, instead of elevated reflection, she may become only sentimental, or perhaps, sober and restrained, she may sit down and evaluate her profession in a less mythologized light. Architecture, which is not a battle of one individual against social and natural entropy. Architecture, which is placed in the middle of everyday life and which can also reflect about what is unforeseeable and only possible. Where planning is not precisely defined by an authoritative screenplay with a multitude of stage directions (and the all-important prompter), but rather is an outline of living possibilities. For the architect, this kind of planning is unusual or even undesirable, while for the gardener and the landscape architect it is self-evident and necessary. When I learned about the fruit trees in the Kočevsko region, I began to think about architecture as I would about a gardening plan. In such a plan, a building would be interconnected with the long-term possibilities of the use and life of the structure; architecture would adapt to accepted standards, but also from time to time the standards would adapt to architecture. Just as the house suits the needs of those who live in it, those who live in it also adapt to the house and discover new ways of living freely in their

Church ruin at Nemška Loka in Kočevsko forests.

abode. It is more than just a one-way transfer of desires. Just as when we encounter the overgrown roots of some great tree in an old garden or park, or branches hanging above a path, we do not simply think of a saw or an axe. Rather, we quietly marvel as we bend down to avoid the tangle of branches or step over the roots, and, whether we want to or not, we bow down to the great living creatures and the people who planted them, even though they knew they would never see them grow to their full size. G&M

Gardens as Spaces of Collective Imagination

Lilli Lička

The term "garden" has different uses in colloquial speech and professional terminology, but even in the latter is used in a range of different ways; moreover, like all sociocultural expressions, it is subject to constant transformation of meaning. In a general sense, it is futile to assert with any certainty which object is meant by the word garden. "What on earth is a garden?"[1] asks John Dixon Hunt in his treatise on garden theory. The sheer scope of the concept makes it impossible to delineate. The meaning in the word stem, pointing to a boundary,[2] was lost long ago. "Garden" became synonymous with park, a fact that runs through the cultural history of the art of the garden,[3] as well as through the history of professional landscape architecture. What is more, not only public but also private green spaces are called gardens. "Garden" as a term with an obvious or even offensively positive connotation is also used for places (i.e., tourist destinations) or projects (i.e. housing or shopping malls) for the sake of economic exploitation, which is particularly convenient in relation to real estate. In the image-laden language of marketing, real estate also almost always boasts of gardens; but in what is actually built, gardens are no longer as prominent. The observation that the concept of the garden is applied to embellish our imagination allows conclusions about its meaning which seem to lead back to paradisiacal origins. And in the professional context, five decades ago, when landscape architecture began to gain ground beyond

1 John Dixon Hunt, *Greater Perfections, The Practice of Garden Theory*, London: Thames and Hudson, 2000.

2 The word can be traced to the late 13th century and comes from Old North French *gardin,* denoting a (kitchen) garden, an orchard, or palace grounds. It is related to Old French *jardin*, from Vulgar Latin *hortus gardinus*, in the sense of "enclosed garden". The Frankish word *gardo* and Germanic *gardan* is also the source of Old Frisian *garda*, Old Saxon *gardo*, Old High German *garto*, and German *Garten.* Old English *geard* and Gothic *gards* means "enclosure" which is derived from the Proto-Indo-European root *gher-*, "to grasp, to enclose". Italian *giardino* and Spanish *jardin* come from French.

3 See, amongst others, Gabriele Uerscheln and Michaela Kalusok, *Kleines Wörterbuch der europäischen Gartenkunst*, Stuttgart: Reclam, 2001.

A garden or a public park? The former royal garden of Jardin du Luxemburg has acquired a new meaning through its contemporary use.

A designed "natural" garden in Parc André Citroën, Paris, Gilles Clément and Alain Provost, 1992.

Translating the environmental movement into landscape architecture. Park Hönggerberg, ETH Zürich, Stern und Partner and Eduard Neuenschwander, 1980.

the borders of its Swiss and German places of origin, gardens were of rather minor importance. It was a time when concepts like landscape, public and social spaces, and environmental awareness were en vogue, with nature almost at the top of the agenda. Landscape architecture for garden design was limited to private individuals, at least in Austria, where this has not changed to this day. Even the great Swiss landscape architect Dieter Kienast was at that time writing about the sociology of plants and diversity of species. Later, in 1990, Kienast wrote one of the most cited sentences in this context about the garden as the last luxury of our times that requires above all time, care, and space.[4]

The garden as wilderness

This luxury has nowadays been somewhat distributed throughout cities and partially also in the countryside, where the possibility of gardening has been created in public and semi-public open spaces and parks, i.e. to grow and water plants, to weed and to harvest. The components of the social sphere and of production are again combined with closeness to nature and longing for the integrity of the ecological system. The climate crisis has directed the wave from natural via artistic, landscape architectural design back to the green cause. The opportunity of connecting with the soil and therefore of surviving, which is here symbolized by the garden, is perhaps the determining emblem which is also reflected in the aesthetic transformation. Gardens should appear raw again, as wilderness; species and plant diversity are of key importance.

The landscape architects from atelier le balto in Berlin, for example, work at the crossroads of (garden) production and

4 Dieter Kienast, *Die Poetik des Gartens. Über Chaos und Ordnung in der Landschaftsarchitektur*, Professur für Landschaftsarchitektur ETH Zürich (ed.), Basel: Birkhäuser, 2002, p. 76.

The garden as wilderness: diversity of plants in the urban realm of Reininghauspark, Graz.

The aesthetic transformation: Queen Elizabeth Hall Roof Garden, London.

A wide variety of tree species such as oaks (*Quercus robur, Q. phellos, Q. palustris, Q. cerris*), birch (*Betula pendula*) and robinia (*Robinia pseudoacacia*) was used in Nike Campus, Hilversum, Bureau B+B, 2020.

Natural chaos within the order of a constructed space: the atrium garden "Asphalt Jungle", Paris, Wagon Landscaping, 2022.

poetics, and use plant material in their two-dimensional and three-dimensional spatial designs. The Amsterdam-based Bureau B+B opts for a variety of tree species when designing public parks. Even allees are no longer inevitably comprised of a single species, a method of replication that was also employed in forestry to tackle the climate-induced vulnerability of monotonous tree populations. Wagon Landscaping from Paris lets the ground, i.e. the soil, shape their designs and create natural chaos within the order of a constructed space.[5]

Gardens are mirror images of contemporary conceptions of nature. Accordingly, today's question of human survival on Earth with regard to food and climate indeed shapes our imagination. The expression and perception of the garden transcends its objective image. Erik A. de Jong describes the garden as an imaginative space.[6] The individual and collective imagination also feeds off of cultural and societal topics which are predominant during a certain epoch. Nowadays, it is – maybe again – one of a better world. G&M

5 Wagon Landscaping embraces the "wild garden" strategy developed by Louis Le Roy in the 1970s. Le Roy's approach was an attempt at a rather generalized transposition of ecological laws into the urban landscape design, unconventionally leaving the "design" of the urban landscape to natural succession. Such attempts – intended to prevail as an overall strategy – have so far proved to be of limited value because spontaneous, wild, and unpredictable "natural landscape" can only partially meet the manifold human needs. Reviving the model, however, raises the question of whether key changes occurred in the latter (editor's note).

6 Erik A. de Jong, "Hortus conclusus: 'Das Gesetz des Gartens'", in Adriaan Van Der Staay et al., *Public Garden*, Rotterdam: NAi Publishers, 2002.

At the crossroads of (garden) production and poetics: "Printemps à KW", Berlin, atelier le balto, 2017.

Garden as Enchantment

Katsura Rikyu, Kyoto, Japan, 17th century.

Need a Garden Be a Metaphor?

Marc Treib

Posing the question "Can a garden today still be a metaphor?" assumes that there was ever a good reason for the garden to serve as one. We might ask: what is gained by attaching cognitive associations to the garden that reach beyond our direct experience of it as an artefact and environment? The bee requires only pollen to create honey. Are not flowers, shrubs, trees, and grass sufficient for our encounter with the garden in a rich sensual way? Must we require an additional cognitive dimension to profit from being in the garden – or even studying its design? Without question – like virtually any other aspect of our lives – a garden could serve as a metaphor, but why should it? Or are we proposing that a landscape architect's reliance on metaphor can help create and enhance the garden's design? Perhaps considering the garden as an earthly paradise, or as a localized recollection of a distant mountain or lake, may instigate a set of design ideas that may never have arrived without the use of these allusions. George Lakoff and Mark Johnson define a metaphor as "in essence ... understanding and experiencing one

Katsura peninsula and pond, evoking Ama-no-Hashidate, the famous pine-covered sandbar north of Kyoto.

thing in terms of another."[1] Is not the "one thing" of the garden sufficient in and of itself?

On a daily basis any garden can be encountered, experienced, and enjoyed, but only at very few times, and by rather few people, is it pondered in terms of its meaning or related to places or ideas beyond its physical boundaries. As humans, our experience usually arrives in this way: it is first sensed, then perceived, and finally – if ever – interpreted. Here I would distinguish *sensed* from *perceived* because only during perception are the mental faculties involved – our past experience colours, and perhaps modifies, our immediate sensations. Interpretation assumes that at some point – although not always – one thinks about the possible meanings for the garden, whether personal, social, or metaphorical. I suspect that few people ever consider the garden in this light, unless perhaps only many years later when they reflect upon their past experiences in that garden. Perhaps the garden was the site of one's first kiss, or a bad sunburn, or a bad bee sting, or our first success at growing vegetables. This is what we remember, and what gives meaning to this landscape.

The use of metaphor assumes shared references through which the allusion is constructed. If we do not share those references, whether through a common culture or mediated experience such as print, pixel, or film, the metaphor is not read, much less deciphered. In the 18th-century English garden, or those of imperial Japan, visitors often shared class status and education and were thus able to interpret certain features as metaphors or representatives of another landscape beyond the garden – perhaps references to places in the realm of religion, literature, or poetry. Encountering the Elysian Fields at Stowe might bring thoughts of scenes from Virgil's *Eclogues* or Greek mythology; seeing the stone-covered peninsula at the Katsura

1 George Lakoff and Mark Johnson, *Metaphors We Live By*, Chicago: University of Chicago Press, 2003, p. 5.

Imperial Villa in Kyoto might trigger associations with Amano-Hashidate, a revered scenic site with a pine-covered sandbar in northern Japan. But metaphors exist in more than one form. A broad, vague metaphor might pose that the garden is the "lung" of the house or the "lungs" of the community. A more personal metaphor might link the shape of a pond to one from childhood, in a historical landscape, or seen as a young adult in a foreign land. Or could the pond, more broadly, suggest a vast sea once viewed only in a photograph, but hardly present on this particular landlocked garden site?

In some previous writings I have considered the meaning of gardens and reached the conclusion that meaning cannot be embedded by the designer in any original design.[2] To clarify my point: the design might mean something in the mind of its creator at the time of design and realization, but there is a good risk that any intended meaning remains privy only to its maker and not to anyone first visiting the garden.[3] Meaning accrues only over time, over the years the garden is used and associations with it accumulate. Meaning becomes personal to those who experience the garden, experience which may or may not be shared by other members of a community of people. Meaning *can* be created and shared of course, perhaps through social events such as county fairs, political demonstrations, or even sporting events – but I hold that meaning is ultimately personal. At the turn of the 20th century the Swiss linguist Ferdinand de Saussure, distinguished between *langue* (language) and *parole* (speech).[4] Language is the broad vehicle that provides the structure, grammar, and vocabulary for communication within a linguistic group. Speech, in contrast, is the individual use of that linguistic system – use shaped by personal encounters gathered over time, whether positive or negative. I hold that the construction of meaning follows a similar

2 Marc Treib, "Must Landscapes Mean? Approaches to Significance in Recent Landscape Architecture", Landscape Journal, Spring 1995, pp. 46–62, reprinted in Marc Treib (ed.), *Meaning in Landscape Architecture & Gardens*, Oxon: Routledge, 2011, pp. 82–125.

3 In teaching design, one of the precepts was to make students understand the difference between "the intended perception" (what is proposed by the designer) and "the perceived in- tention" (what is understood by the user). The two are rarely the same.

4 Ferdinand de Saussure; Charles Bally and Albert Sechehaye (eds.), *Cours de lin-guistique générale*, Lausanne/Paris: Librairie Payot & Cie, 1916. First English edition: *Course in general linguistics*, translated by Wade Baskin, New York: The Philosophical Society, 1959. Reprint: New York: McGraw- Hill, 1966.

pattern: personal interpretation within a shared cultural environment. "Cultural assumptions, values, and attitudes", assert Lakoff and Johnson, "are not a conceptual overlay which we may or may not place upon experience as we choose. ... All experience is cultural through and through, and ... our culture is already present in the very experience itself."[5] True; but experience and its interpretation are also ultimately unique to the individual.

Desired readings

Any attempt to inject meaning into a garden – for example, through metaphor – risks being a useless effort. Certainly, inscriptions support a desired reading, and possibly, interpretation. On a tombstone the text might tell how beloved was the departed family member and his or her value to the community. Or, at Little Sparta – the garden of the poet Ian Hamilton Finlay in Scotland – inscriptions and objects construct and colour the reading of the place. One work tells us to "See Lorrain, Hear Poussin", making reference to landscape views by these two celebrated 17th-century painters. At another point, Finlay uses Hegel's proposal of the dialectic to describe the stile used to traverse a fence. The poet proposes the fence as the thesis, the gate as its antithesis, and the stile as the synthesis that shapes the new thesis. Here the metaphor – or at least, allusion – is given concrete form in wood and word, and causes us to consider the artefact of the stile at a deeper cognitive level. But without words, or considering the entire garden as a metaphor for heaven, assumes a great deal from the visitor. Sensually there may be no doubt that the garden is indeed a haven removed from the hubbub of everyday life and the pressures

5 Lakoff and Johnson, *Metaphors We Live By*, op. cit.,

Front Garden, Little Sparta, Dunsyre, Scotland, Ian Hamilton Finlay, 1970s.

Saint Just, Lochan Eck Garden, Little Sparta.

of the workplace. Need it also be considered a mental haven as well? Perhaps it should, and in rare instances I would have to agree that it does. Constructing metaphors today is even more difficult than in the past, given the plethora of sources like the internet that fragment, and augment, our experience and thought, as well as the existence of so many subcultures, each possessing its own set of codes and beliefs. Today, it may be more reasonable to have fewer ambitions and pursue humbler goals: that is, to provide in the garden a comfortable place graced by flowers, grass, trees, and even vegetables. We can think about what else it might mean later, after we settle in, get comfortable, and enjoy the place. G&M

The Garden as a Metaphor of Contemporary Paradise

Davorin Gazvoda

In the history of garden art in many cultures around the world, the garden has often functioned as a metaphor for paradise: the Garden of Paradise. The design of gardens, particularly during the early development of garden design, adhered to the description of paradise found in the holy books of various religions. It was also grounded in the understanding of nature in specific historical periods, and materialized through the gradual development of culture, the establishment of certain aesthetic rules, and the technical capacity to create specific gardens. In short, human faith and the understanding of nature combined with the image of paradise led to the realization of a range of uniquely designed gardens.

An approximation of Renaissance Arcadia: Villa Medici in Fiesole above Florence. A country villa offering wealthy families to retreat to an idyllic landscape with superbly designed gardens and peaceful surroundings.

Here faith is understood as a specific religion or, in the case of atheists, as a social understanding of idealized Nature. We recognize the metaphor of paradise in the creation of gardens that imitate specific religious models in their design – for example, in Islamic culture, the use of the motif of the four rivers of paradise, and, in Asian gardens, the homes of spirits in certain garden elements – but it is also present in non-religious models, such as the equally idealized and utopian Arcadias of Western civilization.

The garden as Arcadia

The garden remains a metaphor for paradise in postmodern society at the beginning of the 21st century. In order to defend this claim, I will first explain how I understand today's faith in a sacred landscape, not in the religious sense, but in the understanding of the essence of the garden as a search for a utopian Arcadia, a physical world in perfect harmony with nature that is no longer similar to the bucolic and pastoral idyll presented in rural landscapes from Antiquity and the Renaissance or in the English landscapes from the 18th century onwards. In Slovenia, with its blurred borders between urban and rural areas and the migration of urban dwellers to the countryside, we still believe that the most desirable form of living is a single-family house with a garden located outside of the city in the countryside: in other words, a sort of new pastoralism. Nevertheless, today's faith in this new Arcadia surpasses the banal notion of the ideal place to live, especially

Community garden "Beyond a Construction Site" in Ljubljana as a temporary use for an abandoned construction pit.

Since 2020, an attractive kitchen garden at Schloss Dyck in Jüchen, Germany, designed by the Danish garden architect Jacob Fischer, shows how the useful can be combined with the beautiful. The layout of the beds and the planting of fruit and vegetables follow a geometric pattern and also relate to the old brick wall.

for the many who wish to remain in the city. For this reason, representations of the healthy life and the understanding of nature and ecology that we observe today, especially among the young urban generation, are important for the articulation of themes related to the metaphor of the garden as paradise. Young people have become increasingly obsessed with healthy food, vegetarianism, veganism, and also with control of the food chain. Thus, it is no surprise that we observe a growing enthusiasm for urban gardening, permaculture gardens, bee-keeping, organic farms, etc. At the same time, this generation dedicates enormous attention to ecological practices such as recycling, reducing livestock farming, trash separation etc. and is concerned about sustainability issues. However, knowledge on what comprises a healthy living environment is often lacking and sometimes rather superficial information from the internet prevails. For some people, the new garden of paradise is a natural landscape in which healthy food is cultivated. In short, they are believers. But the result of these efforts may be a banal and amateurishly designed landscape.

As long as these urban gardens remain in the private realm – for example, a vegetable patch beside an apartment house – it poses no problem. But, unfortunately, this utilitarian understanding of the garden also occurs in the planning of public green spaces where sometimes authorities in charge who do not have the skills to design outdoor spaces, who have no knowledge of horticulture and are not familiar with natural processes, are responsible for the planning of urban gardens. Sometimes, landscape architects are not involved in the planning of these utilitarian gardens, because the history of the

Vegetable beds in front of the Lone Hotel in Rovinj, Croatia. The surrounding open space was designed by Studio Kappo landscape architects simultaneously with the architecture (3LHD) to form a quality space.

gardening arts has deemed that such gardens are not art. Nevertheless, they are a constituent part of many important historical garden forms such as the vegetable or kitchen garden. It is, of course, necessary to include the principles of sustainability in the design of landscapes, parks, and gardens. Landscape architecture must actively collaborate in creating a new understanding of nature and thus redefine a metaphor of the garden (of paradise) in the 21st century.

Respect for natural processes

This will lead into the next phase: the definition of specific programmes and structural segments for modernized urban green areas. Landscape architects must develop carefully defined categories that respect natural processes and introduce them into the space: in short, they would imitate nature. This is something that contemporary landscape architecture has been dealing with since its inception. During the past century, the field consistently retreated from the imitation of nature and then, in the 1990s, it was forced to confront yet again the question of how to define ecological and environmental aesthetics. It is yet unclear, though, whether a garden described as more natural is also more beautiful to the non-professionals using it. Let us assume that the answer is affirmative and that the role of landscape architecture is to create "gardens for the people" and, as a result, respect the conservationist mindset of the potential users of the space. Would respect for the characteristics of the living material – the plants used in the design – and for natural processes represent a sufficient depiction of nature to satisfy an average visitor? Probably not, which is why it makes sense to think about the new themes that represent a display of natural processes in a manner that is understandable to everyone. These newly emerged green spaces in cities with an ecological programme often emerge during the restoration of derelict or devastated landscapes. During the planning stage of such projects, interdisciplinary teams can facilitate the reinstatement of natural processes. As a landscape designer, I am most interested in questions of what forms these designed natural spaces might take. Numerous examples of designed green spaces in the city include a display of nature but they also comprise facilities such as paths, park furniture, buildings and infrastructure, for instance playgrounds, educational trails, or research centres. It is important to differentiate between nature conservation and the provision of ordinary park features: the newly created green spaces that to some extent replace lost habitats or preserve threatened ones, cater to users at the same time, satisfying their passing need for communing with nature without exploring whether these processes are truly natural. G&M

Kirkkojärvi Flood Park in Espoo, Finland, by Loci Landscape Architects is an excellent example of urban green space design, subordinated to the hydrological dynamics of the site and potential flooding (simulated in the bottom image).

Heterotopia: The Garden as a Metaphor

Martin Rein-Cano

> "*The heterotopia is capable of juxtaposing in a single real place several spaces, several sites that are in themselves incompatible.*"
>
> Michel Foucault[1]

It is not an exaggeration to say that the cradle of humanity is in the garden. In our collective narratives, God does not create houses – God creates landscapes and gardens. An important founding myth of mankind and human culture hence starts here. The lost paradise nourishes manifold subsequent narratives in which the garden is the metaphor for an intact reality and an existence of ease. Today, the garden is a man-made utopia. While the paradise is the work of God, we become creators ourselves when we make gardens. Yet in doing so, our achievements are doomed to fail: like Camus' Sisyphus, maintaining a garden means to start over and over again – a mode of being that allegorizes the human condition already quite accurately.

The English garden as a collage

As a metaphor, the garden expresses realities and utopias simultaneously. Gardens symbolize visions – be it individual desires or collective dreams. This is especially true for public gardens that possess imaginative functions for the communities who

1 Michel Foucault, "Des espaces autres: Hétérotopies", March 1967. English edition: "Of Other Spaces: Utopias and Heterotopias", translated by Jay Miskowiec, in *Diacritics*, 16, 1986, 1, pp. 22–27, John Hopkins University Press. https://www.jstor.org/stable/464648

cultivate and inhabit them. Throughout history, horticultural places have had representative, communicative, and identity functions. Drawing the line from historical forms, important references for public gardens are certainly the Baroque garden, the Renaissance garden, and especially the English landscape garden. The latter also points out a conceptual shift in the history of garden typologies: in the concept of a cultivated "wilderness", the transformative forces and dynamisms of nature define a new paradigm. The romantic ideal of a powerful *Übernatur*, which is still productive today, became a conceptual archetype, especially for the public park as an important garden typology.

As a process-based fabric that is constantly transforming and forever in the making, the English landscape garden teaches us an important lesson on culture. This lesson originates from the fact that its typology was initially one hundred per cent foreign. By no means English, this garden is a polyglot assembly of plants and follies – pictures actually – taken from various geographic and cultural contexts.[2] What results are collages – constructed and multiple identities mounted so carefully that the ensemble eventually appears as a unity. It is the active dislocation and copy-pasting, the migration of forms and images and their translation, in which the English garden is set up as an allegoric cultural space. In the resulting hybridity, I would localize its potential for contemporary garden design – and also its powerful metaphorical potential for cooperation and collective forms of living: like a catalyst, this conceptual archetype of a public park can be capable of incorporating a vast multitude of things of different forms, sizes, ages, and origins. Like a small-scale version of a diverse culture, it creates a space where a splendid variety can playfully be experienced, tested, and rehearsed.

2 Rein-Cano refers here to the affectated, pretentious landscape "improvements", including exotic follies such as Chinese buildings promoted by Sir William Chambers (1723–1796) which indeed were estranged from the idea of the true English landscape advocated by William Gilpin (1724–1804). For the quest for the Englishness of the English "style", the "true English picturesque", see Simon Schama, *Landscape and Memory*, New York: Alfred A. Knopf, 1995, pp. 135–139 (editor's note).

Aerial view of Superkilen park, Copenhagen.

An assortment of narratives

If we look at the conceptual basis of the English garden (and forget for a moment all the kitsch and bad taste this typology has accumulated), the interesting point of this traditional form is that it can serve as creative groundwork for contemporary urban space design. Taking the garden as a starting point to reflect upon social territories, it becomes conceivable as a site that is open for an assortment of narratives and projections. As a dynamic typology, the garden then functions as a productive place for the many ideas, practices, and expectations a pluralist society may generate: it gives us a space to coexist, a place of visibility, and a protected site for acting out. As such, it is what Michel Foucault described as a heterotopia: an alternative to a predefined and normative reality; a space that allows for constant re-definition, for ambiguity, and for playful aesthetic experiences. Like Baudelaire's novels, the garden establishes an aesthetic regime that traverses ethical and representative norms, and – like the concept of the English garden – this regime is based on dislocation, transformation, and integration. Constructing itself out of the broadest cultural fundus, the productive simulacrum of the garden succeeds to eventually become all the multiple elements it adapts.

As a tissue of quotations drawn from the innumerable centres of culture, the garden is a bastard. In this sense, it is a radical form. Behind the apparent harmony of the garden, there hides no paradise lost, but a mesmerizing *Überreality*. At times being crushed beneath the weight of disintegrated multiplicities, the hopeful aspect is that the garden is a big playground, where falling and failure has no real-life consequence. What the garden makes visible in glances is a picture puzzle of failure, as it does not solve conflicts, but stages them – just as Sisyphus teaches us that there is no solution to find and no achievement to reach. Because parks and gardens are a remaining cultural play area, they are rather emancipatory spaces than battle zones. Due to their ambivalent being and simulative functions, they allow for a gentle ironic notion. Emancipated from tradition, contemporary parks tend to produce idiosyncratic effects: a barbecue by an Arab family can happen next to a feminist yoga circle, children can play next to students drinking beer, politics can be discussed while Freeletics groups pass by, dogs chase squirrels while rabbits witness drug deals in the bushes.

Superkilen in Copenhagen

By all means, the garden allows for things to come together that are usually separated. In this sense, it has a vital capacity for unforeseen encounter and hybrid forms of identification. A significant example, which for me functions as a metaphor in just this sense, is the public park Superkilen, which Topotek 1 completed in 2012. The idea of this project was to create an urban garden in the spirit of multitude – an attractive as well as sustainable space for the hybrid identity of Nørrebro, Copenhagen's most diverse district. Today, the site offers a stage for the encounter of Denmark's multi-cultural post-migrant community. In the tradition of the cultural technique of gardening, Superkilen can be understood as an updated version of the English landscape garden: a process-oriented growing site, which is never complete and has been made to endure constituent diversity. Instead of solving conflicts, it allows them to appear and take their place, embracing tension and heterogeneity as powerful opportunity.

The most important metaphorical function in Superkilen has been attributed to the urban elements. Comparable to the English garden, a variety of things populate the terrain. Finally, these objects increased the symbolic potential of the whole space, citing personal and cultural narratives. In a collaborative process, the inhabitants of the neighbourhood were asked what kind of objects with special meaning they would like to place in their new urban garden. In the end, 108 objects and eleven trees species from all over the world were chosen and either imported or reproduced on site – for instance a Moroccan fountain, a Kazakh bus stop, a Japanese play structure in the shape of an octopus, a Thai boxing ring, a Qatar dentist's sign, a swing bench from Baghdad, the Spanish Osborne bull, neon advertising posts from different countries, and even soil from Palestine. To me, these iconic follies, which were planted here to grow in a new bed, refer to the many cultural identities that shaped this contemporary urban landscape. And in doing so, they represent a novel typology, where the hermeneutic circle of the original was projected forwards to a new every-day cultural imaginary in the classical picturesque tradition of figurative design techniques. In their reconnection to the social realities, the site becomes legible again.

More than one hundred objects from different countries enliven Superkilen park.

As such, Superkilen is a proliferating urban garden, and it is a metaphor. It is an example of a hybrid iconic public space with identifying potential, which lastingly interrelates the people in an extremely diversified sociocultural context. Instead of resolving tensions, it creates an allegoric space where they can be displayed and experienced. And like any good garden, it is a place where the dynamism of plurality becomes aesthetically productive. In this sense, Superkilen is my personal metaphor for the realistic utopia of a heterogeneous society – a *heterotopia* which performs within the aesthetics of conflict that constitutes us as individuals and as society, and that is also in the essence of the garden. G&M

In Superkilen park, neon advertising posts act as modern-day follies.

The Garden as Microcosmos

Aleš Vodopivec

The most poetic architectural works have always, almost without exception, emerged in dialogue with nature. This is true even of the last century. In Frank Lloyd Wright's Fallingwater House, in Alvar Aalto's Villa Mairea, in Álvaro Siza's Boa Nova Tea House, the interior space extends without interruption far into the environment and nature reaches deep into the interior of these buildings. Unfortunately, Mies van der Rohe's iconic project for the Brick Villa Country House remained unbuilt. Its floor plan recalls the paintings of De Stijl with the dynamic composition of walls continuing far outside the perimeter of the building, beyond the edge of the drawing, the walls being comprised of panoramic glass panels that merely suggest the borders of the interior space. This unrealized project is perhaps the most radical illustration of the ideals of life in direct connection with nature. Mies' house is a representation of both a safe shelter and the wider world.

Villa Mairea, Noormarkku, Finland, Alvar Aalto, 1939, exterior view.

Villa Mairea, covered walkway.

Space in constant transformation

Man's devotion to nature is difficult to explain only rationally, as experience of the environment and space is very personal and emotional. I lived in the Ljubljana city centre for more than half a century in an apartment building built at the beginning of the 20th century. I always experienced nature as the opposite of the city, believing that the excitement of urban life is a counterweight to the natural environment. This belief led me to the conclusion that the preference of most Slovenians to live in a house with a garden was thus an expression of a unique anachronism, a legacy of our historical attachment to the soil.

Casa Barragán, Mexico City, Mexico, Luis Barragán, 1948, living room.

Casa Barragán, studio patio.

Only after I moved into a house with a garden did I gradually recognize the inexplicable power of the daily presence of nature. The constant transformation of the quality of the light, temperature, vegetation, precipitation, sounds, scents, and other phenomena, causes the space and image of the garden to ceaselessly change as well, and the person living amidst that environment becomes a part of the rhythm of those natural changes. With the help of the garden, the experience of time and space becomes more pristine and nature's authenticity touches us in the most direct manner possible.

And yet people in the developed part of the world today value comfort in their living spaces that excludes the influences of the outside environment. In contemporary buildings, the heating and cooling of the space with artificial ventilation, the reduction of openings in the façade, the additional insulation of the external walls, and even the airtight surface of the façade ensure constant conditions of temperature, moisture, light, and fresh air regardless of the weather and climate changes that take place at different times of day and in different seasons. The consequence of this is that a person in the interior of a building is more isolated and has few possibilities for the authentic experience of changes in the environment, space, and time.

Our first universe

In the 1930s, Alvar Aalto, disillusioned by the prevailing faith in the power of technocratic rationalism that neglected the psycho-physical feelings of people, drew attention to the humane goals of architecture and worked to integrate architecture with the natural environment. He claimed that architecture was a part of biology and that the building functioned as a mediator between man and nature. In his opinion, this was also reflected in the ceaseless striving of architects to create paradise: "Every building, every architectural product that is its symbol, is intended to show that we wish to build a paradise on Earth for man." [1]

Luis Barragán's enclosed gardens are perhaps the most beautiful metaphor of paradise. Located in Mexico City, one of the loudest, most polluted, and populated cities in the world, they create surprising oases of peace and silence in which the dignity of nature "combines the poetic and the mysterious with a feeling of serenity and joy."[2] Barragán demonstrates that the garden can, regardless of its size and in any time period (including the present), create a unique microcosmos and is therefore "the most efficient haven against the aggressive tendencies of contemporary life".[3] And because the world is day by day becoming more unpleasant and alien to mankind, it seems that only because of the garden do we, to quote Gaston Bachelard, experience the house or rather the home as "our corner of the world ... our first universe ... a real cosmos in every sense of the word."[4] G&M

1 Göran Schildt, *Alvar Aalto in His Own Words*, Helsinki: Otava, 1997, p. 215.

2 Luis Barragán, "Composing the Enclosure – A Poetics of Space", Interview by Alejandro Ramirez Ugarte. in "En el mundo de Luis Barragán", special issue, *Artes de México, Nueva época*, no. 23, spring 1994, pp. 88–112; p. 90.

3 Ibid.

4 Gaston Bachelard, *La Poétique de l'Espace,* Paris: Presses universitaires de France, 1958. English edition: *The Poetics of Space*, translated by Maria Jolas, London: Orion Press, 1964; reprint: Boston: Beacon Press, 1969, p. 4.

Casa Barragán, views of walled rooftop patio.

The Garden as a Photographic Image in the Era of Digitalization

Jure Mikuž

In the 2010 film *Certified Copy,* Abbas Kiarostami looks for answers to the eternal question of verisimilitude in art and life. Is the *Mona Lisa* not merely a reproduction of the model? Why do everyday objects, such as those painted by Jasper Johns or Andy Warhol, become valuable when they are exhibited in a museum? Are we not all DNA replicas of our ancestors? What does the fact that no cypress growing at the side of the road is identical to another say about art and reality? Does it mean that each is an original work of art?

The two main characters in the film drive through a Tuscan landscape of cypress trees, the beauty of which had already been imprinted in the consciousness of a much larger audience in a previous and more famous film, Ridley Scott's *Gladiator* from 2000. In particular, there are two small but renowned groves known by the locals as "i cipressini" located some thirty-five kilometres southeast of Siena in San Quirico d'Orcia on the hills beside the SS2 motorway. Today, the Via Cassia still runs along the route that begins where Via Flaminia ends in Rome, crosses the Pons Mulvius, and then continues through the Etruscan countryside towards Florence. The road was constructed around 187 BCE and, according to ancient records, was well maintained because it was a heavily travelled route. With the expansion of the Roman Empire, military units passed along this route on their way to conquer territory to the west and the north, and also towards what is today Slovenia:

first through Primorska, Emona, and Poetovia, and then to Pont in the eastern provinces. Travelling along with the military units was the whole administrative apparatus, the soldiers' families, and merchants. After the fall of the Roman Empire, tribes of barbarians moved in the opposite direction along the very same road, this time towards Rome. Throughout the Middle Ages and in subsequent centuries, the barbarians were followed by Christian pilgrims, crusaders, and countless others for whom the Papal city represented the pinnacle of their aspirations, both spiritual and aesthetic.

All roads leading to and from Rome comprised the transportation system known as the Via Francigena (the French road) that was first mentioned in historical sources in 876 CE. Travellers made use not only of the roads but of the excellent infrastructure that had been built alongside them as early as in Antiquity: a network of bridges, guest houses, hospitals, and rest areas. Amenities also included small groves of cypress trees that were especially welcome during the season when the hot Tuscan sun scorched the meadows and wheat fields.

The legend of Gildas the Wise

However, the quality of the impressive system declined over time. Supplies dwindled and the condition of the roads, and also their safety, deteriorated. Roadside parks were no longer pleasant havens, places for relaxation and merrymaking, but traps used by robbers and other gangs. One record, probably from the 9th century, describes what befell the British monk Gildas who was travelling on a pilgrimage to Rome during the 6th century. The record offers a general description, warning of murderers, adulterers, infidels, and other good-for-nothings, and also provides prayers to protect the pilgrims. One can easily imagine the fears conjured in the minds of listeners to and readers of these passages as they passed through the vicinity of San Quirico, an important station between Pienza and Montalcino. The chronicler writes that when the thieves spotted Gildas' shimmering personage, some wanted to kidnap him, others to kill him. He called Christ's name upon them, and with God's assistance, the legs of the thieves were driven into the ground and their bodies went numb as if they had been turned to stone. As Gildas walked on, he turned around and freed them, and they never harmed anyone ever again. The other adventure narrated in the chronicle refers to a dragon that lived in a cave in these same hills and poisoned the populace with its pestilent breath. When Gildas heard of the dragon, he went to the cave and in Christ's name ordered the monster to die, and that is what happened, and the plague ended.

Perhaps the cypresses on the hills above the valley of the Orcia River witnessed these and similar events. Peter Wohlleben, a German forester, believes that trees feel and, if they grow together, communicate with each other.[1] Perhaps scientists will one day be able to understand their speech. Cypresses live two thousand years, sometimes even four thousand, and it would no doubt be interesting to hear what they have to say. Who knows? They might even tell us what the good-natured monk, who later became a saint, actually experienced on his donkey as he travelled through the summer heat, lugging a barrel filled with the best Italian Brunello wine from nearby Montalcino. The cypresses on these hills certainly have an excellent view of what happens in the region because there are no other trees high enough block to it, and perhaps they would report that Gildas was simply so enchanted by their magnificent display that these visions were conjured only in his mind.

1 Peter Wohlleben, *Das geheime Leben der Bäume: Was sie fühlen, wie sie kommunizieren - die Entdeckung einer verborgenen Welt,* Munich: Ludwig Verlag, 2015. English edition: *The Hidden Life of Trees: What They Feel, How They Communicate – Discoveries from A Secret World,* translated by Jane Billinghurst, Vancouver: Greystone Books, 2016.

Views of the cypress grove, San Quirico d'Orcia, near Siena.

The cypress as symbol of eternity

The Etruscans moved from the eastern Mediterranean and settled in Tuscany (long before the Romans) and brought the cypress tree with them. There are many types of cypresses and they thrive in relatively warm climates on all continents. The principle characteristics of cypress trees – that they are evergreen, long-lived, supple, and have tall, elegant forms – created the impression that they were eternal. Thus, they have long been considered a holy plant, their flame-like growth providing a link between the terrestrial and the supernatural, connecting the materiality of their earthly nature to the spirituality of the heavenly creator. That is why it is almost obligatory to plant them in cemeteries where, according to the Christian faith, souls leave the bodies of the dead and ascend into heaven for divine judgement. In the Old Testament, the evergreen cypress was equated to eternal faith in God, the tree's abundance and fertility symbolizing infinite divine wisdom. Isaiah 55:12–13 made the follow prophecy:

> For you shall go out in joy and be led forth in peace; the mountains and hills before you shall break forth in singing, and all the trees of the field shall clap their hands. Instead of the thorn shall come up the cypress; instead of the brier shall come up the myrtle; and it shall make a name for the Lord, and everlasting sign that shall not be cut off.

Homer also sang the praises of the sharp-scented cypress tree, which, even in his time, was a symbol of mourning for death. Ovid absorbed these beliefs from Antiquity and encapsulated them in his verses about the unhappy Cyparissus, the young beloved of the god Apollo. Ovid relates the story of how the boy inadvertently killed the sacred stag, a powerful and divine animal to which he was deeply attached. Apollo "counselled him to moderate his grief in proportion to the cause. The young boy still continued grieving and asked the gods, as a last gift, to let him mourn forever. By now, as his blood was being consumed in constant tears, his limbs began to change, turning a shade of green, and then his hair, which a moment ago was hanging down his snow-white forehead, grew bushy and stiff, pointing upwards in a graceful spiky crest to the starry sky. The god Apollo groaned and sighed with grief: 'I will mourn for you. And you, in your turn, will mourn for others and become a part of people's grieving.'" ... The young boy "loved by the god who strings the bow and lyre" was transformed by grief into a tree that was then named after him, into "a cypress ... shaped like a cone."[2]

In the Middle Ages and the Renaissance, it was believed that people born in places where olive and cypress trees grew, where the sun shines brightly and the wind blows from the sea, were gifted with the disposition to become giants of spirituality and art. In the late 19th century, the French philosopher and historian, Hyppolite Taine, developed the theory that the artist is influenced by the place and time in which he creates. Like Homer, many Italian writers sang the praises of cypresses in their works, among them Giordano Bruno, Ugo Foscolo, Giosuè Carducci, and Gabriele d'Annunzio. Cypresses are also significant in the paintings of the early and high Renaissance, their undulating beauty used to designate specific landscapes and the apparent deepening of nature into the background. Paolo Uccello, Fra Angelico, Piero della Francesca, Benozzo Gozzoli, Filippino Lippi, Leonardo da Vinci, and others used the image of these trees to invent and perfect both aerial and

2 Ovid, *The Metamorphoses*, translated by Ian Johnston, Vancouver Island University, Nanaimo, BC, 2012, http://johnstoniatexts.x10host.com/ovid/ovid10html.html

linear perspective. Gardeners and architects with a heightened aesthetic sensibility used cypresses as natural fences in Italian parks and created geometricized mazes to emphasize the nobility of the spaces around statues, villas, churches, and other buildings. Cypresses were planted along roads and allees to deepen the perspective and in cemeteries to create a solemn atmosphere. Of course all of this was done following the traditions of previous generations, and the simple inhabitants of these places understood both the purpose and meaning of these trees: they served to strengthen the terrain by protecting the soil from wind and rain, and as symbolic markers, flowing into the harmonious rhythm of the calming and safe landscape.

The cypresses of Orcia Valley

Precisely the two groves of cypress trees in the Orcia Valley mentioned at the beginning have become a favourite motif on postcards, as well as appearing in guide books and other tourist material about Tuscany. That is why many travellers look for the two parks as they drive past on the SS2 motorway.

Views of the cypress grove, San Quirico d'Orcia, near Siena.

Countless photographs and videos are posted on social media. We may glean from the comments below the postings that there is too little space to actually pull a car up, that it is an unsuitable place to stop, and that the visitor would have to walk quite a distance to actually get close to the trees. But, in fact, it is not advisable to go all the way to the parks themselves because the area around them is still used occasionally as a garbage dump for locals.

In short, there are increasingly few people who would bother, like the late Kiarostami, to wonder if each cypress is an original work of art, and even fewer who would stop in the grove and listen to the whisper of memories rustling through their crowns. The park has become a victim of an amateur photo spree from which the trees cannot escape. Thus, the cypresses end up in the pitiless digital digestive system, passing through winding intestines that metastasize like a cancer that paralyzes human memory, consciousness, and curiosity, as well as the desire for knowledge and a sense of beauty. G&M

Summer Splendour

Photographs by *Anne Schwalbe*

OLAF

Garden as Art

Hans Haacke, *DER BEVÖLKERUNG*, 2000.

Garden as an Open Work

Jože Barši

In the year 2000, the artist Hans Haacke launched a project entitled *DER BEVÖLKERUNG* (for the populace, for the folk) in the context of the construction of the parliament building (Bundestag) in Berlin, the capital of united Germany. The purpose of the work commissioned by the German government was to symbolize the politics of the new Germany. One of Haacke's starting points in terms of his reflections on the theme of the project were the words under the tympanum on the Eastern part of the parliament building. The caption from 1916 was *DEM DEUTSCHEN VOLKE* (for the German people), suggesting at the time that the focus of political activities in parliament was the care of the Germans, specifically people who were German by blood, or the nation sharing a common history, cultural legacy, and affiliation. The contentiousness of this slogan was the starting point of Haacke's artistic project. The artwork *DER BEVÖLKERUNG* is a response to the previous text visible on the façade of the building, using the same font – developed by Peter Behrens – as the 1916 inscription. The words *DER BEVÖLKERUNG* written with neon letters ninety centimetres high constituted the central part of a garden that Haacke placed in the northern atrium of the parliament building. He conceived of the symbolism of the territory and politics of Germany in the form of a twenty-one metre long and seven metre wide garden surrounded by a thirty centimetre high frame. In contrast to the title on the façade that we see from below, Haacke's project is visible from the roof of the parliament, which is accessible to all visitors.[1]

1 More on the topic: Rachel Churner (ed.), *Hans Haacke*, October Files 18, Cambridge, MA: MIT Press, 2015; Walter Grasskamp, Molly Nesbit, Jon Bird, *Hans Haacke*, London/New York: Phaidon, 2004.

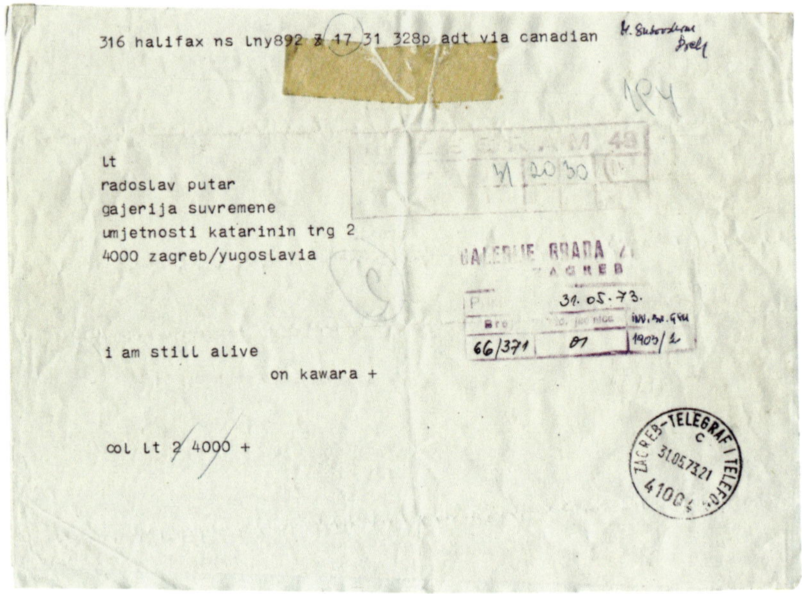
316 halifax ns lny892 7 17 31 328p adt via canadian

lt
radoslav putar
gajerija suvremene
umjetnosti katarinin trg 2
4000 zagreb/yugoslavia

i am still alive
on kawara +

col lt 2 4000 +

On Kawara, "I am still alive" (31.05.1973), from the series of five telegrams, 1973.

Each member of parliament contributed fifty kilogrammes of soil for the garden, bringing it from their own voting districts. During a 2001 lecture in Pittsburgh, Haacke showed photographs of elected politicians carrying soil in bags and depositing it within the frame. The soil contained seeds and roots that sprouted and grew over time, creating the image of an informal garden, i.e. a garden not planned or formalized by the artist or anyone else. Over the years a garden without gardening emerged. It is possible to observe, also on images posted on the internet, the wildly growing garden over longer periods of time.

The contrast between the two phrases symbolizes past and current politics in relation to the population (or the folk) that members of parliament represent. The phrase on the façade that is based on the idea of nation or ethnicity ("blood" Germans) is replaced in Haacke's project by the idea of all the people who live on the territory that is Germany, regardless of ethnicity or country of origin. The parliament thus also became the voice of those who are not heard, some of whom might not having voting rights, but nevertheless live in Germany. The artwork triggered a great deal of discussion during its implementation. Many people were not favourable towards the project because they connected it to, among other things, the Nazi slogan *Blut und Boden* (blood and soil). In contrast, supporters saw in the project something that went beyond such notions. However, the focus here is the theme of the garden and its anti-formalism.

Spontaneous vegetation

During the 2001 Pittsburgh lecture, Haacke said the idea for the unrefined soil that would be donated by members of parliament came to him when he noticed plants sprouting from a small pile of dirt that had been left on the roof of the building where he lived at the time. The use of plants in the work of contemporary artists is not entirely new. We may recall the period of Arte Povera and the artist Jannis Kounellis' use of cactuses and also Haacke's experimentation as early as the 1960s with water and plants in a gallery. In these cases, it had less to do with formal research of the media but rather with artists taking an interest in processes and materials that create forms independent of the artist's will. The practice might be defined as the delegation of the creation of form to something other than the artist. There are many samples of this kind of work. For example, the artist On Kawara sent a telegram with the message

The individual neon letters overgrown by spontaneous vegetation.

"I am still alive" to various addresses. The artist determines the content of the message but cannot influence the form of the artistic work, which is dependent on the post office and the country to which the message is sent. These types of projects inspire artists for many reasons, but mainly because of the surprising manifestations of form that are not dependant on the artists themselves. With On Kawara, who was exceptionally precise about his projects (and also about their formalization), it is especially interesting because the "I am still alive" project is the only one of his works in which the artist leaves the final form of the artistic work to someone else. This does not mean that the artistic work is entirely delegated to someone else, but rather that the reflection on or rather the content of the artistic work shifts from form to other aspects: for example, processes, participation, or other elements that interest the artist and are not a formal research of the media. The concept expands – form as such remains in the background and the space opens to different considerations. Formalization is disconnected from the will of the creator and delegated to other procedures or actors: human, nature, or machine. The delegation of formalization to something else, whether to another artist or to nature itself, represents a possible starting point for reflections about nature and the totality of its activities.

This kind of work does necessarily eliminate all familiar material and use only combinatorics that create new formalistic solutions. Differently conceptualized means of production offer different solutions that are often surprising in their relation to the procedures that the artist anticipates or controls. In his book *Difference and Repetition,* Deleuze, in the seventh postulate of the chapter entitled "The Image of Thought", precisely summarizes the difficulty of separating the question from its solution.[2] The solution or response to a problem is always

2 Gilles Deleuze, *Différence et répétition,* Paris: Presses universitaires de France, 1968. English edition : *Difference and Repetition*, translated by Paul R. Patton, New York: Columbia University Press, 1994.

directly connected to how the question is formulated. The problem, or more accurately the formulation of the question, is that which produces the answer. For this reason, the realization of a certain task is not only dependent on the solution but has a direct connection to the way the question itself was articulated. The problems or questions themselves are often erroneous or even false. Similarly, the separation of the problem from its solution also creates misunderstandings. By forgetting the question, an answer is generated that becomes absolute. But answers are always concrete and particular or, if you like, temporary, being relevant only in the environment or conditions that prevailed during the time the question was articulated. We don't function in an entirely empty space. Without even wanting to be, we are submerged in a concrete, local, historical world that comprises a very specific environment. Thus, a problem is always multi-layered. It is dependent on the specific circumstances of the space and time in which it is possible to articulate a certain question. The question of the relationship between nature and human beings functioning in nature is extremely relevant in the contemporary world.

As a sculptor, I see the world not as a dualistic relationship between thinking subjects and unthinking objects. Relevant are the processes, how something becomes something. This is not about the division into a world of active creators and a world of objective materiality into which the former interferes. It seems that a much more fruitful idea is that we are things among things, and that we are engaged in a reciprocal interaction between human beings, unformed material, and formed bodies. The creation of new reality therefore presupposes precisely this reciprocal response to various things. Materiality, and we sculptors know this very well, is as thinking as we are – or try to be – ourselves. G&M

The Silent Garden

Miklavž Komelj

The image of the garden has the capacity to combine a range of symbolic messages – including some which are extremely contradictory: from *The Garden of Earthly Delights* in which people, their bodies interwoven in positions of perverse innocence, seem to be approaching the condition of flora and fauna, to *hortus conclusus* in which the unicorn seeks refuge with the Virgin Mary; from the dreamlike landscape of *Hypnerotomachia Poliphili* to Amida Buddha's allusions to the Pure Land; from the Rococo *fêtes galantes* to the garden on the Mount of Olives where the terrible drama of redemption took place.

Controlled tension

Regardless of how serene it is, regardless of how it appears to offer shelter – the garden is in fact characterized by extreme tension. Controlled tension. The garden represents the control of what seems most uncontrollable: mastery over nature itself, which remains nature in the garden, but at the same time either carries the external impression of human design, or, put another way, the control and direction of nature's own power to create form. The garden, whether it is luxurious or ascetic, represents a fragile balance that must be maintained with constant mindfulness.

Vapours blow through Dante's earthly *Paradiso*, the biblical Garden of Eden, which is full of flowers but at the same time described as a "divine forest, dense and green". The vapours do not emerge from the atmosphere but directly from the movement of the heavenly spheres. We can sense the expectation of such a breeze in all gardens when we walk through them with the mindful gaze of the gardener. When we walk through Renaissance or Baroque gardens that emerged from a humanist vision, which is in itself "profane", our response has less to do with simple enjoyment and more with something demanding, strict, and noble. Even gardens that were not inspired by religious thought incite a sort of contemplation: the contemplation of the cosmically ordered principle.

The garden only strikes the most vulgar gaze as mere luxury. Slovenian landscape architect and great teacher of landscape design Dušan Ogrin, at the beginning of his magnificent publication *The World Heritage of Gardens* – a book that has inspired me on many occasions – purports that the garden was humanity's first form of organized space, older than the hut, which represents the first example of architecture and construction. Biblical myth assumes that the garden existed before any other human ordering of physical space, that the garden was the first direct form of the divine arrangement of space. If the first city was founded by Cain, the first garden was designed by God.

Dante describes the garden of paradise as a place made especially for the human race. But precisely as such it offers man no shelter but rather demands self-transcendence. Man finds himself in a place made especially for him but only because he is already abandoning it. When Dante arrives in earthly paradise, he observes with surprise that he has begun to levitate. Beatrice remarks to him that he should be no more surprised at this than that a stream flows down from the mountain heights. If Dante, now when he is free of all hindrances, remained on the ground of earthly paradise, it would be as much of a wonder as if there were stillness in a living flame on Earth.

A place without memory

The garden is the image of what is most demanding. Something that is the most difficult to endure. Of all the images of the garden in literature, I was most affected by the end of Yukio Mishima's "The Sea of Fertility", a tetralogy of novels published between 1969 and 1971. In the final volume, *The Decay of the Angel*, Shikeguni Honda searches for his friend Kiyoaki, who died of his tragic love for Satoko, through encounters with a series of his supposed reincarnations. In the end, after sixty years has passed, Honda makes his way to Satoko who, after she was separated by her family from Kiyoaki, became a nun and then an abbess. When he comes to her and speaks of Kiyoaki, she says that she doesn't know such a person. When Honda attempts to convince her that they did know each other, she asks him if he himself actually knew a person by the name of Kiyoaki. What if from the beginning that person did not exist – anywhere? And Honda begins to wonder whether he himself had ever existed. She answers him: "That too is as it is in each heart."

> A long silence ensured. The Abbess clapped gently.
> The novice appeared and knelt in the doorway.
> "Mr Honda has been kind enough to come all this way.
> I think he should see the south garden.
> I will take him there."
> The novice led her by the hand. Honda stood up as if pulled by strings, and followed them through the dark rooms.
> The novice slid open a door and led him to the veranda.
> The lawn, with the hills behind it, blazed in the summer sun.

> "We have had cuckoos since morning", said the novice.
> The grove beyond the lawn was dominated by maples. A wattle gate led to the hills. Some of the maples were red even now in the summer, flames among the green. Stepping stones were scattered easily over the lawn, and wild carnations bloomed shyly among them. In the corner to the left were a well and a well wheel. A celadon stool on the lawn seemed so hot in the sun it would surely burn anyone who sat on it. Summer clouds ranged their dizzying shoulders over the green hills.
> It was a bright, quiet garden without striking features. Like a rosary rubbed between the hands, the shrilling of cicadas held sway.
> There was no other sound. The garden was empty. He had come, thought Honda, to a place that had no memories, nothing.
> The noontide sun of summer flowed over the still garden.[1]

These words are followed by a date: 25 November 1970. On that day Mishima put the manuscript of the novel in an envelope to be sent to his publishing house. He also left a sheet of paper on his writing desk on which the following words were written: "Human life is limited, but I would like to live forever." Then, after a laughable attempt at a coup d'état, he committed ritual *seppuku*. This image of the garden was his last message. A symbol of something inexpressible because everything in it is perfectly expressed and nothing is hidden. G&M

1 Yukio Mishima, 天人五衰 - *Tennin Gosui*, Tokyo: Shinchosha Publishing, 1971. English edition: *The Decay of the Angel*, translated by Edward G. Seidensticker, New York: First Vintage International Edition, 1990, pp. 235–236.

Apology of a Garden

Erika Bordon

Natura artis magistra. The garden is indisputably a part of nature. It is also a work of art. That we can call it so and separate it from "nature itself", *prima natura*, as Cicero called it, it must fulfil the following condition: the garden must be fenced-in, separated from the rest of the world. The world is in a state of ceaseless transformation not only because of the activities of nature but also because of the ceaseless activities of man. Man identifies the places that are suitable for him to live and thus marks his place. He does not merely change nature, but also gives to her when he creates his work.

The garden is an expression of the spiritual state of its owner, an expression of his inner balance. In the garden, man finds a certain comfort. The garden becomes a sort of spiritual or "holy" place where he can find seclusion, that constantly sought-after virtue, and either engage in contemplation or dedicate himself to work on his own piece of land, resulting in a desired sense of purification. In the memory of Western civilization, the garden remains a living representation of the original garden of paradise, the womb of life, *il grembo della vita*, as Massimo Venturi Ferriolo characterized it.[1] Human life was conceived in the garden of paradise; the human race was placed there. Regardless

1 Massimo Venturi Ferriolo, *Nel grembo della vita. Le origini dell'idea di giardino*, Milan: Guerini e Associati, 1989.

Garden pavilion at Trsteno Arboretum, near Dubrovnik, Croatia, late 15th to early 16th century.

Transversal axis near the villa at Trsteno Arboretum.

of the present, the garden lives in the mnemonic image of humanity as a metaphor of paradise; the classic *topos* of comfort, pleasure, immeasurable human happiness, *paradeisos*, the garden of paradise. Evoking comfort, a place of pleasure, it is the legacy of the ancient Persian garden in which Cyrus the Great searched for the source of authentic life and was not ashamed to cultivate the earth and plant trees with his own hands. Even the great authorities of the ancient world, such as Seneca and Scipio Africanus, would withdraw from urban pollution and corruption into their remote estates to be cleansed of the burdens of the city by working their own land and dedicating themselves to the contemplation of their own reality or to the worldly enjoyments that the space of the garden offers. Enjoyment and comfort implied a space that was lost to the living, worldly man. Contemporary man does the same; the phenomenon of rustic life, so well-known in the Western world, still echoes in our time. Today, in the culture of *otium* or contemplative life, retreat into the countryside has been replaced by the cultivation of one's own vegetable or flower garden or vineyard on a little piece of land outside the city. It is an escape from the city into an "idyllic" place of purification, an escape from quotidian obligations. It merges all the elements known from the history of gardens into the positive category of *otium*; creative idleness, creative relaxation.

Soothing the confused intellect

All of this also applies to the contemporary transformation of the social field. Changes are first seen on the level of aesthetic ideals and art, and then continue into the delicate theoretical paradigm of the space that creates art. A garden is certainly that; when we enter a garden, we enter a work of art. There are divergences between the possibilities created by certain technological advances and mental, logical, and moral sensitivities, and the capacity of society to absorb these new possibilities. This seems particularly relevant in today's chaotic and turbulent times where, on the one hand, we have amazing technological development and, on the other, we have our somewhat slower and chaotically confused intellect that becomes agitated as it attempts to absorb a dimly defined future.

Garden as emanation of memory

Art is an exceptionally sensitive recorder of history. We transform: *historia magistra memoriae.*[2] The cultural-historical installation of transcriptions of the landscape ideal, the space of gardens, is an expression of hopes and desires unconnected to space and time. The words of gardens and the space of the garden, all the gardens that we have ever read or heard or saw, are etched into our consciousness with constant repetition. They

2 "Historia magistra vitae est", which can be translated as "History (is the) teacher of life", is a phrase from Cicero, *De oratore*, II 36.

are the emanations of our memory that, with mnemonic support, appear and become the cornerstones of the garden, the other, the material space removed from the unpredictability of the outside world. What kind of garden, and of what it is a metaphor, emerges and remains in the mnemonic image of each individual. It is a part of the individual's historical memory perceptions, mnemonic images, and thus it remains elusive, diverse, unspoken, and indeterminate. G&M

Part of the Renaissance parterre at Trsteno Arboretum.

Access to the villa through the garden at Trsteno Arboretum.

The Garden in the Knot of Meaning

Nadja Zgonik

In order to reflect on the garden, we must begin at the beginning. We must ask whether what we would today define as essential to the garden differs from past definitions. Has the garden become a particularly relevant theme in contemporary society, its rhizomatic structure technologically appropriating our perceptions of the world to the point that we have become increasingly alienated from nature? Has the role of the garden essentially changed as a result of the globalized information society in which we increasingly speak of threatened nature?

Geometric patterns at Kyoto Botanical Gardens, Kyoto, Japan, founded in 1924.

Throughout history, the garden has proved to be an amazingly complex phenomenon that is difficult to define unambiguously. It is a specific art form, the meaning of which has migrated in the past from the aesthetic to the natural, from the social to the political. What was once a vegetable and fruit garden soon became a space for leisure. Then, in the Middle Ages, the garden was enclosed within monastery walls and became a sacred space. As *hortus conclusus*, it acquired a symbolic significance – an enclosed garden separated from the rest of the world – and became a metaphor for the garden of paradise. It was a space where answers to the fundamental existential questions could be found through meditation, and a connection could be established both with oneself and with the divine in nature. Entering this earthly paradise introduced the possibility of transformation just as entering the first biblical garden of paradise and the confrontation with original sin transformed and permanently marked all of humanity. In subsequent centuries, the garden acquired new meaning. With Louis XIV, it became political, the garden suggesting that the king's right to rule came from God. In the 19th century, the garden as a public city park became the space that returned to the rural population the connection with nature that they had lost as a result of industrialization.

Let us instead begin by shifting away from a contextual reading of the garden to reflections about the specificity of the medium. During the 20th century, the modernist analytical spirit of art was directed towards the exploration of that which was essential to a specific medium and was expressed in the process of abstracting the material and the formal. The process resembled a sort of purification that would lead to the complete autonomy of the medium. In other words, each specific medium would not engage with anything not inherent to it, but rather only with itself, and the discovery of its true nature. In "Modernist Painting" (1960), the influential essay that defined high modernism, Clement Greenberg concluded that what makes painting exceptional is its own specific properties: its flatness and the two-dimensionality of the canvas, the character of the brushstrokes, the quality of the pigment, and the chemical and physical properties of the paint.[1] The painting can only be what it truly is; it should conceive of itself only through its own painterly means. The process of stripping away the less intrinsic facts that we know about an object is characteristic of the modernist approach and can be applied to all artistic phenomena, including the field of landscape architecture. When we think about the garden in the material sense, the surface of the earth can be viewed as the fundamental medium, analogous to the painter's canvas, the earth being the surface upon which the relief of the garden is formed: whether it is low or high, with the material of the garden being comprised of both living and non-living nature.

The garden as a two-dimensional image

As with modernist painting, sculpture, and architecture, considerations about the medium – its characteristic, type, and above all the specific qualities of the medium's identity – can be applied to the garden, which must also be stripped of its unessential elements. The latter includes, in the first place, the constituent parts of the garden that are foreign to nature. We must first strip away elements from related disciplines – architectural and sculptural – such as the gazebo, pergola, grotto, ruins, fountains, cascades, statues, monuments, and even benches, all of which have served to romanticize or classicize the garden while being alien to its essence. The primary function of these

1 Clement Greenberg, "Modernist Painting", Forum Lectures, Washington, D.C.: Voice of America, 1960. Various reprints: *Arts Yearbook* 4, 1961 (unrevised); *Art and Literature*, Spring 1965 (slightly revised); Gregory Battcock (ed.), *The New Art: A Critical Anthology*, New York: E. P. Dutton, 1966; Francis Frascina and Charles Harrison (eds.), *Modern Art and Modernism: A Critical Anthology*, London: Routledge, 1982.

elements is to rhetorically address visitors to the garden with an architectural or sculptural language and direct their attention towards the urban and cultural content that is not taken from nature. Thus, the first step is to disregard anything in the garden that is not nature or that emerged as a product of human hands. Only then can we continue the procedure with the simplification of the garden's natural volumes. We then attempt the process of flattening the relief of the garden from high and varied to something flatter and more uniform. By reducing the volume of the tree crowns and bushes, by shrinking both into a low growth, by eliminating the vertical components and flattening everything into low flower beds and grassy surfaces, the ambience of the garden becomes that of a two-dimensional image. Continuing to move towards absolute clarity of form, we eliminate unbalanced and dispersed forms with amorphous contours and replace them with forms that are larger, more uniform, and geometrical. The garden is thus transformed into a clear and uncomplicated geometric pattern. Finally, we simplify the textures of the surfaces that are contained within the contours of the geometrical shapes and at last arrive at the abstract clarity of the garden surface.

Simplified outlines and uniform surfacaes at Parc Burle Marx, São Paolo, Brazil, Roberto Burle Marx, 1950, restored 1991.

The approach of Roberto Burle Marx

In the 20th century, the most radical reductive formal approaches to the garden were pursued by the Brazilian landscape architect, Roberto Burle Marx. At the beginning of his career, he introduced exotic plants with large and shining leaves, endlessly playful shapes, blossoms of saturated colours combined in complementary contrasts into his garden designs. He was fascinated by the abundance of volume, colours, and textures in these new "materials". Later, under the influence of the trends of abstract art in the 20th century, and above all geometric abstraction, Burle Marx began to simplify the outlines of the garden surface. He ordered them into geometric patterns and reduced the variety of textures, making increasingly large uniform surfaces. He also diminished the number of colours and began to make use of mostly green hues with similar tones, and with this reduction of the colour palette he sometimes evoked the effect of the huge rectangular forms as being monochromatic paintings. In this way, he transformed the garden into a pattern on a vast surface of soil, which visitors to the garden, simply because of the sheer size of the planes, could not take in all at once. In the Lúcio Costa Monumental Axis Garden in Brasília, for example, visitors can only enjoy a perspective from an elevated position, namely platforms on a viewing tower that can be reached by elevator. This transformation of the garden produced an alienated individual, characteristic of the modernist observer, comprehending the garden only as a form without meaning. The ideal perspective of a work of land art, in which the experience of reducing the spatial presence of natural elements is pursued to an extreme degree, is even more radical and distanced. In these projects of monumental proportions, landscape design achieved the utmost reduction, with the replacement of living with non-living nature, the use of stones and sand, and the choice of setting, the American desert for example. This process involved the disregard and flattening of the landscape elements themselves, down to bare stone or the sand floor. The related process of making meaning equivalent, of taking materials from nature and transforming them into materials for art, represents the extension of the field of media practices, which took place during the 1960s. By using non-living materials in the design – for example, stone and sand – and fixing the form, a third nature was consciously created in order to achieve an artistic effect akin to a minimalistic spatial drawing, a spiral, a line. All that remained of nature was the pattern on the foundation, which we cannot understand directly because it exceeds human measure, the ideal perspective for land art being from space.

The garden as pattern

The process of material, technical, and formal reductionism has brought us to the garden as pure image. The garden is a formally ordered whole that has pushed out the ordinary human being on a stroll and replaced it with a viewer, the eye of whom travels along the surface and searches for impulses that it perceives as surfaces and colour sensations. Can the garden be realized as a "carpet" woven from natural elements? From grass of different textures, sand, gravel, earth, bricks, concrete, metal, and other materials that mark the barrier between surfaces and thus become ornaments, ornaments that comprise the surface structure and are defined as the relationship between pattern and foundation? In the case of the garden, this means the relationship between materials from nature and the natural foundation. That which actively interferes with the foundation is the pattern – and this can introduce elements that are not only a question of form, material, and technique. The word "pattern" offers a stimulating starting point for reflection. A pattern can be something that expresses a two-dimensional division of the surfaces of a plane or a three-dimensional object this is arranged with motifs using the compositional principle of repetition. At the same time, a pattern is also a paradigm that uses a small scale to give us a view of a larger whole. Even the word "garden", looking at its etymological roots – the Latin phrase *hortus gardinus* means "enclosed space" – implies, in the spatial sense, the contraction of something larger. To enclose something means to take a part of the whole, and this part can be understood as a representation or a deliberately planned paradigm of the whole. We can also treat the image of the garden that we have subjected to formal analysis as a conceptual model that serves to represent the garden as nature. We can understand the garden today as a pattern of nature that through the experience of the medium (the awareness of the "nature" of nature – from acquired experience we know how living nature behaves) and with information that the medium (the garden) mediates, allows us to expand our awareness of nature. Today the garden as a medium that usefully mediates information no longer evokes a feeling of happiness, nor can it be a neutral image of nature. It has increasingly become a manifestation of our relationship to nature – it has been transformed from a neutral pattern to a contextualized, rhetorical surface that exposes the essential processes of nature, not the forms, that are a consequence of human intervention into nature.

If *hortus conclusus* provided the metaphor of the garden of paradise in the Middle Ages, the symbolic potential of the contemporary garden has become its de-idealized opposite. Once a space for mystical revelation, the garden has been transformed into the carrier of a realist message communicating the inescapable fact that the history of our civilization has been based on the subordination of nature. The awareness that floods, droughts, and wildfires are the consequence of the exploitation of nature by human beings has increasingly become part of our perception of the world – even the garden has become a reminder of our catastrophic treatment of nature. The garden remains one of civilization's most powerful artistic metaphors with a wide spectrum of meaning. Many institutions make use of the garden therapeutically to contribute to the mental health of society. The community garden unites individuals through work, weaving together torn social ties and revealing lost communities. The garden's essential task in contemporary society is to trigger an awareness of the close human connection to and our dependence on nature, and this in turn should create new conditions in which the subordination of nature by human beings will be replaced by the subordination of human beings by nature. G&M

TV Tower and Monumental Axis Garden, Distrito Federal, Novacap, Brasília, Brazil, Lúcio Costa, 1965–1966.

The Metaphorical Life of the Garden

Lev Kreft

The Greek expression *techne* is translated into Latin as *ars*. In modernity, craft and art are understood as opposites, whereas in the beginning they were one and the same, a feature of human behaviour. They were considered characteristic of humanity because they could be carried out in accordance with rules and did not require divine inspiration. Other behaviours also existed, which, as Aristotle claimed in *The Nichomachean Ethics*, were either divine or bestial. For the divine, the favour of the gods was necessary, and the ancient gods, as we know, were often capricious and uncontrollable. You had to use all your seductive allure when you asked them for inspiration, without which divine behaviour could not be summoned. Bestial behaviours were more characteristic of barbarians than of Greeks, and in the latter emerged only in the case of a fundamental lack or error in the human condition. Art-craft is performed according to rules that are learned while this is not true of divine and bestial behaviours.

This hierarchy of skills did not change with the advent of Christianity. Art and craftsmanship were seen as one and the same, and together they extended from unskilled amateurism to virtuosity. When the first two human beings tasted fruit from the tree of knowledge, they illegally partook of divine knowledge that should have remained divine. As a result, God expelled them from the Garden of Eden and cursed man to a lifetime of hard labour by the sweat of his brow and woman to give birth in no less torment. Human abilities, divided between higher free and lower quotidian skills, could never change this condition but only alleviate it slightly because no tool or skill of man could compel, much less earn divine grace. *Gratia* does not care for or respond to orders or negotiation about merits. The keys to the garden of paradise, guarded by the archangel with his sword, are in the hands of God and the path to the Lord is mysterious.

When did the equivalence between art and craft dissolve? It is clear that it began to fray during the Renaissance, and that this process was given additional momentum by the Protestant ethic, and that a hard border was established between them on the basis of new definitions that emerged during the Enlightenment. But the revolution that first set this process in motion was the discovery that the earth was not the centre of the universe but rather "the third rock from the sun", and, what's more, that the sun itself was not all that special, since the universe extended from finity on to infinity. If on the physical level, we are insignificant and worthless specks, then we must rescue man's dignity and greatness on the metaphysical level where there was a connection between theology and anthropology. No matter that our solar system is lost in an infinite universe, that the Earth is ordinary flotsam thrown off by the centrifugal force of the Sun, that man is a powerless creature, he is nevertheless entitled to a certain dignity and elevated purpose. This dignity, that God cannot possess, is the free will to choose between good and evil. Because the possibility of choice rests on the ability to recognize, the mission of man is not to wait, calmly following all of the rules, for life after death and the final judgement that will come with the end of the world, but rather to build a paradise here on Earth and in this way to earn grace. Alexander Gottlieb Baumgarten, the founder of aesthetics, stated that man can be *quasi factor sive creator* – as if he were Creator and creator. "As if" is added because the true creator of new worlds can only be God, at least that was the case before Nietzsche's announcement that God was dead. That "as if" was discarded after God's death, and the artist who creates new worlds has now taken his place. Hence the modern battle between art and craft in which craft is associated with function and use and the scientific exploration of what the world offers, and art is associated with creativity that opens new worlds beyond this one. According to the plan of the Enlightenment, both should participate in the conquest of new spaces of human freedom and the freedom of humanity, but this project did not proceed as anticipated.

Mexico vs. the United States

In 1932, Frida Kahlo, Mexican painter and wife of the muralist Diego Rivera, went for the first time to the United States with her husband. In 1933, she painted *Self-Portrait on the Borderline between Mexico and the United States*, addressing the themes of transition and opposition between the two sides of the demarcation line. The work is heavily weighted and indeed subordinate to connotations, among them the relationship between Mexico and the United States articulated as the contradiction between a spiritually wealthy although materially impoverished garden on one side, and destructive technology that exhausts nature on the other, transforming it into a poisoned desert and an artificially mechanized garden of lifeless growth. The Sun and Moon shine on one side of the painting, the Mexican side, both representing ancient deities from Mexican culture, which has a long tradition that the United States

Frida Kahlo, *Self-Portrait on the Borderline between Mexico and the United States*, 1933.

has not. There are also a number of small sculptures left behind by this culture that remain objects of cults and rituals for the descendants of the native peoples. La Calavera Catrina, the skull which is the symbol of natural death, is also featured on this side of the painting as well as blooming flowers that sprout from a deep connection with their roots in the earth, another ancient divinity. On the American side of the painting, clouds of smog gather above factories, including the Ford factory with the first assembly line conveyor belt, steel production, and bland and unsympathetic structures that reach far into the sky above the clouds of pollution. A curtain of smoke almost covers the American flag with its stars and stripes. Rather than roots, branches, and flowers, cables exhaust the earth that can no longer produce life.

Frida Kahlo herself occupies the centre of the painting. Around the time this painting was created, she began to use Frida instead of the Germanic Frieda and in this work, she defined herself as Carmen Rivera, inscribed on the border stone beneath her feet, her full name being Magdalena Carmen Frieda Kahlo y Calderón. Regardless of her strong association with her Mexican homeland – in this self-portrait she also holds a small Mexican flag in her hand – she reigns like a queen over a border that divides two mutually exclusive social and life principles: the deep and elevated spirituality on the vertical plane between the Earth and Sun/Moon on the Mexican side of border, and the holy profanity on the American side where the Earth is only earth, a field for the extraction of energy that generates a passion for material comfort and constant accumulation with no spiritual content. This metaphor/image of modern civilization and its principle contradictions did not grow in Frida Kahlo's garden (although it must be said that the garden around her Blue House is no less famous than her paintings) but indeed was the formational identity and self-image of Latin America at the turn of the 20th century. The Uruguayan writer and thinker José Enrique Rodó, contributed to this conversation about cultural identity in his essay "Ariel" in which he presented the dualism of Ariel and Caliban, two figures from Shakespeare's *The Tempest*.[1] Arielism became the positive pole of Latin American spirituality and the identifying characteristic of native culture, while Calibanism (which might easily be mispronounced as cannibalism) became the negative pole of the materialistic and gluttonous characteristics of the United States of America, which no self-respecting Latin American would ever simply call "America".

A garden of surrogates and simulators

This conflict between the authentic garden of culture and the artificial desert of civilization is not a characteristic of post-colonialism that belongs only to the Latin orbit of the United States. The confidence that science will be able to solve all the difficulties caused by global capitalism because it will always discover new ways to exploit natural sources, thus making prosperity available to all people, is a constant feature that elevates the artificial garden of civilization in which only surrogates and simulators thrive. The other side of the coin of modernity is the notion that humanity seeks its self-realization in the living gardens of natural, pure, and authentic existence. This reflects the divergence of interpretations of the modernized world that emerged in Germany at the end of the 19th century when the debate turned towards too rapid progress that people, although they were themselves the creators of this progress, could no longer keep up with. Academic thinkers of

1 José Enrique Rodó, *Ariel*, Montevideo: Impr. de Dornaleche y Reyes, 1900. English edition: *Ariel*, translated by F. J. Stimson, 1905, reprint Boston: Houghton Mifflin, 1922.

the time believed that culture needed to act as a counterweight to the progress of civilization in order to make it bearable. And although different visions about the future garden in which the whole of global humanity could live still exist today, the choice between the artificial garden of civilization and the authentic garden of culture was rejected more than a hundred years ago after the experience of mass death on the battlefields of the First World War. Only one conclusion could be drawn from this: that culture itself is a part of the problem of our civilization, not the solution to the problem. When Jean-François Lyotard[2] pronounced the end of grand narratives about the progress of humanity towards perfection, Arthur Danto[3] added that everything was acceptable because criteria no longer existed that would define the progressiveness or conservatism of cultural positions or styles. Both statements express the desire that the conflict between nature and art would be resolved as the sole purpose of the conflict is ideological. But this resolution did not take place, and this may be the reason that for at least the last ten years we again prefer to use the term "modernity" instead of "post-modernity".

Faust's lesson

When we say that we are living in the Anthropocene, this is a powerful denial of the choice between natural and cultural. The Anthropocene means that in the history of nature and the history of humanity, nature, and culture are so closely linked that humanity dictates what will happen in nature – but this mastery is only apparent because unwanted and unanticipated consequences are constantly taking place. In this context, it could be said that the earth in its entirety has become the garden of

2 Jean-François Lyotard, *La condition postmoderne,* Paris: Les Editions de Minuit, 1979. English edition: *The Postmodern Condition: A Report on Knowledge,* translated by Geoff Bennington and Brian Massumi, Minneapolis: University of Minnesota Press, 1984, here: "Introduction", pp. xxiii–xiv: "I will use the term 'modern' to designate any science that legitimates itself with reference to a metadiscourse of this kind making an explicit appeal to some grand narrative, such as the dialectics of Spirit, the hermeneutics of meaning, the emancipation of the rational or working subject, or the creation of wealth... I define 'postmodern' as incredulity toward metanarratives."

3 Arthur Danto, Charles Altieri, Anne M. Wagner, Anthony J. Cascardi, *"Anything Goes": The Work of Art and the Historical Future.* Berkeley: Doreen B. Townsend Center for the Humanities, 1998.

humanity – the space that we cultivate and shape in accordance with our own cultural concepts. This in turn implies that Western civilization achieved its goal when it colonized the whole world. The goal itself is expressed in the cultural symbol of Dr Faustus, a man willing to sell his soul to the devil for unlimited knowledge, and for love as well, but ends up reclaiming polders from the sea in the Netherlands and thereby creating new tracts of arable land. Because we live in the Anthropocene, we know that Faust's story, even in the Netherlands, will end badly: that the earth that has been reclaimed from the sea will, because of global warming and rising sea levels, have to be given back. It will soon take much more work to cultivate a field of tulips. The metaphor of the garden as the earthly goal of humanity, considered the highest achievement of natural history and as the beginning of the supernatural mastery of humanity over the earth, lost its attraction the moment it was realized. That which global humanity has imprinted on nature is the work of the sorcerer's apprentice, not of the master himself, and this process has unleashed forces that we cannot control and that now threaten humanity and its current way of life on the planet.

If the garden is both image and metaphor, it is an image of powerlessness and limits. Even as we push towards the creation of artificial intelligence, towards discovering the mystery of life and infinity in service of our own immortality, creation itself is beyond the reach of humanity. In the garden that humanity has cultivated, life can be rearranged and forced into metamorphosis but it cannot be created from inanimate material. The reverse process, of course, has proved to be no problem at all. All of the skills from the fields of art and craft will not be enough because we are no longer choosing between divine and bestial behaviours. That is the problem: Aristotle had already concluded that it is impossible to define the best path between these two antipodes – the middle path. Perhaps it is merely the recognition that divine power is not within our reach, and the admission that bestiality is not something that is only present in others, but also in us. It would be better to cultivate a garden that we can never fully master than to master a garden that we can never fully bring to life. G&M

paradise-darkness

Olaf Nicolai

without light. with closed eyes. it works best like this – you can go far.

Carl sits in a heated room. a walk would be just the thing now. with closed eyes of course ... outside it began snowing hours ago. and there's rumbling.

in the tiny cinema below his studio they're showing *Star Wars* – today for the third time. not surprising, since thirty people can barely fit into that small space. who even let them call it a cinema? and then there's *Gloria*. should be titled something more like *Sputnik* or *Nautilus*. but: it's the perfect soundtrack for a walk! just don't go out ... a sheet of paper. and you're off, like Stifter, stuck in a snowstorm writing letters: *In the darkness, not seeing the shimmering, you had to imagine it, and you imagined it to be worse than it would've looked in the light of day. And ultimately, you didn't know if it wasn't worse.*

And ultimately, you didn't know if it wasn't worse ... if it was even snowing. and how it would look then! was he, Stifter, perhaps aware of Poe's little text "The Landscape Garden"? *The original beauty is never so great as that which may be introduced* ... Carl looks at the photo he pinned to the wall next to the table. a crossroads in the country, muddy surfaces in the spring, cloudy sky. on the horizon leafless trees. and in front of the crossing, along the edge of the meadow, a landmark: a chopped off treetop, delimbed, four strong arms branching out from the trunk, reaching above. screaming, you could say. the ends sawn straight off into little plateaus. a picturesque pedestal. for four figures, two stand on top: Garden Dwarf and

Snow White... without the two the treetop seems like a huge construction part, a coupling made of wood. every time he sees the photo, Carl has to think of the dutch linden in the palace garden of the neighbouring town. its branches almost extend horizontally from the trunk, a roof under which five or six cars could very well park. if there weren't all those supporting posts. as kids they were told the tree was planted upside down, as a divine judgement. if the tree started to bud then the accused was not guilty. so, it's the roots that rise up to the heavens. Garden Dwarf and Snow White fit in quite nicely with this. Snow White in a white dress. the beauty which may be introduced ...

snow white also the paper. the pen glides – not too fast. just keep pausing, tracing, slowly. see how the hand feels, as it turns, how the pen flows or slashes, stumbles. burying itself in a point – the printing changing over coffee, or when the espresso begins to kick in ... drink, but not too fast – it's supposed to go far. and start again. little islands. like eyes with huge circles – between them the lines, some of them almost straight, others temperature curves, zig zagging, without a goal. from garden to garden. Carl has to smile. when he shows these sheets they will happily be labelled landscapes. and if so, then these are now gardens. little paradise gardens. between them nice white emptiness, that you must pass through – with closed eyes. and what about black gardens – without light?

there goes the door. Ana comes in.
– what are you doing here?
– taking a walk ... are they done down there?
must still be running ...
– yes, but the bar is closed now, have to go down there again.
you should turn on the light!
– no, it's better like this.
– alright. what are you working on?
– it's about gardens, or rather: the garden.
– that's why you have all these books on the table?

Ana briefly browses through the stack.
– Runge, Poe ... who is Eduard Wimmer? what does it have to do with gardens? because of the ornaments and paper cuttings?
– yes, no ...

Carl turns to Ana:
– i just found it fitting. supposedly Wimmer was shocked when he visited Palais Stoclet in Brussels and saw the hostess there. in his opinion, the way the lady of the manor was dressed did not fit with the house at all. so then, back in Vienna, that's allegedly why he started the fashion workshops. so that people are dressed to fit with the interiors, not clash with them. seems fitting, doesn't it?
- and that's why you have these twenty-year-old newspapers lying here?

Ana unfolds one of the pages, printed completely in abbreviations.
– is this some kind of code ...?

– yes. they printed it on the front page back when the genomes were decoded. without comment. i inserted it into the book about the garden by Gregor Mendel. the garden as a laboratory where Mendel discovers the laws of heredity.
– or as a plantation.
– what are you saying?
– you yourself spoke of it yesterday, the poem by the danish author, about the apricots. in there, it said. where gardens are, plantations aren't far off. but, hey, i need to go down now ... to my plantation ... don't wander off too far ... and turn the light on.

Carl stops short ... apricots ... yes! *the apricot trees exist, the apricot trees exist.* he goes to the bookshelf. this is how *alfabet* begins, the cycle of poems by Inger Christensen. *but the darkness / is white, say the children, the paradise-darkness is white ... the darkness is whiter, eyes melt.* from outside, now, a blue grey light descends on the room. the snow glows. back to the table, walk on. coffee again – like feathers in the mouth. skipping lightly – then an unstable pressure, almost a hole in the paper. one would have to be able to touch all these islands that surface. or connect them with tunnels. beautiful places need distance. one doesn't always want to see the in-between. a tunnel like the czech general had planned. so that everyone could drive south – below the Alps – from Bohemia to the Adriatic, for vacation. not far from here, would've been the entrance into Jadran. and then a few hundred kilometres under the earth into the blue, towards Piran. just like that under the iron curtain, through it and back. from paradise to paradise. he doesn't know exactly where the landscape lies the creators of his old favourite game "Day Z" had so accurately reconstructed – but this piece of land, about ten × ten kilometres in size, is found in Bohemia as well! he read that. each street, all paths and small woods, not only the buildings, were accurately reconstructed for the game. so, it can also work differently with "walled gardens". playfully wandering about, barely being able to get out. if everything that is drawn can be transformed, you can no longer think nothing. *the borders are there, the streets, the forgetting* ... the sheet is quite good like that. it wasn't far, but it's enough for today.

Carl briefly glances at the time on his phone and then looks out the window. out of the movie theatre a furious finale resonates. *the darkness is whiter, the eyes melt.* somewhere out there Garden Dwarf and Snow White are being buried in a mountain of snow. perfect for walks! G&M

Bibliography

Annaberger Kunst- und Kulturverein (ed.), *Carlfriedrich Claus*, Annaberg-Buchholz: Annaberger Kunst- und Kulturverein e.V., 2000.

Inger Christensen, *alfabet*, Copenhagen: Lyrikbogklubben Borgen-Gyldendal, 1981; English edition: Inger Christensen, *alphabet*, translated by Susanna Nied, Newcastle upon Tyne: Bloodaxe Books, 2000 (New York: New Directions, 2001).

Frankfurter Allgemeine Zeitung, 27 June 2000.

Luigi Ghirri, *Collazione sull'Erba*, London: Mack, 2019.

Geert Lovnik, *Networks without a Cause*, Cambridge: Polity Press, 2011.

Edgar Allan Poe, *The Collected Works*, vol. 2, Cambridge: Belknap Press, 1978.

Adalbert Stifter, Winterbriefe aus Kirchschlag, in: *Adalbert Stifter, Sämmtliche Werke. Vermischte Schriften. Zweite Abteilung*, Reichenberg (Liberec): Sudetendeutscher Verlag Franz Kraus, 1935.

Photographs by *Anne Schwalbe*

Garden as Reflection

Paul Klee, *drawing for Candide*, 1911.

ZEICHNUNG ZU „CANDIDE". ERSCHEINT IM KURT WOLFF-VERLAG. 1911/12.

Let Us Cultivate Our Garden

Mladen Dolar

In all of world literature and philosophy, there is no more famous sentence about gardens than the one that ends Voltaire's *Candide*: "*Il faut cultiver notre jardin.*" Let us cultivate our garden. As soon as the sentence was published, it immediately turned into a proverb, a maxim, and remains one to this day. *Candide*, the "philosophical novel" written in 1759, retains the same freshness, spirit, and nonchalance as it had in the era when it was published. It was written amidst the controversies of the Enlightenment century, which today seem a bit distant and forgotten, and yet the freshness and lucidity of this work reaches straight into present times. The absurd difficulties of the condition of the world that Voltaire so drastically and grotesquely caricatures seem a perfect match for the absurdity of our own times.

The story begins with a garden, an apparent garden of paradise, situated in Westphalia, and shot through with the bizarre extravagance of the then German nobility, but in the light of all that follows it still seems like paradise. It is here that Candide meets his teacher, the high-minded philosopher Pangloss, a follower of the philosophy of Gottfried Wilhelm Leibniz, who maintained that we live in the best of all possible worlds in which all things have a sufficient reason. In the first chapter Candide is expelled from this alleged Garden of Eden, and is subsequently condemned to experience all imaginable afflictions and calamities: the senseless slaughter of war, deceit, and hypocrisy, stupidity and greed, the perversity of the Church and its clerics (this was Voltaire's particular grievance), cruelty and humiliation, robbery and rape, slavery and brutal exploitation. He must experience himself all of the injustice of the world undermining the Enlightenment's optimistic faith in the rational order of the universe, in justice and progress. The novel's hero, of course, always miraculously escapes the catastrophes that follow his every step in this best of all possible worlds. His life is constantly in jeopardy, but nevertheless he also finds on his long journey a handful of brave and upright people who help him. In the end he settles with them on a patch of land they find near Constantinople and there they establish their own garden which they must create with their own work, a curious counterpart of the garden from which he was expelled at the beginning.

The framework of the novel is simple: on one side there is Leibniz's philosophy which prevailed in the early 18th century and that the unrelenting optimist Pangloss tirelessly promotes, the view that we live in the best of all possible worlds. At the time of creation, God rationally considered all possible worlds and, in his infinite wisdom and justice, decided on the best among them; if it strikes us as imperfect and miserable, then that is because we, with our limitations, are unable to discern God's plan concealed within it. On the other side there is the empirical experience of immeasurable suffering, evil, injustice, and terror that exist in blatant opposition to this metaphysical reasoning and abstract optimism. Candide and his company move through a world ruled by contingency, chaos, and evil. What can they do – or, for that matter, what can we? The answer to this question emerges as the maxim towards which the entire novel is directed: let us cultivate our garden. (We must, it's our duty, *il faut.*) Of course, there is an actual garden that Candide and his friends devotedly cultivate and in this way defy the chaos. But the garden is clearly a metaphor that reaches beyond its borders, ultimately to the human condition in this non-rational universe and to the answer to the oldest of questions: what can we do in face of our limitations and impotence?

The sentence itself appears simple and yet its simplicity has occasioned endless debates. First, we must note that the French word *cultiver* (cultivate) shares its etymology with the word "culture", so what is at stake is the entirety of human culture, culture as an elementary struggle against evil and chaos. The sentence takes us directly from horticulture to culture as such. Culture is our garden, and the garden is the source of culture. We must also be attentive to the fact that Candide speaks about "our garden". The garden in question is a collective effort, although the group that remains together at the end is small, not more than eight people. Tiny in comparison to the unfathomable amount of injustice, but still. As if Voltaire wanted to say: we the enlightened ones are few, only a handful, but if we persistently cultivate our garden, i.e. take care of our culture, we can hope and trust that this will have consequences.

Retreat into privacy

It is possible to read Candide's sentence in two opposed ways. Many critics reproached him for promoting a retreat into privacy, away from political and intellectual engagement, leaving the unjust world be. What could be further from the risky combat with the social injustice than gardening? What's more, they reproached him for pursuing his own selfishness and private interest, turning away from the radical demands that would call for revolution – and the dreadful circumstances that are so drastically and graphically described in the novel call for nothing less than revolution – not the cultivation of gardens. In other words: instead of the universal project of emancipation imposed by the Enlightenment, a retreat into "horticultural quietism".[1] The sentence sounds like a letter of resignation – if we cannot change the world, in its immense meaningless cruelty, then let us at least tackle this little garden that we can master and abandon the illusory great projects of changing the world.

And yet, precisely thirty years after the first publication of *Candide*, the French Revolution indeed took place, eleven years after Voltaire's own death, and Candide's sentence was one of the significant elements in the process leading to it. Thus, a different reading of the sentence could find not the rejection of universalism, but the search for a new entry to universality, an incentive for collective engagement that, despite the limitation of its starting point, reaches far beyond the garden and its fence. The garden then appears as a particular limited starting point, removed from the general havoc, a small but highly telling reflection on the condition of the world. The adage was also intended as a sharp critique of the old metaphysics that prevailed at the time and this critique permeates the entire novel and announces a new era: it presents a contingent and senseless universe that bids farewell to the metaphysical rational arrangement of the world, a view that astonishingly evokes the modern age.[2] The garden is not merely a retreat but a point of view.

1 Even the always lucid Julian Barnes attributes to Voltaire "horticultural quietism" in "A Candid View of Candide", *The Guardian*, 1 July 2011.

The end of history

From here one can make a direct step into our own times. The idea of the end of history that Francis Fukuyama[3] proposed after the fall of socialism could be read as a new secularized version of the best of all possible worlds. History has presumably come to an end when it allegedly became clear that liberal democracy and global capitalism were the best possible world we could hope for. It is impossible to imagine an alternative to it, and if it is shot through with contradictions, that would be taken care of by the development of more capitalism. Instead of the divine plan and the invisible divine hand that guided the theodicy, all would be set right by the invisible hand of the market, if we only put our trust in it, as in other times we have trusted the divine plan. Economics is our theology and our metaphysics.

And so finally we come to the question of Candide's garden today and what it is the metaphor of. Just as we can directly relate the absurdities of the time, so vividly conjured in *Candide*, to the mishaps of our own era, so too does Candide's maxim place us before the very same dilemma. On the one hand, we can interpret the garden as a shelter where one can retreat from all the absurdity and injustice, a space of privacy that we can share with a handful of like-minded friends. The garden as a comfortable asylum far away from dirty politics, a safe haven, a fenced-in little piece of the world where we can tailor nature to our own measure. But on the other hand, the garden was never just a garden and has always also functioned as a counterimage, a reflection, a *mise en abyme*; it has always transcended its borders and reached out to the world from which it was excepted. It always represented the totality of the world and, as an exception to the world, it stood for its universality.

2 In the 20th century, *Candide* produced many echoes, various theatrical and film adaptations, from which I arbitrarily mention two: the illustrated serial *Candide* by Paul Klee in 1912–1913, at the very birth of modernism; and the operetta *Candide* written by Leonard Bernstein in 1965, which despite its early lack of success was increasingly appreciated and frequently staged in subsequent decades.

3 Francis Fukuyama, *The End of History and the Last Man,* New York: Free Press, 1992.

As a heterotopia in the midst of our world, the garden opens a different idea of space, it offers a different reality that persists in interaction and in tension with the outside world, providing an antithesis to it. Not a retreat into seclusion, but a demand for a different public space; not privacy, but the source of a different collectivism; not a flight from participation, but engagement and a call for change; not retreat, but an intervention. Thus, Candide's simple appeal retains all of its initial tension and ambivalence, and a message for our own times. G&M

"C'est à ce prix que vous mangez du sucre en Europe" ("This is the price for the sugar you eat in Europe"), illustration from the 1787 edition of Voltaire's *Candide*.

Gardengraph

Dean Komel

A written description of a garden begs the question: is not writing itself also a sort of "gardening"? Or perhaps writing is more similar to travelling. Plato refers to it in Phaedrus. Someone who travelled the world with writing might have just as well spent that time in a garden.

"Working in the garden" means something different to us than "preparing a meal", "setting a table", "tidying an apartment", "ironing", or "doing our homework". We do not have a garden in the same way as we have clothes in the closet, a car in the garage, water in the pipes, or a roof on our house. A garden lies beside the house in a different way than a front yard. Just as the garden belongs to the house, the hut belongs to the garden. A garden on a balcony bestows onto a living place a different expression and face, making it a home. Working in the garden is one of our many quotidian chores that is not exactly "quotidian", and also not exactly a "chore". It is different, for example, from working in a field, as it expressly includes the concept of a break, of rest and relaxation. The garden can be a business: a nursery for plants for example. But such work does not capture the whole of gardening, does not capture horticulture, still less the amateur habit of gardening.

We can go to the garden just to sit. We can sit and listen to the warbling of a blackbird while it pecks at the cherries – almost as if it knew how those from Igor's garden are the sweetest of all. We can put together some chairs and a table, spread out a pretty tablecloth, decide to have a garden party. Otherwise Voltaire, summoning biblical authority, suggests that man was placed in the garden of paradise, not to relax, but to cultivate it. If that is the case, the purpose of the garden is not only to make man work but also that in man's work we find a trace of divinity. How else could the garden remind the enlightened Voltaire of the best of all possible worlds? We do not need the elevated beauty of Schwetzingen or other castle gardens for such high praise. The divine is sooner given to humanity through poverty than with the inflated majesty of being too human.

In any case, the garden does not serve the sole purpose of being a place for us to cultivate garden crops. Flowers in a blossoming garden are not vegetables, a tree in a botanical garden is not a forest plant, stones and sand in the dry garden of a Buddhist monastery are not building materials. We do not build gardens at all. But we do. Like to build. Fences around them. Vegetable patches and flower beds and the paths running between them are an elemental method of weaving together the fabric of the garden. Terraces offer a more elevated method of weaving. Fences and fence posts are situated closer to the ground and, because they provide more solid measurements of the garden, they also reveal complex interpersonal

Ripe cherries in a cherry tree.

The garden and its hut.

relationships and the limitations of human wisdom. The hedgerow constitutes a unique example of this practice, being both a method of repelling the gaze of unwanted observers and a decoration for the house or garden. The hedgehog holds the hedgerow in particularly high regard because it can slip into the garden that man cultivates for himself and for which he has set the rules of whom the garden serves and who serves the garden. Of course, the zoological garden is established for the precise purpose of viewing animals although we would probably not call it a garden if it were not suitably fenced. Can cages be a garden?

The kindergarten perhaps reminds us that human gardens also exist but here we find ourselves in an even greater dilemma as to how to make rules for it. Peter Sloterdijk wrote an article entitled "Rules for the Human Zoo"[1] in which he describes the technological breeding of intelligent animals. However, man cannot essentially be "placed" in a garden. The garden is written on the heart and soul of man, and, though it may never be fully understood how, fulfils his humanity.

What is the actual measure of the space for the garden where man spends his time? A garden is not merely a piece of cultivated land. Man can conjure a garden anywhere and anytime. He can find it in himself, as desire, dream, passion, serenity. It is a little harder to tuck it into a backpack and take it along with you. Someone on the run – deserter, fugitive, refugee, economic exile, political exile – would probably not even attempt to take it at all, or only in thoughts and feelings. Blind Oedipus is led by his daughter Antigone into a garden that is the site of his destiny. Parks, where homeless people often conjure a refuge and sanctuary for themselves (until someone chases them away of course), have the manner of bridging the near and distant but always possess traces of the garden. Perhaps

1 Peter Sloterdijk, "Regeln für den Menschenpark", lecture held 15 June 1997 in Basel, published on 9 September 1999 in the newspaper *Die Zeit* and then as *Regeln für den Menschenpark. Ein Antwortschreiben zu Heideggers Brief über den Humanismus,* Frankfurt: Suhrkamp, 2001. English edition: "Rules for the Human Zoo: a Response to the Letter on Humanism", *Environment and Planning D: Society and Space*, 27, 2009, pp. 12–28.

they recall the expulsion from paradise. By contrast, the cohabitation of bridges and gardens in Venice conjures the heavenly host, something that the architect Maks Fabiani knew full well when he designed the Ferrari garden in Štanjel.[2]

We like to walk through parks and gardens. We like to admire them. We find in them blessed peace. If we search in the garden for a connection to nature, the connection is intimate. But what kind of intimacy is it? The time that we give to the garden is time that we give to ourselves. The intimacy of the garden is actually extimate and therefore transitory. But not in the same way a walk through nature is or a rest in the hills, a holiday at the seaside, the creation of an artwork, sinking into our own thoughts, the consecration of prayer. The space of the garden, which allows us to move in and out of it without the opening or closing of doors and windows, creates a special dimension that relaxes us, makes us free in what is human and at the same time extends, like a bridge, to a place beyond, a place different from man. Without these others – without plants, animals, stones, earth, water, air, fire, gods, and our fellow men – humanity would not be humanity.

Enthralling forms

I remember the garden best as a paradise in my youth, where, full of a sense of importance, I helped my grandfather Kazimir with various tasks. I was not allowed to play in the garden. Neither were the birds. There is of course nothing more playful than a scarecrow that frightens the children more than the birds that visit the garden. But child's play takes place in the sandbox where we find neither birds nor scarecrows. Perhaps this is a distant pattern for the kindergarten that, in contrast to

2 Maks Fabiani, a Vienna-based Slovenian architect from Trieste, designed Villa Ferrari with adjacent garden on the slopes of the Karst village Štanjel, cleverly utilizing the old ramparts of the fortified settlement, developed in terraces around the 363 metres high hill (editor's note).

school, still allows playfulness, although it is subordinated to education and upbringing. The relationships of superiority and subordination that are characteristic of education and upbringing are not decisive in cultivating and growing. The cultivation and growing of a garden establish an order that is satisfying and fulfilling. In cultivation we are not perfecting forms that education transforms into patterns, but rather images that invite attention and even enthrallment. Form exists within the whole while the image stands out of the whole – and thrives. Of all things that thrive through cultivation, the grove stands out most of all, so much that it almost seems untouchable, but of course many things spring from the word "garden" – kindergarten, gardener, gardenia. In Slovenian – the word for garden is *vrt* – the list is even longer: *vrtiček* (allotment), *vrtec* (kindergarten), *vrtnica* (rose), even *vrtača* (karstic sinkhole) which evokes the image of an abandoned garden.

The parallel offered at the beginning between writing and gardening becomes clearer with the insight of how both offer a touch that returns us to a human measure. When I write, I search, with the touch of the pen on paper, for what I am recording and describing, the matter of my thoughts and my

The lower terrace of the Ferrari garden, Maks Fabiani, 1920–1930, pond and bridge.

A flower bed with roses and lavender, in a Karst village.

feelings, the demands of my condition and emotions, my reflections and imagination. A similar search for meaningful connection takes place when I am gardening and I take up the shears, the hoe, the rake, shovel, stakes, and watering can. With the possibility of touch, the possibility of meaningful connection grows, and work in the garden, like writing, becomes art and radiates beauty.

Garden as handiwork

Thus, both writing and gardening are connected to what we might loosely call "handiwork". We need our hands to use a range of tools, but the hand is more than a tool. The hand is not merely an organ that performs functions for the organism. The hand and hands reach into the organization of the space. The hand and hands are not meant only for grabbing and holding, hand-shaking, embracing, and slapping. We indicate with our finger this one or the other, we extend our hand in greeting, we lift our hand as a sign of support. When there is nothing more to do, we cross our hands. Even when we hold nothing in our hands, or we cannot do the business at hand, that hand is still full of connection, insofar as it initially vouches spatial connectivity. A space is above all created by the hands and only afterwards is its dimensions perceived by the eyes. From this perspective the garden is above all the utterance of the hands and their handiness. The garden is man's handwriting. G&M

Karstic sinkhole, *vrtača*, near Jurišiči village.

Architecture and the Supplement of Nature

Sven-Olov Wallenstein

From the early Enlightenment onwards, architecture gradually began to sever its ties to the classical canon: the authority of the Vitruvian text began to crumble, the normative role of the classical order was questioned, both because of archaeological findings and new theoretical agendas. Instead, an appeal to nature emerged, a nature no longer exclusively predicated on a series of existing models, but also on a claim to universality. At the same time, new intermediary models emerged (the garden, the park), which were designed spaces that yet could lay claim to being closer to nature, and thus provide a link between constructive and natural elements: neither pure nature nor pure culture, they became means to *think* the passage between them while still perceiving it as somehow already emerging out of nature itself.

With respect to the classical tradition, the first step in this transformation was the quarrel between the ancients and the moderns at the end of the 17th century, which in architecture found its paradigmatic form in the writings of Claude Perrault. His brother Charles had been the instigator of the *querelle*, and Claude, with his solid training in the natural sciences as well as in the humanities, was well equipped to take on the new task, both of producing a new translation of Vitruvius[1] and subjecting the legacy of the classical orders to a rationalist examination. In his *Ordonnance des cinq espèces des colonnes selon la méthode des Anciens* (1683),[2] he launches a fundamental attack

1 Perrault's translation of Vitruvius has been re-edited as *Les dix livres d'architecture,* Brussels: Mardaga, 1979.

2 Claude Perrault, *Ordonnance des cinq espèces des colonnes selon la méthode des Anciens,* 1683. English edition: *Ordonnance for the Five Kinds of Columns After the Method of the Ancients,* translated by Indra Kagis McEwen, with a preface by Alberto Pérez-Gómez, Santa Monica: Getty Center, 1993.

on the classical doctrines in asking whether there exists a unified system behind the orders, and concludes by proposing a distinction between "positive" and "arbitrary" beauty. Positive beauty, he suggests, rests on reason and is available to everyone at all times, whereas its arbitrary counterpart is contingent, dependent on particular circumstances, traditions, and associative habits that provide no firm basis. In this, Perrault takes a decisive step towards the dissolution of mimetic continuity between nature, presumed to anticipate art and provide guidelines for its development, and history, in turn regulated by a set of examples assumed as natural paradigms. In this equation, the ancient models must be upheld simply because their beauty is inscribed in nature: they are our nature, whereas Perrault's distinction between positive and arbitrary beauty opens a rift that will only deepen.

As this new type of rationalism evolved, the ancient authorities were subjected to a critical reading, which however did not displace the structure of mimesis as such, but rather rendered it more abstract. A century after Perrault, the Italian architect and historian Francesco Milizia, in the introduction to his *Memorie degli architetti antichi et moderni* (1768), provides a dense formula for this tendency to abstraction: "Architecture is just as much as the other arts an art of imitation. The only difference is that some of them have a natural model on which their imitation may be based. Architecture lacks such a model, instead it has an alternative model offered by the man's natural course of action when he builds his first settlements."[3] The mimesis of architecture no longer bears on particular objects erected as models, but on a sequence of actions binding together nature and culture in a complex way that does not relate to pre-existing things, but in a temporal twist allows both to become *what they will have been*: nature becomes the origin

3 Francesco Milizia, *Memorie degli architetti antichi et moderni,* Parma: Stamperia Reale, 1781, vol. 1, xii. For a discussion of this and similar passages, see Joseph Rykwert, *On Adam's House in Paradise: The Idea of the Primitive Hut in Architectural History*, 2nd ed., Cambridge, MA: MIT Press, 1981, pp. 65–69.

of our interventions only when superseded, transcended, and perfected by human interventions. On the one hand art imitates nature, but on the other hand also completes it, supplements the lack in nature that prevents it from being fully itself, fully natural.[4]

The first hut

The paradigmatic case of this new tale of origins can be found in Abbé Laugier's *Essai sur l'architecture* (1753). He sketches a picture of a human being who through his instincts and primary needs must compensate for nature's shortcoming – the sun is too hot, the shade too cool – in creating the first hut. Four branches form a square, then four crossbars are added on top, and finally a tilted roof covered with leaves as protection against the rain.[5] Art begins by imitating nature's own processes, and man's natural spontaneity makes it pass over into the order of culture. "Such is the simple course of nature", Laugier writes in the introduction, and "the birth of art resides in the imitation of its procedures (*c'est à l'imitation de ses procédes qui l'art doit sa naissance*)".[6] And yet nature is as such not sufficient, which is why man must "through his industry (*industrie*) compensate for nature's oversights (*inattentions*) and negligence (*néglicences*)".[7] Nature is already moral, but also flawed, and man, poised between its incompletion and a developed culture, is called on to supplement nature's lack through his industrious practices that would as it were restore it to what it should have been, and only then allows it to become a full-fledged model for the architecture of the future.

The best way to avoid mistakes in the future, Laugier continues, is this to hold onto the lucidity of the first paradigm: "The

4 This equation has its roots in Aristotle, whose *Physics* proposes two ideas that would remain decisive for a long tradition: "Generally, art imitates nature" (*techne mimetai ten fysin*, 194a 23), but also that art "in one sense seems to complete, bring to its end (*epitelei*) that which nature generally is incapable of achieving (*adynatei apergasasthai*), in another sense it imitates". (199a 15–16) This logic of the supplement has been worked out in great detail in relation to Rousseau in Jacques Derrida, *De la grammatologie* (Paris: Minuit, 1967; English edition: *Of Grammatology*, translated by Gayatri Chakravorty Spivak, introduction by Judith Butler, Baltimore: Johns Hopkins University Press, 2016 [1976]), many of whose arguments have a direct bearing on my proposals here.

5 This hut represents already an improvement over what Claude-Nicolas Ledoux (1736–1806) envisioned around the same time in his engraving "L'abri du pauvre" as the shelter of the poor, namely a tree. *L'Architecture considérée sour le rapport de l'art, des moeurs, et de la legislation*, Paris, 1804, plate 33.

6 Abbé [Marc-Antoine] Laugier, *Essai sur l'architecture*, Genéve: Minkoff Reprint, 1972 [1755], p. 2. For more details on this figure in Laugier, see Joseph Rykwert, *On Adam's House in Paradise*, op. cit., pp. 43–49, and Daniel Payot, *Le philosophie et l'architecte,* Paris: Aubier, 1982, pp. 69–70, and, more generally, Wolfgang Herrmann, *Laugier and 18th Century French Theory*, London: Zwemmer, 1962.

7 Laugier, *Essai sur l'architecture*, p. 2.

small hut that I have just described is the model by which one can arrive at all the great works of architecture. It is by sticking to the simplicity of this first model in all further execution that one can avoid fatal errors and achieve perfection proper."[8] This primordial model is nature and culture in one, or better, the link between them, the folding over of one into the other, and it is no coincidence that its structural form is that of the temple, laying bare the basic relations between load and load-bearing.

Other origins were proposed, notably by Piranesi, who locates Egypt as the true origin of architecture. But the loosening of the traditional Roman and Greek references that still implicitly prevailed in most writers, even though henceforth divested of their normative singularity and instead read as pointing towards a new kind of universality, in fact renders the underlying new logic visible. Architecture is doubly mimetic: nature is already proto-architectural, which is why architecture can become *archi-tectural*, a rebuilding, restoration, rejoining (*tikto*) of what was left unconnected or merely implicit in origin (*arche*), supplementing its lack in the origin and in this becoming the art of foundations, becoming archi-tecture. Even though the origin still needs to be located somewhere, in empirical space and time (a people, a place, a culture) – and many more or less fanciful origins were suggested – it must also transcend the empirical origin in the direction of principles, the universal.

In 1783, the architect and writer Ribart de Chamoust publishes a work, today little noticed and to some extent already outdated when it appeared, but which summarizes this logic in a

8 Laugier, *Essai sur l'architecture*, p. 2.

The frontispiece of Marc-Antoine Laugier's *Essai sur l'architecture*, 1753, with the engraving by Jacques Aliamet showing "the first hut".

slightly hilarious way: *L'ordre françois trouvé dans la nature*, "The French order found in nature". We have to "return to the primitive theory" (*remonter à la théorie primitive*), Chamoust writes, a theory that is nothing less than nature itself, which in turn will reveal itself to be the expression of the "French order". Imagining a walk in the forest, Chamoust observes how the trees, "placed fairly regularly in threes, even though they were planted randomly ... formed ... a natural hall of sorts, hexagonal in shape and quite extraordinary. Faced with this sight, my first idea of the transformation of volumes arose, and it was further strengthened when it proved to be fully consonant with the idea of a French order that I already had formed."[9] What here may seem as a perfect vicious circle – nature is already French, because the French order has always been nature – is in fact essential for this theory, even though it is here displayed in a charmingly naïve fashion: here the wholly natural and the arbitrary, perhaps for the last time, coincide, without contradiction, since the analysis of our ideas down to their origin also shows what nature is in itself.

9 Ribart de Chamoust, *L'ordre françois trouvé dans la nature,* Farnborough: Gregg Press, 1967 [1783]), p. 6; see also Rykwert, *On Adam's House in Paradise,* op. cit., pp. 80–82, and Payot, *Le philosophie et l'architecte,* pp. 72–73. Little is known about the author, and even his first name (Charles-François or François-Joseph) is in doubt. The first was the author of books on finance; the second, and more likely alternative, the author of *Architecture singulière* (1758) and *Lettre de M. Ribart* (1770), and is thought to have been an engineer.

Nature, city, park

In the reading proposed by Manfredo Tafuri, who focuses on the later *Observations sur l'architecture* (1765), Laugier's claims indicate that the mimetic exchange between art and nature enters into a new phase organized around the *city*, in which the image of the park, at once artificial nature and natural artifice, plays a crucial role as a mediating function. On this level – which does

Detail from Claude Nicolas Ledoux's engraving "L'abri du pauvre" (The shelter of the poor), 18th century.

not contradict the theory in Laugier's earlier book, but develops it on a higher level – it is not the primordial hut that is at stake, but rather architecture's encounter with a new urban order. Here it is called upon to take on the task of shaping social relations that are required by the emerging capitalist order, which in turn generates a tension between urban form and the solitary object. This opposition between object and milieu is spelled out by Laugier, Tafuri suggests, when he reduces not the first hut but instead the city to nature, by portraying it in terms of painting and the newly emerging theory of the "picturesque", i.e. understands it as an image. "Whoever knows how to design a park well will have no difficulty in tracing the plan for the building of a city", Laugier writes, for in both there must be "regularity and fantasy, relationship and oppositions, and casual, unexpected elements that vary the scene; great order in the details, confusion, uproar, and tumult in the whole".[10] Laugier's anti-perspective and anti-Cartesian gesture places nature and reason, landscape and townscape, on the same level, and just as the metaphorical grasp of the city as a piece of nature dehistoricizes it, it also turns the process of industrialization into a natural phenomenon. Urban naturalism covers over the rift between the emerging city and a pre-capitalist rural order, and the task of architecture, or rather a certain discourse of architecture, Tafuri claims, is to allow the Enlightenment to avoid confronting its own premises. In this way, Tafuri's narrative of modern architecture combines the logic of Capital with the dialectic of the Enlightenment: to hide the contradictions by formal manipulations, and by making it possible for us to enjoy them as aesthetic-picturesque complexity, is at this stage the properly ideological role of architecture.

This compensatory role of architecture, to cover over those contradictions that it is itself unable to solve, produces an inner

10 Abbé Laugier, *Observations sur l'Architecture* (1765; reprint Westmead, Farnborough Hants: Gregg Press, 1996), pp. 312–313, cited in Manfredo Tafuri, *Progetto e utopia: Architettura e sviluppo capitalistico*, Bari: Laterza, 2007 [1973], pp. 7–8. English edition: *Architecture and Utopia: Design and Capitalist Development*, translated by Barbara Luigia La Penta, Cambridge, MA: MIT Press, 1976, p. 16.

unease, which comes across in the 18th century fascination for the exotic, for Indian and Chinese architecture, pavilions and fake ruins – all of which are different ways of finding an "authentication from outside architecture", but that in fact initiated a "systematic and fatal autopsy of architecture and all its conventions".[11] For Tafuri, this anxiety bears the name "Piranesi", to whom he would return in many later publications. Piranesi stages a violent fragmenting of the tradition, where a plethora of historical references whirl by in the desperate attempt of architecture to provide form to a reason whose newfound wakefulness seems to breed ever more monsters. In this, his work forebodes the danger of a complete loss of organic form, Tafuri suggests, which leads to a situation when rationality and irrationality can no longer be separated. In the visions of Piranesi's *Campo Marzio dell'antica Roma* (1761–1762) we see the struggle between architecture and city, and how the ensuing crisis takes on "epic" dimensions, where the excesses of architecture, turning back to face its own aporias, disclose the truth of the Enlightenment dialectic: "In the attempt to absorb all of its own contradictions, architectural 'reasoning' applies the technique of shock to its very foundations",[12] and the city, whose overall unity was intended to provide a meaningful milieu for the single edifice, becomes a "gigantic 'useless machine'".[13] Similarly, and perhaps even more threatening, the infinite interiors of the *Carceri* (1760) become co-extensive with reality, showing "the new existential condition of human collectivism, liberated and condemned at the same time by its own reason",[14] a condition of anonymity that reflects the "silence of things". Nature has ceased to speak, which prepares the emergence of new vocabularies in the discourses that followed. G&M

11 Ibid, p. 22.

12 Ibid, p. 26.

13 Ibid, p. 26.

14 Ibid, p. 29.

Giovanni Battista Piranesi's *Campo Marzio dell'antica Roma*, 1761–1762.

The Garden, Pleasure, and Epicurus

Mateja Kurir

In this reflection on the interdependence of the garden and pleasure, I will attempt to show that the garden is a *space of pleasure* that is simultaneously the *pleasure of space*. This attempt is not so much about expanding the meaning of pleasure as it is about tracing the nuances of changed conceptions of the meaning of the garden.

The garden is a *space of pleasure*, in which, because of the space itself, we can surrender to leisure, from reading to conversation, from strolling to lounging to quiet contemplation, from the cultivation of green vegetables to enjoying food and drink, some of which might have even been made from the products of the garden. The specificities of the garden space offer pleasures of a unique kind. When we speak of the garden, we usually mean an enclosed and ordered outdoor area. The enclosed place generally is located beside a private building, or it may be a cultivated public space, such as a park, the greenery of which gives meaning to the built structures around it.

Temple of Hephaestus from 415 BCE, view from the Acropolis in Athens.

Regardless of whether we are speaking of a private garden or an expansive park, the implication is generally that the garden is a space of pleasure, which is at the same time the *pleasure of space*. The garden, its plants, mild aromas, serenity, the intermingling layers of time revealed in newly opened blossoms and those that have already withered, the different kinds of fruit, the colourful shadows and silhouettes that provide a backdrop: all almost necessarily trigger a sense of enjoyment. The garden may be a space of pleasure because it embodies emergence and blossoming, and of passage, the immanent dialectic of the cycle of life. The garden in and of itself arouses pleasure.[1]

Epicurus' garden in Athens

The proximity of the garden and pleasure was noted at the very inception of philosophy. One of the most renowned Greek philosophers swore by both the garden and pleasure. Indeed, Epicurus (341–270 BCE) named his philosophical school, which in its later incarnation became a comprehensive philosophical system known as Epicureanism,[2] nothing other than the Garden. Epicurus[3] was said to have been born in Samos, only settling in the Athenian capital near Plato's Academy in his mature years. Historical sources report that Epicurus bought a garden

1 There are certain exceptions: cemeteries which are landscape interventions, memorial parks, and other spaces of memory that are designed by landscape architects or other professionals. These and similar examples are not included in these reflections.

2 The ideas of Epicureanism, especially regarding its ethics and methods of discovery, saw their first fiery opponents with the advent of Christianity. Epicureanism, which strived to know the senses and to vanquish the fear of death when both the soul and body dies, did not suit Christian dogma and its notions of abstinence and eternal life. Epicureanism experienced its last period of great popularity during the 17th and 18th century, i.e. the period of Enlightenment. Later, paradoxically because of the dominance of the new empiricism that in many ways corresponded to the ideas of Epicureanism, it was no longer as popular.

3 Because of the opposition of religion and the development of atomism, Karl Marx declared Epicurus "the greatest Greek enlightener". Marx's doctoral dissertation *The Difference Between the Democritean and Epicurian Philosophy of Nature* is dedicated to Epicurus.

Temple of Apollo Patroos from 340–320 BCE, Athens.

in Athens and "founded a school of 'philosophers in the garden'".[4] It is suggested in many sources that the Garden was situated close to Plato's Academy while Epicurus' house was in the centre of Athens, and the master commuted every day between the two locations. It is possible that the location near the Academy was specifically chosen to draw more visitors and students to the lectures and debates that eventually came to attract a wide array of listeners, including women and slaves who were welcome to attend in opposition to the accepted customs of the time. In the scarce literature that remains on this topic, we find descriptions of the Garden as being not a crowded or busy hub, but, at least during Epicurus' lifetime, more of a meeting place where his friends and fellow thinkers could share intimate thoughts, life wisdom, and tell personal stories. The Garden was a version of the classical Greek philosophy school that was in many ways comparable to a wealthy household filled with interesting guests. Thus, Epicurus' Garden functioned both as an intimate and a public space. In the Garden, socialization, conversation, and the exchange of opinions took place in tranquillity and comfort, discussion of the daily news mingling with the wisdom of Epicurus.

Epicurus is mostly known as the philosopher of pleasure, although very few of his writings, including those about pleasure, remain.[5] Epicurus' letters and sayings, as well as writings by his students, emphasize notions such as pleasure, the senses, and serenity (*ataraxia*), the achievement of happiness and the avoidance of suffering as the meaning of life. However, it is worth noting that Epicurus does not view pleasure as something to achieve at all costs – his point is more complex as he values pleasure when it is connected to virtue and wisdom. The following is one of his most famous sayings that captures this particular axis of thought: "It is impossible to live plea-

4 R. E. Wycherley, "The Garden of Epicurus", *Phoenix* 13(2), 1959, pp. 73–77. doi:10.2307/1086973

5 Most of the preserved writings were published in: Diogenes Laërtius, *Life and Opinions of Eminent Philosophers*, probably written in the 4th century, translated by C. D. Yonge, London: G. Bell and Sons, 1915.

surably without living prudently, and honourably, and justly; or to live prudently, and honourably, and justly, without living pleasurably."[6] The maxim to achieve knowledge in comfort and pleasure, Epicurus' greatest challenge during the course of his life, made him popular among the people and elevated him among the notables of Antiquity. And yet we know even less about the Garden today than we do about his writings.[7]

Several writers from Antiquity reported with pride that they had been at Epicurus' Garden. Cicero, among them, mentioned that he was there on a visit to Athens. Seneca in his *Moral Letters to Lucillius*, recommends that his friend also visit the Garden and describes the motto above the entryway, which while perhaps a later invention, is nevertheless telling as it captures the essence of Epicurus' teachings: "Stranger, here you will do well to tarry: here our highest good is pleasure."[8] Seneca adds that visitors to the Garden are welcomed by a custodian who says:

> Have you not been well entertained? This garden does not whet your appetite, but quenches it. Nor does it make you thirstier with every drink; it slakes the thirst with a natural cure – a cure that requires no fee. It is with this type of pleasure that I have grown old.[9]

With these possibly also imaginary words of the Garden's custodian, Seneca indicates that it is always necessary to interpret Epicurus's dedication to pleasure, which many had assumed to be delight as the greatest good or the open advocacy of hedonism, in close connection with virtue and morality. In general, Roman philosophy understood Epicurus and his Garden more as a space of unbridled hedonism than as a place in harmony with respect for virtue and the power of reflection. For Seneca,

6 Attributed to Epicurus, quoted in: Samuel Johnson, *A Dictionary of the English Language; in which the Words are Deduced from their Originals; and Illustrated in Their Different Significations by Examples from the Best Writers: Together with a History of the Language, and an English Grammar*, vol. III, London: Longman, Hurst, Rees, Orme, and Brown, 1818.

7 For more about this see Wycherley, "The Garden of Epicurus", op. cit. Also well-known is the so-called Memmius incident which occurred in 51 BCE during Cicero's visit to Athens. At that time, Epicurus' Garden was already in ruins, and the Roman nobleman Memmius intended to buy the property with the purpose of constructing a building on it. The Epicureans were horrified and asked Cicero to intercede because they did not want the sacred location to be defiled. The outcome of the affair is unknown because the exact location of the Garden also remains obscure.

8 Seneca, *Epistulae morales ad Lucilium – Moral Letters to Lucillius*, translated by Richard Mott Gummere, Loeb Classical Library edition, published 1917–1925.

9 Ibid.

the garden was a place of restraint and virtue where pleasure in a green ambient was also present.

With this emphasis on virtue, the Garden, which in Antiquity became a sort of symbolic, philosophical temple of wisdom, functioned more as a place of intellect than as a place of sensual pleasure. The Garden in its heyday was full of students, friends, acquaintances discussing and debating philosophical questions. The primary purpose of Epicurus' Garden was socializing, debating, discussing, and exchanging viewpoints in the pleasant atmosphere of the garden. This suggests that the greatest pleasure in the Garden was precisely discussion, and that conversation in the form of questioning existing hypotheses and conclusions about the cosmos and matter, society and nature, was the central work carried out in the Garden. Discussion was, in fact, what primarily gave pleasure.

Might we, based on this meaning of Epicurus' Garden, draw some parallels with the meaning of the garden today? More precisely, could we draw from the meaning and message of Epicurus' Garden a conclusion about the role of the garden in recent times when the world had to confront on a global scale the pandemic caused by the corona virus?

The garden as a pandemic sanctuary

First, we should note that before the outbreak of the Covid pandemic in 2020 – that is during the peak of neoliberalism, the fourth industrial revolution, the Anthropocene, and the climate crisis – the meaning of the garden had already changed in comparison to previous periods. In this regard, we also note that, during both the previous and current century, there has been an intense preoccupation with and critical

An ordinary garden in Ljubljana during the pandemic, offering a place of refuge.

transformation of the meaning of representation, among other things, representation on the level of the environment and nature, and this had also led to a different understanding of the garden.[10] Post-humanist approaches under these new conditions opened up a range of social tensions (in society, politics, the economy, and other arenas of social life), which were often ascribed to the environmental and spatial situation, or put another way, to social conditions that have always been reflected in our environment and the way we arrange the space around us. It has become evident during the 21st century, which ushered in a period of multiple crises, that the Anthropocentrism and the Cartesian paradigm that have dominated for centuries have run their course and we now need a new social contract. In Anthropocentrism, nature is viewed as the *object* of humanity, completely subordinate to man as master, and this culminated in the so-called Cartesian paradigm.[11] The current series of looming crises we now face ruthlessly expose the fact that we have driven nature to the very edge of survival, and that nature – whether individual plants and animals, or complex ecosystems – needs a more suitable and forceful expression of its rights and a way to establish them. The garden, as an approximation of nature, comes into proximity with humanity, and thus finds itself in a similar situation. During these perilous times, the garden remains above all a *topos* that expresses current conflicts and social frictions.

During the urban rebirth of the 20th and 21st centuries, the garden increasingly became an important status symbol. The garden remains a specific, enclosed, and cultivated space, ranging from private property adjacent to houses to public green spaces next to multi-dwelling residential buildings and public parks. It could be argued that the garden acquired even more status and prestige in densely populated areas and during

10 For more about this see Giovanni Aloi (ed.), *Why Look at Plants? The Botanical Emergence in Contemporary Art*, Leiden: Brill/Rodopi, 2019.

11 The Cartesian paradigm refers to the entire civilizational framework of modern perceptions of culture and society, which includes man's dominance over nature through the use of technology. Within this framework, man embraced Enlightenment ideas and became the unlimited master of nature which could be exploited for his uses. In the most extreme interpretations of this paradigm, the environment is completely subordinated to the satisfaction of man's needs, and animals and plants are understood as mere "automata".

periods of rising inequality, and that this prestigious status is even greater because of the garden's role as a unique space of pleasure. The garden is a place that provides unique pleasure in and of the space. We could also say that, before the Covid pandemic, during an era when Western society persistently advocated the pleasure principle, the garden became a sort of idealized shelter, an ideal space for pleasure. Perhaps it was precisely because of the mandate for pleasure that the garden was elevated in the post-industrial society of the 21st century as the place of all places, an emblematic space of pleasure that metaphorically functions on all levels. Above all, it seems that pleasure in the garden is of a transitory nature, with almost all necessary elements – such as a grill, sometimes a swimming pool, and other leisure items – ensuring the stipulated enjoyment. On the symbolic level, the garden of the 21st century is increasingly remote from what it was in the past.

The Covid pandemic went even further in highlighting the meaning of the garden as either a private or public good. During a period when people have for more than a year been overwhelmed with an onslaught of negative news, death, lockdowns, and restrictive measures that recall conditions of war, the garden has become the ideal sanctuary to escape the machinery of systemic changes in social conditions caused by the virus.[12] Thus, the garden acquired greater significance, and this was then reflected in both its symbolic and material value. In countries where residents could not leave the house at all, the garden added the greatest surplus value to real estate as it allowed for movement, mental health, and joy. If residents had no garden, they were forced to remain inside, between four walls. All of a sudden, we recognized as a society the significance of parks and gardens. In these constrained circumstances, Epicurus' adage – "Stranger, here you will do well to tarry: here

12 For more about this see Renata Salecl, *Človek človeku virus*, Ljubljana: Mladinska knjiga, 2020, p. 14.

our highest good is pleasure" – found its greatest relevance precisely on the level of the garden. The prices of houses with gardens went up. Even the most prestigious apartments in city centres were no longer as attractive as real estate with a garden on the periphery of the city or even in the countryside. The world – and also the garden – was turned upside down.

During the Covid crisis, the value of the garden increased on all levels, perhaps because the garden was the only place of enjoyment that remained during the pandemic and one of the few places where we could temporarily forget the rules imposed on our behaviour, the social disputes, and the overwhelmingly negative news that poured from all screens. In the garden, we could immerse ourselves in plants and sometimes also animals. We could get temporary relief from society. In the context of a cultivated environment that functions as an approximation of and substitute for nature, we could calm down, collect ourselves, and breathe. The garden, by becoming a luxurious station of repose, once again performs the spatial and curative roles that it had in previous epidemics and wars – with the additional value that, in the era of the fourth industrial revolution which revolves around information, the garden is a space where there is almost no data in the contemporary sense of the word. This new value of the garden may well accompany us into our uncertain future, and might become part of a new social contract that will reflect the quality and accessibility of green public spaces for the entire community. G&M

The garden as a place of enjoyment.

Gardens of Others

Photographs by *Anne Schwalbe*

DAIKIN

Post Scriptum

This book is dedicated to the memory of Dušan Ogrin (1929–2019) and thus the last essay in this anthology will tell the story of his most important publication *The World Heritage of Gardens*. I met Professor Dušan Ogrin in the early 1990s when I worked as an editor for the EWO publishing house based in

The garden of the author's grandfather in the Slovenian countryside.

Ljubljana. During this era when Eastern Europe began to open to the West, the fundamental mission of EWO, under the leadership of Slavko Pregl, was to act as a mediator between publishers in Eastern and Western Europe and make available to the reading public high-quality books, many of which were filled with abundant illustrations. We often published such books with a co publisher simply to make the printing affordable. The project that Professor Ogrin offered us was astonishing and ambitious in every way. Within the green canvas box that he gently put on the table before us was a complete layout of an extensive overview of the world heritage of gardens. The layout had been created down to the last detail, the text and the photographs already arranged in the format of a finished book. In that moment, I knew that what lay before me on the table was nothing other than the lifework of this remarkable man. Professor Ogrin had thought out every single detail, had conceived the book based on his erudition. During our chats, he revealed his great love and admiration for the artistic gardens of the Far East, and so in the spirit of the *chanoyu*, I instituted a ritual of tea-drinking with him, meticulously preparing Gyukoro, his favourite Japanese green tea. We could not, unfortunately, walk along a garden path, or *roji,* to a tea pavilion but had conversations in my office.

The author as a girl in her grandmother's orchard.

Sadly, the production of such a luxurious book in Slovenia without a sponsor was impossible. And so we endeavoured to set up a cooperation with a foreign publishing house to achieve the publication of the book in English, a process that took several years. But finally, the moment came when Mr Werner Guttmann, the charming director of Thames and Hudson, presented to me not only precise instructions on how to plant roses but also a signed contract.

The book came out in 1993 in both a Slovenian and a British/American versions edition.[1] The two publications had different covers: the Slovenian edition showed a Japanese garden, while the English book cover presented of course an English landscape garden. Both were produced by the printing company Gorenjski tisk. The presentation of both versions took place at Cankarjev dom, the most important cultural centre in Ljubljana, in the presence of Professor Ogrin and other distinguished persons from the world of architecture such as Vladimir Braco Mušič, Janez Lajovic, as well as the prominent American historian and geographer David Lowenthal, renowned for his work on heritage. Later, in 1995, an Italian version of the book was published by the Fenice 2000 publishing house.[2] As an integral authorial work, the book is unquestionably exceptional, and its importance goes far beyond Slovenia's borders.

Hortus conclusus?

Personally, I grew up in a garden with an orchard; it was my world. The garden had vegetables, daffodils, Turkish carnations, hydrangeas, pansies, and lilacs, and extensive orchard of fruit trees where a mighty oak also grew. My grandmother used to cut the lawn with a scythe only when the grass was very high and already blooming with colourful little flowers. I would often lay on a lacy rug of meadow bittercress. I gathered lilac blossoms. I climbed the trees, ate their fruit, swung on a swing hanging from one of their branches, and sat in their shade. I

1 Dušan Ogrin, *The World Heritage of Gardens*, London, New York: Thames & Hudson, 1993; Dušan Ogrin, *Vrtna umetnost sveta: pregled svetovne dediščine,* Ljubljana: Pudon and Ewo, 1993.

2 Dušan Ogrin, *Giardini del mondo. Storia, protagonisti, stili dei giardini di tutti i paesi dall'antichità al XX secolo*, Milano: Fenice 2000, 1995.

observed and came to know all the different animals that lived in our garden. I helped to cultivate the garden and enjoyed its fruits and other produce. I was a child, in the animist phase, and the trees still spoke to me. My grandmother's garden no longer exists and, somewhere along the path to growing up, I lost the ability to talk to trees, but I never really lost that inner garden, that little piece of domesticated nature where I feel connected to life. When I think about my childhood home, my memory does not linger in the dim rooms with their old furniture. Rather it pauses in the kitchen and most of all in the garden. That is the mandala I carry inside of me. The garden was the place where I moved freely, exploring and admiring it, feeling safe and connected in it. The garden was not only a spiritual haven, not only beauty, but above all a space for the body and the senses.

The garden as a lost paradise is perhaps one of the oldest archetypes of our collective subconscious that we harbour within us. The garden as an expression of our human creativity, in service to a range of efforts, has earned a place in history. It is a special sphere of the visual arts, but unlike the other visual arts, it is created from what is already given. Perhaps today we no longer live in the time of formidable gardens through which individuals, and most of all rulers, displayed their power and brilliance. Gardens are not profitable, and today passion and prestige take on other conceptual forms. It is difficult to imagine that today anyone would ever end up in a dungeon because of a garden as one of the miserable subjects of Louis XIV[3] did; or that a ruler would lose his throne because of an expensive passion for tulips, as happened to Ahmed III[4] at the beginning of the 18th century. And yet the passion for botanical collection has existed since the birth of great civilizations, embodied in travellers, soldiers, and professional hunters of various plants.

3 The King's Minister of Finance, Nicolas Fouquet, had the audacity to build a chateau with a garden in Vaux, designed by the famous trio of Louis Le Vau, André Le Nôtre, and Charles Le Brun, which was far more splendid than anything in the King's possession. Two weeks after the spectacular opening, the King had Fouquet arrested and imprisoned. Fouquet would remain incarcerated in harsh conditions until his death in 1680. After the arrest, the King hired the same trinity of artists to design Versailles (editor's note).

4 Ahmed III (1673–1736) was Sultan of the Ottoman Empire from 1703 until 1730. Also called the ruler of the Tulip Age (*Lale Devra*), because his fascination with tulips sparked a true tulipomania that extended beyond the borders of the Ottoman Empire. The flowering of art and culture, extravagance and openness to the West, led to strong resistance from more conservative forces and, coupled with a complicated political situation, the Sultan was forced to resign and ended up under house arrest (editor's note).

It is also difficult today to conjure the single-minded dedication of Vita Sackville-West and Harold Nichols,[5] the creators of Sissinghurst Gardens.

Sissinghurst Garden in Kent, Vita Sackville-West and Sir Harold George Nicolson, between 1930 and 1960.

Today the taste for gardens is globalized and eclectic. Thus, we find Zen dry gardens in Slovenian suburbs and English gardens around Tuscan villas. I once was walking through a Scottish wood when suddenly there appeared beside a stream a wall of flowering rhododendrons; when I stepped out of the wood, I was greeted by a river of Himalayan blue poppies on a hillside. In front of the house where I live, a linden tree and a fan-like Japanese maple gently touch each other like fingertips. Wild garlic grows happily beneath a magnolia. Now that we live in a time of change where we question our very existence, our survival, gardening is once again in fashion. The design of gardens

5 Vita Sackville-West (1892–1962), aristocrat, poet and writer, and her husband, Sir Harold George Nicolson (1886–1968), author and diplomat, created one of the world's most famous and influential gardens, the Sissinghurst Garden in Kent, between 1930 and 1960, with extraordinary dedication and passion.

is now the most democratic of arts: anyone can create a garden. The garden is a space of spirituality and physicality. Perhaps we are truly grounded only when we plunge our hands into the soil.

The beginnings of the European garden reach back to the mediaeval enclosed garden, *hortus conclusus*: a small, cosy, arranged space for recreation and relaxation within high walls that protected those inside from the dangers of the outside world. Today the enclosed and safe garden is once again the spiritual axis of our reflections. The garden as a space of recreation/re-creation has regained its original meaning. We must create ourselves anew, otherwise we are threatened by destruction. The garden has to do with the re-creation of our humanness, which has lost contact with the earth and therefore has betrayed it. The following is the way Milton articulated the internal garden in *Paradise Lost* during the dialogue between Adam and the Archangel Michael:

> This having learnt, thou hast attained the summe
> Of wisdom; hope no higher, though all the Starrs
> Thou knewst by name, and all th' ethereal Powers,
> All secrets of the deep, all Natures works,
> Or works of God in Heav'n, Aire, Earth, or Sea,
> And all the riches of this World enjoydst,
>
> And all the rule, one Empire; onely add
> Deeds to thy knowledge answerable, add Faith,
> Add vertue, Patience, Temperance, add Love,
> By name to come call'd Charitie, the soul
> Of all the rest: then wilt thou not be loath
> To leave this Paradise, but shalt possess
> A Paradise within thee, happier farr.[6] G&M

6 John Milton, *Paradise Lost: Book I and II*. London: Macmillan, 1946.

Temple of Ancient Virtue, Elysian Fields, Stowe landscape gardens, England, William Kent, mid-18th century.

About the Authors

Jože Barši (1955) graduated in architecture and sculpture at the University of Ljubljana. His work ranges from site-specific artworks to radio broadcasting, from public talks to sound and textual art, such as those first presented in 2007 at the exhibition *Close reading* (Galerija Gregor Podnar, Ljubljana). In 1997, Barši represented Slovenia at the Venice Biennale with the work *There are many answers to the question about why to grow vegetables…* He was invited by René Block to the 4th Biennale in Istanbul (1995) and was awarded the *Golden Bird* for visual arts (2010) and the Jakopič Award (2014). Barši is Professor at the Academy of Fine Arts and Design at the University of Ljubljana.

Andrew Benjamin (1952) is Distinguished Professor of Architectural Theory at the University of Technology, Sydney. He was teaching philosophy in the United Kingdom (Architectural Association in London, University in Warwick, Kingston University) as well as in Australia (Monash University, Melbourne, where he is a Professor of Philosophy Emeritus). His publications, which touch upon architecture, art history, and philosophy include *Architectural Philosophy* (London: Continuum, 2001); *Writing Art and Architecture* (Melbourne: re.press Books, 2010); *Architectural Projections* (Melbourne: RMIT Press, 2012); *Art's Philosophy Work* (Lanham, MD: Rowman & Littlefield Publishers, 2015). He is currently working with Gerard Reinmuth in an ongoing studio investigation of relational architecture.

Erika Bordon (1972) graduated in art history and sociology of culture at the University of Ljubljana. She taught art history at the Academy of Visual Arts in Ljubljana and works as a cultural programme manager. Her research interest is the interdisciplinary study of the historiography of gardens and cultural landscape, a platform where humanities, fine arts, history, philosophy, literature, and the poetics of space meet. Bordon focuses on the history of gardens, the history of ideas in the production of space, the history of humanities, cultural history, the philosophy of nature, and art history.

Lisa Diedrich (1965) studied architecture and urbanism in Paris, Marseille, and Stuttgart, journalism in Berlin, and landscape architecture in Copenhagen. She has been teaching and researching in the field of contemporary landscape architecture for universities in Europe and worldwide. Currently she is Professor of Landscape Architecture at the Swedish University of Agricultural Sciences (SLU) in Alnarp, Malmö. She also works as the editor-in-chief of the book series *Landscape Architecture Europe* and of *'scape the international magazine for landscape architecture and urbanism*. She lives in Berlin.

Mladen Dolar (1951) is Professor and Senior Research Fellow at the Department of Philosophy, University of Ljubljana. His principal areas of research are psychoanalysis, modern French philosophy, German idealism, and art theory. He has lectured extensively at universities in USA and across Europe, and he is author of over hundred and fifty papers in scholarly journals and collective volumes. Apart from twelve books in Slovenian, his publications include most notably *A Voice and Nothing More* (Cambridge, MA: MIT Press, 2006, translated into ten languages) and *Opera's Second Death* (with Slavoj Žižek, London/New York: Routledge 2001, also translated into several languages). He is one of the founders of the Ljubljana Lacanian School.

Pavel Gantar (1949) is a sociologist with professional interest and activity in urban sociology, urban and regional development, planning theories, and environmental sociology. Gantar was from 1974 to 1994 a full-time lecturer and researcher at the Faculty of Social Sciences at the University of Ljubljana, and after entering politics, continued part-time. From 1994 to 2000 he served as the Minister of Environment and Spatial Planning, and from 2001 to 2004 as Minister for the Information Society. He was a Member of the Parliament of the Republic of Slovenia and from 2008 to 2011 he also served as its President (Speaker). After leaving professional politics, he retired, yet he still continues to work with various research institutions in Slovenia and abroad. He published numerous articles on urban development, planning theories, and environmental and climate change policies.

Davorin Gazvoda (1965) is Professor of Landscape Design at the Biotechnical Faculty, University of Ljubljana, and has been teaching studios in landscape design for over thirty years. He conducted landscape design workshops at various universities in Turkey, China, Serbia, Croatia, Russia, and the USA. His research includes published articles, papers at international conferences and research reports, focusing on methods of teaching landscape arhitecture. In the field of landscape design, he accomplished dozens of landscape architecture and urban design projects and competitions, most of them awarded and some of them built. From 2006 to 2020 he served as Vice Dean for Landscape Architecture and Vice Dean of Study Affairs and for one term (2014–2016) also as the Dean of the Biotechnical Faculty.

João Gomes da Silva (1962) is a landscape architect, Partner and Director of Global Arquitectura Paisagista and Professor at Accademia di Architettura di Mendrisio. He lectured at several universities and participated in conferences and workshops focused on the theory and practice in landscape architecture, both nationally and internationally. In 2015, he was, with João Nunes, invited as a visiting professor in Landscape Architecture at Harvard Graduate School of Design. He is a recipient of several national and international prizes and awards, among them the Schinkel Prize (1991), the Piranesi Award (2010) and the Audience Award at the Barcelona Landscape Biennial (2008). Since 1987, he has dedicated his professional life to the critical production of landscape.

Barbara Habič Pregl (1958) graduated in philosophy and comparative literature. She started her career in newspapers and magazines devoted to the field of culture, especially film. For ten years she was a curator at ARS Gallery in Ljubljana and worked as an editor of art monographs and other books at the publishing houses of EWO and Arkadija. She is also the author of several books for children, a translator of non-fiction publications, and a yoga teacher.

Urška Jurman (1973) is an art historian and a sociologist of culture. She is active as a curator, editor, and writer in the field of contemporary art. Her work centres on the intersection of art, spatial practices, ecology, and active citizenship. She is a co-founder of the Obrat Culture and Art Association with which she co-authored a number of spatial interventions in Ljubljana, among which is also the community garden Beyond a Construction Site. In 2021, she co-initiated (with Elke Krasny) the Ecologies of Care network. Since 2013, she has been the programme director of the Igor Zabel Association for Culture and Theory in Ljubljana.

Dževad Karahasan (1953–2023) was an author and Professor of Drama and History of Drama and Theatre. He was educated in Duvno and Sarajevo, worked as a dramaturgist in Zenica, Salzburg, and Sarajevo, and lectured at universities in Sarajevo, Salzburg, Göttingen, Berlin, Basel, and Graz. Besides many novels, that often revolve around Sarajevo, such as *Istočni diwan* (*The Eastern Divan*), *Šahrijarov prsten* (*The Ring of Shahriyar*), *Sara i Serafina* (*Sara and Serafina*), *Noćno vijeće* (*Night Council*), *Što pepeo priča* (*The Solace of the Night Sky*), and *Uvod u lebdenje* (*Introduction to Floating*), he published several collections of stories such as *Kraljevske legende* (King's Legends), *Izvjestaji iz tamnog vilajeta* (Reports from the Dark World), *Kuća za umorne* (*A House for the Wearied*), and essays *O jeziku i strahu* (The Smell of Fear), *Dnevnik selidbe* (*Exodus from a City*), and *Knjiga vrtova* (*The Book of Gardens*) among others. Karahasan received numerous awards, including the Charles Veillon Prize, Leipzig Book Award for European Understanding, the Goethe Prize, the Herder Prize, and the Vilenica Prize. Sadly, he passed away in 2023.

Dean Komel (1960) is Professor of Contemporary Philosophy and Philosophy of Culture at the Faculty of Arts, University of Ljubljana, the head of research at the Institute Nova Revija, and president of the Phenomenological Society of Ljubljana. In 2003, he received the Zois Award of the Republic of Slovenia for highest scientific achievements in the field of philosophy. He published his works in prominent journals and book series for phenomenological and hermeneutical philosophy and was the initiator of several humanistic institutions in Slovenia and abroad. He is the member of many editorial boards of journals for philosophy and culture, and the organizer of more than fifty international scientific conferences. With his critical stance concerning cultural and social questions, he regularly contributes to public discussions on television and other media.

Miklavž Komelj (1973) is a Slovenian poet and historian of art. He has published fourteen books of poetry (the book *Hippodrome* is available also in an English translation), three books of prose, a scientific monograph about Slovenian partisan art, two collections of essays, several other books and scholarly articles and essays about the theory and history of art and literature. He is a recipient of numerous awards, including the Prešeren Foundation Prize, Jenko Prize, Veronika Prize and Igor Zabel working grant.

Miloš Kosec (1986) is an architect, architectural historian, and writer. He is a curator for architecture at the Museum of Architecture and Design and a researcher and assistant professor at the Faculty of Architecture, University of Ljubljana. He completed his master's degree in 2014 in Ljubljana with the thesis "Ruin as an Architectural Object" and his PhD in 2019 at Birkbeck College, University of London, with the dissertation "Passivism: Activism and Passivity in Contemporary Architecture". His research is focused on the questions of contemporary architectural agency, the notion of passivity, and the intangible strategies in transforming space.

Lev Kreft (1951) is an editor, philosopher, and sociologist, and a retired Professor at the Faculty of Arts of the University of Ljubljana. In the late 1980is, Kreft was director of the Marxist Centre of the League of Communists of Slovenia, and later, in 1990–1996, a member of the first and the second Parliament of the Republic of Slovenia, acting also as Deputy Speaker during the second term. In the new millennium he headed The Peace Institute of Slovenia. He still lectures on aesthetics, philosophy of art, and philosophy of sport. He focuses on contemporary art, historical avant-garde, struggles at the artistic left, Marxist aesthetics, totalitarian art, postmodern and postsocialist art as well as the aesthetics and philosophy of sport. Kreft is still a Marxist.

Ana Kučan (1964) is a landscape architect, Professor of Landscape Design and Theory at the Biotechnical Faculty, University of Ljubljana. She received a master's degree in urban design from Harvard University, Graduate School of Design. Since 2007, her office Studio AKKA has designed award-winning projects which were presented at exhibitions and lectures internationally. She represented Slovenia at the 12th Biennale of Architecture in Venice (2010) and has received numerous national and international awards, including three Plečnik Awards (2003, 2016, 2021). She was a finalist for the Rosa Barba Prize (2006). Kučan is a critical author and editor of publications on landscape design such as *Krajina kot nacionalni simbol* (Landscape as National Symbol), 1998.

Mateja Kurir (1978) is a philosopher, researcher, and editor. She was a visiting researcher at the Department of Architecture, KU Leuven (2015), and postdoc researcher at the University of Rijeka (2017). Currently she is the manager of LINA platform. She published *Arhitektura moderne in das Unheimliche* (2018) and co-edited *Vrt in prispodoba* (2021), the Slovenian edition of *Garden and Metaphor*. As the editor of *O oblasti v arhitekturi* (*On Power in Architecture,* 2021), Kurir received the Plečnik Medal 2022 in the field of architectural theory, criticism, and publication.

Lilli Lička (1963) is Professor of Landscape Architecture as well as a consultant, jury member, and activist. She studied landscape ecology and design. Currently Lička is heading the Institute of Landscape Architecture and LArchiv at the University of Natural Resources and Life Sciences BOKU Vienna and is principal of studio LL-Landscape architecture. She is active in research, teaching, the design of parks, squares, streets, heritage sites, and gardens. Lička is part of the BLA (Büro für lustige

Angelegenheiten) collective, who, in a performative manner, question societal issues, which become manifest in public space.

Janez Marušič (1939) is Professor Emeritus at the Biotechnical Faculty, University of Ljubljana. He studied in Ljubljana, Scotland, and the USA, and is known as one of the pioneers of Environmental Impact Assessment in Slovenia, where he introduced and further developed methods of landscape planning. Marušič has conceived a package of programmes for spatial evaluation, *Prostor*, and co-authored the *ProVal* computer system for spatial planning. His bibliography is extensive. Besides teaching landscape planning at the universities of Ljubljana and Zagreb, Marušič lectured at the TU Vienna, SLU Alnarp, Malmö, and the University of Beijing. In 2022, he published *On Landscape: Creative Protection of the World* (Ljubljana: Biotechnical Faculty, University of Ljubljana).

Jure Mikuž (1949) is a leading representative of an art-history school that goes beyond the boundaries of an otherwise conservative and rigid field of humanities. He has written twenty books and the list of his publications comprises over seven hundred items. In addition to research, he also worked as a curator, director of the Gallery of Modern Arts in Ljubljana between 1972 and 1992 and Deputy Minister of Culture between 1993 and 1994. He was a lecturer and Head of Historical Anthropology of Visual Arts at the Institutum Studiorum Humanitatis and Professor at the Academy of Fine Arts and Design of the University of Ljubljana.

Olaf Nicolai (1962) is a German conceptual artist. He grew up in Chemnitz in the German Democratic Republic. He studied German language and literature in Leipzig, Vienna, and Budapest, holds a doctorate from Leipzig University and a diploma in applied arts from the Technical College at Schneeberg in Saxony. Since the early 1990s, Nicolai has participated in numerous international solo and group exhibitions at important crossroads of contemporary arts. Several of his works can be found in public collections, such as the Museum of Modern Art, New York, and at the Friedrich Christian Flick Collection, Berlin. Olaf Nicolai lives and works in Berlin.

Martin Prominski (1965) is Professor and Chair of Designing Urban Landscapes at Leibniz University Hannover, Germany. After three years of apprenticeship and work experience as a landscape gardener, he studied landscape planning at TU Berlin and received a master's degree in landscape architecture from Harvard University, Graduate School of Design. He has a PhD from TU Berlin (2003). His current research focuses on design research strategies, new concepts of nature and culture in the Anthropocene, and landscape architectural strategies to address the challenges of biodiversity loss and climate change. He is a registered landscape architect and co-founded mesh landscape architects, Hannover/Tokyo in 2018 with three partners.

Martin Rein-Cano (1967) was born in Buenos Aires. He studied art history at Frankfurt University and landscape architecture at the Technical Universities of Hannover and Karlsruhe. Since 1996, the international office TOPOTEK 1, that he founded, has created and designed German and international projects ranging from master plans to gardens. Martin Rein-Cano has been appointed as guest professor in Europe and North America. He frequently lectures at internationally renowned universities and cultural institutions, and regularly serves in competition juries. Several professional books and articles have been published on his work, which has been honoured with many awards and prizes.

Gerard Reinmuth (1970) is a Founding Director of TERROIR and Professor in Practice at the School of Architecture at the University of Technology Sydney. TERROIR is an architectural practice which emerged from conversations around the potential for architecture to open up and work into questions of cultural consequence. The practice has been featured in numerous international publications, biennales, and awards programmes for its built work, while Gerard's research and teaching specifically explores the agency of the architect, given contemporary economic and political tendencies. His current research project, "Towards a Relational Architecture" (with Andrew Benjamin), suggests that the re-thinking of the discipline in the context of the impact of neo-liberalism, and in particular the global climate emergency, might inform a new conception of the profession.

Anne Schwalbe (1974) is an internationally renowned photographer based in Berlin. Her focus is on gardens, plants, and other natural phenomena. In 2001, she received her master's degree in German Language and Literature Studies and Cultural Studies from Humboldt University, Berlin. Subsequently, she undertook photography studies with Ute and Werner Mahler at Ostkreuz School of Photography, Berlin (2003–2007), and attended Arno Fischer's master class (2008–2009), also at Ostkreuz School of Photography. Her work is exhibited in galleries and museums worldwide and she is the author of many publications and catalogues of her work. Since 2018, she has been the garden columnist at *ZEIT Magazin* with the regular column "Die Gärten der Anderen" (Gardens of Others)

Carl Steinitz (1937) is the Alexander and Victoria Wiley Professor of Landscape Architecture and Planning Emeritus, at Harvard University, Graduate School of Design. Steinitz has devoted much of his academic and professional career to improving methods to analyse large land areas and make design decisions about conservation and development. The focus of his applied research and teaching is on highly valued landscapes that are undergoing substantial pressures for change. Steinitz has lectured and given workshops at more than 170 universities. He is currently Honorary Professor at the Centre for Advanced Spatial Analysis at University College London.

Kinga Szilágyi (1953) is a landscape architect and senior researcher at the Doctoral School of Landscape Architecture, Budapest. Her professional activity, research, and publications focus on both main fields of landscape architecture, i.e. planning and design. She developed the education programme at her school for urban green system planning and urban ecology and, lately, urban green infrastructure. She runs a set of public open space analyses of planning history, structure, design, and public use. Her papers about Budapest's two hundred years old public park, the Városliget, provide valuable knowledge about public park design in the Central European region. Her research interests are centred on historic gardens and sites, as well as on methods of their revitalization.

Marc Treib (1943) is Professor of Architecture Emeritus, University of California, Berkeley, and a historian and critic of landscape and architecture who has published widely on modern and historical subjects in the United States, Japan, and Scandinavia. Recent books include *Austere Gardens: Thoughts on Landscape, Restraint, and Attending* (Novato, CA: ORO Editions, 2016); *Pietro Porcinai and the Landscape of Modern Italy* (co-editor, London/New York: Routledge, 2016); *Landscapes of Modern Architecture: Wright, Mies, Neutra, Aalto, Barragán* (New Haven: Yale University Press, 2017); and *The Landscapes of Georges Descombes: Doing Almost Nothing* (Novato, CA: ORO Editions, 2018).

Aleš Vodopivec (1949) is a renown Slovenian architect and Professor of Architectural Practice and Theory at the Faculty of Architecture, University of Ljubljana. He has published widely on architectural theory. He has been a guest professor and guest lecturer at various European universities, as well as at universities in Israel and USA and at international symposia and conferences. Vodopivec is a recipient of numerous national and international awards, including the Prešeren Foundation Prize, Piranesi Prize, Piranesi honorary mention, Plečnik Award, three Plečnik medals, and the Ernst A. Plischke Award, Vienna.

Sven-Olov Wallenstein (1960) is Professor of Philosophy at Södertörn University, Stockholm. He is the translator of works by Baumgarten, Winckelmann, Lessing, Kant, Hegel, Frege, Husserl, Heidegger, Levinas, Derrida, Deleuze, Foucault, Rancière, and Agamben, as well as the author of numerous books on philosophy, contemporary art, and architecture. Recent publications include *Upplysningens estetik: Nedslag i 1700-talet* (Göteborg: Paletten, 2019), *Spacing Philosophy: Lyotard and the Idea of the Exhibition* (London: Sternberg Press, 2019, with Daniel Birnbaum), and *Adorno: Negative dialektik och estetisk teori* (Gothenburg: Glänta produktion, 2019), as well as translations of Adorno's *Negative Dialektik, Ästhetische Theorie*, and *Mahler: Eine musikalische Physiognomie*.

Catharine Ward Thompson (1952) is Professor of Landscape Architecture and Director of OPENspace Research Centre at the University of Edinburgh. Her work focuses on inclusive access to outdoor environments and links between landscape and health. It includes work with children, young and older people; it covers environment-behaviour interactions, historical landscapes, and contemporary needs, and salutogenic environments. She was a member of the Scottish Government's "Good Places Better Health" Evaluation Group. Currently she is exploring whether an urban woodland intervention programme improves psychological well-being and early childhood development in deprived communities.

Udo Weilacher (1963) is Professor at the Technical University Munich at Weihenstephan. Prior to that and until 2009, he was a Professor of Landscape Architecture and Design at the University of Hannover (from 2002 on) where he also served as the Dean (2006–2008). He researches the links between modern landscape architecture, visual arts, and garden design history in conjunction with forward-looking landscape developments, focusing on the sustainable transformation of industrial landscapes. After graduation from TUM in 1993 he was a research fellow and lecturer at the University of Karlsruhe and the Swiss Federal Institute of Technology (ETH) Zurich. He has published numerous papers and books, including the seminal *Between Landscape Architecture and Land Art* (Basel: Birkhäuser, 1995).

Saskia de Wit (1969) is Assistant Professor at the department of Landscape Architecture, Delft University of Technology, the Netherlands. She combines teaching and research with design practice at her own firm Saskia de Wit tuin en landschap. Her research focuses on the garden as a core concept of landscape architecture and as a lens to unravel notions such as perception of place, sensory landscape qualities, contemporary concepts of nature, and metropolitan landscapes. She recently published *Hidden Landscapes* (Amsterdam: Architectura & Natura Press, 2018), a book in which she connects the concept of the walled garden with contemporary urban practices.

Nadja Zgonik (1964) is an art historian and art critic, Associate Professor at the Academy of Fine Arts, University of Ljubljana. As a student, she was employed at the Gallery of Modern Arts in Ljubljana at the Department of Documentary Studies, from 1986 to 1987. She has been teaching at the Academy since 1989. Her research interests include Slovenian modernism, postmodernism, contemporary art, art theory, and the theory of art historiography. She writes critiques, essays, scientific discussions, accompanying studies in exhibition catalogues. She published several monographs on Slovenian painters from the 20th century.

Dedication

Dušan Ogrin (1929–2019) was a pioneering Slovenian landscape architect and Professor Emeritus at the Biotechnical Faculty, University of Ljubljana. In 1972, he founded a study of landscape architecture at the University of Ljubljana and organized one of the first conferences on landscape planning worldwide. His contributions to landscape architecture made a deep impression on both Slovenian and international spatial planning. Ogrin was a member of the IFLA (International Federation of Landscape Architects) Executive Council and the president of the IUCN (International Union for Conservation of Nature) committee, a founder and the first president of the Association of Landscape Architects of Yugoslavia and member of the Slovenian Association of Landscape Architects (SALA) till his death. He was awarded the Sckell Ring, Lenné Gold Medal as well as several national awards for landscape architecture and design, and was a renowned lecturer and guest professor at several universities, including Harvard University and Beijing University. Finally, Ogrin was an avid photographer and documented all the gardens he visited.

Cover and frontispiece
Anne Schwalbe

First There Was the Garden
Ana Kučan

Ana Kučan
12

Marc Treib
14, 17

Alan Sonfist
20

Alison C. Meier
21

© Holt/Smithson Foundation/Licensed by Artists Rights Society (ARS), NY
22

Marc Treib
31, 32, 33

Japanese Gardens
Anne Schwalbe

34–41

The Garden of Life: From Birth to Death, Where Else but a Garden?
Catharine Ward Thompson

Public Domain
44, 48

© RHS/Sarah Cuttle
46

Marc Treib
47

Catharine Ward Thompson
49

The Garden as the Experience of a Promised World
Janez Marušič

Public Domain
52, 62

Zaš Brezar
54

Ben Skála, Benfoto/Wikimedia Commons
55

Ana Kučan
59

On Mistaking Garden for Nature
Pavel Gantar

Igor Andjelić
65

Taking Responsibility for Landscape
Kinga Szilágyi

Mőcsényi archive, Entz Ferenc Library and Archive, University of Agriculture and Life Sciences, Hungary Budapest
70, 73

Kinga Szilágyi
75

Annamária Gerzánics
76

The Garden as a Spatial Idea
João Gomes da Silva

Duarte Belo
78

Ana Kučan
80

Dušan Ogrin
81

The Garden as an Expression of Supernature
Saskia de Wit

Sebastiaan Kaal
84, 86, 89, 91

Garden Thinking and Garden Action
Udo Weilacher

Udo Weilacher
96, 97, 99, 100

The Garden's Complex Instrumentality
Andrew Benjamin and *Gerard Reinmuth*

Arcaid Images/Alamy Stock Foto
107

Public Domain
109

Dongsei Kim
113

Winterscapes
Anne Schwalbe

118–127

Radical Gardens
Lisa Diedrich

Lisa Diedrich
130, 135

The Community Garden as a Metaphor of Coexistence
Urška Jurman

top row left Suzana Kajba; top row right Toni Poljanec
139

centre row left and middle Suzana Kajba; centre row right Drago Kos
139

bottom row left Drago Kos; bottom row middle KUD Obrat; bottom row right Toni Poljanec
139

bottom Gregor Gobec
139

Drago Kos
142

The City as a Garden
Dževad Karahasan

Public Domain
147

Overgrown Plans
Miloš Kosec

Lan Hočevar
148, 149

Miloš Kosec
150, 151

http://www.kocevsko.com
153

Thanks to Tanja Štajdohar

Gardens as Spaces of Collective Imagination
Lilli Lička

Lilli Lička
155, 157

top Bureau B+B
158

bottom Yann Monel/
Wagon Landscaping
158

atelier le balto
159

Need a Garden Be a Metaphor?
Marc Treib

Marc Treib
162, 163, 167

The Garden as a Metaphor of Contemporary Paradise
Davorin Gazvoda

Davorin Gazvoda
169

Maja Simoneti
170

Davorin Gazvoda
171, 172

Pyry Kantonen Photography, flooding simulation Loci Landscape Architects
174

Heterotopia: The Garden as a Metaphor
Martin Rein-Cano

Iwan Baan
177, 180, 181

The Garden as Microcosmos
Aleš Vodopivec

Nena Gabrovec
182, 183

top Marc Treib
184

bottom Aleš Vodopivec
184

Mateja Kurir
187

The Garden as a Photographic Image in the Era of Digitalization
Jure Mikuž

Luka Javornik
191

Roberto Baroni (Costaetrusca)/
WikiCommons
194

Summer Splendour
Anne Schwalbe

196–203

Garden as an Open Work
Jože Barši

top DPA/PIXSELL
206

Muzej suvremene umjetnosti Zagreb (The Museum of Contemporary Art Zagreb) Croatia, inv. br. MSU 1903 (1-5)-2
208

bottom Hans Haacke, 2001–2008/
VG Bild Kunst
206, 210

Thanks to Zdenka Badovinac and Oliver Schwarz

Apology of a Garden
Erika Bordon

Erika Bordon
217, 218, 220, 221

The Garden in the Knot of Meaning
Nadja Zgonik

Nadja Zgonik
222, 225, 229

The Metaphorical Life of the Garden
Lev Kreft

WikiArt
233

Fruits of the Garden
Anne Schwalbe

244–251

Let Us Cultivate Our Garden
Mladen Dolar

WikiArt
254

Public Domain
260

Gardengraph
Dean Komel

Dean Komel
262, 265, 266

J. Hajna
267

Architecture and the Supplement of Nature
Sven-Olov Wallenstein

Public Domain/from: Marc-Antoine Laugier's *Essai sur l'architecture*, 1753
271

Public Domain/from: *L'Architecture considérée sous le rapport de l'art, des moeurs, et de la legislation*, 1804, plate 33
272

Giovanni Battista Piranesi, Campo Marzio dell'antica Roma, 1761–1762. Ministerio di cultura Italia
275

The Garden, Pleasure, and Epicurus
Mateja Kurir

Mateja Kurir
276, 277, 281, 285

Gardens of Others
Anne Schwalbe

286–293

Post Scriptum
Barbara Habič Pregl

Archive Barbara Habič Pregl
295, 296

Dušan Ogrin
299, 301

Dedication

Eva Zupan, Department of Landscape Architecture, Biotechnical Faculty, University of Ljubljana.
312

#

A

B

C

D

E

F

G

H

I

J

K

L

M

N

O

P

Q

R

S

T

U

V

W

Z